his

UMI
BOOKS ON DEMAND™

UMI
A Bell & Howell Company
300 North Zeeb Road
P.O. Box 1346
Ann Arbor, Michigan 48106-1346

1-800-521-0600 734-761-4700
http://www.bellhowell.inforlearning.com

Printed in 2000 by xerographic process on acid-free paper

VARIANT FAMILY FORMS

FAMILIES IN TROUBLE SERIES

Series Editors: CATHERINE S. CHILMAN, ELAM W. NUNNALLY, FRED M. COX
all at University of Wisconsin—Milwaukee

Families in Trouble Series is an edited five-volume set designed to enhance the understanding and skills of human services professionals in such fields as social work, clinical psychology, education, health, counseling, and family therapy. Written by recognized scholars from several academic disciplines, this impressive series provides practice guidelines, state-of-the-art research, and implications for public policies from a family systems perspective. No other book or integrated series of books provides such an authoritative overview of information about the wide range of economic, employment, physical, behavioral, and relational problems and lifestyles that commonly affect today's families.

VOLUMES IN THIS SERIES:

Volume 1
Employment and Economic Problems

Volume 2
Chronic Illness and Disability

Volume 3
Troubled Relationships

Volume 4
Mental Illness, Delinquency, Addictions, and Neglect

Volume 5
Variant Family Forms

VARIANT FAMILY FORMS

Families in Trouble Series, Volume 5

Edited by:
Catherine S. Chilman
Elam W. Nunnally
Fred M. Cox

SAGE PUBLICATIONS
The Publishers of Professional Social Science
Newbury Park Beverly Hills London New Delhi

To our spouses, children, and grandchildren

For information address:

SAGE Publications, Inc.
2111 West Hillcrest Drive
Newbury Park, California 91320

SAGE Publications Inc.
275 South Beverly Drive
Beverly Hills
California 90212

SAGE Publications Ltd.
28 Banner Street
London EC1Y 8QE
England

SAGE PUBLICATIONS India Pvt. Ltd.
M-32 Market
Greater Kailash I
New Delhi 110 048 India

Printed in the United States of America

Library of Congress Cataloging-in-Publication Data

Families in trouble : knowledge and practice perspectives for professionals in the human services / edited by Catherine S. Chilman, Fred M. Cox, Elam W. Nunnally.

p. cm.

Includes bibliographies and indexes.

Contents: v. 1. Employment and economic problems—v. 2. Chronic illness and disability—v. 3. Troubled relationships—v. 4. Mental illness, delinquency, addictions, and neglect—v. 5. Variant family forms.

ISBN 0-8039-2709-6 (v. 5) ISBN 0-8039-2710-X (pbk.: v. 5)

1. Problem families—United States. 2. Family social work—United States. 3. Problem families—Counseling of—United States. 4. Problem families—Government policy—United States. I. Chilman, Catherine S. II. Cox, Fred M. III. Nunnally, Elam W.

HV699.F316 1988 88-6539
362.8'2'0973—dc19 CIP

FIRST PRINTING 1988

Contents

Introduction to the Series

CATHERINE S. CHILMAN, ELAM W. NUNNALLY AND FRED M. COX

MAJOR PURPOSES AND CONCEPTS

The major purpose of this series of books is to enhance the understanding and skills of human services professionals in such fields as social work, education, health, counseling, clinical psychology, and family therapy so that they can more effectively assist families in trouble. There is no need to elaborate here that many of today's families are in serious trouble, as rising rates of divorce, unmarried parenthood, poverty, and family violence suggest. The stresses imposed by a rapidly changing society are creating severe strains for families and their members. There are also positive aspects of these changes, however, including improved health care and freedom from backbreaking toil, as well as increasing knowledge about family-related problems and ways to minimize them.

Thus, to reduce the negatives that are afflicting families and to enhance the positives, it is important to marshal the social and psychological knowledge and practice wisdom now available to enrich professional family-related practice, policies, and programs. The editors fully recognize that current knowledge is all too meager; much more needs to be developed. However, let us use the knowledge we do have while the search for more continues.

This series proposes to function as a basic knowledge, theory, and practice resource of the highest scholarly and professional quality. It is directed to practitioners and graduate students in the human service professions who work with troubled families. It emphasizes families in trouble, rather than families in general. As far as the editors can ascertain, no other book or integrated series of books combines an authoritative overview of information about the wide range of economic, employment, physical, behavioral, and relational problems and lifestyles that commonly affect today's families.[1]

This is especially true with respect to books that link up-to-date, research-based knowledge about common family-related problems to implications both for clinical practice and for policy and program development and implementation. For the most part, publications and curricula for the human services tend to be presented in discrete, specialized units. In the family field, for instance, knowledge from the social and behavioral sciences is often presented in a separate course with its own texts that emphasize basic knowledge and theory, with little or no mention of the applications of this knowledge and theory to professional practice. Quite different courses and texts deal with clinical practice applications, often with little reference to the related knowledge and theory base. Another set of courses and texts deals with planning and policy strategies for programs to meet individual and family needs, with little reference either to clinical practice techniques or to basic knowledge and theory foundations on which program and policy development should rest.

Thus, professionals tend to have serious difficulty forming clear links along the continuum of theory, knowledge, policies, programs, and clinical practice. Yet professional services cannot be adequately designed and delivered unless these links are made and applied, in an integrated way, to meeting the needs of families and their members.

Family Systems Perspective

A family systems perspective forms the fundamental conceptual scheme of this series. Families are seen as small, open systems, deeply affected by their internal, interpersonal dynamics and by the many aspects of the external environment with which they interact. From the internal dynamics perspective, everything that happens to one member of the family affects all members. The internal systems of families can vary in a number of ways, some of them dysfunctional. For example, the members of some families are so tightly and rigidly interconnected, or "fused," that members have virtually no sense of personal identity. Flexible changes of family patterns in order to meet changing conditions from within and from outside the family then become virtually impossible. Moreover, in such instances individual family members find they cannot extricate themselves from the poorly functioning family system.

In addition, some families form dysfunctional subsystems, such as a closed partnership between a father and son in competition with a closed mother-daughter partnership. Such alignments tend to undermine the parents' marriage and the development of sons and daughters as maturing individuals.

Some families with interpersonal problems, such as poor husband-wife relationships, deny their real difficulties and displace them onto another family member, such as a child, who may then become the problem-laden scapegoat for both parents.

There are many other variations on the internal systems theme, briefly sketched here. The chief point is that efforts aimed at treating individual members of families are often fruitless unless the operation of the whole family system is better understood and included in treatment plans, as well as in programs and policies. Moreover, individual treatment, without regard to family system dynamics, may increase rather than decrease the problems of the whole system and its members.

In seeking to understand family systems, it is also important to study the many "family actors"—older, middle, and younger generations and interactive members of the extended family such as grandparents, aunts, uncles, brothers, sisters, steprelations, former spouses, and close friends.

It is also essential to consider the development of families and their dynamics over the life span, with the recognition that family interactions, concerns, and tasks vary at different life cycle stages and crucial transition points such as marriage, childbirth, launching children into schools and jobs, retirement, illness, and death.

Family structures and lifestyles vary, especially at this time in society when a variety of family forms is becoming more common, including single-parent, divorced, widowed, separated, reconstituted, gay or lesbian, extended, foster and adoptive, and two-career families; cohabiting, never-married couples who may also have children; childless couples; and, of course, the traditional two-parent nuclear family with one or more children. Each of these family forms has its own particular strengths and vulnerabilities.

When families have particular problems such as unemployment, low income, chronic physical illness or death of a member, chemical dependency, mental illness, conflict with the law, and so on, their strengths are likely to be seriously undermined. The nature and extent of the stresses they experience will be affected by a number of factors, including family system characteristics and family developmental stage. It is crucially important, therefore, to consider family-related problems, such as those mentioned above, in a family-focused context rather than in the more usual framework that seeks to treat or plan for individuals without appropriate consideration and understanding of the complexities of family dynamics, both internal and external.

External factors affecting families are all too frequently overlooked or brushed aside by human service professionals, especially those in clinical practice. Viewing families ecologically, as open systems, leads to the recognition that many factors in the environment have a strong impact on them. These factors include the state of the economy, employment conditions, the availability of needed resources in the community, racism and other forms of discrimination, and so forth. When environmental conditions are adverse and community resources are inadequate, the stresses on families escalate, especially for families of relatively low income and low educational and occupational status. It then becomes the responsibility of professionals to help vulnerable families develop strategies to deal more effectively with these stresses. Professionals may also need to serve as advocates to assist families in obtaining available resources and to work with other local, state, and national groups to promote improved conditions and resources.

In light of the above, the proposed series includes overview chapters about existing and needed policies and programs that are directed toward more effective problem management in support of family well-being. It is hoped that this material will serve as a stimulus and information base for professionals in their larger community responsibilities.

CONTENT

With these purposes and concepts in mind, the editors offer a series of five books, each of which has the following underlying structure (a) research-based theory and knowledge about each topic, (b) suggested guidelines for methods of family-centered practice, and (c) implications for public programs and policy. At our invitation, recognized specialists from their respective fields have prepared chapters dealing with particular aspects of this overall plan. Specific problem areas that are often associated with trouble for families are covered in the five books. Volume 1, *Families with Problems with Work and Financial Resources,* discusses employment and income. Volume 2, *Families with Physically Impaired Members,* deals with physical illness and disabilities. Volume 3, *Families with Disturbed Family Relationships,* covers that problem area. Behavior that the community finds unacceptable is discussed in Volume 4, *Families with Mental Disorder, Addiction, Delinquency, and Neglect*. Volume 5, *Families with Problems Related to Alternate Lifestyles,* covers participation in alternative family forms that are sometimes accompanied by difficulties for the families involved.

We recognize that not all problem topics are covered. Space

constraints require that we select a set of subjects that seem to be most widespread and most apt to be related to serious troubles for families. We also do not cover all major methods of human service delivery. Our discussion is limited, for the most part, to methods of direct practice in the provision of social and psychological services. The reasons for this limitation are (a) the editors' expertise lies in the social/psychological area, (b) we believe these practice approaches to be of major importance in assisting families, and (c) the majority of human service professionals today are in direct practice.

Although we believe the methods of social planning, administration, and legislative advocacy, to name a few, also are essential to the human services enterprise, adequate coverage of these topics is beyond the scope of the present series.

Underlying Concepts

Definition of the Family

We define a family to mean two or more people in a committed relationship from which they derive a sense of identity as a family. This definition permits us to include many nontraditional family forms that are outside the traditional legal perspective, including families not related by blood, marriage, or adoption. This broad definition is essential if we are to recognize the full variety of family forms found in modern society.

"Families in Trouble" versus "Troubled Families"

We begin with the premise that most, if not all, families are apt to encounter stresses at one time or another in their lives. Due to these stresses they may, from time to time, be "in trouble." This concept is quite different from that which proposes that some families are inherently troubled, largely because of their own internal problems.

We build on the work of such systems theorists as Bertalanffy (1968), Buckley (1967), and Bateson (1972, 1979); family stress and coping theorists such as Hill (1949), Olson and McCubbin (1983), and McCubbin, Cauble, and Patterson (1982); and such clinical theorists as Haley (1963, 1976), Minuchin (1974), Watzlawick, Weakland, and Fisch (1974), and Satir (1967, 1983). We amplify their concepts to develop a multifaceted set of interrelated principles which are reflected to one degree or another in the various chapters.

In so doing, we weave together knowledge and theory from a number of the social, behavioral, and biological sciences and integrate them within a family systems framework. Although such a complex approach may seem overly ambitious, we believe it is important, especially if knowledge and theory about families are to be effectively applied to the fields of practice, programs, and policies.

Our basic theoretical position is that the reactions of family systems and their members to stressful experiences depend on the following major interacting factors:

1. The nature, severity, and duration of the stress and its effects on each family member and the family structure.
2. The perception of each member of the family system (which often includes the extended family) of what the stress is and what it means to each member in terms of that person's beliefs, values, and goals.
3. The size and structure of the family (such as number, gender, and spacing of children); the marital status of the parents; the presence of other kin or friends in the household.
4. The stage of family development and age of each member.
5. The psychological characteristics of each family member (including personality and cognitive factors).
6. The physical characteristics of each family member (such as state of health and special physical assets and liabilities).
7. The previous life experiences that each family member brings to the present stressor event. For instance, a series of losses of loved ones during childhood and adolescence can make a parent, as an adult, particularly sensitive to another severe illness or death.
8. The characteristics of the family system, including the clarity or ambiguity of its boundaries, the rigidity or flexibility of behavioral patterns, the existence of subsystems and their nature, the degree of fusion or distancing of relationships, interaction with external systems, and patterns of communication, plus social, psychological, and material resources available from within the family and its network.
9. Social, psychological, and material resources available to families from communities. This includes not only the existence of a wide variety of community services and resources that are potentially supportive of the well-being of families and their members, but the recognition that families are apt to vary in their access to community resources depending on such factors as the degree of social stratification, racism, ethnocentrism, and power politics within the community.

In summary, the above formulation proposes that families are not inherently "stable" or "healthy" or, conversely, "unstable," "troubled," or "sick," but that most families encounter external or internal stresses at different points in the life span of each member. These stresses vary from one family to another depending on many factors in the environment and within the family. Families also differ in their capacity to cope with these stresses; their coping capacities depend on the nature of these stresses, plus a complex of family system and structure variables together with the social, psychological, and physical characteristics of each member.

To differing degrees, human service professionals can be of important assistance to families and their members at times when stressful events threaten to overwhelm their coping capacities. This assistance may consist of direct treatment, resource mobilization, or efforts to improve public policies or programs, all central topics covered in this series. These efforts are most apt to be effective if the professional approaches his or her work objectively, rather than judgmentally, and with a high level of competence solidly based on the best available scientific knowledge and skills derived from that knowledge, also a major focus of this series.

Our choice of authors was made partly on the basis of their reputations for scholarly or clinical achievements and partly on the basis of their affinity to a systems approach to understanding families and their environments. All of our invited authors were requested to relate their contributions to a systems frame of reference. We have not excluded other theoretical views, however, and the reader will find articles which contain, for example, learning theory and behavioral concepts as well as systems thinking.

We chose a systems paradigm as the orientation for these volumes for several reasons. First, this paradigm readily permits one to view the interplay of individual, family group, and community or societal factors in understanding how troubles arise for families and how families cope. Second, the systems paradigm is hospitable to developmental analyses of families and their difficulties and strengths. Third, at this juncture some of the most fruitful research studies and most exciting clinical developments reported in the scholarly and clinical literature are systems oriented.

We have asked the authors of the various chapters to pay careful attention to the available research in their fields and to view this research in a critical fashion so that they can make distinctions between what knowledge has been clearly established, what has been only partially established, and what still exists largely in the area of clinical impressions and speculation. Although much more and better research, both basic and applied, is needed on most of the topics covered in this series, the needs of families are such that it is essential for human service professionals to proceed in the most effective way they can, on the basis of what knowledge and theory is available. It is also essential for researchers to continue with the many studies that are needed, for them to disseminate their results, and for practitioners to study the research in their fields as new information becomes available. The editors have made a serious attempt to ensure that the present series brings together, in summarized and applicable form, the most pertinent, up-to-date research available on the various topics that are covered here.

Topics Included Throughout the Series: Racism, Ethnocentrism, and Sexism

As sketched above, each of the five books in the series deals with a set of issues that often cause trouble for families. Although the titles of the volumes do not include the subjects of racism, ethnocentrism, and sexism, we recognize that these factors are of central importance and have a profound impact on the whole of our society, as well as on many individual families and their members. Because these factors tend to have pervasive effects on numerous aspects of family lives, we incorporate a discussion of them as an integral part of many of the topics covered, including chapters on poverty, employment, interpersonal difficulties within families, variations in family forms, family-community conflict, and implications both for direct practice and public policies and programs.

NOTE

1. As of this writing (early 1987), there appears to be one partial exception to this statement. A recent two-volume text by McCubbin and Figley, *Stress and the Family* (1983), includes some of the topics that we have dealt with. However, the following important family-related subjects are not included in that book: poverty, long-term unemployment, alcoholism, marital and parent-child conflict, family violence, cohabitation, gay and lesbian lifestyles, nonmarital pregnancy and parenthood, chronic illness or disability of a parent, delinquency and crime, and aging. Moreover, the material on treatment in these volumes is rather sketchy and that on programs and policy almost nonexistent.

Preface

VARIANT FAMILY FORMS

A wide range of family lifestyles are discussed in this volume: single, adolescent parents; cohabiting couples; gays and lesbians; widows and widowers; adoptive families; and remarried families.

Research and theory regarding these various lifestyles are presented by recognized scholars in their particular fields, as follows: single, adolescent parents—Catherine Chilman; cohabitation—Eleanor Macklin; gays and lesbians—Joseph Harry; widows—Helena Lopata; widowers—Jane Burgess; adoptive families—Ron Kral and Judith Schaffer; remarriage and stepfamilies—Kay Pasley.

Treatment chapters, building on the lifestyle topics, are also authored by specialists in their respective fields. Richard Weatherley and Virginia Cartoof describe a variety of methods of working with teenage parents. Treatment of cohabitants in difficulty is described by Charles Cole; Susan Rice and James Kelly do the same with respect to troubled gays and lesbians. Helena Lopata and Jane Burgess write about treatment of widows and widowers in need of help. Ron Kral and Judith Schaffer discuss working with adoptive families in difficulty, while Emily and John Visher share their treatment expertise regarding reconstituted families.

Implications for public policies and programs addressed to the difficulties often encountered by people with alternate lifestyles are presented by Roger Rubin, a well-known specialist in related policy fields.

Important and highly useful new material is provided in this volume on topics rarely, if ever, thoroughly discussed in a scholarly fashion in the professional literature. This appears to be especially true of those chapters dealing with family treatment approaches to troubled cohabitants, widowers, gays and lesbians, and adoptive parents.

Acknowledgments

We extend our gratitude to a number of people whose help has been of enormous importance in the development of this five-volume series:

To the Johnson Foundation, which graciously extended the hospitality of its Wingspread Conference Center in Racine, Wisconsin, for a two-day planning meeting of most of our authors at the start of this book project.

To the Milwaukee Foundation of Milwaukee, Wisconsin, which generously provided funds to meet some of the costs of the above-named planning conference.

To MaryAnn Riggs, Word Processor Extraordinary, who with unusual skill and pertinacity typed many of the chapters and prepared the bibliographies in standardized formats.

To Carolyn Kott Washburne, expert technical editor, who polished the writing of each chapter promptly and efficiently.

To all our authors, who cooperated gallantly with this project and who tolerated the frequently heavy revisions suggested by the series editors who have consistently held to the ideal of a high-quality product that would be of important use to human service professionals, both as students and practitioners.

To families everywhere whose strengths and vulnerabilities have provided the basic inspiration for this series.

CATHERINE S. CHILMAN
ELAM W. NUNNALLY
FRED M. COX

1

Never-Married, Single, Adolescent Parents

CATHERINE S. CHILMAN

INTRODUCTION

The focus of this chapter is on parents whose children are born outside of marriage, with a particular emphasis on adolescent parents. The reasons for this focus are to avoid duplication with other chapters in this series that deal with divorce, separation, and widowhood. Moreover, adolescent parents and their children appear to be particularly vulnerable. More information is presented here about adolescent mothers largely because there has been much more research about them than about adolescent fathers, and the mothers are more apt to have custody of their children.

Adolescent pregnancy and parenthood have been much in the news and have been a prime program focus for both public and private human services agencies. Although a somewhat similar observation might be made about many topics discussed in this series, it appears that the subject of teenage pregnancy and parenthood has been particularly publicized and often over-dramatized. So much publicity has been given to the topic that a good deal of misinformation has been disseminated as well as correct information. This chapter is based on an analytic study of all available research of adequate quality; it attempts to modify the sensationalism and hasty generalizations so often made about adolescent parents and their children.

TRENDS IN SINGLE-PARENT FAMILIES

General Trends

Norton and Glick (1986) provide the most recent data regarding one-parent families in general. From 1970 to 1984 the number of these families doubled (3.2 million in 1970 and 6.7 million in 1984); 88% of these families were mother-child families. Fifty percent of black families and 15% of white families were headed by one parent in 1984.

From 1970 to 1984 the number of divorced couples increased by almost 300%, and the number of unmarried mothers increased even more, by 500%. In 1985 the latter represented 20% of all mother-child families. About 12% of the births to white women in 1985 were out of wedlock, compared with 55% of births to black women (U.S. Bureau of the Census, 1986). Over a child's life from birth to age 18, it is estimated that 12% of all children will experience being in a female-headed, unmarried family situation. In general, these families are apt to have a high rate of poverty, a high rate of minority representation, relatively low education, and little status in society.

Trends in Adolescent, Unmarried Parenthood

To put early childbearing into perspective, it is important to understand the post–World War II "baby boom," which constituted a rise in the birth rate that lasted into the early 1960s (1948–1962). The aging of the baby boom babies meant that during the 1970s the number of teenagers was 43% higher than in the preceding decades. This created more potential adolescent parents, with the result that although the birth rates for most teens were declining in the 1970s, the number of births rose through 1970 and declined slowly thereafter. Since birth rates and numbers of births were falling faster for older women, the proportion of births to teens actually rose (Baldwin, 1983).

Most teen births are to young women between the ages of 15 and 19. However, this groups together women who may have completed high school and who have very good pregnancy outcomes with young women who may be in junior high school and who are high-risk obstetrical patients. During the 1970s the birth rate fell fastest for the oldest teens and rose for the very youngest, those under age 15, who are viewed as high-risk mothers from both social and medical standpoints. Births to this group constitute a very small percentage of all births (less than one half of 1%); while births to women under age 15 were less than 7,500 in 1960, they rose to almost 13,000 in 1973 before declining to under 10,000 by 1983, the last date for which this information is currently available (November, 1987). Most teen births are to women ages 18 to 19, and birth rates have fallen fastest for this group (Select Committee on Children, Youth and Families, 1986).

The rate of nonmarital childbearing is much higher among black adolescents, with 86% of babies born to this group being to unmarried mothers, compared to about 19% of white babies. As Burden and Klerman (1984) point out, whites are much more likely to marry if they are pregnant, and they are also more apt to place their child for adoption (19% of whites and 2% of blacks). Although the abortion rate for black teenagers was relatively low in the past, by 1983 it had risen to 66% compared to a rate of 38.3% for white teenagers (Henshaw & O'Reilly, 1983). Then, too, blacks are far more apt to have their first child when they are aged 16 or less and to have a second child before the age of 20. Some of the reasons for these differentials between the races will be explored in a later section.

Although the rate of pregnancies to teenage women rose markedly during the 1970s and early 1980s, the birthrate declined, chiefly owing to the fact that almost half of these pregnancies were terminated by abortion. For example, in 1970 the birth rate for teenagers was about 9% of teenagers, and in 1980 it was 5.3%.

The number of births outside marriage is higher for adult women than for adolescents. For example, a 1983 survey of unmarried women found that 83% of the single women ages 20 to 29 said they had had nonmarital coitus. One third had had at least one pregnancy; 14% of the white women and 62% of the black women had had at least one out-of-wedlock birth. The incidence of nonmarital childbearing in this age group, as in the younger one, is higher for people who are black, unemployed, not currently enrolled in school, and have no education past high school. All in all, it seems likely that the problems thought to be associated only with nonmarital teenage parenthood are also associated with parenthood in the older group. The assumption that the difficulties teenage parents are often found to have pertain to their age alone is doubtless an error, as we shall see in more detail later.

Throughout this chapter research concerning both white and black adolescents is cited. There is little substantive information available regarding Hispanic, Native American, or Asian groups because they have not been studied. Rates of teenage childbearing appear to be very low in the Asian population but high among both Native Americans and Hispanic Americans. Much more research is needed regarding these groups.

APPARENT CAUSES OF ADOLESCENT UNMARRIED CHILDBEARING

Although older age groups of single parents probably require more attention than is commonly given them, the following discussion centers on the apparent causes of adolescent childbearing, chiefly because the vast majority of related research has been for this age group. Adolescents become unmarried parents through a series of behaviors: having nonmarital intercourse, not using effective contraceptives or (less usual) experiencing contraceptive failure, becoming pregnant, not obtaining an abortion, carrying a pregnancy to term, failing to marry before the child's birth, and not placing the child for adoption. Thus, attempting to understand the causes of adolescent childbearing requires a look at what the research reveals to be the factors associated with each of these behaviors.

Nonmarital Intercourse among Adolescents

The rates of nonmarital intercourse among adolescents increased sharply from the end of the 1960s through the 1970s. Since that time the rise in rates seems to have leveled off but still remains fairly high. The increase was especially the case for white girls, for whom, prior to the late 1960s, the rates had been around 15% by age 18. By 1979 these rates were 53% for white females and 76% for black ones by age 18 (Zelnik & Kantner, 1980a). There are no adequate studies with national samples of adolescent male sex activity, partly because young males are so difficult to reach for research purposes. However, it appears that 80% or more of both white and black men have had coitus by age 18 or so (Zelnik & Kantner, 1980a).

Table 1.1 presents a summary of research findings regarding factors associated with participation in nonmarital intercourse by young people under the age of 18.

Some cautions are in order when reading Table 1.1. Only findings from recent American studies judged to be of a high scientific quality are reported. However, small local samples (indicated by an "a") are sometimes used, and it is dubious whether findings from these studies can be generalized to other groups. Other findings were obtained from national probability samples, and, thus, they can be viewed as applicable on the average to groups of adolescents throughout the country during the 1970s and early 1980s. Note the use of the words "average" and "groups" in the preceding sentence. Since research findings pertain to group averages, individual adolescents may differ widely in their traits from the findings shown in this table. These findings pertain to group tendencies and are likely to be more useful to program and policy planners than to practitioners working with individuals.

Moreover, research findings that deal with group averages may well mask clusters of traits belonging to subgroups within the larger whole. For example, clinical studies with a number of adolescents

Table 1.1
Major Factors Apparently Associated with Nonmarital Intercourse among Adolescents under Age 18: A Summary of Research Findings

Factors	Males	Females
Social Situation		
Not living in a middle-class, family-focused neighborhood	yes	yes
Parents having less than a college education	unknown	yes, especially for blacks
Low level of religiousness	yes	yes, especially for whites
Norms favoring equality between the sexes	probably	yes
Permissive sexual norms of the larger society and reference group	yes	yes
Racism and poverty	yes	yes
Migration from rural to urban areas	unknown	yes
High youth unemployment	yes	yes, especially for blacks
Peer-group pressure	yes	not clear
Lower social class	yes	yes
Sexually active friends	yes	yes
Single-parent (usually low-income) family, especially if parent is dating	unknown	yes
Mother having been a teenage parent	unknown	yes[a]
Psychological		
Use of drugs and alcohol	yes	no
Low self-esteem	no[a]	yes[a]
Desire for affection	no[a]	yes[a]
Dysfunctional family system	unknown	yes[a]
Low education goals and poor educational achievement	yes	yes
Alienation	no[a]	yes[a]
Deviant attitudes	yes	yes
High social criticism	no[a]	yes[a]
Permissive attitudes of parents	yes[a]	yes[a]
Going steady; being in love	yes[a]	yes[a]
Steady love partner with permissive attitudes		
Risk-taking attitudes	yes[a]	yes[a]
Passivity and dependence	no[a]	yes[a]
Aggression; high levels of activity	yes	no[a]
Biological		
Older than 16	yes	yes
Early puberty	yes	yes

a. Variables supported by only one or two small studies. Other variables are supported by a number of investigations.

Note. The major studies on which this table is based are: Furstenberg (1976); Jessor and Jessor (1975); Sorenson (1973); Kantner and Zelnik (1972); Udry et al. (1975); Simon et al. (1972); Zelnik and Kantner (1977); Fox (1980); Cvetkovich and Grote (1975); Schulz, (1977); Pressor (1978); Zelnik, (1980); DeLameter and MacCorquodale, (1979); Zelnik, Kantner, and Ford, (1982); Furstenberg and Crawford (1978); Reiss and Miller (1979); Peterson et al. (1985); Thornton (1985); Udry (1985); and Hagan, Astone, and Kitigawa (1985).

drawn from a variety of social class, racial, and family backgrounds reveal that some sexually active young people experience serious pathology in their families of origin (such as alcoholism, promiscuity on the part of parents and siblings, family violence, and the like). At the other extreme, some sexually active adolescents come from far more stable families, tend to be over age 16, and report that they engage in coitus largely because they have liberal parents, are going steady, are in love, and believe that intercourse within a committed relationship is acceptable if it includes the use of effective contraceptives.

Other case examples tend to fall somewhere between the extremes sketched above. Although clinical studies reveal the importance of family system factors in affecting the sexual behavior of adolescents, no large formal studies have adequately taken these variables into account in their research designs. There are numerous reasons for this oversight, including the lack of training in this field on the part of many researchers and the complexity of the dynamics of family systems, complexities that are difficult to pin down in the usual quantitative research design. Particularly missing, though shown to be important in clinical experience and case studies, are such factors as family size and structure, kinship networks, multigenerational issues, family enmeshment or distancing, family developmental stage, family communication patterns, the quality of the relationship between the parents, scapegoating of family members, and horizontal and vertical stresses in families.

Despite these cautionary remarks regarding research in this field, the findings reported in Table 1.1 are useful in developing further understanding of some of the factors that on the average tend to be associated with early nonmarital coitus. Note, too, that these cautions also apply to research reported later in this chapter regarding contraceptive usage, abortions, and apparent outcomes of adolescent childbearing.

Social, psychological, and biological factors all play a part in nonmarital adolescent coitus. These factors have numerous aspects and interact in such a way that no single trait, such as early maturation or poor educational achievement, can be held accountable for the young person's behavior. However, an increasing number of studies show the central part played by the following factors: poverty, living in a one-parent family, minority group membership, low education and occupation level of parents, low educational achievement, and low educational/occupational goals of the young person. Such psychological traits as low self-esteem, alienation, and feelings of powerlessness tend to derive from the life situation that involves these factors. However, such traits can also be present and important with respect to early nonmarital intercourse among middle- and upper-class adolescents. It is probable that for the latter groups psychological difficulties are more salient than for their less advantaged peers because social and economic problems are less apt to be present in the lives of middle- and upper-class youngsters.

Another consideration is that early nonmarital intercourse may be both expected and accepted among certain cultural groups. This tends to be true especially for black teens, particularly for males. According to Peterson et al. (1985), data from a recent national study reveal so many sharp differences between white and black adolescents regarding nonmarital intercourse attitudes and behaviors that further studies of adolescent sexuality should look at white and black teenagers as separate groups. These differences are particularly marked for those black teens who attend racially segregated schools, perhaps because cultural norms are particularly reinforced under those circumstances.

Contraceptive Behaviors

At least half of sexually active teenagers engage in coitus a year or more before using contraceptives, and many more use poor methods or use them inconsistently thereafter. Table 1.2 presents the findings of a number of recent studies. As in the case of research regarding early, nonmarital intercourse, these findings pertain to average group tendencies.

Although it is frequently speculated that poor contraceptive use is particularly characteristic of adolescents, this theory has been recently undermined by various studies that indicate that older women, especially those who are single, also frequently fail to use contraceptives when they have intercourse. Recent research on this subject with adult subjects, however, is meager.

Table 1.2 presents a summary of factors found to be significantly associated with nonuse or poor use of contraceptives by adolescents. As in the case of the apparent causes of early nonmarital intercourse, adolescent attitudes related to nonuse of contraceptives include feelings of helplessness, fatalism, a sense of personal incompetence, and lack of self-esteem.

Table 1.2 also shows the importance of the ready availability of

Table 1.2
Major Factors Associated with Nonuse or Inconsistent Use of Contraceptives by Sexually Active, Unmarried Adolescent Women: A Summary of Research Findings

Demographic

Age lower than 18
Low socioeconomic status of parents, self, and partner
Non-attendance of college
Fundamentalist Protestant affiliation
Being black or Hispanic

Situational

Not in a steady, committed dating relationship
Not having experienced pregnancy
Having unplanned, sporadic intercourse
Contraceptives not available at time of need
Being in a high stress situation
Poor mother-daughter relationship
Lack of access to a high-quality, confidential, free family planning service
Living in a ghetto neighborhood

Psychological

Low educational/occupational achievement and goals
High fertility values and desiring a pregnancy
Attitudes of risk-taking, alienation, personal incompetence, powerlessness, fatalism, low self-esteem, dependence on others
Lack of acceptance of reality of one's own sexual behavior
Poor partner communication skills about sex and contraceptives
Lack of partner cooperation
Fear of contraceptive side effects and of possible infertility
Ignorance of family planning services
Thinking they are at "safe time of month" (often incorrect information about time of ovulation)

Note. The major studies on which this table are based are: Lindeman (1974); Luker (1975); Cvetkovich and Grote (1975); DeLameter and MacCorquodale (1979); Fox and Inazu (1975); Finkel and Finkel (1975); Furstenberg (1976); Hornick et al. (1979); Miller (1976); Presser (1977); Rosen, Martindale, and Hudson (1976); Shah et al. (1975); Zelnik, Kantner, and Ford (1982); Jorgensen et al. (1981); and Hagan, Astone, and Kitagawa (1985).

confidential, free, or low-cost family planning services as well as sound information about pregnancy and varieties of contraceptives plus their relative effectiveness and effects. While family planning clinic services expanded greatly during the 1970s, there remains considerable unmet need among teenagers. Skill in communication about sex and contraceptives, especially with partners, is also important. For further details see Chilman (1983).

The foregoing discussion has centered on young *women*, largely because nearly all the studies have had only female samples. This is partly because of the sexism in the whole field of reproduction and family planning—the focus is on women "because they are the ones who get pregnant." However, men are the persons who get women pregnant; thus, far more research and program attention should include them (Chilman, 1985; Chilman, 1987b). Another reason for the research focus on adolescent women is that they are much more reachable and willing than adolescent men to participate in studies regarding their sexual behavior.

However, a few investigations with adolescent male samples show that the majority believe that the primary responsibility for contraception lies with females. This is especially true if they are not in a committed, steady relationship. Although the condom as a contraceptive method is especially appropriate for adolescents because of their generally infrequent, sporadic, unplanned intercourse, many males have negative attitudes regarding this method, even though condoms have been greatly improved in recent years and have a high rate of contraceptive effectiveness if used correctly.

Important findings about contraceptive methods are reported by Zelnik and Kantner (1980a), who found that in 1979 about 40% of sexually active females, both white and black, depended on male methods of contraception. Because the majority of adolescent males seem to be markedly inconsistent and perhaps unconcerned about contraceptive use, there is a central problem with respect to their attitudes and behavior and the reliance of so many adolescent girls on the inadequate contraceptive vigilance of boys (Brown et al., 1975; Finkel & Finkel, 1975; Kantner & Zelnik, 1972; Zelnik & Kantner, 1980a; Sorenson, 1973). If the few available studies are correct in their findings and can be generalized, a particular problem seems to reside with the contraceptive behavior of black males, especially because 80 to 90% of these males are sexually active by age 16. At present, a number of organizations, for example the national and local Urban Leagues, are engaged in a welcome effort to push more

Table 1.3
Factors Associated with Adolescent Women's Decision to Carry Pregnancy to Term

High religiosity (especially fundamentalist Protestant and non-Caucasian Catholic)
Low education of parents
Low educational-occupational goals
Low educational achievement
Having dropped out of high school
Mother opposed to abortion
Peer group, including boyfriend, opposed to abortion
Teenage friends and/or siblings who are parents
Wanting to have a child
Access to financial aid from family and/or the government
Traditional conservative attitudes including "abortion is murder" and "woman's place is in the home"

Note. The major studies on which this table is based are: Leibowitz, Eisen, and Chow (1980); Luker (1975); Smetana and Adler (1979); O'Connell and Moore (1980); Klerman et al. (1982); Rosen (1982); Rosen and Stack (1982); Eisen et al. (1983); Henshaw and O'Reilly (1983); Rosen (1983); Eisen and Zellman (1984); and Rickels (1985).

"contraceptive responsibility" on the part of males as well as females. Perhaps the growing concern about such sexually transmitted diseases as herpes, AIDS, and gonorrhea will promote more acceptance of condoms on the part of males.

Abortion

So far this discussion has centered on behavioral factors among adolescents that lead to pregnancy. However, as shown earlier, about half of teenage pregnancies are resolved by abortion. A few studies have looked at the characteristics of young women who do not choose to terminate a pregnancy versus those who elect an abortion. The findings, shown in Table 1.3, again show the salience in the adolescent's decision to carry a pregnancy to term of having low educational/occupational goals, low socioeconomic status of family of origin, and high fertility and anti-abortion values.

It is also estimated that the lack of financial resources to defray abortion costs and the unavailability of abortion services in some parts of the country prevent the termination of pregnancy by about one fourth of the pregnant adolescents who desire an abortion (Rodman, Lewis, & Griffith, 1984). This lack of resources has become especially important since the so-called Hyde Amendment was passed by Congress in 1976 and upheld by the Supreme Court in 1979. This amendment prevents the use of federal funds for meeting the costs of abortion for low-income women unless their lives are endangered by the pregnancy. However, about 20 states were continuing to meet these expenses out of their own funds as of 1986.

Failure to Marry

One more component needs to be considered in searching for the factors associated with becoming an unmarried teenage mother. It will be recalled that more than 80% of black teenage mothers are unmarried, as are about 20% of white teenage mothers. One reason for this difference between the rates is the relatively greater acceptability of unwed adolescent motherhood among black people, especially people from low socioeconomic backgrounds. This in turn may be a response to a situation in which the shortage of economically secure, marriageable males makes marriage an option available to relatively few.

It is becoming increasingly clear that the shortage of marriageable black men, especially black men with secure, steady employment, is a major contributor to the rise in the rates of unwed parenthood among black women. For example, federal government figures show that the proportion of employed young black men in the population has declined sharply since 1972. This is especially true of young men ages 18 and 19. As of 1982 only about one-third of these young men held regular jobs, contrasted with two-thirds of young white men. Wilson and Neckerman (1986) write that only recently has it been hypothesized that the rise in female-headed families among blacks is strongly related to the declining rates of male employment. They conclude that there is a strong case for placing the problem of black joblessness, which underlies nonmarital childbearing, as a top-priority item in policies designed to enhance the status of families.

The incident of unemployment among black youths is only one of the reasons for the low marriage rate in this population. There is also a marked shortage of young black men compared to the number of young black women. This is the result of high rates for black male youth of homicide, accidents, and incarceration. Largely as a result of this shortage, a young black man may form sexual relationships with a number of young women and become the father of children in two or more young families (Farley, 1980, Blumstein, 1982).

Low-income black males tend to have negative attitudes toward marriage. However, a number of studies have found that many of them continue an interest in their children and the mothers of the children even if they are not married (Furstenberg, 1976; Ladner, 1971; Liebow, 1967; Sauber, 1970).

Furstenberg's 5-year longitudinal study of adolescent mothers showed that these young women were most apt to return to school if they remained single and had help from their families in many respects, including child care. Marrying a young man who was a school dropout often meant a young mother also stayed out of school. Furstenberg also found that marriage could have an adverse effect on the adolescent mother's total situation if the marriage were followed by separation, which tended to occur in over half the cases. Understandably, adolescent mothers were in the best economic position if they and their husbands were both employed and child care resources were available through either informal or formal arrangements.

Few young husbands were able to support their families adequately through their sole efforts. As mentioned previously, this was because of high unemployment rates and poor wages for black inner city youths. Moreover, welfare policy tends to discriminate against the adolescent family if the young father is present. All in all, it is essential to recognize that marriage does not necessarily solve the problems of adolescent parents, or of older parents either, for that matter. The high rates of unemployment and poverty for teenagers suggest that remaining single may be a better strategy for young parents than getting married. This is especially true if, through marriage, the young mother cannot get a range of AFDC benefits including Medicaid and if, as is frequently the case, marriage brings with it another child in a short space of time.

It is frequently claimed that unwed adolescent childbearing is caused by the desire of teenagers to have children in order to "get on welfare." However, a number of studies refute this. For example, national data show no association between differences in AFDC benefit levels in different states and the rates of illegitimacy or adolescent childbearing in those states. Moreover, benefit levels have been falling in recent years, but the rates of unwed pregnancy have risen (Ellwood & Bane, 1986). For a highly competent analysis of research concerning this and related issues, see Danziger and Weinberger (1986).

In conclusion, it can be seen that on the average adolescent parents tend to have suffered from multiple deficits in the larger environments in which they grew up as well as in their own families. As shown in tables 1.1, 1.2, and 1.3, a cluster of generally similar social, psychological, familial, and economic factors tends to be significantly associated with early nonmarital coitus, lack of contraceptive use, not terminating a pregnancy through abortion, and not marrying before a child's birth. On the average, problems in the individual development of these adolescents interact with the poverty situation within which many currently live. Thus, a total complex of factors tends to make them particularly vulnerable to life stresses, including those associated with early parenthood. These problematic factors may often be exacerbated by difficulties associated with stages of adolescent development plus early parenthood, but these difficulties are not attributable to youthful age alone. Moreover, it is essential to recognize that on average most of these adolescents had a number of problems that predated their parenthood. It appears that in essence the people who seem the least likely to be able to bear the stresses of early parenthood are the ones who are the most likely to become teenage mothers and fathers.

PROBABLE EFFECTS OF ADOLESCENT PARENTHOOD

It is a common error on the part of both the mass media and writers in scholarly journals to state, as they often do, that teenage childbearing invariably has severe consequences such as welfare dependence, early school leaving, larger completed family size, high rates of divorce, unemployment, and poor developmental outcomes for children. Statements like these often represent unfortunate misinterpretations of the data. For one thing, they overlook the variability within groups of adolescent parents. Even more seriously, these statements frequently assume that an association between one set of factors and another necessarily means that this association indicates either a cause or a consequence. An apparent association of two sets of factors often (but not always) indicates a relationship between the two sets, but a relationship does not necessarily mean that one set of factors is either a cause or a consequence of the other set.

There are further problems, including the fact that some of the frequently quoted research projects use data from samples studied in the early 1960s (Card, 1978; Maracek, 1979; Russ-Eft, Spring, & Beever, 1979; Bowerman et al., 1966). Their findings must be viewed with caution with respect to their possible application to today's adolescent parents. Societal changes create a different environmental context at different periods of time, so that the effects of behaviors today may be quite different from those of 5 or more years ago. For example, public attitudes toward unwed parents tend to be much more lenient today (1987) than they were 25 years ago, so that unmarried mothers and their children are far less likely to become social outcasts than was true at earlier periods. Other examples of recent changes include the following: that rates of youth unemployment, especially minority youth unemployment, have risen; health, employment, and welfare programs have been cut; and public opposition to abortion has increased. All these contextual changes affect both the incidence and outcomes of teenage childbearing, especially unwed childbearing.

Studies using more recent data are emphasized here. They include those of Presser (1976); Kellam (1979); Kellam et al. (1982); McCarthy and Menken (1979); Millman and Hendershot (1980); Furstenberg (1976); Furstenberg (1981); Moore and Hofferth (1978); Burden and Klerman (1984); Klerman (1986); Mott (1986); Roosa and Vaughan (1984); Brooks-Gunn and Furstenberg (1985); Moore and Wertheim (1985); Gershenson (1983); Elster and Lamb (1986); Bane, 1986. Some of these investigations involved very small samples, but others used populations from national probability surveys. Again, teenage mothers have been studied much more frequently than teenage fathers.

With all the foregoing cautions in mind, let us consider the findings from recent investigations of the apparent effects of adolescent childbearing on young parents and their families, especially on young mothers. Unfortunately, few studies have looked at the effects of this childbearing either on fathers or on the adolescent's family of origin.

Educational Factors

Adolescent pregnancy and parenthood have been a factor in dropping out of high school. However, as noted earlier, a number of teenagers drop out of school or have serious school problems before they become pregnant (Brooks-Gunn & Furstenberg, 1985). They are especially apt to withdraw from school if they get married.

Early school leaving does not necessarily mean that adolescent mothers do not obtain further education. In the 17-year follow-up study of Furstenberg's earlier research, it was found that almost one-third of low-income, urban, black women obtained some education past high school, and 5% had graduated from college (Brooks-Gunn & Furstenberg, 1985). These accomplishments reflect another aspect of the effects of environmental change in the past 20 years, during which time the higher quality and integration of schools have greatly improved opportunities for black students. Moreover, both GED programs and free or low-cost, post–high school education have become much more readily available to people of all races, ages, and income levels.

In general, black teenage mothers are more likely than white ones to continue in school and to complete high school after becoming mothers. This is probably because fewer marry; the extended black family is more apt to provide child care and other assistance; and youthful, unwed parenthood is apt to be more normative and acceptable in black communities, especially in low-income communities (Furstenberg & Crawford, 1978; Presser, 1980; Kellam et al., 1982; Brooks-Gunn & Furstenberg, 1985).

Later Family Size

Data from the late 1950s and early 1960s showed that adolescent childbearing was associated with larger-than-average family size over the following years. However, childbearing patterns have clearly changed since that time. For instance, Brooks-Gunn and Furstenberg found in their 17-year follow-up study that the average family size was 2.2 children and that over half of the mothers had had voluntary sterilization (well beyond the national average). According to an analysis by Mott (1986), the factors associated with a second birth to teenagers are: being black, low socioeconomic status of family of origin, high fertility values, being a fundamentalist Protestant, and being married. In summarizing the findings, Mott emphasizes, as did Brooks-Gunn and Furstenberg, that adolescent mothers are a very heterogeneous group and should not be considered as one type in terms of either etiology or outcomes.

Family Structure

Kellam and associates (1982) carried out a 10-year follow-up study of a large sample of chiefly black, low-income children and their families in a section of Chicago. They found five major types of family structure: mother alone; mother/father; mother/grandmother; mother/aunt; and mother/second husband. Mother/father families occurred somewhat more frequently for people who had married after age 20 (about one-half of older first marriers compared to about one-third of younger ones). Women who had borne a second child while they were still teeangers were especially apt to be in a mother-alone situation.

Mother-alone families at first child's birth tended to remain mother-alone families 10 years later. About 60% of the women in these mother-alone families said they had had no help in childrearing, compared to 6% of mothers in other family structures. Assessment of the social/psychological well-being of children in these different family structures showed that those at highest risk were children in mother-alone families. (See also a later section of this chapter regarding apparent effects on children.)

Welfare Dependency

Although it has become conventional wisdom to state that welfare dependency is a leading result of adolescent childbearing, this is an overly simple formulation. Many adolescent parents come from poverty backgrounds and might well remain or become dependent on welfare whether or not they have children. However, having a child increases their vulnerability to economic dependency and, of course, adds a child who may be welfare-dependent at least in her or his early childhood years.

Through an overview of related research Burden and Klerman (1984) conclude that although 60% of teenage mothers are dependent on welfare at one time or another, their dependency tends to last for only a few years, and as they and their children grow older, there is an increasing reliance on income through employment and marriage.

Brooks-Gunn and Furstenberg (1985) also find that adolescent mothers in later years tend to become independent of welfare. In their 17-year follow-up study they learned that two-thirds of their sample had not had any public assistance in the past 5 years, and only 13% had been welfare-dependent most of that 5-year period. Those women with the highest and most secure incomes were married to employed men. However, recall that marriage is not a "cure-all" for the economic problems of young mothers, especially black mothers, in that there is a very high, and increasing, unemployment rate among young men, especially black men.

Employment

Although the unemployment of young women is frequently claimed to be the result of adolescent childbearing, this, too, is an overly simple conclusion. For instance, there is a high youth unemployment rate for women and men in general, especially for blacks. However, having a child to care for adds another barrier to a young person's employment, especially if that person is a high school dropout. On the other hand, as we have seen, a number of these young women return to school after the child is born. Then, too, a number obtain employment, especially if they have help with child care—a crucial ingredient to their employment. Such help is most often provided by family members. However, the basic point remains: Unemployment problems lie chiefly in the structure of our economy rather than in the characteristics of individuals. Whether or not a young parent obtains a job depends primarily on the availability of employment; whether or not this job creates economic self-sufficiency depends on the wages and job security this employment offers.

Marriage

As already indicated, the majority of white, pregnant, adolescent women marry before the birth of the baby, but this is true of only a minority of black pregnant teenagers. This difference is probably attributable to a number of factors discussed earlier in this chapter, such as the unavailability of young employed black men and the norms of the black community.

A number of studies in the 1960s and early 1970s showed that early, forced marriages to legitimate a pregnancy are particularly apt to end in divorce and are especially apt to be unhappy and characterized by low income (Burchinal, 1965; Glick & Mills, 1974; Bacon, 1974; Freedman, 1970). However, again we have the question of what may be causes and what may be consequences. For instance, as shown earlier, young women who bear children as adolescents are especially likely to have a number of predisposing social, psychological, familial, and economic problems. The same is probably true of young fathers. Thus, the characteristics that they bring to marriage, plus their low employment opportunities, may well play an important part in negative marital outcomes. Marrying at a later age, not being pregnant, or not having a child would probably lessen but not erase the marital stresses observed to be likely for this group.

Furstenberg (1976) found high rates of divorce for his urban black sample of adolescent parents. The marriages that were most likely to last involved young people who had a long history of partner commitment before marriage and in which the young man had a steady job. Eighty percent of their sample at the 17-year follow-up had been married, but two-thirds of the first marriages had ended in divorce, and half of the second marriages had dissolved. These divorce rates were somewhat higher than those found in a comparable black population of women who had their first child after age 19 or so.

Families of Origin

Most studies of early parenthood show that the parents of teenage childbearers do, in fact, assume much of the associated economic burden. The availability of public assistance may contribute to the support furnished by the extended family, but parents of adolescent mothers (and sometimes parents of adolescent fathers) seem to be willing to lend assistance whether or not they receive welfare supplements (Furstenberg & Crawford, 1978; Presser, 1980; Kellam et al., 1982).

In general, however, there is a serious lack of adequate studies concerning the impact of adolescent parenthood on family systems. Furstenberg (1981) reports on nine clinical studies at the Philadelphia Child Guidance Clinic regarding the impact of the teenage mother and child living with her parents. It was observed that in a number of cases the advent of the baby of the adolescent mother seemed to pull the family together. Care of the baby sometimes seemed to strengthen the marital relationship of the grandparents. However, the girl's parents frequently resisted involving the young father and in effect the girl had to choose between a close relationship with her family or the child's father.

With respect to child care some of the families seemed to have well-organized plans, while others were somewhat haphazard. Also, in some cases the grandparents treated the adolescent mother like the baby's sibling rather than his or her mother. All in all, some families appeared to become reorganized by the child, and a cut-off of the adolescent mother was prevented. However, in some cases this lack of cut-off was accompanied by overenmeshment.

Brooks-Gunn and Furstenberg found further that the teenage mothers usually lived with their parents for only a short period. The great majority left home when they were ready to marry or become self-supporting.

Fathers

A large proportion of fathers in the Brooks-Gunn and Furstenberg follow-up study had never acknowledged their parenthood, many saying they felt unable to provide either emotional or financial support. On the other hand, about one-fourth of the fathers living outside the home continued to visit for 5 years, and one-sixth were still involved with the child for 17 years. Never-married fathers were as apt to be involved as married ones. Rather similar findings have been obtained in other studies, as discussed in the following chapter.

The many contributions that the adolescent father often makes or wishes to make may be obscured by society's harsh, punitive attitudes toward these young men. Usually the major effort of the law and welfare agencies is to establish paternity and require child support, with the assumption often being that the young man is a "no-good" Don Juan. Partly as a result of such attitudes and behaviors, young fathers are apt to become highly elusive and distrustful of the establishment (Furstenberg, 1976; Miller, 1983).

Elster and Lamb (1986), in summarizing the results of the few available (and small) studies of teenage fathers, write that the immediate events around pregnancy and parenthood tend to be stressful for them. They often have concerns about their financial responsibilities, parenting skills, education, employment, and relationships with their girlfriends. These researchers make a strong and welcome plea for clinicians to work with adolescent fathers as well as mothers in a total family context.

Child Rearing and Children

Although it was thought earlier that the youthful age of adolescent mothers was the cause of observed higher rates of prematurity and associated birth defects in their children, it has been learned more recently that these outcomes were largely, perhaps totally, a result of the higher average rates of poverty backgrounds among adolescent mothers and their greater tendency to not obtain early prenatal care. When free, high-quality care is provided to adolescent mothers, adverse birth outcomes tend to disappear, although age-related difficulties may still pertain to very young mothers (ages about 12 to 14 years) (Baldwin & Cain, 1980; Hamburg, 1986).

Other frequently claimed adverse developmental outcomes have been overstated when they are attributed to youthful age alone. However, the few available studies indicate that on the average the sons, but not the daughters, of early childbearers have a somewhat greater tendency than sons of older comparable mothers to present behavioral problems, such as hyperactivity and high levels of aggression (Bromen, 1981; Maracek, 1979).

By adolescence school achievement among children of early childbearing mothers is lower on the average. In both the 17-year follow-up in the Baltimore study and in the National Survey of Children, about half of these youngsters had repeated a grade, whereas this was true for only 20% of teenagers whose otherwise comparable mothers had been older at their birth. Also, on the average the rates of learning problems and school disinterest were somewhat higher for this group (Brooks-Gunn & Furstenberg, 1985).

Despite these adverse findings, a number of pertinent studies, mostly carried out with low-income, black adolescents, show that the majority of these mothers are as loving, conscientious, and competent as older mothers of similar socioeconomic status and race. They are especially apt to be "good" mothers when they are given support by their own families and their boyfriends, the fathers of their children (Miller, 1982; Furstenberg, 1976). However, children of adolescent parents are somewhat more likely to grow up in homes marked by marital disruption, single-parent households, and remarriage; thus, they are more apt to be exposed to the stresses often associated with these conditions (Maracek, 1979; Presser, 1976, 1978; Russ-Eft, Spring, & Beever, 1979; Sandler, 1979; Miller, 1982).

In summarizing research regarding child development outcomes, Brooks-Gunn and Furstenberg (1985) write that few differences have been found between the children of teenage and older mothers of comparable backgrounds. A few small studies show that on the average teenage mothers are less apt to talk to their young children. This may be a reason that their youngsters tend to obtain lower cognitive development scores in early childhood (Field, 1980). Then, too, although some have claimed higher rates of child abuse among teenage parents, the research evidence to date does not support this claim (Gelles, 1985).

The major studies have been of adolescents who bore infants in the 1950s and 1960s. The present data suggest that the mothering skills and childbearing practices of today's adolescent women have yet to be evaluated adequately. Parenting skills and maternal readiness rather than age per se may well be the critical determinants in the long-range outcome of infants born to adolescent mothers.

These outcomes are also affected by a number of other factors including whether or not the adolescent father is also involved in child care; whether or not the young couple is able to establish a stable, satisfying marriage; and whether or not essential resources and services are available to the youthful family including continuing education, employment, adequate income, child care, housing, and health care.

SUMMARY

The birth rate to adolescents has been declining ever since the 1960s, but the rates of both pregnancy and nonmarital births have risen markedly since the early 1970s. This decline in births has been largely owing to an increased use of abortion to terminate unwanted pregnancies. The highest birth rates have been for 18- and 19-year-old women, and the lowest are for teenagers under age 15. The rise in nonmarital births has been associated mainly with an increase in permissive attitudes towards nonmarital intercourse and childbearing (chiefly affecting white teenagers) and the marked rise in the unemployment of young black males, with jobless rates being well over 50% for inner city youth. This is a major cause of the high rate of nonmarital births (close to 90% of them) to black, adolescent mothers.

In general, much more is known about the sexual behaviors of adolescent women than of adolescent men. Partly because of sexism in our society, the major research focus has been on the female, with the result that the information presented here can be more confidently applied to young women than to young men.

A complex of biological, social, psychological, familial, and economic factors tends to be associated with the behaviors that lead to nonmarital, adolescent childbearing among adolescents. These behaviors are nonmarital intercourse, failure to consistently use effective contraceptives, failure to terminate the pregnancy through abortion, and failure to marry before the child's birth. Although adolescent parents are a highly variable group, on the average these behaviors are particularly associated with: the poverty and low socioeconomic status of their families of origin; being black; growing up in female-headed families; low occupational/educational goals; low self-esteem; and high rates of unemployment, especially for minority youth. Lack of low-cost, readily available contraceptive and abortion services also plays a part.

Factors associated with the outcomes of adolescent, nonmarital parenthood vary in relation to the characteristics young mothers and fathers bring to their new roles; the prenatal and obstetrical services they receive; the living arrangements available to them (often with the young mother's family); the nature of comprehensive educational, child care, medical, and vocational services provided for young families; and, of central importance, the availability to them of jobs at adequate wages.

Outcomes for the children of adolescent parents also vary. When appropriate controls are used to take into account the effects of socioeconomic status and racism, few if any differences can be found between the children of adolescent mothers and those of comparable mothers who had their first child when they were in their 20s or older. More longitudinal research is needed on this topic in order to further clarify the somewhat greater tendency sometimes found for a small group of children of teenage parents (especially their sons) to have behavioral problems in school.

As indicated earlier, it is unfortunate and sexist that the chief focus of research attention has been on adolescent mothers, with only slight heed given to young fathers who are of equal importance. This lack also applies to current programs set up to serve teenagers, usually the mothers, and their children, a topic that is discussed more thoroughly in the following chapter.

It is a common and unfortunate error to conclude, as many do, that adolescent parenthood is the main cause of early school leaving, youth unemployment, poverty, and welfare dependency or that these factors are the *consequences* of this parenthood. The chief *causes* of these problems lie in the structure of our society, with its institutional racism and social stratification and with the structure of our economy, with its increasing high rates of unemployment, especially among minority youth.

Many of the problems faced by adolescent parents are more likely to be an outcome of the societal and economic deficits that have often shaped their lives from their early childhood. These problems are apt to be exacerbated by their youthful childbearing but not fundamentally caused by it. The difficulties they have encountered in the past and may well encounter in the future are not centrally a matter of their age alone. Rather, these problems are, in the majority of cases, symptoms of deeper difficulties of an imperfect society that differentially imposes its deficits on those families at the most vulnerable end of the social and economic spectrum. This has significant implications for public policies, as addressed in the final chapter of this volume and in Volume 1 of this series.

2

Helping Single Adolescent Parents

RICHARD A. WEATHERLEY AND VIRGINIA G. CARTOOF

This chapter describes a continuum of services thought to be appropriate at various stages of adolescent pregnancy and parenthood. We will explore programs that address specific aspects of problems encountered by pregnant and parenting youth as well as programs that attempt to integrate service components into a comprehensive package. In considering these programs, the reader should bear in mind that there are many kinds of adolescents with many sorts of needs and characteristics. As emphasized in the preceding chapter, adolescent parents are a heterogeneous group, although they are frequently seen as just one type. Therefore programs, services, and methods of working with young parents should depend on differential diagnosis and a careful consideration of the particular characteristics of each adolescent family.

PRIMARY PREVENTION: SEX EDUCATION, BIRTH CONTROL, AND THE PROMOTION OF CHASTITY

Numerous studies have shown a widespread ignorance among adolescents about the basic facts of reproduction and the likelihood of pregnancy. Research has also confirmed that while millions of adolescent pregnancies have been averted by the availability of birth control since the late 1960s, a high percentage of sexually active teenagers still fail to use contraceptives or use the least reliable methods. To some extent these problems can be addressed through increased and more effective sex education and by making birth control more accessible to teens. Moore, Simms, and Betsey's review of research (1986, pp. 58–59) points to several factors that predict clinic use by adolescents: free services, an absence of parental notification, convenient hours for students, walk-in service, a diversity of locations, and warm and caring staff. Promising results have been reported for school-based and school-related comprehensive health clinics that offer contraceptive services. Such clinics may reduce the psychological and economic costs of birth control for adolescents (Center For Population Options; Dryfoos, 1985; Kenney, 1986).

A comprehensive review of the literature on sex education found that such programs can increase students' knowledge about sexuality and may increase the use of effective contraception, especially when linked to specific birth control services. However, these programs do not appear to have much effect on sexual behavior, and their impact on pregnancy rates is not known (Kirby, Alter, & Scales, 1979; Scales, 1983). While it may be desirable to encourage adolescents to delay the initiation of sexual activity, there is as yet no evidence that campaigns promoting chastity have that effect.

These somewhat discouraging findings underscore the complexity of the problem and the limitations of any one approach or intervention. As shown in the preceding chapter, adolescent pregnancy and parenthood seem rooted in one's total life situation and are related to social conditions such as poverty, racism, unemployment, and sex-role attitudes that inhibit contraceptive utilization by young men and women. On the other hand, while not a panacea, accessible birth control services and early, comprehensive sex education should be a major part of a community's effort to reduce unintended pregnancies among adolescents.

PREGNANT ADOLESCENTS AND HELPING PROFESSIONALS

Women of all ages commonly experience anxiety and depression during pregnancy (Bassoff, 1983), but many pregnant adolescents may respond with "denial and a facade of indifference" (LaBarre, 1972, p. 34). In contrast to the views of some helping professionals, adolescents, like many other fathers and mothers, do not necessarily view parenthood as problematic. The discrepancy between the views of young parents and service providers may lead to frustration for both: Pregnant and parenting adolescents may suspect they are being treated for a problem that does not exist, and counselors may despair over their inability to establish a therapeutic relationship (McGee, 1982). These adolescents may miss appointments and may appear indifferent to attempts to engage them (O'Leary, Shore, & Wieder 1984; Provence & Naylor, 1983; Taylor, et al. 1983). Not surprisingly, many professionals describe this population as "hard to reach" and "unmotivated" (O'Leary, Shore, & Wieder, 1984). This may be partly because of their youth but also because of the problem-filled backgrounds from which so many come.

The developmental tasks of adolescence may complicate work with pregnant adolescents. Adolescents' age-appropriate struggles toward autonomy may prevent them from seeking help, and, especially for young adolescents, their underdeveloped capacity for abstract thinking, complex decision making, and expressing feelings may further impede the development of a helping relationship (O'Leary, Shore, & Wieder, 1984; Taylor et al., 1983). It should be recognized, however, that the vast majority of older parents, including those in difficult situations, also tend to reject offers of psychological counseling (Chilman, 1980). And studies have shown that, contrary to popular belief, adolescent parents have no greater problems than somewhat older ones of comparable socioeconomic status (Furstenberg, 1976; Zitner & Miller, 1980).

OUTREACH

Adolescents who are pregnant or have children rarely seek services on their own. They may be unaware of the services available to them, lack transportation and child care, and have hopes of being rescued by parents and boyfriends (McGee, 1982). Furthermore, not all are in need of services, although financial and other concrete forms of assistance may be welcome. Agency fees, parental consent requirements, and concerns about confidentiality, restricted hours, and inconvenient locations may also inhibit service utilization (Chamie et al., 1982; Dryfoos and Heisler, 1978).

Aggressive, personal, and persistent outreach is generally required to recruit and serve pregnant girls and young parents who are having problems. Programs and services must be perceived as valuable and accessible. Child care and transportation are especially important, and staff members should be comfortable working with adolescents and able to secure their trust. This may require the assignment of peer counselors, male staff (to reach adolescent fathers), and staff from specific racial and ethnic backgrounds to reach minority youngsters.

Home visits to all adolescents who enroll in a community prenatal clinic or who are known by school personnel to be pregnant or parenting appears to be an effective outreach technique. Some programs have established in-school or in-clinic outreach centers where adolescents can learn about services before enrolling.

SOCIAL ISOLATION AND SOURCES OF SUPPORT

Reliable support networks are vitally important to adolescent mothers during pregnancy and the early years of parenthood. Social support tends to be associated with reduced emotional stress, an enhanced sense of efficacy, greater maternal satisfaction, more skillful and responsive parenting, and improved developmental status of infants (Colletta, 1981; Colletta & Gregg, 1981; Klerman, 1985; Schinke & Gilchrist, 1984; Unger & Wandersman, 1985).

While peer relationships are developmentally important (Adams et al., 1976), many adolescents tend to isolate themselves from peers when pregnant (Cannon-Bonaventure & Kahn, 1979; Colletta, Hadler, & Hunter, 1981; Colletta & Lee, 1983). Families are usually the most consistent sociocultural group providing assistance in coping with early parenthood (Fine & Pape, 1982). After the initial shock most families accept a daughter's pregnancy positively, and their acceptance, especially that of the maternal grandmother, may enhance the adolescent's ability to deal with her new role (Furstenberg, 1976; Mercer, 1979; Presser, 1980). Most unmarried adolescent parents remain at home and receive considerable help from their families—emotional support, child care, financial aid, and assistance negotiating social and health service systems. Mothers who remain at home are more likely to defer having a second child (Chilman, 1983; Furstenberg, 1976; Presser, 1980). Family support, especially the provision of child care, enables many to make educational and employment advances that would not otherwise be possible. Current public assistance policies, however, fail to reinforce family support. AFDC grants do not provide assistance for grandparents unless they had already been receiving public assistance, and their child care is uncompensated. Consequently, young mothers are most likely to remain in households when there are two grandparents, sufficient income to support an additional dependent, more living space, and the possibility that the grandmother will provide child care (Furstenberg, 1980; Furstenberg & Crawford, 1978).

Family contact is not synonymous with support, however. Social support is a function of the quality of one's relationships and the resources they provide (Unger & Wandersman, 1985). Dense and conflicted social networks can be intrusive and demanding and may engender increased anxiety, dependency, and difficulties in adjusting to parenthood (Barrera, 1981; Barth & Schinke, 1984; Unger & Wandersman, 1985). The adolescent's reliance on her mother or other kin entails reciprocal obligations; the help she receives may be conditional on her compliance with parental dictates and may supercede her developmental need to separate (Presser, 1980). Further studies are needed on the long-term psychological and social effects on young parents and their children of alternative ways of adapting to early parenthood: living with either the young mother's or father's family, marriage, cohabitation, living as a single parent, or adoption.

SERVICES TO EXTENDED FAMILIES

Teenage mothers are at the same time parents, daughters, partners, and siblings, and their pregnancies are apt to be a crisis for the entire family. These pregnancies both affect and are affected by the family system (Authier & Authier, 1980), but only recently has the role of the family been recognized in public policy or professional practice (Chilman, 1983; Forbush, 1979; Ooms, 1981). Adolescents are generally treated as autonomous decision makers, reflecting the individualistic bias that characterizes our approach to most social problems (Furstenberg, 1980).

There has been little effort to date to work with the extended families of adolescent fathers and mothers. However, most of the teenage mothers and fathers remain with their families of origin. The families often face the multiple problems of poor housing, inadequate income, unemployment, and interpersonal conflict that may embroil the young parents and inhibit their development and threaten the well-being of the infant. Thus, while family situations may differ, careful attention to the family system, including assessment and family-focused services, is indicated.

The benefits of parenthood may include an elevation of status for the adolescent mother, improved family relations, and the provision of a replacement for older siblings who have moved out—filling the empty nest. Family members may view the teenage mother as more adult than before and may extend greater privileges and resources to her as a result. Motherhood may enhance an adolescent's ability to identify and communicate with her own mother, and earlier conflicts between them may be resolved.

However, the young mother's gain in status may be at the expense of a sibling, and additional strains can develop as the infant becomes older and more difficult to manage, or when a second pregnancy occurs. Especially in families with limited incomes and restricted space, the baby's arrival can stretch meager resources to the breaking point (Furstenberg, 1980; Furstenberg & Crawford, 1978; Leishman, 1978).

The involvement of the family can begin with the decision about the resolution of the pregnancy (Abel et al., 1982). Professional intervention may help to mobilize family support and other resources and at the same time strengthen the family's decision-making and problem-solving skills (Authier & Authier, 1980; Barth & Schinke, 1984; Fine & Pape, 1979; Unger & Wandersman, 1985). Families differ in terms of structure, cohesion and adaptability, and stage of development (Authier & Authier, 1980; Russell, 1980). Grandparents may themselves be young and still coping with child-bearing and rearing (Leishman, 1978; Smith, 1975), or they may be much older and confronting the problems of aging (Stokes & Greenstone, 1981).

Family assessments should be based on direct contact with all members in order to get a better picture of family dynamics (Fine & Pape, 1979; Palmer, 1981). Families are apt to maintain entrenched attitudes toward pregnancy that should be respected by the worker (Fine & Pape, 1979). Since families differ in cultural, psychological, and system characteristics, considerable clinical skill is required in working with family members. If the decision is to relinquish the child for adoption or to abort, the counselor may be able to help the family grieve for the loss. If the decision is to keep the child, parents and siblings may need help incorporating the child in the family, repositioning the adolescent from daughter to mother, and making arrangements for prenatal care and delivery (Authier & Authier, 1980; Furstenberg, 1980).

SERVICES TO FATHERS AND THEIR FAMILIES

Contrary to popular views, the adolescent father is usually involved in his child's life and makes some material and personal contribution to the child's support in the early years. The father's involvement usually drops off after the first 2 to 5 years, although the duration of support may be related to his economic situation (Furstenberg, 1986; Presser, 1980; Rivara, Sweeney, & Henderson, 1986). Also, paternal support depends to a large extent on whether or not either parent marries or has additional children by other partners. Aside from the material benefits such involvement may bring, paternal visitation, play, and child care have been found to be usually associated with better parenting and life satisfaction for young mothers and for their children increased responsiveness and cognitive development and fewer behavior problems (Furstenberg, 1976, 1980; Parke et al, 1980; Unger & Wandersman, 1985). In recognition of this under the 1972 U.S. Supreme Court decision in *Stanley v. Illinois,* adoption agencies must attempt to locate unmarried natural fathers to secure their approval for custody dispositions (Barret & Robinson, 1982; Connolly, 1978).

Studies of adult prospective fathers reveal a pattern of somatic symptoms and psychological problems often associated with their partner's pregnancy; adolescent fathers also face the additional stresses of premature role transition (Elster & Panzarine, 1983). Early intervention with young fathers may serve to prepare them for parenting, reinforce their support for the mother, enlist their cooperation in avoiding a second pregnancy, and facilitate links with the paternal family (Allen-Meares, 1984; Earls & Siegel, 1980; Hendricks, 1983; Parke et al, 1980). Help with school completion and job training may be instrumental in providing the material basis for responsible parenting (Earls & Siegel, 1980; Hendricks, 1983).

Title IV-D of the Social Security Act was adopted in 1974 to help states secure child support from absent fathers; however, most states do not take action when the father is under 18 years of age (Rivera-Casale, Klerman, & Manela, 1984). Those advocating child support actions against teen fathers argue that these might secure contributions from his family, tap his future earnings, and deter out-of-wedlock pregnancies. The deterrence theory is reflected in the provision of a 1985 Wisconsin law that establishes "grandparent liability" for the support of a child born to an unmarried mother or father under age 18. The reasoning underlying this provision is that parents would be more inclined to counsel contraceptive responsibility for their sons if faced with the likelihood of having to support a grandchild born out of wedlock. Others, however, maintain that legal proceedings could endanger current unrecorded support payments, alienate the father, and deter the mother from seeking essential Medicaid or public assistance benefits (Cartoof, 1982; Rivera-Casale, Klerman, & Manela, 1984).

COUNSELING DURING EARLY PREGNANCY

Denial and procrastination characterize most teenagers' response to a suspected pregnancy (Bierman & Street, 1982). Professionals should help young women to confront their suspicions about pregnancy, arrange for a pregnancy test, review their options, and share the news with their parents (Klerman, Jekel, & Chilman, 1983). Adolescents may experience great difficulty over the abortion decision, obtaining an abortion, and the associated sequelae. Teenagers who abort are less likely to discuss their decision with significant others, and they receive less support than those who deliver (Klerman et al., 1982). They may need help locating a reputable clinic, negotiating parental consent or notification requirements, communicating with their partners, and confronting their feelings about the abortion. They may also need help meeting the cost of an abortion. The Hyde amendment prohibits the expenditure of federal funds for this procedure, although some states do provide for Medicaid abortions financed by state revenues. Counselors should attempt to maintain contact during the grieving period following the abortion and reinforce continued contraceptive use.

Few pregnant adolescents (5 to 10 %) choose adoption today, and as a result counselors may neglect discussing this option (Greer, 1982; Mech, 1986). Those wishing to consider this alternative should be helped to locate a licensed child-placing agency and to recognize and cope with their feelings about surrender. Support should continue after the infant's placement, as many young women experience a period of acute mourning for at least several months (Deykin, Campbell, & Petti, 1984.

While pregnant adolescents who decide to parent appear to have less difficulty making this decision and receive more support for it during pregnancy (Klerman, Jekel, & Chilman, 1983), they too need concrete assistance securing prenatal care, considering educational alternatives, and negotiating relationships with parents, peers, and partners.

INDIVIDUAL COUNSELING AND CASE MANAGEMENT

Traditional counseling strategies may be less effective with pregnant and parenting adolescents than a combination of supportive counseling, home visiting, and offers of help with concrete tasks. Young parents, like their older counterparts, are often more comfortable discussing material, external concerns than internal or interpersonal problems. Helping professionals should respect each adolescent's capacity for direct questions about feelings and relationships and should avoid offering unsolicited advice (Heger, 1977; Provence & Naylor, 1983).

Individual counseling should be combined with case management, including assistance locating services needed by young parents and advocacy for them with other agencies and institutions. Referrals for medical care, financial assistance, WIC, day care, housing, education, and employment head the list of services needed by pregnant and parenting teenagers. Counselors should take an active part in orchestrating these services by role modeling the referral process, providing transportation, offering to accompany the teen parent to community agencies, and following up after the initial visit. As Zitner and Miller (1979) observe, many adolescent mothers "need help to seek help" (p. 79). Young parents express high satisfaction with services that include case management; they find their workers helpful, experience positive feelings about the relationship, and describe the help as consistent with their own view of their problems (Brindis, Barth, & Williams, 1985; Cannon-Bonaventure & Kahn, 1979; Rubenstein & Bloch, 1978).

GROUP COUNSELING

A number of benefits of group counseling for adolescents who are pregnant or have young infants are suggested in the literature. Groups are thought to provide support and information, decrease isolation, and enable members to express their feelings and consider a range of problems, opinions, and options (Adams et al., 1976; Brindis, Barth, & Williams, 1985; St. Pierre & St. Pierre, 1980). They may provide young parents a "moratorium on growth," allowing a gradual movement into adulthood (Erf, 1981). Those who are threatened by the intimacy of individual counseling may benefit from a less intrusive group setting (O'Leary, Shore, & Wieder, 1984). Groups also offer staff members a forum in which to reinforce program goals (Quint & Riccio, 1985).

Despite these acclaimed benefits, groups do not involve or benefit all participants equally, nor do they eliminate the need for individual counseling (Brindis, Barth, & Williams, 1985). Limited verbal and conceptual skills and a mistrust of adults may make it difficult for adolescents to participate in counseling groups (O'Leary, Shore, & Wieder, 1984).

Programs that provide successful group sessions find that concrete supports, especially transportation and baby-sitting, must be offered to enable young parents to attend (Kilburn, 1983). Group membership should be proposed on the basis of each individual's needs; members should be contacted prior to each meeting and called or visited following an absence (St. Pierre & St. Pierre, 1980).

Group counseling should begin no later than the third trimester of pregnancy and should continue at least until all members have delivered. Initial sessions might focus on the young women's anticipation of labor and delivery, comparisons of due dates, and preparations for the hospital stay. The leader might introduce topics such as circumcision, rooming-in, and postnatal emotional changes (O'Leary, Shore, & Wieder, 1984). Group visits to a hospital maternity ward can help reduce anxiety about delivery (Adams et al. 1976).

Subsequent sessions are likely to focus on the adolescents' relationships with partners, peers, and parents. Bierman & Street (1982) note that in group settings most teenage expectant parents are more interested in talking about typical adolescent issues than their imminent parenthood.

There is increasing recognition of the need for individual and group services for teen fathers. While this requires considerable effort, projects that have done so report that the fathers do want assistance and do participate when appropriate services and approaches are offered. Generally, comprehensive services are needed, including personal counseling, GED classes and vocational training, and parenting education. Some projects have used peer couselors to reach the young fathers (Klinman et al., 1985; Sandler, 1979).

SERVICES AFTER DELIVERY

For teenagers who choose to raise their children the postdelivery period is generally the time when they most need support and services (Zitner & Miller, 1980). Long-term follow-up services may yield substantial benefits, as the effects of short-term interventions are often not maintained after services are terminated (Furstenberg, 1976; Klerman, 1979; Polit & Kahn, 1985; Quint & Riccio, 1985; Zitner & Miller, 1980).

The postdelivery service needs of young parents are varied and extensive. They may require help with child care, employment and training, educational services including GED preparation, medical care, birth control, transportation, and financial and housing assistance (Clapp & Raab, 1978; McGee, 1982; Mott & Marsiglio, 1985; Zitner & Miller, 1980). While case management may go a long way toward ensuring that young parents receive services, Quint and Riccio (1985) warn that the brokerage model may not respond adequately to young mothers' needs. Direct provision of these services may be a far more effective way of monitoring services and teens' participation in them.

Perhaps the most effective long-term follow-up is through home visiting (Badger, 1982; Brindis, Barth, & Williams, 1985; Cartoof,

1979; Dawson, Robinson, & Johanson, 1982; Mercer, 1979; Polit & Kahn, 1985; Provence & Naylor, 1984). Periodic maintenance visits should focus on social supports, school attendance, employment, infant health and development, and avoidance of additional pregnancies (Cartoof, 1979). Further studies are needed to assess the costs and effectiveness of these approaches.

Programs that continue to provide services for adolescents during the early child rearing years generally focus on achieving three goals: enhancing parenting skills, encouraging avoidance of additional pregnancies, and supporting education and employment goals.

PARENTING EDUCATION

Despite the lack of research support for the popular view of adolescents as inadequate parents (Furstenberg, 1976), programs generally recognize that parenting tends to place extraordinary burdens on many teenagers, especially those under age 18. Studies of parenting education have established that it is best offered following delivery rather than during pregnancy (McGee, 1982) and is most effective when instruction is flexible, informal, and individualized (Badger, 1982). Parenting courses should also target the family caregivers and father as well as the mother (Furstenberg & Crawford, 1978).

Parenting classes will not make one an expert mother nor necessarily change patterns of child care (Bierman & Street, 1982; Weigle, 1974). Heger (1977) found that structured parenting classes were often viewed by young mothers as conveying the deprecatory message that "you must learn to be better parents" (p. 3), a view sometimes reinforced by characterizations of such programs as preventing child abuse. Nevertheless, some promising results have been reported from parenting programs with differing formats and content. The various approaches have included individualized goals and instructional programs (Bell, Casto, & Daniels, 1983; Unger & Wandersman, 1985); modeling by an instructor; material incentives for participation (free toys and baby photos), transportation, and home visits (Badger, 1980); home-based training in communication, developmental milestones, and sensorimotor and interaction exercises; and training young mothers as child care workers (Field & Widmayer, 1982; Field et al., 1980; Unger & Wandersman, 1985).

Field and associates (1980) conclude that "an important caveat for [the] fairly dramatic benefits [of this program] . . . is that the results may derive simply from increased contact of a supportive nature with these mothers" (p. 435). This view is supported by the fact that the reported benefits of this and several other experimental projects were not limited to improved parenting or better developmental outcomes; they also included increased employment and school continuation rates (Bell, Casto, & Daniels, 1983; Unger & Wandersman, 1985) and fewer repeat pregnancies (Badger, 1982; Field et al., 1980; Field & Widmayer, 1982). However, caution is urged in planning parent education programs, since education alone cannot alter individual temperaments or environmental factors. Effective parenting is not primarily a matter of acquiring information but rather a response to the possibilities present in one's total life situation. To be most effective, parenting education should be offered as one of a continuum of services including employment opportunities and support services for all family members.

ENCOURAGING AVOIDANCE OF SUBSEQUENT PREGNANCIES

While most young mothers wish to prevent conception during the early years of parenting, their compliance with family planning methods often falters (Aires & Klerman, 1982; Burt et al., 1984; Polit & Kahn, 1985; Quint & Riccio, 1985). Ways of helping young mothers avoid additional conceptions include educational sessions focusing on birth control and the risk of pregnancy (Quint & Riccio, 1985) and constant, supportive reinforcement of birth control use (Cartoof, 1979; Furstenberg, 1979). The involvement of male partners in discussions of birth control is especially important, and Gilchrist and Schinke (1983) suggest several techniques for helping boys and girls communicate about contraception.

While free, accessible family planning services are an essential prerequisite, birth control information is of little use unless adolescents are motivated to use contraception. Researchers have noted a link between pregnancy prevention and school continuation. Young mothers seem to be more motivated to avoid additional pregnancies if they believe their educational goals are attainable (Furstenberg, 1976; Quint & Riccio, 1985; St. Pierre & St. Pierre, 1980). Adolescent parents are apt to have had a long history of educational problems. Therefore, a very careful assessment is needed of their academic aptitude, level of achievement, and educational deficits. Individual tutoring in basic skills and the provision of day care would go a long way toward helping young parents remain in school.

RETURN TO SCHOOL

Teenage mothers who return to school following childbirth often do so within a few months of delivery (Badger, 1982). Those who do not return then are substantially less likely to complete their high school education (Miller & Miller, 1983), and most programs actively discourage young mothers from taking time off from school for this reason. Evaluative studies have found that in programs that explicitly seek to encourage school continuation, 80 to 90% of young mothers return to school immediately after delivery (Aires & Klerman, 1982; Hardy et al., 1978); Nelson et al., 1982). However, school continuation subsequently drops off—only 55% of OAPP (Office of Adolescent Pregnancy Programs, DHHS) project clients were still attending or had completed school 2 years after delivery (Burt et al., 1984); and only 43% of Project Redirection clients were still in school 2 years after enrollment (Quint & Riccio, 1985).

Teen parents sometimes prefer alternative school programs that offer more individualized attention, smaller classes, and more flexible scheduling (Quint & Riccio, 1985). Forty percent of young mothers who complete school obtain GED diplomas (Mott & Marsiglio, 1986), suggesting the importance of providers establishing or referring to GED programs.

EMPLOYMENT

While the vast majority of young mothers report that they plan to work (Zitner & Miller, 1980) and that they would prefer employment to public assistance (Quint & Riccio, 1985), many do not succeed in realizing this goal (Burt et al., 1982). Thus, service providers have increasingly turned to employment preparation, job training, and job development (MDRC, 1986; Schinke & Gilchrist, 1984). WIN (Work Incentive) programs that succeeded in placing low-income and AFDC mothers in jobs found that certain basic services were required: child care, transportation, job search assistance, and counseling and job development based on individual needs and interests (Feldman, 1985). More attention also needs to be paid to increasing employment opportunities for young fathers (Polit, 1986). With persistent high rates of youth unemployment, especially for minority youth, such services are likely to have only limited success. A more promising approach is the creation of public sector jobs for hard-to-place unemployed youth. (See Volume 1, chapters 1 and 2 of this series.)

SERVICES FOR THE CHILDREN OF TEENAGE PARENTS

Difficulty locating reliable child care is the chief reason given by young mothers for dropping out of school. The lack of free or low-cost infant care has led a number of school-based programs to develop on-site day care facilities for participants' children, and many of these use the center as a learning laboratory for young mothers to acquire parenting skills (Klerman, 1983; Palmer, 1981; Sung, 1981; Wiegle, 1974).

Teen-tot clinics have been established by hospital- and clinic-based programs to provide comprehensive health care to mother and baby by the same providers and during the same clinic hours. Such programs strive to increase compliance with well-child checkups, provide family planning services, and offer counseling and education (Miller & Miller, 1983; Nelson et al., 1982).

The St. Paul, Minnesota, Maternal and Infant Care Project sponsors a public school-based program that has gained national attention because of its on-site clinic that provides pregnancy testing, prenatal and pediatric care, and family planning services. A day care center provides care for the babies of parenting students, who are required to attend a for-credit child development course (Berg et al., 1979; Edwards, Steenman, & Hakanson, 1977; Taylor et al., 1983, 1979).

SERVICE SITES AND PROGRAM MODELS: COMPREHENSIVE PROGRAMS

An approach long favored by many service advocates has been that of fostering local, comprehensive service programs that combine a variety of social, education, and health services at a single site or at multiple sites that are linked through referral arrangements. Core services include pregnancy testing, maternity and adoption counseling and referral, family planning, pre- and postnatal care, nutrition information, and family life education (Jekel & Klerman, 1982; Weatherley et al., 1986, pp. 73–74; Weatherley et al., 1985, pp. 7–12). With the enactment of the Adolescent Health Services and Pregnancy Prevention Act of 1978 and its extension in 1981 as Title XX of the Public Health Service Act, the comprehensive service model became official federal policy. Although service advocates welcomed the legislation as providing needed support for the development of model programs, many faulted it for its lack of emphasis on birth control and for its meager funding (Ooms, 1981, p. 39).

Furthermore, most communities lack the complement of essential health and welfare services, administrative funds, and other resources on which to build a comprehensive program (Weatherley et al., 1985, 1986).

Any program or site may be effective in delivering and managing comprehensive services, with the key elements of apparent success lying in "competent management, good community relations, and proper coordination" (Burt & Sonenstein, 1985, p. 32). While projects based in schools or social agencies offer more diversity of services than those in health agencies or hospitals (Burt et al., 1984), hospital and clinic-sponsored programs are perhaps best at offering pregnancy verification, pre- and postnatal health care, and family planning. Adolescent prenatal clinics have proven successful at improving obstetrical outcomes for this high-risk group (Cooper, 1982; Felice et al., 1981). However, health agencies face constraints in recruitment and in providing ancillary social and educational services (Jekel & Klerman, 1982; Aires & Klerman, 1981).

DATA COLLECTION AND PROGRAM EVALUATION

A program's ability to collect and report quantified data regarding who is being served, the nature and amount of services received, and participants' outcomes following service provision can result in better understanding of needs and can assist programs to compete for scarce funds. Klerman (1979) suggests that programs begin planning an evaluation by defining the specific changes that participants will have to undergo to avoid the negative consequences of young parenthood as well as the program elements designed to help them achieve those goals. Whenever possible, enrollees' outcomes should be compared to those of comparable nonparticipants. At a minimum a program should be able to determine the proportion of a community's pregnant adolescents that is being served and to identify gaps in services.

An adequate evaluation should take into account the findings of other studies of similar programs and populations. While individual programs may define a unique intervention, client outcomes may lend themselves to comparisons across program types. The per-client cost of providing services should be measured as well, so that the benefits of participation can be weighed against the resources required to achieve them. Specialists in program evaluation should be hired by projects wishing to evaluate their effectiveness, as technical expertise is required to perform quantitative analysis of program effects.

Despite the urgings of most researchers to utilize a control or comparison group in evaluating a program's impact, providers have considerable difficulty locating and maintaining contact with adolescents who do not receive services. Young mothers recruited for comparison groups tended to be hostile and suspicious.toward interviewers, although each was paid for cooperating. Considerable staff time and resources, neither of which is readily available in most programs, must be devoted to identifying and interviewing control group members. Despite these constraints, program evaluators must recognize that client outcomes can best be measured by controlling for the effects of personal motivation through the use of a comparison group.

Data collection can be time-consuming and tedious for busy program staff. Agency administrators should assist providers to comply with data collection schedules through incentives (time off, extra pay) and by allocating realistic time to this task. The results of a data collection effort should be shared with staff and utilized as a tool for improving services.

CONCLUSION

Those seeking to provide services for adolescent parents, their children, and their families face difficult challenges. Many of the deleterious outcomes often associated with early childbearing reflect the adverse effects of poverty and racism on the lives of pregnant and parenting adolescents rather than their youth. Adolescent parents may be able to achieve substantial goals with help from service providers, but the chronic deprivation, including high rates of youth unemployment, that characterizes the lives of many may mean that the gains are often not enduring.

Funding is scarce, and existing local health and social services are generally insufficient to meet the needs of this population. Where special programs exist, service providers often find that resources are unavailable for such essential functions as outreach, home visiting, coordination, and evaluation. With limited resources it is difficult to serve fathers and extended families and to provide infant care and long-term follow-up. As a result, providers are often forced to concentrate on less effective short-term crisis intervention services for pregnant girls. Many communities remain unserved by any kind of special program.

The problem is as much political as technical. We are not certain which interventions are most effective, and we lack the resources to implement and test various interventions. What is needed is both a national commitment to prevention to reduce the number of unintended adolescent pregnancies and births together with an adequately funded national program supporting local services for young single parents. In addition, the impact of such services should be evaluated. For maximum effectiveness these approaches need to be carried out in the context of broader reforms to reduce the poverty, unemployment, racism, and associated ills of our society.

3
Heterosexual Couples Who Cohabit Nonmaritally
SOME COMMON PROBLEMS AND ISSUES

ELEANOR D. MACKLIN

INTRODUCTION

In 1986 there were about 2.2 million unmarried-couple households in the United States (U.S. Bureau of the Census, 1986b, pp. 2–3, 5). Thirty percent of these households had children under 15 years of age residing in the home, and an unknown number had children from a previous relationship who visited on occasion. Thus, in discussing the problems commonly experienced by unmarried couples, we will be considering problems potentially faced at any given time in the United States by a minimum of 4.5 million persons and their children and other kin.

Unmarried couples include persons of all ages, with the majority under 35 years of age. About one in five such households includes two persons under the age of 25. In 1986 the median age of all unmarried-couple householders (61% of whom were men) was 31.6; 22% were under 25 years; 43%, 25–34 years; 18%, 35–44 years; and 17%, 45 years and older. About 52% of the householders were persons who had never been married, and 40% were either separated or divorced. Unmarried households can be divided into three general categories: two persons who have never been married, one never-married person and one previously or currently married person, and two persons currently or previously married to others, with roughly equivalent numbers in each category (see Macklin, 1985).

The number of such households has increased dramatically over the past 25 years (see U.S. Bureau of the Census, 1986a, pp. 14–15, 75), with the primary escalation occurring in the 1970s. From 439,000 unmarried-couple households in 1960, the number rose to 523,000 in 1970 and 1,589,000 in 1980, with about four times as many unmarried couples in 1986 as in 1970. Further documentation of this trend comes from data on marriage license applicants. For example, in Lane County, Oregon, the number of couples residing together before marriage (as evidenced by both persons using the same address) increased from 13% in 1970 to 53% in 1980 (Gwartney-Gibbs, 1986).

In a sample of 159 newly married couples in Los Angeles in the late 1970s (Newcomb & Bentler, 1980b), 47% reported having lived together for some time before their marriage (35% for 3 months or more).

It should be noted that in spite of this increase, only about 4% of all couple households in the United States in 1986 consisted of nonmaritally cohabiting couples. Moreover, the rate of increase appears to have slowed somewhat in recent years, dropping from 11% per year in the 1970s to 5.6% annually from 1980 to 1986 (U.S. Bureau of the Census, 1986b, pp. 2–3).

One can only hypothesize about the reasons for the sudden increase of persons living together unmarried during the 1970s. Numerous factors apparently combined to create an atmosphere in which such a lifestyle could be both comfortable and functional. Major factors initially were the improved availability of effective contraception, the growing acceptance of nonmarital sexual interaction for both men and women, and the increasing demand that women be granted the same liberal housing policies on college campuses normally accorded men. The rising divorce rate and the increasing concern for the quality of the marital relationship prompted persons to move more cautiously than before into both first and second marriages, thus creating large numbers of persons who wanted to "try out" a relationship before making a permanent commitment.

In response to changing gender roles, increasing numbers of women were postponing marriage in order to pursue advanced education and establish themselves in careers prior to assuming family responsibilities. In 1986 the median age of first marriage was 25.7 years for men and 23.1 years for women, compared to 23.2 and 20.8 in 1970; 58% of women aged 20 to 24 in 1986 had not married, compared to 36% in 1970 (U.S. Bureau of the Census, 1986b, p. 4). With societal norms allowing persons the opportunity for a fully intimate relationship while unmarried, and technology and the availability of abortion reducing the likelihood that unwanted pregnancy would force marriage, couples could now elect to live together while testing the relationship and/or growing to the point where marriage was desired and feasible.

It is important to recognize that there is no standard "nonmarital cohabitation relationship." Persons engage in and continue nonmarital cohabitation for a host of reasons, ranging from the convenience of sharing companionship and household facilities to a belief that society should not be in the business of legitimizing marital relationships. The age and previous life experience of the individuals, their degree of commitment to the relationship, and the particular context of their cohabitation (e.g., previous marital relationships, the presence and age of children, financial or professional pressures, and extent of support from kin) will all play an important role in determining the nature of the relationship, the type of stressors experienced, and the degree of perceived satisfaction.

In order to understand the range of cohabitation relationships, it is sometimes useful to classify them in terms of degree of emotional and behavioral commitment to the relationship. Using such a continuum, at least five types become immediately obvious (see Macklin, 1985; Petty, 1975; Storm, 1973):

1. *Temporary casual convenience* (including "contract cohabitation" as described by Van Deusen, 1974), in which two persons share the same living quarters because it is advantageous to do so, with interaction ranging from none to friendly companionship
2. *Affectionate, going-together relationship,* in which the couple lives together because they enjoy being together and will continue to live together as long as this is true
3. *"Trial marriage,"* in which the couple is together because the partners are seriously contemplating a permanent commitment and wish to test the wisdom of it
4. *Temporary alternative to marriage,* in which the partners have made a commitment to marry but are living together until it is more convenient to do so
5. *Permanent or semipermanent alternative to marriage,* in which the couple is living together in a long-term committed relationship similar to marriage but without the legal and religious sanctions

Classification is complicated because any given cohabiting couple may exemplify a number of these types or stages as their relationship evolves, and partners within the same relationship may not necessarily be at the same point at the same time.

It is impossible from available data to say what proportion of the 2.2 million cohabiting couples reported by the Census in 1986 fall into each of the five categories. When college cohabitants were asked during the 1970s to describe their relationship, most designated themselves as being in a "strong, affectionate, monogamous" Type 2 relationship (Macklin, 1978). They often shared a strong emotional relationship with each other but had not yet reached the point of long-term commitment; the women were somewhat more likely than the men to indicate plans to marry their partner (Lyness, Lipetz, & Davis, 1972; Risman et al., 1981). However, it is not at all clear that these couples are representative of the average cohabiting couple, who are considerably older, nor do we know if this is still the norm for college couples.

Data to date on U.S. couples indicate that few choose to cohabit on a long-term basis without marriage and that most nonmarital cohabiting relationships either terminate or result in marriage, usually within a year of the initiation of the cohabitation (Hanna & Knaub, 1981; Newcomb & Bentler, 1980a; Rank, 1981). These data have led researchers to conclude that cohabitation in the United States is an added stage in the courtship/mate selection process rather than an alternative to marriage (see Macklin, 1978, 1985). Rather than serving as a threat to the institution of marriage, nonmarital cohabitation appears to be "a new normative step leading to marriage" (Gwartney-Gibbs, 1986).

Researchers are also clear that knowing that a couple has lived together before marriage tells one little about the probable quality of the later marital relationship. The general findings are that there are few differences between married couples who have and have not lived together (Budd, 1976; Macklin, 1985). Some researchers have suggested that persons who cohabit before marriage may, as a group, express less marital satisfaction than noncohabitors (DeMaris & Leslie, 1984; Watson, 1983), although this may be due more to characteristics of cohabitors than to the experience of cohabitation per se.

Other researchers have suggested that couples who have lived together before marriage are just as likely to divorce as those who have not (Newcomb & Bentler, 1980a). Premarital cohabitation is clearly not an effective spousal selection device (see, for example, Clatworthy & Scheid, 1977; Jacques & Chason, 1979; Rank, 1981). This may be because some cohabitors drift into marriage as they drifted into cohabitation, do not consciously use the cohabitation experience as a way to improve their relationship skills, and often marry for the wrong reasons such as a search for security, to legitimize a pregnancy, to conform to social pressure, or to remedy a failing relationship.

In a rare, 4-year follow-up of 34 premaritally cohabiting couples first interviewed soon after marriage, those who had the most successful marriages tended to be older, previously divorced, better educated, and more traditional (Newcomb & Bentler, 1980a). Perhaps it is these couples who had the maturity and motivation to best utilize the cohabitation experience.

It is interesting, however, to note that those premarital cohabitors who later divorced had higher marital adjustment scores at the time of divorce than did the noncohabitors who divorced. Do premarital cohabitors give up on relationships more easily, or do they handle conflict with less animosity and independence with more comfort? The data do not provide the answers.

Given that nonmarital cohabitation has been an increasingly prevalent lifestyle within the majority culture for well over a decade, what have we learned about the characteristic problems experienced by persons who choose this living pattern? What issues might couples living together unmarried have to face? What stressors might persons considering the possibility of living together be advised to anticipate? We will review the problems commonly reported by persons who have cohabited and suggest possible ways in which couples can help themselves deal constructively with these problems.

Discussion of the issues will be organized by the portion of the couple's system in which they are likely to originate: (a) issues arising from within the couple relationship itself, (b) issues growing out of the family system of which the couple is a part, and (c) issues arising from forces external to the family system.

ISSUES WITHIN THE COUPLE SYSTEM

Issues of Territoriality and Separateness

Because for most Americans cohabitation is a step toward rather than a symbol of long-term commitment, "living together" tends to be a fairly ambiguous and somewhat tentative state, at least initially. Persons frequently "drift" into living together (see Jackson, 1983), staying for an increasing number of nights or days on an increasingly regular basis and gradually accumulating clothes and other possessions until such time as a lease must be renewed, a job beckons in another location, or some other factor forces a more definitive decision to be made about the future of the relationship.

Because of this, partners often cannot agree as to the exact date when they began living together, one perhaps marking it from when he began sleeping over or when he moved out of his own apartment while the other marks it from when they bought a house together or made a public declaration of their relationship. Sometimes it will be an old apartment mate who first acknowledges the new arrangement, observing out loud that "Jeff doesn't live here anymore."

Because cohabiting persons on the average are some 6 or 7 years older than persons at first marriage and one of the two partners is likely to have been previously separated or divorced, many persons enter cohabitation having lived a rather independent, autonomous life for some period of time. Unlike a first marriage in one's early 20s, when persons receive their first household possessions as joint wedding gifts, seek out their first residence together, and move in feeling that they each have an equal right to be there, cohabiting couples frequently begin life together with separate possessions, surrounded by "your things" and "my things" that remind them daily of their separateness.

Frequently cohabitation means that one person literally moves into the physical space of the other, feeling to some extent like a guest who is welcome only at the pleasure of the other. There may well be on the part of the host partner a sense of having one's territory invaded ("He's messing up my bathroom with his things!") and on the part of the guest partner a sense of invading someone else's territory ("I wonder if it will be OK if I put my things in his bathroom?"). Unlike marriage, cohabitation carries an air of tentativeness about the future of the relationship, causing partners to hesitate to give up the symbols of their independence and become overly dependent on an as yet unsure thing.

Thus, whereas marriage has classically been plagued by the risk of too much togetherness, too much "couple front," and not enough space for separateness and individuality, cohabitation, by the very nature of the relationship stage that it represents, may run the risk of too much separateness, too much self-protection, and too little openness to vulnerability (Blumstein & Schwartz, 1983).

Issues of Commitment

For most persons in this society marriage is still the primary symbol of emotional commitment between lovers, and for the majority a sincere declaration from one's partner that he or she wishes to marry you is still a necessary step in the commitment process. Therefore, for most cohabitants issues of commitment will be present until the decision has been made either to marry or to break up. Marriage, of course, does not magically remove these issues, for frequently after marriage the question of commitment will resurface.

Many couples, even after years of marriage, may find themselves once again essentially uncommitted cohabitants, in a state of emotional limbo while they search to see if there is sufficient basis to reaffirm the marriage.

Researchers in the field (e.g., Johnson, 1973) have typically viewed commitment as having at least two components: personal commitment, or the extent to which one is personally dedicated to continuing the relationship; and behavioral commitment, or acts and the consequences of those acts that tend to bind one into a relationship (e.g., possessions owned in common, informing others about the relationship). Both of these criteria can be used to assess the level of commitment between cohabiting partners.

Cohabiting partners frequently vary in the extent to which they are committed to the relationship, with one having, at least temporarily, less commitment than the other. It is important to recognize the "principle of least interest" that typically operates in such circumstances, meaning that the person with the least interest in or commitment to the relationship has the most power in it. The more committed partner will typically sacrifice more, work harder to please, and give in more easily to the desires of the other in an effort to maintain the relationship.

Because of the tendency for women to be more committed to marriage than men and because cohabiting women are more likely than cohabiting men to express an intent to marry their partner (Budd, 1976; Johnson, 1973; Kieffer, 1972; Lyness, Lipetz, & Davis, 1972; Lewis et al., 1977; Risman et al., 1981), women may more likely become victims of "least interest" than men. It is unclear whether this will continue as women become more concerned about professional careers and as alternatives to marriage become more viable for them. The level of emotional investment characteristic of lesbian couples, however, suggests that commitment is particularly important to women irrespective of their professional aspirations.

There has been little description to date of the internal dynamics of the cohabiting relationship as it evolves over time. Hennon (1981) has noted that "commitment balance" (i.e., both partners have equal commitment to the relationship) is an important factor in how cohabiting couples handle conflict. In addition to being more open to experiencing conflict, "symmetrical couples" are better able to manage conflict and to keep it from threatening the relationship. Because they are equally invested emotionally, they are more likely to invest equal amounts of energy in conscious efforts at relationship maintenance. The willingness to self-disclose and the ability to deal constructively with the conflict that may ensue from that disclosure have been found to be related to the degree of relationship satisfaction reported by nonmarital cohabiting couples (Cole & Goettsch, 1981). To achieve the quality of communication that this suggests will obviously require both good problem-solving skills and a high degree of commitment to working on the relationship.

Some have hypothesized that because of the relatively few societal supports for the nonmarital cohabiting relationship more effort must be expended by the couple themselves to sustain the relationship (Macklin, 1985). Montgomery (1973) has suggested that there is a hierarchy of behavioral symbols of gradually evolving mutual commitment that must occur if a cohabitation relationship is to last and that there is a form of circular reciprocity that must occur between the partners in order to allow the commitment to escalate safely. For example when one partner agrees to move in, the other agrees to cut off other relationships; as she agrees to be sexually exclusive, he begins to include her in his visits to his parents; as she feels accepted by his family, she adds his name to her answering tape, and so forth.

Each member of the couple uses the behavior of the partner as an external sign of the other's growing investment, thus making it safer to invest oneself further and creating a mutual upward spiraling of both emotional and behavioral commitment. Each partner weighs, often unconsciously, the relative costs and benefits of further vulnerability, the two engaged in a kind of cautious dance, each ever-vigilant and assessing whether the other is approaching at the same rate and risking in the same proportion. Persons who have been badly damaged in earlier relationships may be unwilling to take these necessary risks, and couples composed of two such persons may find themselves stuck, each unwilling to give emotionally until the other demonstrates that it will be safe to do so.

After a survey of 6,000 American couples (of whom 650 were nonmarital, heterosexual cohabitants), Blumstein and Schwartz (1983) conclude that cohabiting couples "hold interdependence at arm's length until they decide to get married." Both persons tend to work, and most do not pool their monies. Cohabitation is usually a "pay-as-you-go" system with each paying an equal share, at least initially. Pooling resources begins when they think the relationship is going to last, and the pooling is a fundamental part of the commitment process. Until then there is a concerted determination to maintain independence. It is this tension between independence and commitment that is the core issue of many cohabitation relationships.

Ambiguous or Incompatible Expectations

Whenever persons enter into a nonnormative relationship in which there are no clearly understood roles and rules, they must assume the burden of clarifying and negotiating the attitudes and behaviors that will be expected of one another. Such is certainly often the case in cohabiting relationships, in which there are no generally accepted norms regarding what is to be expected of a cohabiting partner. The issue of role clarification as discussed here includes, but goes far beyond, the usual issues of division of labor and home/career role conflicts experienced by many marital couples.

The most crucial expectation about which cohabiting couples need to be explicit is the meaning to be attached to their living together. Because people cohabit for a wide range of reasons, and often on the assumption that they are doing so for the same reason, it seems important that individuals be "up front" both with themselves and their partner about what it is they are expecting when they agree to live together. Does it imply a commitment to a long-term relationship? An agreement to live together nonmaritally on a temporary basis until they can see if they should make a long-term commitment? A desire to be together, but only for as long as it is convenient to do so? An emotional need for a housemate because one does not wish to be alone but has no desire for true partnership or real intimacy? Subtle differences perhaps, but very distressing if the two persons are not in agreement about which of these applies to them.

The role of wife or husband used to be quite clear, and the privileges and responsibilities associated with marriage were generally understood. And while this is certainly no longer true for the roles in marriage, it is even less true for the role of cohabitant. For example, does one's partner expect him to share her financial liabilities, serve as a quasi-stepparent to her children, accompany her on the holidays to her relatives, add his signature to the Christmas cards, share equally in the rent even though their incomes may differ, move if her company requires a relocation? To what extent will decisions be made jointly? Is it all right to spontaneously move the furniture or hang one's pictures on the wall? What happens to the division of assets if there is a "divorce" or death? What if pregnancy occurs?

Many persons find it presumptuous even to raise such issues, suggesting that their relationship is not yet at a stage at which such questions would be appropriate, or that they will handle such issues when the time comes. Even the most well-intended, long-term marriages often flounder on the shoals of hurt and bitterness because of unconscious and unexpressed expectations that underlie the inexplicit contract to which they both unwittingly agreed when they exchanged their wedding vows (Sager, 1976). Certainly this is even more likely to happen in the case of the more ambiguous relationship of nonmarital cohabitation in which a lack of predictability and an absence of clear understanding about the meaning of the relationship are intrinsic to the lifestyle (Blumstein & Schwartz, 1983).

Transition to Termination

In addition to the issues surrounding the decision to initiate cohabitation are those associated with the decision to terminate the relationship, whether by parting or marriage.

From his observations, Cole (1976) listed the following as common reasons that unmarried cohabiting relationships fail: emotional immaturity, insufficient or unequal commitment, crises external to the relationship (e.g., physical separation), and value differences regarding such things as use of money and division of labor. Studies of young cohabiting couples (Ganson, 1975) found that the major reasons given for breaking up were "growing apart," overdependency, and loss of identity, with women reporting more problems than men (see also Risman et al., 1981). It is hypothesized that the higher incidence of problems reported by women occurs perhaps because women are more apt to be sensitive to relationship issues, more emotionally invested in relationships and hence more likely to experience emotional dependency, and desirous of a more egalitarian relationship than is often reported by nonmaritally cohabiting couples.

Although it is commonly stated that a good reason to live together rather than to marry is the relative ease of termination, anecdotal evidence suggests that this is not always the case. Persons ending a cohabitation relationship are likely to experience the same emotions associated with any divorce experience (denial, anger, grief, and gradual reintegration into single life), with the amount of stress proportional to the degree of emotional involvement and the length of time together. Because there is less social stigma attached to ending a cohabitation relationship and less legal hassle involved and because cohabiting relationships are generally of shorter duration than marriage, with less initial expectation of permanence, it seems likely that most "divorcing" cohabitants will experience less guilt, less sense of failure, and a quicker adjustment to separation than married persons who divorce (Macklin, 1985).

There are few systematic data regarding the effect of the transition from living together unmarried to living together married. Folklore is full of cases in which marriage apparently destroyed a good relationship, but it seems likely that this was because of an unshared expectation that relationship roles would change with marriage. Berger (1974) noted after interviews with a small sample of 21 married couples who had cohabited premaritally that marriage did not lead to any dramatic change in their relationship and that the relationship after marriage usually reflected the quality of the relationship before marriage.

Rank (1981), who studied married and divorced couples, some of whom had cohabited before marriage, reported that the marriages that ended in divorce tended to have one member who saw the marriage as having led to new and undesired demands and expectations. Divorced couples reflecting on their marriage were more likely to report that they had inaccurately predicted how their partner would behave after marriage, had married for the wrong reasons (e.g. parental pressure, fear of losing the partner, or insecurity), and had assumed that marriage would solve their relationship problems. Still-married couples who had cohabited premaritally reported having had similar expectations of married life and apparently had made a conscious effort to minimize the transition to marriage and to treat the marriage as a natural continuation of the cohabiting relationship.

ISSUES WITHIN THE FAMILY SYSTEM

When Nonmarital Cohabitation Is Viewed as Unacceptable

When nonmarital cohabitation first emerged in middle-class America in the early 1970s, attitudes of the general public were strongly and consistently opposed. The great majority of parents viewed cohabitation as either immoral or unwise, and couples used any number of strategies to conceal their cohabitation from their parents (Macklin, 1974; Smith & Kimmel, 1970; Steiner, 1975). Parents who were most opposed threatened disinheritance, and even the most tolerant wrestled with the question of whether to allow the young couple to sleep together when they came to visit. In 1974 when the CBS *60 Minutes* staff approached the author to do a segment on cohabiting couples and their parents, not a single set of parents agreed to participate, although the families selected were those in which the young couple felt their parents had accepted their relationship. While the particular parents had learned to tolerate the behavior, they clearly were not at ease with it and did not relish having neighbors, relatives, clients, and other associates become aware of their "disgrace."

However, by the time Yankelovich and associates (1981) did a national survey in 1978, 52% of the respondents indicated that it was not "morally wrong for couples who are not married to live together." In the 10 years since that time attitudes have shifted even more dramatically, with large numbers of families having experienced members of various ages living with partners to whom they were not married. Rather than condemn the behavior per se, parents today tend to base their reactions on their perception of the maturity of the persons involved and the degree of responsibility with which the individuals appear to handle their emotional relationships.

The most significant negative familial reaction to nonmarital cohabitation is now likely to be experienced by once-married persons with children. The ex-spouse may object to having his or her children live with or visit the divorced spouse who is cohabiting nonmaritally. Although verbalized as moral indignation or concern for the socialization of the children, the reaction may at least partly reflect jealousy of the new partner or fear that one's parental role will be usurped by the potential stepparent. Grandparents may fear that their grandchildren are being subjected to an unhealthy degree of instability, particularly if there are several successive cohabitations. The children themselves may see the parent's new partner as an undesirable intrusion into their home life or as a threat to their parents' reuniting.

In the case of divorced persons there is some indication that the incidence of cohabitation may decline as the age of the children involved increases. In a study of 80 remarried families 14% of those who had cohabited before remarriage had children aged 11 to 17, compared to 30% of those who had younger children (Hanna & Knaub, 1981). This may reflect the fact that adolescent children as a group tend to experience more problems with being part of a newly formed stepfamily than do younger children, are more angered by divorce, and are more likely to resent their parents' love life and the changes it may impose on the household.

Ambiguity of Family Relationships

Parents of adult offspring who are cohabiting nonmaritally frequently report confusion in knowing how to relate to their child's partner. First, there is the issue of terminology. How does one introduce the cohabiting partner of one's 24-year-old daughter? "This is Mary's boyfriend?" (Too juvenile.) "Fiance?" (Not technically correct.) "POSSLQ" (person-of-opposite-sex-same-living-quarters, a term designed by the Bureau of the Census)? (A bit awkward.) Society is still seeking an appropriate and easily mouthed word for the status of cohabitant. "Housemate," "partner," "significant other," and "friend" all appear to have sifted through the filter of social usage and are now among the terms most commonly used.

More troubling is the degree of emotional investment a family member should appropriately make in such a person. When formal engagements were "de rigueur" and one's daughter became engaged, it was clear that it was time for the family to open its ranks, begin to make overtures to the new in-laws, invite the son-to-be to "call me Dad," and plan for the future. What similar clue do families now use to signal such transitions? Announcement of a wedding date has perhaps replaced the engagement ring. Length of time together is also a factor—the longer the cohabitation the more likely the partner is to be accepted as "family." However, after a period of time parents may press for a more formal definition of the relationship, if for no other reason than their desire to have and to legitimize grandchildren.

It is clear that in most families marriage denotes a more definitive place in the family than does cohabitation. As one woman remarked after a visit to her partner's parents' home, "When I heard Jim's niece refer to his brother's new wife as Aunt Jill, I felt a wave of anger . . . more at Jim than anyone. Jill had been dating Bob for only a year and yet was already firmly ensconced in the family, while I who had lived with Jim for 5 years was still merely Mary."

This lack of legitimacy becomes even more evident in the event of a dissolution of the cohabiting relationship. It is hard enough to know whether and how to relate to in-laws after the end of a marriage. How does one relate after the "divorce" of cohabitation?

Relationships become even more ambiguous in the event of death, especially when there has been no will, for the deceased partner's family in that case has full legal authority to claim any and all of his or her possessions despite whatever wishes the remaining partner may have.

Once-married cohabitants with children from the former marital relationship must be prepared to deal with the special set of problems that cohabitation may present for their children and for their role as parents. In addition to the concerns identified in the previous section, divorced parents may experience some discomfort at exploring an emotionally and sexually intimate nonmarital relationship when their children are also in the house. Often the effect of this is to deny the new couple normal opportunities for the spontaneous and unself-conscious interaction that are desirable for the healthy evolution of a relationship.

The normal issues of role ambiguity experienced by many stepparents will be experienced even more intensely by a live-in partner. What role does the parent expect this person to assume with regard to the children? What role does the individual him- or herself want to play? What role will the children allow? Some parents are very cautious about permitting or encouraging a partner/child relationship, with their degree of caution mirroring the caution or uncertainty that they themselves feel about the couple relationship. Some will resent anyone who may appear to be interfering in or critical of their own child rearing. Some children, particularly adolescents, may react with embarrassment to the renewed sexuality that they sense in their parent and judge the new relationship to be inappropriate for a person of their parent's age. Because of the unclear boundary that often exists between a stepparent and stepchild, a boundary that is even more unclear if the live-in partner is seen as the parent's "girlfriend" or "boyfriend," there may be some latent or even explicit sexual energy between the adolescent and this person.

Some children prematurely adopt their parent's live-in partner, so intense is their longing for a sense of normalcy and stability. Some are joyful at the signs of increasing permanence and eagerly anticipate an eventual wedding ceremony. Some have been so hurt by previous loss that they panic at any signs of conflict, fearful that this relationship will also end. Whatever the situation the partners and their family members will experience, there will be, at least for a time, the underlying question: How are we to relate to each other, and what role are we to play in each other's lives? The question is not quite as likely to be asked by persons in a first marriage or even in a remarriage.

ISSUES WITHIN THE EXTERNAL SYSTEM

In the early 1970s, when nonmarital cohabitation was more of an anomaly, cohabitors often found themselves having to be somewhat wary about the extent to which they publicized the status of their relationship. Landlords might be leery about renting or banks about lending to an unmarried couple, considering a nonmarital relationship to be a rather risky investment. Church groups struggled over the question of whether such persons were "living in sin" and whether unmarried couples should be allowed to remain in the congregation or be housed together at church-sponsored retreats (Mace & Mace, 1981). Trust officers wondered if monies left in trust funds should be granted to young women if they were "shacking up." College housing officers wrestled with how to provide adequate privacy for students whose roommates wanted to have their lovers share the bedroom. Employers such as schools and police departments often threatened to fire their cohabiting employees for immoral conduct unfitting a person in their position. Companies were cautious about hiring young persons who were not more traditionally mated. These attitudes still exist to some extent in parts of the United States today, especially in rural areas and among more conservative groups.

Numerous books were written in the mid- to late 1970s in order to advise persons in "meretricious" relationships about their legal rights and liabilities (e.g., Douthwaite, 1979; Hirsch, 1976; King, 1975; Lavori, 1976; Massey & Warner, 1974). Included were such issues as protection against discrimination, the legal rights of children of cohabitors, the effect of cohabitation on child custody and alimony decisions, the extension of insurance benefits, and the division of property at termination (e.g., Bernstein, 1977; Myricks, 1983). An important precedent was set in 1976 with the famous "palimony" case, *Marvin v. Marvin*, in which the California Supreme Court ruled that courts could uphold oral or written agreements between nonmarital partners regarding earnings, property, and expenses (*Marvin v. Marvin*, 1976; Myricks, 1980). It is indicative that few such books have been written in the 1980s. As the Court observed in *Marvin v. Marvin* in 1976:

> The mores of society have indeed changed so radically in regard to cohabitation that we cannot impose a standard based on alleged moral considerations that have apparently been so widely abandoned by so many. (p. 106)

CONCLUSION

Cohabiting couples, whether of the same or opposite sex, are often among those known to human service professionals. However, cohabitation per se is rarely the central issue, and the presenting problems are apt to be the same as for any couple: poor communication, unequal commitment or emotional involvement, finances, parenting, disagreements regarding lifestyle or roles, family of origin issues, sexual problems, erosion of the love relationship, autonomy/mutuality issues, issues caused by normative and nonnormative stressors, and so forth.

Much as one might like persons to evaluate thoughtfully their decision to cohabit, rarely do clients present with the question of whether or not to live together. Much as in the case of married persons, people are most apt to seek help with their problems after the relationship has been formed. However, cohabitation does present its particular challenges, as shown in the preceding sections. These challenges include role and status ambiguity, lack of legal protections, social stigma, and special problematic issues if children are involved.

Premarital cohabitation appears to neither strengthen nor undermine a later marriage. Ridley and colleagues (1978), based on their clinical and research observations, suggest that the effect of cohabitation will vary with the goals, the expectations, and the skills of the individuals involved. They hypothesize that it will be a more productive experience if the participants share a goal of greater understanding of self and relationships, have realistic and mutually agreed-upon expectations of the relationship, have interpersonal skills, are developmentally ready for an intimate living relationship, and maintain a strong support network that operates against overdependency on the relationship. As Cole and Vincent (1975) have so aptly observed:

> Apparently it is not so much the legal nature of the relationship that encourages or discourages satisfaction. Instead, it is more likely a factor of how the partners behave toward each other and define their roles that is predictive of happiness.

NOTE

1. The U.S. Bureau of the Census (1986a, pp. 78–79) defines an unmarried couple as "two unrelated adults of the opposite sex (one of whom is the householder) who share a leasing unit with or without the presence of children under 15 years old." A householder is the person in whose name the housing unit is owned or rented; if owned or rented jointly by the couple, the householder may be either the man or the woman, depending on whose name is listed first on the questionnaire. It should be noted that the Census Bureau does not inquire about the nature of the relationship between the two persons. Therefore, while the majority are, in fact, couples, some of the persons in this category may be paid employees or renters residing in the household. It is likely that these census figures are somewhat conservative in that there are cohabiting couples who are not counted as such by the census because they do not accurately report their living situation.

4

Family and Couples Therapy with Nonmarital Cohabiting Couples: Treatment Issues and Case Studies

CHARLES LEE COLE

INTRODUCTION

Nonmarital cohabiting couples asking for help from marital and family therapists is not a new phenomenon. In a review article on the history of marital and family therapy, Broderick and Schrader (1981) point out that in the 1920s marriage counseling clinics were established in Germany partially for the purpose of seeing unmarried couples who were seeking guidance with regard to whether to marry or not. Although the incidence of nonmarital cohabitation has no doubt increased in recent years (Spanier, 1983; Gwartney-Gibbs, 1986; Blanc, 1987), it has not become institutionalized as an alternative to marriage as much as it has as a stage in the developmental process of the relationship (Davidoff, 1977; Macklin, 1985).

The influence of therapists' predispositional bias toward marriage is a less significant factor than it was in earlier years (Berman & Goldberg, 1986). Similarly, biases against variant lifestyle options such as divorce, single-parent families, remarriage, and so forth have waned as a variety of societal changes have given impetus to the acknowledgment of pluralistic life choices. The training of marital and family therapists also has changed to provide adequate information and experience in working with couples from various lifestyles.

As the incidence of nonmarital cohabitation has changed the contextual meaning of marriage and family life, it has produced concomitant shifts in the role of providing services for couples and families experiencing these changes. Some of these changes have necessitated that professional marital and family therapists adapt what they do and how they do it in the course of making their services available.

AUTHOR'S NOTE: The author would like to express appreciation to Anna L. Cole, M.S., for providing constructive comments and editorial suggestions on this manuscript. The author also would like to acknowledge appreciation to the Department of Family Environment and the Home Economics Research Institute at Iowa State University for providing support during the writing of this paper.

No systematic data are available on the prevalence of nonmarital cohabiting couples who seek therapy. Berman and Goldberg (1986) note that 13% of the cases seen at the Marriage Council of Philadelphia were made up of nonmarital cohabiting couples. My own experience in private practice in Iowa tends to confirm that a considerable percentage of a marital and family therapist's load is of nonmarital cohabiting couples.

The purpose of this chapter is to examine issues relevant for treating nonmarital cohabiting couples who seek the services of marital and family therapists. Because the spectrum of types of cohabitation spans a broad range, it is difficult to generalize the nature of the problems experienced. Macklin notes in the foregoing chapter that cohabitation for nonmarital couples is both similar to and yet different from cohabitation for married couples.

There is not much written on therapy with nonmarital cohabiting couples. Berman and Goldberg (1986) as well as Kaslow (1985) provide the best material on treating them, citing a number of examples of how such couples are served by therapists (1986). They conceptualize the nonmarital cohabiting couple as having a type of dyad that needs to be examined in the context of the larger family system. They further suggest that cohabitation can be placed on a continuum that ranges from remaining single to getting married.

It is possible to view cohabitation as a quasi-marriage since the couple is functioning in a manner similar to that of married couples. The key difference is the nature of the commitments that the partners make to each other. As Blumstein and Schwartz (1983) point out, cohabiting couples seem to value independence and autonomy more than do married couples. The cost of maintaining this independence is the lack of the interdependence and security derived from joint efforts to build a future together as a couple.

Many nonmarital cohabiting couples are not aware of the laws regarding cohabitation in their state. For example, in many states nonmarital cohabitation legally becomes common-law marriage after a specified number of years, or a couple may be considered to have a common-law marriage if they present themselves to the community as being married. The nature of the commitment will not differ, however, if the partners do not consider themselves to be married, and, indeed, they may never encounter a need to abide with the laws governing marriage. An exception I have seen in my private practice was a couple who had cohabited for 9 years and found that they were legally married when the women tried to apply for Aid to

Families with Dependent Children after her partner thought that he had ended the relationship by moving out. The couple then found that they had to abide by the laws governing legal separation and divorce.

Couples, regardless of whether they view themselves as married or as cohabiting nonmaritally, have explicit and implicit contracts. In this chapter dyadic relationship contracts will be discussed to illustrate how therapists might work with nonmarital cohabiting couples. Sager (1976, 1981) notes that these explicit and implicit contracts specify each partner's perception of what the relationship should entail and how it should be established and maintained. For cohabiting couples the private implicit and explicit contracts become crucial as mechanisms for defining and governing their relationship. The individually developed contracts are the products of each partner's life history, experiences, dreams, fears, and expectations. Sager (1986) advises that in working with cohabiting couples it is useful to examine interrelated aspects of their individual contracts and notes that the couple's cohabitation contract contains an "interactional script" and "behavioral profiles."

In this sense the interactional script details the "rules of the game" that emerge in the course of day-to-day living as a cohabiting couple. It entails rules governing how they will communicate, make decisions, manage conflict, handle problems, make love, and so forth.

The therapist needs to examine the interaction patterns to determine where and how the couple fall into negative and destructive interactions (Sager, 1986). The task of the therapist is to facilitate calming the storm of negative interaction by intentionally disrupting the behavioral sequence, thus altering the feedback loop before conflicts escalate. This can be done by restructuring the negative patterns and shifting the roles played by the two partners in the exchange. According to Kantor and Lehr (1975), each partner has four basic options of response roles: mover (initiating the interaction), follower (supporting either mover or opposer along a course of action), opposer (resisting and countering the efforts and direction of the mover), and bystander (staying out of the action and observing and possibly analyzing what is going on).

The behavioral profiles are the unique ways that each partner acts to try to meet personal expectations for the relationship (Sager, 1986). Profiles can and probably will change over time. Although each profile contains "normal and socially acceptable behavior," it can become dysfunctional if the behaviors are exaggerated. The seven major profiles are: (1) romantic, (2) rational, (3) parallel, (4) equal, (5) compassionate, (6) parental, and (7) childlike. Sager (1986) suggests combining the profiles (e.g., parental/equal) to provide the therapist and couple with a brief description of the couple's interaction.

A variety of therapeutic techniques can be used to alter negative interactional scripts. For example, incorporating the families of origin can be useful in helping the couple clarify where their various expectations originate. By analyzing their behavior patterns in the past, the couple can make choices in terms of whether these are functional in getting the couple's current needs met. Behavioral and strategic tasks can be assigned to break dysfunctional cycles and teach new skills. Structural realignments and boundary marking can facilitate change in the cohabiting couple's structural boundaries or cycles of closeness/distance. Cohabiting couples create boundaries around their dyadic union as do married couples. For some couples the boundaries can be too tightly woven and may not allow enough space for individuality to be expressed. For other couples the boundaries can be too loose and not allow the couple to form a bond strong enough to sustain their relationship.

The following sections will discuss clinical issues that may arise with three categories of cohabiting couples: never-married cohabitors, cohabitors previously married to other partners, and cohabitors previously married to each other. Case studies and possible therapeutic approaches are presented. The chapter concludes with a discussion of issues related to cohabitation separation and dissolution.

CLINICAL ISSUES WITH NEVER-MARRIED COHABITORS

There are basically three types of situations that never-married cohabitors bring to therapy: (a) relationship maintenance problems both interpersonally induced and situationally evoked by outside forces; (b) commitment problems including conflicts over whether to marry, continue cohabiting, or split up; and (c) enrichment or growth issues that involve the couple's wanting to sharpen their skills and enhance their ability to meet both couple and individual needs.

Relationship Maintenance Struggles

Nonmarital cohabiting couples are vulnerable to the same types of relationship maintenance struggles as are married couples. Interpersonal competency skill issues such as the quality of the sexual relationship, quality and effectiveness of the communication system, anger and conflict management skills, and development and implementation efficiency will strongly affect the degree to which couples can effectively maintain their relationship.

Macklin (1985) and Jackson (1983) note that parents of cohabitors frequently have a difficult time accepting the arrangement. Berman and Goldberg (1986) contend that dealing with families can be problematic and stressful for cohabiting couples. Parents are sometimes reluctant to become close to a person their child is living with outside of marriage because they view the situation as temporary. This coolness toward or rejection of the partner may anger and upset the cohabiting couple and might require family of origin sessions. The job of the therapist in this situation is to help the couple clarify what they want, help them develop strategies for redefining their relationships with each partner's family of origin, and help them avoid emotional cutoffs and keep their relationships aligned. Each partner needs to remain the best expert on his or her own family, taking the initiative for communicating directly with the family and working to maintain healthy connections with members of his or her family of origin.

Case Example

Bob and Ellen had been living together for 6 months when they came for therapy. They had started living together the summer after Bob's first year in graduate school and Ellen's senior year in college. Ellen was employed in a part-time job while she tried to decide whether she and Bob had a future together. Bob was working as a teaching assistant while completing his graduate studies. The presenting problem that brought them to therapy centered around their inability to accept and appreciate the differences the two of them had over ways of doing things. Some of the complaints focused on simple everyday habits and patterns such as the ubiquitous issue of how to squeeze the toothpaste tube. Other complaints ranged from when they went to bed, talking on the phone to friends during meals, how much television to watch, and so forth. In short, the problems centered around issues related to the establishment of patterns in their interpersonal routine.

Furthermore, it became apparent that the couple had poor communication skills and were prone to angry outbursts when they became frustrated over their inability to reach agreement. A combination of cognitive-behavioral techniques was used in teaching the couple the requisite skills for developing an effective communication system that served to increase self/other awareness, empathy, and affirmation as messages were clearly and completely sent, received, acknowledged, and verified. As a result of the foundation supports afforded by the improved communication system, the couple was able to begin the tasks of learning to handle their anger and conflict in better ways that consequently improved their overall problem-solving abilities.

A year later Ellen was offered a job in her chosen field that required a move to another city. For a while Bob and Ellen tried to maintain a long-distance relationship, but the stress of the move and separation made them reevaluate their commitment. About 6 months later Ellen made a decision to invest less and less of herself in trying to keep the relationship going. This was due in part to work demands in her new job and in part to her feeling that Bob was likely to expect more from her than he was willing to give to her. Consequently she began to feel resentful and less comfortable with Bob. Without talking it over together, Bob had come to similar conclusions, to the effect that there did not seem to be much future potential for meeting his needs. In actuality the relationship had been primarily one of convenience, and since it was getting harder to maintain it, they simply drifted farther apart without ever ending it.

It is clear as we examine this relationship that it failed as a result of a combination of situationally induced stressors plus interpersonal competency skill deficits. While this case is somewhat uncommon in that Bob and Ellen both made some effort in therapy, it is typical of many cohabiting situations that were originally formed out of convenience.

Commitment Issues

Mace (1982) notes that commitment is the glue that holds a couple together and provides a basis for building a shared future. In an earlier paper (Cole, 1977) I pointed out that cohabiting couples must develop interpersonal commitments to the maintenance and growth of each other's individuality and of the relationship. Similarly Johnson (1973) notes that personal and structural (relationship-defined interactions) commitments serve as a mechanism for developing a relationship that affords the cohabiting couple some predictability and consistency.

The research literature on nonmarital cohabitation (Blumstein &

Schwartz, 1983; Macklin, 1985) suggests that cohabiting couples make fewer commitments to the relationship and to their partner than do married couples. Blumstein and Schwartz (1983) explain this in terms of the cohabiting couples making fewer joint investments together, such as pooling financial resources. The fear of forming a strong interdependence interferes with making behavioral commitments that might serve to cement the partnership. For cohabiting couples commitments are tenuous, with the partners staying only as long as their needs are met. Furthermore, since normative investments in the couple's relationship by significant others, such as family and friends, are weak and ambiguous, and since the interests of societal institutions, such as the church, school, and so forth, are without malice at best, the cohabiting couple may have considerable difficulty forming and maintaining a cohesive dyadic bond.

Berman and Goldberg (1986) note that cohabiting couples may experience problems with the meanings attached to the commitments that each partner makes. The behavioral acts that each makes will be interpreted and evaluated as signs of stability and a change in the level of commitment that each perceives that the other has made. Montgomery (1973) uses the concept of circular reciprocity to describe how cohabiting partners gauge each other's vulnerability level in terms of these behavioral acts. According to Montgomery (1973), as one increases the level of vulnerability, the other partner may feel more comfortable reciprocating. There are times, however, when one partner's shift in vulnerability level threatens the other partner and is interpreted as a symbolic request for more inclusion, pair identity, and commitment than she or he feels comfortable with, thereby increasing the level of dissonance.

When this happens, the tension will drive the uncomfortable partner away to a safer level of commitment, which in turn will cause the partner who has risked increased vulnerability to feel rejected and hurt. This commitment imbalance increases the amount of conflict the cohabiting couple experiences and pushes them into more defensive conflict management styles (Hennon, 1981). The consequences of this defensive conflict management approach are to reduce self/other disclosures and thereby inhibit open, honest communication.

Case Example

Betty and Ray had been living together for nearly 4 years. Up to a year and a half ago their levels of commitment were balanced, that is, both were content with their present level of commitment. At that time, however, the commitment balance became misaligned. Betty told Ray that after they were married she would like to have a child. Even though the subject of marriage had been raised before, this was the first time that Betty had mentioned anything about wanting children. For some time she had felt a stronger commitment than Ray but was reluctant to push the issue for fear that Ray would back off. A commitment imbalance gives the partner with the least interest greater power because he or she likely will distance him- or herself and will possibly end the relationship when suggestions for more commitment are made.

As Betty became bolder in her declarations of intention to marry and began to talk about how they would plan the ceremony, Ray became more reluctant to reciprocate and began to look for ways to lessen the commitments that he had already made to her. In an effort to decrease the pressure he was under, Ray began spending more and more time away from home and began using another woman, with whom he had worked for the past couple of years, as a confidante to gain a clearer perspective on what he wanted to do. Eventually he began a sexual affair with the other woman. In the course of his discomfort and guilt over the sexual infidelity, Ray found himself alternating between wanting to reconcile with Betty and wanting to break the relationship off completely. This discomfort motivated him to tell Betty directly about his ambivalence. The result was for Betty to insist that they see a marital and family therapist, and in the course of treatment it became clear that the affair had served as a distancing mechanism for Ray to slow down the escalating commitment.

Therapeutic Approaches

The treatment strategy included a series of moves to work through the ambivalence, realign the commitment balance, and help the couple synchronize their closeness/distance cycles. New ground rules had to be forged that clarified the meaning of each other's commitments and gave safety valves for times in which one of them was pushed beyond her or his tolerance level.

Individuals vary in terms of the amount of separateness and togetherness they need. When cohabiting partners differ in their desire for intimacy and connectedness as well as privacy and space away from each other, they must learn to respect these differences and allow the needs of both partners to be met. Therapists working with such problems might find it useful to combine elements of structural and strategic family therapy (Stanton, 1981). Both are systemic approaches toward changing the couple's interaction patterns.

Structural family therapy (see Minuchin, 1974) is concerned with how the cohabiting couple (as well as other family systems and subsystems) is organized in terms of spatial connections that determine distance and proximity and define boundaries. For example, the therapist would be concerned with issues such as hierarchies (who is in charge of whom and how the power is established); rules governing interaction patterns (how, when, and where the partners interact); and alliances and coalitions among family members. The therapist joins with the cohabiting couple as well as with other elements of the family system that may have a direct bearing on the couple's level of functioning. The couple and/or family enact (show by interacting together in the therapy session) rather than talk about their problems. And the therapist uses the therapy session to produce the desired change in the way in which the family system is organized (which, in turn, affects and governs how they will interact with each other) by using a variety of techniques such as restructuring the system (e.g., establishing or loosening boundaries). This approach takes into account in constructing a treatment plan the social and cultural as well as developmental context in which the family exists.

Strategic family therapy (see Haley, 1976) focuses on temporal patterning (interaction sequences) within the family system. It is based on communication theory and focuses on the recursiveness (nonlinear circularity) of feedback loops within interaction sequences. For example, what one family member (actor) does affects other members (reactors) who in turn alter their behavior in response to that action, which creates a reaction that reverberates to the original actor, making him or her a reactor.

For example, Betty makes a request that Ray come to bed with her instead of staying up watching a late television show and receives an offhand response of, "No. I'm interested in this." This reaction results in a reaction from Betty of anger and frustration because she feels rejected. She may angrily say, "You care more about television than you do about me!" Ray may then also respond with anger, and the situation soon escalates into an argument.

Strategic therapy focuses on each interaction sequence and how it affects the next reaction. The goal is to change interaction patterns and develop problem-solving strategies created and directed by the therapist. To accomplish this, the therapist assigns tasks and gives directives to be carried out between sessions by the couple and/or family. They are prepared for the assignments by practicing the directive in the session under the direct supervision of the therapist. Attention is given to symptoms, and the therapist develops hypotheses related to what would happen to the family if the symptom were removed, how the symptom is maintained by the family system, and so forth.

The rejection intrusion pattern (Napier, 1978) of Betty pushing for more closeness and commitment and Ray withdrawing and distancing himself when he felt threatened by engulfment can also be explained from a psychodynamic transgenerational perspective (Bowen, 1978; Kramer, 1985). From this perspective it can be seen that the partners were attempting to fill the void they brought into the relationship from their respective families of origin. Bowen (1978) would see the pattern in terms of the lack of differentiation and individuation achieved in their earlier families, which makes them vulnerable to being sucked into similar patterns in the dyad that they have formed by cohabiting together. Napier (1978) would characterize the pattern in terms of one partner seeking closeness and validation while the other strives for independence and freedom. In this sense the partner seeking closeness is probably the product of rejection and abandonment as a child, while the other partner's desire for separateness stems from being smothered and engulfed as a child. This polarized interaction pattern functions to regulate role sets and the frequency and duration of intimacy for a cohabiting couple.

Enrichment and Marriage Preparation Issues

Gwartney-Gibbs (1986) reports that approximately half of the marriage license applicants in Lane County, Oregon, in 1980 were cohabiting at the time of the marriage. It is unclear how many of these cohabiting couples sought the help of a marital and family therapist to enrich their relationship and/or prepare for marriage and increase the probability that marriage would fulfill their expectations. Although the notion of couples living together before marriage as a type of "trial marriage" has been around for the past 75 years or so (Lindsey & Evans, 1927), the research on the effects of cohabitation on subsequent marriages (Macklin, 1985; Newcomb & Bentler,

1980b) fails to show that cohabitors have any more chance of achieving a successful marriage than do couples who have not cohabited prior to marriage. As Macklin points out (see Macklin's chapter in this volume), cohabitation is not an effective screening device for filtering out potential problems in a subsequent marriage primarily because the couple often lacks intentionality and simply drifts into the marriage in much the same fashion that they did into cohabitation. In short, if the couple had interpersonal skill deficits when they were cohabiting, they will likely continue to have the same deficits after they marry unless they intentionally acquire those skills through some type of enhancement program.

Case Example

Jan and Larry had lived together for 7 months when they decided they wanted to make it a more permanent arrangement by getting married. Jan wanted Larry and herself to begin the marriage on a solid footing by going through a preparation program at a local church. Finding that the four sessions on basic marriage skills they attended (communication, conflict, sexuality, and role expectations) merely scratched the surface, they sought the help of a marital and family therapist. In working with the therapist it became clear to both Larry and Jan that although they thought they knew each other very well, they were constantly surprised to find out a wealth of new things about each other. For example, Larry had not known that Jan was close to her family and liked to spend special occasions such as birthdays and anniversaries with them. And Jan learned that Larry was one of four boys and the one who was the most like his father in terms of temperament and disposition.

Therapeutic Approaches

The treatment plan included enrolling the couple in a marriage preparation group led by the therapist that lasted for 10 weeks. It covered a variety of topics using a combination of approaches that facilitated awareness and the acquisition of knowledge and skills. Under the supervision of the therapist they practiced basic training in communication, conflict resolution, and problem-solving. Both Jan and Larry were eager to learn and assimilate the new skills. The task was relatively easy since both came from families of origin that had provided them with good role models for continuing to grow as human beings.

The second phase of the treatment plan called for doing over a period of 2 months some family of origin work that included having each one make visits to the other's family of origin overnight without the partner, as well as joint sessions with both sets of families conducted by the therapist.

Two substantive issues that required more attention in the therapy sessions involved gender role expectations for what being a husband and wife meant to them. Jan's father had been very involved in helping around the house, and her mother was equally involved in outside tasks related to the yard, taking care of maintenance on cars, and so forth. Larry's parents, on the other hand, had developed a more traditional division of labor and responsibility, with his father in charge of outside activities and his mother in charge of the house. It took the couple some time to negotiate and decide on their own interdependent task-sharing arrangement. Knowing that the gender roles and division of labor issues would be difficult adjustments for Larry and Jan gave the therapist a clue to the direction in which follow-up work after the marriage should proceed. A checkup once a month began 3 months after the wedding and continued for the first year of the marriage. This was done to help Jan and Larry develop healthy interaction patterns and establish their marriage on a solid foundation.

The value of checkups for relationship maintenance and development within the first year of marriage has been demonstrated (e.g., Mace, 1982; Guldner, 1971, 1983; Bader & Sinclair, 1983) in shaping healthy interaction patterns. Bader and Sinclair (1983) as well as Guldner (1971) report that marital checkups during the first year of marriage are more effective than premarital counseling programs alone. Premarital counseling without follow-up is less effective since the couple is idealistic and only begins to face the complexities of marriage after it occurs. In a 5-year follow-up study (Bader & Sinclair, 1983), couples who participated in premarital and postmarital enrichment programs showed more improvement and greater intentionality than did a control group.

As Berman and Goldberg (1986) point out, the kind of prevention-oriented, premarital cohabiting couple discussed in this case example is both an exception and a very rewarding experience for the therapist. It is so much easier to help couples develop healthy interaction patterns if they seek assistance before they get into serious trouble. And as Markman and associates (1986) comment, the developmental tasks immediately confronting a couple as they attempt to establish their marriage can be overwhelming. These include developing (a) communication and conflict resolution skills; (b) realistic, constructive expectations and attitudes that provide a compatible fit; (c) interaction patterns that are mutually satisfying and that fulfill basic emotional needs; (d) mutually gratifying emotional interdependence in which the partners confide in each other and assist each other in reducing anxiety; and (e) mechanisms for distance regulation, including togetherness as well as separateness and dependency as well as interdependency.

Lewis (1979) notes that a primary task of developing a strong marital partnership is to complete the unfinished business of separating from families of origin. Part of the process of bonding within the dyad requires the establishment of a separate identity as a couple.

CLINICAL ISSUES WITH COHABITORS PREVIOUSLY MARRIED TO OTHER PARTNERS

Cohabitation for couples in which one or both partners has previously been married is much more complex than for never-married cohabitors. Not only do such cohabitors bring a current cast of characters into their new life, but they also bring the ghosts of former spouses, in-laws, and friends.

Boundary and Role-Strain Issues

Since divorce disrupts the role constellation within a family system, a number of role relationships in the family are permanently altered. Parents and the larger family of origin network frequently choose sides in the marital dispute and consequently alienate one or both of the divorcing partners. This makes family members vulnerable to cutoffs. A number of family therapists (e.g., Boszormenyi-Nagy & Spark, 1973; Bowen, 1978; Kramer, 1985) have described cutoffs as an emotional break from the family by one or more family members who has either voluntarily or involuntarily (by being expelled from the family system) severed emotional and/or social contact with the family. Cutoffs can occur when family members are embedded in conflicts that contravene the family system's rules and value system.

One of the consequences of divorce cutoffs is that the family boundaries become rigid, and the network of support systems becomes less available and smaller as the family members isolate themselves from the primary actors in the divorce. In some cases this will take the shape of an inverted shrinking sponge whereby the parents of the divorcing partner try to pull him or her into the safety of the family, returning the divorcing partner to the status of a child. In other cases the parents may threaten to (and in some instances actually do) expel their own child and rally around the in-law spouse.

Both types of family responses signal how the family will probably respond when and if the divorced member of the family lives with someone in nonmarital cohabitation. In general if family members have not accepted the changes in membership composition and relationship status that resulted when a member divorced, it is unlikely that they will accept cohabitation as a legitimate lifestyle.

Case Example

Al and Karen had been cohabiting for nearly 2 years when Al's mother died. The family did not notify him, and he found out about it by reading her obituary in the newspaper. Karen was the one who called to make the appointment with the therapist. She indicated that she was worried about Al because he had been despondent over his mother's death and the family's exclusion of him from this important time.

Al had been divorced from his ex-wife, Sara, for about 5 months when he met Karen. In some ways there were interesting parallels between Karen and Sara: Both of them were born in November of the same year, wore the same size clothing, had similar taste in decorating their homes, were only children, and were close to their parents. Karen recalled the good time they had had a few weeks earlier celebrating her 40th birthday at her parents' house and had remarked at the time that she thought it was strange that Al never saw his parents.

Al had never told Karen how his parents angrily abandoned him and disinherited him because of his divorce from Sara. Both of his brothers and his younger sister sided with the parents, while his older sister, Alice, who had said or done nothing to defend him at the time, later phoned, saying she thought it was wrong for the family to throw him out. Al kept in touch with Alice occasionally but did not try to have much of a relationship with her, since Alice felt threatened that her parents would disapprove. Since Al was cut off from his family of origin, he tried to substitute Karen and her parents for his absent family. On the surface he handled the disenfranchisement well, but underneath was a painful memory that left him feeling betrayed. He started living with Karen partially because she reminded him so much of his ex-wife whom he had not wanted to divorce (his wife had run away because she could not live with Al's engulfing attachment) and partially because Karen was warm and nurturing, which made him feel accepted and reassured.

Therapeutic Approaches

The treatment plan called for doing some family of origin work in an effort to process the grief Al was feeling over his mother's death and the cutoff from his family. Attention to the connection points that might facilitate Al's rejoining his family was a critical step in reconnecting and repairing the linkages that might bring him back into the family. The clearest connection point was the one sister who had not totally abandoned him.

Together Al, Alice, and Karen evolved a way they thought might bridge the gap. The plan was to have Alice approach each family member directly and separately to share her pain over the loss of their mother and to invite the other family members to open up. When the other members, one by one, began to express their feelings, Alice would suggest that everyone seemed to be having a hard time adjusting to their mother's death and that things in the family had been difficult ever since Al left. This approach is compatible with Kramer's (1985) notion that when a death occurs in a family, the system is ripe for change in role relationships.

While Alice was doing the advance work inside the family, Al was being prepared for the eventual reunion. Karen's role in this was to be coached by the therapist in preparation for the reactions that Al's family might have both to the reunion and to learning about her and their nonmarital cohabitation. Both Al and Karen needed to be prepared for all contingencies, as it was likely that the family, especially Al's father, would disapprove of the nonmarital cohabitation.

Having the family come in for a family of origin session would have been desirable, but this was not possible since the father adamantly refused to have anything to do with Al. His stated reason was that he felt Al's mother would never have approved and that it would be disloyal to go against her will. One of Al's brothers, Tom, did soften his blind allegiance to their parents' rejection of Al, which provided an opportunity for Al and Tom to reconnect.

Parental Inclusion and Children of Cohabitors

Perhaps one of the biggest struggles nonmarital cohabiting couples with children from previous marriages have is trying to establish their relationship while simultaneously adjusting to each other's youngsters. This is similar to the types of problems experienced by remarried families (see Visher and Visher's chapter in this volume for a more complete discussion of treatment issues with stepfamilies). Spanier (1983) notes that over a fourth (28%) of nonmarital cohabitation households have one or more children living in them. It is unclear how many children are included in these households on an occasional basis when they are visiting their noncustodial parent.

Berman and Goldberg (1986) note that children may perceive their parent's new nonmarital cohabitation to be a threat. Divided loyalties (the children versus the new partner) can be a problem for the cohabitant with children in terms of the amount of time, money, and other resources available to meet the needs of everyone involved. Children may feel similar conflicts over loyalties to biological parents, which probably strain the interaction between children of a cohabitor and his or her partner.

A family session with the adult members of the family and the children can be used to clarify expectations about what the rules are for the children when visiting with the noncustodial parent and when living with the custodial parent. Discipline in particular can be a problem for cohabitors with children, and the nonparent cohabitant needs to have some rights and to be able to enforce rules. In most cases the rules and disciplining are left to the parent, with the nonparent partner relegated to a bystander role except when left alone with the children, thus functioning in much the same fashion as a baby-sitter.

The problem can be viewed as a boundary issue in that the parameters of each role relationship are being discovered and challenged. For the cohabiting couple the adjustments can be complicated by blurred boundaries between the partners as well as their relationships with their own and each other's children. In both sectors there are multiple adjustments for all members of the household unit. The cohabitation pair-bond must establish privacy and time alone as a couple. In the parental system the couple needs to develop ground rules that will create and maintain a strong pair-bond coalition in their dealings with the children.

Further, children need time to adjust to the cohabitant partner and for the relationship to emerge gradually and naturally as they get to know each other. The children need to learn how to relate to the cohabitant partner, whom they may resent and distrust. If these issues are not worked out, the couple may split up.

The couple's sexual relationship may be inhibited by the children's presence in the home, especially if the children voice protests about it. This would probably be more difficult for children who are consciously aware of the social norms against sexual intimacy outside marriage. Young children may be unaware of the sexual nature of their parent's relationship with the cohabitant partner but may well resent the affection and attention being given to someone else.

Case Example

Tammy, a 43-year-old mother, had been living with Richard for nearly a year when she called for an appointment with the therapist. Richard, 47, was the father of two boys for whom he had had full responsibility since his divorce 3 years earlier. Tammy's children, 17-year-old Michelle and 13-year-old David, lived with her ex-husband and visited Tammy and Richard for holidays and summer vacations. Richard's sons, Rick, an 18-year-old senior in high school, and Tad, a 14-year-old freshman, lived with Richard and Tammy in the home that Richard had once lived in with his ex-wife.

The couple had a number of problems gaining the acceptance of each other's children, and the children in this blended family arrangement had difficulty getting along with each other. This was most true for the two younger boys, Tad (Richard's son) and David (Tammy's son), who were expected to share a room during visits. Tad felt as if David were taking over his room, and David felt like an unwanted stranger who had no rights. Increasing tensions among quasi-siblings increased the tension for the parents. Richard took the position that Tad should welcome David as a brother and tried to force this on him.

Tammy let Richard take the lead in disciplining his children, and she did the same with her children, expecting that Richard would back her up as she had done for him. Richard was trying so hard to make Tammy's children accept him that he took their side in arguments and contradicted her in front of them. This split in the parental coalition produced more tension between Tammy and Richard.

The children thus learned that they could create a wedge between the cohabitant partners. The usual pattern was for David to complain to his mother that Tad was picking on him and that things were not fair. In this sense David and Tad each hoped that they could destroy the couple's relationship. The goal of their collusion was to reunite their biological parents and thus reconstitute the two original families.

It was during a 10-week visit by Tammy's children that Richard and Tammy sought therapy. During the first three sessions each person was given a turn to tell his or her story. Richard started with his version of the history of their relationship and how it evolved into nonmarital cohabitation. Tammy's story was a similar description of their relationship as one of passion and friendship.

When the children were given their turn, Tad told of feeling uncomfortable having Tammy around and resentful of the inconvenience when David came to visit. He remarked in a sullen tone, "I'm the only one who has to share a room when her kids come to visit. It isn't fair. How come they [Dad and Tammy] don't give up their room or stick David in with Rick?" At this point Rick protested loudly, "That is absolutely ridiculous!" The therapist intervened and told Rick to wait his turn and let Tad finish his story.

When Rick did get his turn he mentioned that he liked having Tammy around, since if she were not there Michelle wouldn't come to visit. Rick and Michelle went out together when she visited, although she liked her more than she did him. Rick went on to say that he thought it was unfair that his Dad and Tammy could have a sexual relationship when they would not let him sleep with Michelle.

Hearing this shocked Tammy, and Richard reacted with anger, saying, "You won't ever sleep with your sister! You hear me!" To this Rick shouted back in an equally angry voice, "She's not my sister! She never has been and she never will be! We're never going to be a family either! You know that my sleeping with Michelle is no different than you sleeping with Michelle's mom!" The therapist held his hand up to stop the exchange which was escalating into an unproductive free-for-all.

The therapist then established control, reassuring the family that what had happened was important to get out in the open but that it needed to wait until later so that the therapist would have a complete picture of what was going on in the family. The next session was spent having David tell his story of feeling like an intruder who was resented and despised. David's account painted a picture of a lonely child whom nobody wanted, abandoned even by his mother.

Michelle's story reflected themes of confusion and anger. She was confused about her feelings toward Rick. Moreover, she harbored feelings of anger toward her mother for betraying her father by leaving him some years earlier.

Therapeutic Approaches

The therapist developed a plan to work structurally to help the parents take charge and provide leadership for reorganizing the family. Serious problems that threatened to undermine the system needed to be corrected. Tension in the sibling and parent/child systems was slowly eroding the loving feeling that Tammy and Richard had shared. Boundaries needed to be clarified and maintained, making it possible for Tammy and Richard to be lovers, friends, and partners and still allowing room for parenting duties.

Using strategic techniques designed to increase problem-solving effectiveness within the family system, the therapist assigned a number of tasks. One task done partially in a session and partially as a homework assignment was to dismiss the two younger boys and have the parents take part in a discussion with Rick and Michelle. Another task was for the parents to develop rules for the family and decide together how to present and implement them.

The chance for success in a case like this is less than in simpler cases without the wide assortment of side issues and changing cast of characters. The couple's strength was their deep feelings of attachment to each other as lovers and friends.

CLINICAL ISSUES WITH COHABITORS PREVIOUSLY MARRIED TO EACH OTHER

In some instances couples once married to each other and later divorced establish their dyadic relationship as a nonmarital cohabiting pair-bond. For them the institution of marriage was what they divorced and not the partner for whom they still have feelings of caring and love.

Case Example

Jenny and Kevin, a couple in their late 30s, had been married for 17 years when they decided to get a divorce because they felt trapped by the conventions of marriage. They lived apart for nearly 2 years but remained in contact with each other, partially because of their joint responsibilities for their three children and partially out of genuine caring for each other. They felt they had taken each other for granted and fallen into the trap of assuming the societal role definitions for husband and wife.

Finally Jenny and Kevin decided to try to live together again but not to remarry, out of a fear that if they did, they would resume the patterns that they both hated and that had driven them to divorce in the first place. They sought the assistance of a therapist to help them forge new roles that better fit their needs and personalities and to work out some mechanism to change their patterns so that neither would take the other for granted.

Therapeutic Approaches

The therapist helped them clarify their expectations and thereby uncover the underlying implicit contracts that they had used to guide their behavior in the marriage (see Sager, 1976 and 1986, for a discussion of this approach). Jenny expected Kevin to be open and share his feelings with her. She also expected him to treat her as an equal who was capable of making her own decisions and solving her own problems, because when they were married Kevin thought it was the role of the husband to shield his wife from problems. Kevin expected Jenny to respect his need to have his own space and not be badgered into doing things he did not want to do. Kevin also expected Jenny to take more initiative in sex.

In all, Kevin brought out 39 specific expectations for Jenny, and she had 61 specific expectations for him. It was decided that several items on each list were unrealistic, so these were discarded, with the remainder serving as a base for their mutual expectations contract.

After the contracts were clarified and agreed on, the therapist began to teach the couple some basic interpersonal competency skills (e.g., communication, conflict resolution, problem-solving, affective awareness and expression, and so forth). There were a few other issues that were dealt with in the therapy, but for the most part the couple had learned to handle their own problems and did not require further assistance from the therapist. The therapist requested that they come back in a year for a checkup to reevaluate the changes they had made and to begin plotting together for the future. The result of that checkup indicated that the couple was doing fairly well on their own but did need to sharpen their interpersonal skills at affective expression.

COHABITATION SEPARATION AND DISSOLUTION ISSUES

Macklin (1978) notes that a vast majority of nonmarital cohabiting couples will terminate their relationship when it fails to meet their needs and/or when the structural barriers (such as job offers that require residential mobility) arise that make it impossible to continue the status quo without increased opportunity costs. Many couples who chose to live together in nonmarital cohabitation did so partially with termination in mind. That is, they felt that the likelihood of a permanent relationship was not high enough to risk the pain and ordeal of a potential divorce. In essence these couples assumed it is easier to terminate nonmarital cohabitation than it is a marriage.

The notion that dissolving nonmarital cohabitation is without pain is illusory. Couples who share part of their lives by living together form attachments and thus suffer much of the same emotional pain that married couples do when they divorce.

It is often as complicated to terminate nonmarital cohabitation as it is to terminate marriage. If the couple has lived together for a while and has acquired communal property, the court might rule that the partners have a financial responsibility to each other even after the dissolution. The *Marvin v. Marvin* (1976) "palimony" case is a good example of this type of legal liability.

Treatment Issues

Rice and Rice (1986) identify seven issues therapists need to attend to when treating couples who are going through the process of dissolution: (a) painful emotions and a sense of crisis; (b) possibilities for psychological growth; (c) learning how to become more mature and less dependent on others; (d) a sense of failure and questions about one's ability to have a lasting relationship; (e) developmental delays coming from family of origin; (f) the need to find support from others; and (g) practical matters such as living arrangements, finances, and legal considerations.

Case Example

Glenn and Mary, a couple in their mid-20s, had been living together for almost 2 years. It was Glenn's second time cohabiting. He had never married and indicated to Mary that he never intended to make their arrangement permanent. Mary had cohabited twice before, including with her ex-husband, whom she had lived with for 8 months before they married. Both experiences had ended in her partner's leaving her and thus making her feel like a failure. When things began going badly with Glenn, Mary had flashbacks to these earlier "failures." She wanted desperately to avoid the empty feeling of being lost and cut off. She therefore sought the help of a therapist to work through the confusion.

Glenn, the partner who wanted out and had in fact left, agreed to come for three sessions (later extended to seven) "to help Mary" but insisted that he was comfortable with his decision to move out and did not need any help himself. In the first session the therapist had them tell their stories of how the relationship had evolved and changed over their years together. They shared the tender moments of joy, ecstasy, frustration, alienation, etcetera, and began to see their time together in a broader context that had both pluses and minuses. For Glenn the sharing was a chance to reflect on his part in making the relationship both work and disintegrate.

Although Mary focused more on the pain of loss than did Glenn, she was able to acknowledge that there had been disappointments all along that she had tried to ignore. Mary's primary tasks were to work through the grief of the loss and say goodbye to Glenn so that she could move on with her life.

Both were interested in learning more from their mistakes in hopes that they would not repeat them with other persons. Part of that process involved doing some family of origin work so that they could each understand what they had brought into the relationship and how that had contributed both strengths and strains.

The therapist referred the couple to an attorney since there seemed to be many questions about property settlement. They found that they were considered to be legally married and would need to proceed with a divorce. The therapist was asked to serve as a mediator in working out a property settlement. If they had not formally dissolved their relationship through the legal system, they would have left themselves vulnerable to future litigation.

When the legal divorce process was completed, Mary decided to continue therapy to work on improving her self-esteem and complete the unfinished business of working through the separation, dissolution, and readjustment as a single person. A combination of individual therapy sessions and divorce group sessions was chosen as the mode of treatment.

CONCLUSION

Nonmarital cohabiting couples experience the same types of presenting problems as do married couples, although there are some concerns unique to the nonmarital couples. The issue is not so much the nonmarital cohabitation status as it is the couple's mastery of or failure to master the interpersonal competencies that are required in forming, maintaining, and changing their relationship so that it meets the needs of both partners. Treatment approaches for nonmarital cohabiting couples are dictated by the presenting problem and contextual reality in much the same fashion that they are for other couples and family forms. To the author's knowledge there have not been any outcome studies on treating nonmarital cohabiting couples. Indeed, few studies have been published on treatment approaches for nonmarital cohabitation. Furthermore, it needs to be recognized that the treatment techniques described in this chapter represent the author's approaches and experience in working with cohabiting couples. More research is needed to answer a variety of questions related to the treatment of cohabiting couples using family and couples therapy models and techniques.

5

Some Problems of Gay/Lesbian Families

JOSEPH HARRY

In attempting to write this chapter, I found that much of the conceptualizing about family systems seems singularly inappropriate to the case of gay and lesbian "families".[1] For example, Carter and McGoldrick (1980) define a family system as "the entire family emotional system of at least three generations." For homosexuals this definition is markedly inappropriate, since the large majority of gay/lesbian households or couples do not and never will contain the third generation; that is, children. Only 20 to 30% of homosexuals ever marry (Bell & Weinberg, 1978). Also, many gays are alienated from their parents and have little or no contact with them. Similarly, notions of the "family life cycle" seem inappropriate, since most of the stages defined as part of that cycle are defined in terms of children or in terms of the child's participation in institutions for children such as school or dating. It is clear that the heterosexual origins of these concepts of family and life cycle render them largely inapplicable to the intimate relationships of gays or lesbians or even those of heterosexual couples without children.

McWhirter and Mattison (1984) have attempted to identify six stages through which gay couples progress. However, their stages lack the clarity or demarcating events that the stages of the heterosexual family life cycle exhibit. Their stages seem more to resemble the processes or focal concerns of couples, which may be of greater salience in relationships of differing lengths. The reason for the greater clarity of stages in the case of heterosexual couples is that society has erected a variety of compelling social institutions, such as marriage, school attendance, adolescence, and children leaving home, that organize the heterosexual stages. Since none of these institutions or events readily applies to most homosexual couples, their careers as couples may not easily be approached through a conceptual apparatus that uses stages. What may be more useful in this context is to identify a set of processes, for example, conflict, dependence, accommodation, individuation. Some of these processes may be cumulative and hence suggest stages. However, others may not exhibit any cumulative nature.

Rather than attempting to adapt these definitions of family and family life cycle to the case of gay/lesbian families, the approach taken here is to treat such families as small social systems attempting to meet the needs of their members while also adapting to an intermittently hostile environment. A "gay/lesbian family" is here defined as a homosexual person tied by affectional and/or erotic needs to either another homosexual person or to children with whom they may cohabit. This definition does not necessarily include the criterion of sharing a common household, since a large minority of gay couples do not share a common domicile (Harry & Lovely, 1979). The exclusion of a common household criterion from this definition differs from most definitions of family, which usually involve the criteria of common residence and a socially recognized or legal marital tie. However, no state in the United States recognizes homosexual unions. (Sweden does provide a civil status for homosexual unions.) The use of a common household criterion, while often employed, seems somewhat arbitrary, since it excludes from the definition many cases that otherwise resemble "families." The discussion of couples to follow is organized around problems in dealing with the environment and then problems in meeting the needs of the members of a homosexual couple. I then discuss the external and internal problems of gay/lesbian households with children. The chapter concludes with a discussion of future research topics.

PROBLEMS WITH THE ENVIRONMENT

Problems in Dealing with Parents

There do not appear to be any systematic studies that focus on the relationships between homosexuals and their parents. Rather, this topic is dealt with in passing in sections of works discussing other aspects of homosexuality or homosexuals generally (e.g. Bell & Weinberg, 1978; Lewin & Lyons, 1982; Mendola, 1980; Spada, 1979). Hence, the following discussion of relationships with parental families attempts to identify various problems and processes that may occur in these relationships without specifying the frequencies with which these problems occur. The term "child" will be used even though the homosexual may be well into his or her adult years as these family issues are played out.

In the course of the formation of a gay/lesbian union or household, problems in dealing with parents arise quite often. These problems seem to proceed down two alternative pathways depending on whether the parents know that their child is homosexual. It appears that about half of gay men have told their parents that they are gay (Bell & Weinberg, 1978; Spada, 1979). In the case in which couple formation precedes parental knowledge of the child's homosexuality, the intergenerational stress seems greater, since the difficulties associated with "coming out" to parents are confounded with those of establishing a union that may or may not be accepted by the parents. In this more difficult case the gay/lesbian couple may either choose to conceal their union from parents or to simultaneously come out to parents and reveal that union.

In the concealment case the lovers may maintain separate residences. If they live together, they may represent each other as roommates. They may also attempt to reduce the frequency of visits by parents to their household and, when parents do drop in, may maintain the appearance of separate sleeping arrangements. The concealment case seems to be more common among homosexuals in their early to mid-20s who have not yet come out to their parents or have not yet sufficiently distanced themselves from their parents so as to attain full adult autonomy.

For some couples concealment may be an enduring approach taken in dealing with parents. In the course of repeated visits between households the couple gives little indication to the parents of the nature of their relationship beyond the fact that they are especially close friends. However, as the years go by, pretenses often wear thin, and parents are apt to become aware of the nature of the union. Sometimes parents, usually the mother, may make inquiries, but these are often responded to with vague parries. Often the concealment case may result in a measure of acceptance by the parents, who have never been presented with a direct confrontation and have not been forced to choose between love for their child and their beliefs about proper sexual relationships. However, that acceptance often comes at the price that the couple never openly expresses physical affection for each other in front of the parents and never makes explicit reference to their union. The concealment case probably works better when parents live in a different city from that of their children or are kept at some distance.

In other instances of concealment the gay couple may eventually decide to come out to the parents both as homosexuals and as a couple. This decision is fraught with dangers because it can produce an ugly scene and result in permanent or long-term rejection of the child. According to the few pertinent studies, coming out to parents either as a gay/lesbian person or as a member of a couple is most commonly done first with a mother rather than a father (Bell & Weinberg, 1978; Weinberg & Williams, 1974). Coming out to fathers is typically more difficult because fathers, like most heterosexual males, are apt to find homosexuality and especially male homosexuality very threatening. However, if the parents are highly religious, mothers can also be intolerant. For example, an acquaintance of the author came out to his mother who responded by saying, "Had I known that 30 years ago when I was carrying you I would have had an abortion." It is impossible to make a recommendation that an individual or member of a gay/lesbian couple should come out to his or her parents without knowing the individual's circumstances. Those circumstances include the religious norms of the parents, the parents' views on homosexuality, whether the child is financially dependent on them, and their psychological stability.

In those cases in which couple formation follows the person's coming out to his or her parents, the eventual result will depend on the post–coming out relationship between parents and child. If the coming out resulted in complete rejection, the situation is simplified, since the rejecting parents can be treated as nonexistent, although there will often be lingering hopes of an eventual reconciliation. In cases in which the parent has fully accepted the child's homosexuality, the establishment of a union can be viewed positively by the parents as individual fulfillment. However, there are also cases in which coming out has been only partially accepted by the parents. For example, a mother may have responded, "That's OK with me, but don't tell your father." This can result in intergenerational relationships full of complicated pretenses and strains.

In the preceding descriptions of possible intergenerational accommodations associated with the formation of a gay/lesbian union, only those milder and more benign situations have been mentioned. More violent or forceful ones may include: attempts by parents at homosexual (usually lesbian) deprogramming, commonly associated with kidnapping the homosexual; pressures for the homosexual to undergo psychotherapy in the usually futile hope that he or she can be rendered heterosexual; threats to financially cut off the child from further support, such as in the case of college students; and threats or attempts to take away the homosexual's children, if there are any.

Problems with the Broader Environment

Since virtually everyone lives within some immediate community, it is necessary to come to an accommodation with that community that is reasonably satisfying. One difference among communities that is highly salient for gay/lesbians is the size of the community. Small communities typically present greater difficulties for gay/lesbian couples than do larger ones. Some communities forbid home ownership by persons unrelated by blood or marriage. In dealing with immediate neighbors, the couple may have to decide whether to be open about their relationship or to attempt to conceal, which may involve such tactics as completely fencing in the house so as to maximize privacy. Another means of concealment is not to host gatherings of large numbers of same-sex persons at a party or picnic.

Research shows that the social world of heterosexuals is sharply separated by marital status. Married persons socialize with married couples and singles with singles. Social invitations from married persons to nonmarried persons are rare, and the latter are generally treated as nonpersons after work hours (Block, 1980). These socializing patterns impinge on gay/lesbian couples in special ways, since no homosexual couples are legally married to their partners. In order to be socially involved in the world of heterosexual marrieds, they must present themselves as a couple. In order to present themselves as a couple, they must come out to heterosexuals. But such coming out is likely to be unacceptable in the world of heterosexual couples. The net result of this in most communities is strong and enduring social segregation between gay/lesbian couples and heterosexual marrieds. This segregation can be particularly isolating in smaller communities where the number of other socially available gays or lesbians, coupled or not, is limited.

Such segregation between the homosexual and heterosexual social worlds may be less isolating in larger cities where there are typically large numbers of gays or lesbians to meet through homophile organizations, bars, churches, and so forth. Within the last 15 years there has occurred within most large American cities an efflorescence of gay and lesbian organizations devoted to a wide variety of social, cultural, and age interests (Harry & DeVall, 1978; Humphreys, 1979). These organizations serve to socially integrate the gay world and also provide gay couples with social settings other than the often highly sexual context of the gay bar. Until the 1970s the gay world may have been one dominated by a largely sexual culture (Gagnon & Simon, 1973). However, the changes of the 1970s resulted in the enrichment of that culture that has provided greater social, rather than predominantly sexual, opportunities for gays. These social opportunities permit gay couples to relate to other gays and gay couples in settings that are less likely to provide erotic temptations to one or both of the partners. A similar but less elaborate expansion of the lesbian world has also occurred, with considerable overlapping of the lesbian world and the social structures associated with the women's movement.

One difference between the social world of homosexuals and that of heterosexuals seems to be that the former is less segregated by couple status than the latter. Both coupled and uncoupled gays relate socially to each other to a greater extent than is true in the heterosexual world. One effect of this may be that the gay world presents to gay couples greater opportunities for extracouple erotic encounters than does the heterosexual world. Also, the typical absence of children in gay male households gives rise to a less home-based lifestyle than is the case among many heterosexual families, in which the presence of children often restricts the extent to which a couple can spend time away from the house. While this nondomestic lifestyle provides many rewards and opportunities, those opportunities include sexual ones. However, an offsetting factor is that many gay couples like and prefer the company of other couples (Harry & Lovely, 1979). This preference seems to parallel that in the heterosexual world because couple-to-couple encounters are less threatening than ones in which couples and singles intermingle. Some gay organizations formally provide activities or settings that cater to this desire of couples to relate to other gay couples.

Another advantage of the large city for gay/lesbian couples is in the area of religion. For those who are religious the history of the relationships between churches and their gay/lesbian members has not been a happy one. Until quite recently all American churches have strongly condemned homosexuality (Irle, 1979). The result of this condemnation has been a common and enduring alienation of homosexuals from their churches (Bell & Weinberg, 1978). In response to an apparent need for religion felt by some gays, there developed during the 1960s and early 1970s the Metropolitan Community Church, an interdenominational church for both male and female homosexuals (Irle, 1979). This church now exists in most large American cities. Slightly later a number of liberal churches developed, affiliated fellowships, albeit sometimes grudgingly, for their gay members who did not want to abandon the churches in which they were raised in favor of the Metropolitan Community Church. Such affiliated fellowships also are principally found in large cities. They, along with the Metropolitan Community Church, provide interactional settings that are often couple-oriented and meet the religious needs of homosexuals.

As a broad generalization it can be said that large cities meet the needs of gays and lesbians, both single and coupled, far better than do smaller communities. This appears to have been historically true and accounts for the large-scale migration of homosexuals to larger cities (Harry & DeVall, 1978; Schofield, 1965). Relocation to a larger city may meet the needs of homosexuals for companionship, reduce the isolation they often find in smaller communities, and provide a greater measure of self-esteem as they become involved in a varied, active, and openly gay or lesbian lifestyle. However, migration to a large city may not be a feasible solution for some because there is often a conflict between leading a gay/lesbian lifestyle and earning a living. Often jobs are not located in communities that homosexuals might consider desirable places to live (DeVall, 1979). Despite this some gays have moved in large numbers to certain homosexual "meccas" such as San Francisco where large numbers have been unemployed or underemployed. For the coupled this may be somewhat less of a problem because it may be possible for one partner to quickly acquire employment and support them both while the other continues to search for work.

PROBLEMS INTERNAL TO THE GAY/LESBIAN FAMILY

Decision Making

Income and Decision Making

It is in their tendency toward egalitarian decision making that homosexual couples shine, although there are a few dark clouds. Power within heterosexual couple relationship has widely been found to be based on age difference, income difference, and gender (Blood, 1972; Blumstein & Schwartz, 1983; Harry, 1984). However, in the case of homosexual couples several strong forces operate to reduce the degree of inequality based on such differences. Since both parties of a homosexual couple are of the same sex, the average income difference between them is likely to be less than in heterosexual households. Income differences between members of a homosexual couple do occur, but are not based on gender.

When there is a nontrivial income difference between the partners to a gay union, it is commonly associated with differences in decision-making power, and this power imbalance seems to be particularly strong among gay men (Blumstein & Schwartz, 1983). Blumstein and Schwartz (1983) found that among lesbians, however, income difference is not apt to give rise to a power difference as it does among gay couples, heterosexual couples, and heterosexual cohabitors. The researchers interpreted this difference between gay and lesbian couples as due to their different gender roles. Gay men, like most men, tend to evaluate themselves and other men by the amount of money they make plus their other accomplishments. Such an instrumental approach to self- and other evaluation leads to the presumption that "he who pays the piper calls the tune." This is most often expressed in disagreements over how money is to be spent, particularly in the area of leisure activities.

An income difference between gay partners can be a source of irritation and self-devaluation for both members. If the member with the higher income wants them to take a trip to Europe and the other cannot afford it, the first is faced with the alternatives of going alone or with others, not going, or paying the way for the other member. In the first case the poorer member may feel abandoned. In the second case he may feel he is an obstacle to the other. While the third case may be acceptable to many heterosexual couples, in the case of gay male couples it gives rise to feelings of unmanly dependency with overtones of being a "kept boy."

Two partial solutions to income disparities are to live in separate households or, if they choose to live together, to not pool their resources. Separate households largely avoid the problem of one partner's partially supporting the other. Those who live in separate households report greater equality in decision making than those who cohabit (Harry, 1984). When partners live together, keeping incomes separate maintains the economic relationship between the two in a fashion similar to that of dating couples while having the advantage of the economies that arise from maintaining only one household.

It was noted that according to the scanty available evidence, income differences do not seem to be a source of decision-making inequality among lesbians. Blumstein and Schwartz (1983) attribute this to two factors. First, women are a good deal less likely than men to evaluate themselves and other women on the basis of their income. Second, many lesbians are feminist in their interpretations of gender roles or at least sensitive to the inequalities historically associated with gender roles. Rather than using income as an evaluative criterion, lesbians are apt to use more personal characteristics. When there are income differences between partners, it appears they go to considerable lengths to minimize the effects of those differences. Typically this involves an agreement on equal contributions to the relationship regardless of their individual incomes.

Gender Roles and Decision Making

Homosexual couples are fortunate in that they rarely fall into role specializations parallel to the gender role patternings often found among heterosexual couples, which are a common source of misunderstanding among the latter. As Tripp (1975, p. 152) observes. "When people who are not familiar with homosexual relationships try to picture one, they almost invariably resort to a heterosexual frame of reference, raising questions of which partner is the 'man' and which is the 'woman.'" However, since both partners in a homosexual relationship are of the same sex, the question of who is to play which gender role is indeterminate, and there appear to be few pressures by one partner to cast the other into a given gender role. While "role playing" may have been practiced by some lesbians prior to 1970 (Ponse, 1978; Wolf, 1979), in the contemporary gay and lesbian worlds this appears to be rare.

The "butch-femme" hypothesis that homosexual couples play heterosexual gender roles in their relationships has received considerable research attention and been found to be nearly totally lacking in support. For example, "kept boys" are quite uncommon. Harry (1979, 1982) found that only 1% of his Detroit gay respondents and none of his Chicago respondents were economically supported by another man. In analyzing the Bell and Weinberg (1978) data, Harry (1984) found that household tasks were not divided along traditional gender role lines. Rather, they tended to be divided according to talents and tastes into a "kitchen cluster" plus a residual cluster that also included some traditionally female-typed household chores. Similarly, in the area of who does what to whom in bed, little support has been found for the butch-femme hypothesis. Most gays prefer to vary their activities in bed and not to specialize in any activities that might be considered as more masculine or feminine (Harry & DeVall, 1978). However, those gays who actually preferred inequality in their relationships did tend to become "butches" or "femmes" in bed.

Not only has the butch-femme hypothesis found little support, it seems to have been maximally misleading. Those gay men who value masculinity in themselves also seem to value masculinity in their partners (Harry, 1982) and are also more masculine in their self-presentation. It thus seems that masculinity is a criterion by which gay persons select partners similar to themselves. Of course, this is the opposite of the butch-femme hypothesis.

Age and Decision Making

Age differences between heterosexual couples have been found to be associated with differences in decision making (Blood, 1972). This has also been found to be true among gay couples (Harry, 1984). Gays who are more than 5 years older than their partners tend to have disproportionate influence in the relationship. (Comparable data do not seem to exist for lesbian couples.) However, partners who are older than their mates are also likely to have more income. Hence, the question may arise whether it is age difference or income difference that gives rise to inequality in decision making. In Harry's (1984) data both kinds of differences were found to be associated with decision-making power, while being older was also found to be associated with having relatively more income than one's partner. It thus seems that age and income may combine in some cases to create an unequal relationship.

Age differences may be somewhat greater among gay couples than among heterosexual ones, with the average age difference among gay couples seeming to be about 5 years (Harry, 1985). The greater difference may arise because the gay world is less age-segregated than are heterosexual institutions. Also, since there are no strong norms among gays that persons should only couple with others closely similar in age, greater age disparities arise. Still, the data seem to show that gays, like heterosexuals, generally prefer partners of approximately the same age. As the gay man ages, his age tastes in partners age increase. However, there is an interesting side effect in that the gay man seems to age faster than his age preferences (Harry, 1984), so that a majority of gay men over 40 prefer other men who are 10 or more years younger.

The import of the greater age differences among gay couples may be that age rather than gender is a notable source of inequality in gay relationships. Harry (1982) found that while age differences do not strongly predict decision-making differences, prediction was much better in the reverse direction. Although there are some age-different couples who are egalitarian, if couples are inegalitarian the majority are likely to be age-different.

Sexual Exclusiveness

It has been uniformly found that the majority of gay couples are not sexually exclusive. Saghir and Robins (1973) reported that only about one-quarter of their coupled gay respondents had been sexually exclusive, while Harry and DeVall (1978) report a similar figure. Blumstein and Schwartz (1983) found that 18% of their coupled gay men had been sexually exclusive compared to 72% of their lesbians, 74% of their heterosexual husbands, and 79% of the heterosexual wives. Sexual exclusiveness is highest during the first year of a relationship but tends to decline over time (Harry, 1984).

Much has been made of the nonexclusiveness of gay men. Hoffman (1968) argues that nonexclusiveness arises because many gay men have internalized the societal disapproval of homosexuality, and this makes it difficult for them to establish enduring and monogamous relationships. Gagnon and Simon (1973) present a more benign interpretation of the nonexclusiveness of gay couples. These authors note that lesbian relationships are typically far more exclusive than gay relationships in a manner parallel to the differences in exclusiveness between married heterosexual males and females. According to available, perhaps outdated, studies, about half of heterosexual husbands are nonexclusive at least once during their married lives compared to one-fifth of married women (Kinsey, Pomeroy, & Martin, 1948; Hunt, 1974).

Authors researching gay nonexclusiveness infer that sex differences in socialization into sexuality are an important factor. Males, both gay and nongay, are socialized to value sexuality both in and outside of an emotionally intimate relationship, while women are principally expected to enjoy sexuality within the context of such a relationship. Given such socialization, considerable nonexclusiveness could be expected in a relationship involving two men, while considerable exclusiveness could be expected in a relationship involving two women. However, it should be noted that recent changes in contemporary norms regarding permissiveness may have increased the percentages of women, both homosexual and heterosexual, who are occasionally nonexclusive. Finally, the impact of AIDS (Acquired Immune Deficiency Syndrome) on the issue of exclusiveness, especially for gay males, is beginning to be felt dramatically and is discussed at the end of this chapter.

Silverstein (1981) suggests that coming to an agreement on exclusiveness or nonexclusiveness is the single largest problem that must be faced by gay couples. The relationship can survive if both of them can agree that they may both be nonexclusive or that they may both be exclusive. Warren (1974) suggests that an agreement on nonexclusiveness is the more viable adaptation in the context of the actual sexual marketplace of the gay world. Harry and DeVall (1978) found that couples in longer-term relationships more often agreed on exclusiveness or nonexclusiveness than disagreed.

While in heterosexual relationships exclusiveness is supported by strong norms and its lack can give rise to considerable conflict between partners, we need not expect this situation to be identical among gay males. Gays are aware of the propensities of other gays to have sex with a variety of partners and hence may consider nonexclusiveness to be just part of the facts of life (Blasband & Peplau, 1985). Hence, as long as nonexclusiveness does not violate a partner's expectations about the relationship, it may not be a problem. Some data do show that relationships characterized by nonexclusiveness are less emotionally intimate; however, the association reported was not very strong (Harry, 1984). The most striking data on nonexclusiveness reported that "among those with partners who don't mind non-exclusiveness, satisfaction is associated with the respondent's not minding his partner's non-exclusiveness, while among those with partners who do mind exclusiveness, satisfaction is associated with their own minding about their partner's exclusiveness" (Harry, 1984). Thus, agreement on exclusiveness or on nonexclusiveness seems to be very important, while the mere fact of exclusiveness or nonexclusiveness seems to matter little to a gay relationship.

Although a large number of gay male couples agree that nonexclusiveness may be practiced by both partners, this does not usually include permission to carry on a continuing affair or relationship with another man. In most relationships in which there is an agreement that they may both be nonexclusive, the agreement places limits on the kind of outside practices that may be indulged in. Casual sex is acceptable, but having an affair is not (Blumstein & Schwartz, 1983). For example, a common understanding is that a partner may engage in casual sex with another man as long as the other man is not brought home. Another variant of the casual sex understanding is that both members of a couple may simultaneously have sex with another man. Such behavior is considered not as disruptive as one of the partner's having a continuing outside affair, which is felt to be a threat to the primary relationship.

Nonexclusiveness plays a different role in lesbian relationships.

First, the data strongly suggest that for the most part lesbians do not engage in casual sex. Rather than engaging in outside "tricking," when they are not nonexclusive, they have affairs. This sex difference is parallel to that among heterosexuals (Blumstein & Schwartz, 1983). The result of this seems to be that outside sex has greater import for lesbian relationships than for gay ones. Blumstein and Schwartz (1983) report that lesbians engaging in outside affairs are often unhappy with their primary relationship and doubt that they want to continue it. Hence, while nonexclusiveness is often a non-problem in gay relationships, it is more likely to be a problem among lesbian couples.

GAY/LESBIAN HOUSEHOLDS WITH CHILDREN

Lesbian households are considerably more likely to contain children than are gay households. This is largely due to the fact that a higher percentage of lesbians have been heterosexually married. Approximately one-third of lesbians have been married compared to one-fifth of gay men (Bell & Weinberg, 1978; Saghir & Robins, 1973; Cotton, 1975; Schafer, 1977). Also contributing to the greater presence of children in lesbian households is the tradition of the courts' awarding custody to the mother as long as the mother's homosexuality is not an issue in the divorce (Maddox, 1982). Another reason is that lesbians tend to come out a few years later than gay men. While gay men usually come out at approximately 18 or 19 years of age (Dank, 1971; Harry & DeVall, 1978; Saghir & Robins, 1973), lesbians do so during their early 20s (Schafer, 1977; Saghir & Robins, 1973). The effect of this is that lesbians are available to marry for a longer time than are gay men, particularly at an age when a large percentage of their heterosexual peers are getting married.

A common threat to gay or lesbian households with children comes from the courts. The courts give two primary reasons for their reluctance to grant custody or even visiting rights to lesbian mothers and gay fathers. The first is the possibility that the children might become homosexual if raised in a homosexual environment. So far as data are available, there appears to be little basis for this concern. Green (1978) examined the erotic fantasies of 37 children raised in lesbian, gay, and transsexual households and found all the children, with one possible exception, to be heterosexual. Hoffer (1981) examined the toy preferences of 20 children of lesbian mothers and 20 children of heterosexual mothers and found no differences between the two groups of children. It should be noted that toy preferences are claimed by some to be the best childhood indicator of future adult gender atypicality, especially among males (Green, 1976; Bell, Weinberg, & Hammersmith, 1981; Whitam, 1980). From the reports of 40 gay fathers on their 21 sons and 27 daughters who were old enough for their sexual orientations to be assessed, it was found that only one of the sons and three of the daughters were homosexual (Miller, 1979).

In another study Hotvedt and Mandel (1982) compared the 56 children of 50 lesbian mothers with the 48 children of 40 heterosexual mothers while controlling on ages of mother and children, race, income, time since separation, education, and religion. For boys there was no difference in toy preferences, with both groups of boys consistently choosing "masculine" toys. The daughters of lesbian mothers chose somewhat less "feminine" toys than did the daughters of the heterosexual mothers, but they did not choose "masculine" ones. These data suggest no disproportionate amount of homosexuality among the children of homosexual parents. However, in Lewis's (1980) study of eight lesbian families several of the children had doubts about their future sexual orientation.

A second concern of the courts is that the children of homosexual parents will be harassed by others because of their parents. Three of the 37 children in 14 families studied by Green (1978) had been teased by other children (e.g., "Your mother is a lezzie," "Your mother is queer," "homoson.") Of the 18 gay fathers studied by Bozett (1980), one reported that his child had been teased about him. However, Hotvedt and Mandel (1982) reported from interviews with the children of lesbian and heterosexual mothers that the two groups of children did not differ in their popularity with other children of either sex. Interviews with the mothers on the children's popularity also showed no differences.

Aside from the courts' concern, homosexual parents are sometimes concerned about their children being harassed because of the parent's sexual orientation. Like gay fathers, lesbian mothers sometimes advise their children to be guarded in providing information about the home life to neighbors and school teachers (Wolf, 1979). It appears that in the cases in which a gay father disclosed his gayness to a child, a common practice was for him to suggest that the child practice discretion in talking about the matter with others (Bozett, 1980). For example, the father's live-in lover is referred to as an "uncle" in the presence of outsiders.

A later study by Bozett of 19 children of gay fathers (1985b) found that some of the children engaged in considerable impression management in order to avoid being harassed by the children of heterosexual parents. They sometimes avoided bringing other children over to their homes and avoided reference to their father's lover. Some did not want to be seen in public with their father if the father was stereotypically homosexual in appearance. The scanty evidence suggests that there may be some basis for the court's concern that the children of gay or lesbian parents may be harassed by others. However, it should be noted that these arguments are often made to justify discrimination by the court against the gay parent on the basis of a presumed probability of discrimination against the child by others.

One environmental problem sometimes faced by homosexual parents is that of adapting their role as parents to values and behaviors of the gay or lesbian worlds (Bozett, 1985a). Those worlds consist largely of singles and childless couples rather than of other parents, and socializing involves considerably more away-from-home activities than is the case for parental families. It may also involve more late-night activity than is compatible with the routines of a household with children. Faced with sometimes conflicting demands between parental obligations and the desire to have a social life, homosexual parents are sometimes forced to make sacrifices. These choices are especially onerous for those who are also without partners. The problems they face are the same as those reported by single-parent households generally, that is, having to choose between parental obligations and social isolation. Of all kinds of households, including single-person households, single parents are the most isolated from the community and from social contact with adults (Institute for Social Research, 1984).

Homosexual parents without partners sometimes try to meet these conflicts by falling back on the help of outside persons since they cannot routinely rely on the assistance of a partner, as occurs in heterosexual marriages (Lewin & Lyons, 1982). Friends can occasionally be relied on for brief stints of baby-sitting. However, this resource can only be called on occasionally since friends will typically revolt if the requests for assistance become either frequent or routine. Single lesbian parents also rely on their own parents for assisting in child care obligations, but this solution is only available in those cases in which the parents have not been alienated by the mother's homosexuality. In a few cases former spouses can be utilized as long as the estrangement is not too great. The best solution to these conflicts is to establish a two-parent household so that the partner can share the responsibilities and pleasures of caring for the children. As in the case of stepfamilies, children of lesbian mothers may require a period of adjusting to the mother's lover (Hall, 1978; Lewis, 1979). However, the scanty literature suggests that most children come to accept and love the mother's lover.

There has been some question about whether male children are out of place or unwelcome in lesbian circles. Hall (1978) described a situation in which persons planning a Mother's Day celebration for lesbians and their children questioned the appropriateness of allowing male children to participate and yet hesitated to exclude them. However, the few available studies indicate that lesbian mothers are usually aware of the needs of their male children and are more likely than single heterosexual mothers to be concerned about providing adult male figures for their boys (Kirkpatrick, Smith, & Roy, 1981). Nungesser (1980) reported that 80% of the male children of lesbian mothers had adult male figures involved in their lives, including a number of gay men. Some have suggested that lesbian mothers may, because of their unique situations, bend over backward to ensure that male children have exposure to both sexes. It does seem that lesbian mothers attempt to raise their children in nonsexist ways and to bring them up without the constraints of traditional gender roles (Kirkpatrick, Smith, & Roy, 1981; Wolf, 1979).

The issue of the acceptance of the parent's homosexuality by male children may arise in both gay and lesbian households. Lewis (1980) found in a study of 21 children of lesbian mothers that older adolescent boys sometimes reacted negatively to the mother's homosexuality. Hints of such nonacceptance by male children are also found in the writings of Bozett (1980; 1985b) and Miller (1979). It is unclear whether the source of these boys' discomfort is threatened gender identity, the intensely homophobic culture of their adolescent peers, or both.

One form of gay family not discussed so far is that arising through adoption or foster parenting by a gay couple. During the 1970s a number of gay foster homes were established in some large cities. Gay adolescents who had either run away from home or had been thrown out by parents after learning of the child's homosexuality have been occasionally placed with gay male couples. Of course, the foster parents have been carefully screened to eliminate the inappropriately motivated. Such placements, typically done by private agencies, sometimes encounter a number of legal problems, since the natural parents usually retain legal custody. Such placements and adoptions seem a promising development, since gay adolescents sometimes do not fare well in institutions for juveniles, in heterosexual foster homes, or in conventional heterosexual public schools where they may be harassed or beaten. In response to this last problem the New York City Board of Education recently established the Harvey Milk High School for gay/lesbian children who do not fit into the regular public schools. Placing young gays in gay foster or adoptive homes may provide them with the first positive relationship with an adult male they have had in their lives.

FUTURE RESEARCH TOPICS

One aspect of the gay/lesbian family that very much needs to be researched is that of family violence. To date there has been no research on this topic. One hypothesis would hold that gay couples would be rather high in interpersonal violence due to the simple fact that they were socialized as males, while lesbian couples would be quite low due to their socialization as females. However, one can derive the opposite hypothesis from a few studies (Harry, 1982; Green, 1976) that report that homosexual children are usually committed to a cross-gender role until they become more gender-conventional by adulthood. Those practicing professionals interested in the problems of homosexual households would certainly benefit from any knowledge to be gained from research on gay/lesbian family violence.

An unfortunate omission in this chapter has been discussion of the impact of AIDS (Acquired Immune Deficiency Syndrome) on the gay or lesbian family. At the present writing there is no published reliable research on the social, rather than medical, impact of AIDS on gay/lesbian relationships. The medical situation surrounding AIDS is constantly changing, and it is likely that the impact of AIDS on the gay and lesbian worlds has not stabilized. Hence, we conclude by raising questions that future research on the impact of AIDS will want to take up. Has AIDS given rise to greater exclusiveness among coupled homosexuals, especially gays? Do single gays experience fewer sexual partners than in the preAIDS era? If so, has this changed the social structures of the gay world such that social, rather than sexual, settings have become more popular? Has the rise of AIDS provided an excuse for so-inclined heterosexuals to practice more overt discrimination than before? It is clear that there have been cases in which gay men have been discriminated against in housing and medical care on the basis of unjustified fears of contagion. Will AIDS provide reason for judges to refuse custody to gay and lesbian parents? Finally, will AIDS provide justification for others to discriminate against children in gay and lesbian households, for example, refuse to admit to school a child living in a gay/lesbian household?

NOTE

1. In this work the expression "gay/lesbian" is synonymous with "homosexual," while "gay" refers to homosexual men only.

6

Choosing a Gay/Lesbian Lifestyle

RELATED ISSUES OF TREATMENT SERVICES

SUSAN RICE AND
JIM KELLY

The purpose of this chapter is to discuss the issues of treatment that are related to working with people who have chosen a gay/lesbian lifestyle. In categorizing the issues likely to be present in treating people who are gay/lesbian, it is important to first examine a general typology of issues. Initially, problems in living generally can be separated from problems in living associated with a person's homosexuality.

If the problem that someone brings to therapy is not related to his or her sexual preference, then that person would be "treated" with the same understanding of the dynamics of the issue as would a heterosexual person. For example, if an individual is suffering from poor relationships with friends, it cannot be assumed that the person's homosexuality is either a reason for that difficulty or even a related dynamic. If it seems in the course of initial assessment that the difficulties stem from poor self-image, poor communication, or the like, then treatment would focus on those issues as well as the individual's relationships with persons of the same gender. With that as a preface, this chapter will focus on those issues that are directly related to one's choice of a homosexual lifestyle.

The point also must be made that there is a difference between sexual preference and choice of lifestyle. Sexual preference primarily occurs on levels outside of people's conscious decision-making arenas. However, choosing to access the variety of resources and types of living that are associated with homosexuality *is* a matter of choice. It is important to try to ascertain the degree to which people have immersed themselves in a homosexual lifestyle, as that will affect treatment in all areas.

In this chapter we will first discuss intrapsychic and interpersonal issues and then environmental concerns. Intrapsychic and interpersonal issues are those self and relationship issues that are directly related to peoples' homosexuality. In this category are included issues of homophobia (self and others); signification, or the labeling process; the coming out process; issues of finding and maintaining social relationships, including concerns about sexual exclusivity;

and decision-making and power within relationships. Special issues related to the adolescent and aging populations will also be discussed.

Environmental issues are those that are raised for people in their environment because of their chosen lifestyle. Included in this category are issues related to parental relationships; children and custodial arrangements; the work environment; religious conflicts; and cultural mores that complicate individuals' adaptation to their environment. We will also briefly discuss problems associated with AIDS.

As a general guideline for intervention, it is important to recognize that dealing with any of these issues does not require a clear and in-depth understanding of why people are gay/lesbian or heterosexual especially since scholars cannot agree on this subject. Unless an understanding of why people have chosen their lifestyle is a concern of the person seeking treatment, it is irrelevant to effective intervention with other specific issues.

Gayness is not a clinical entity (Moses & Hawkins, 1982) and is neither indicative of, nor a causal factor in, psychological disturbance or social malfunctioning in and of itself (Gonsiorek, 1977). It can become a problem, however, through oppression from the larger society and/or through ignorance or conflicts about the matter within the self. Therefore, one of the necessary requirements of effective therapy is to be clear, for the therapist and the person seeking treatment, that a homosexual lifestyle is a viable alternative, so that gays and lesbians can be dealt with *within their own contexts*. Otherwise, the issues that emerge and the ensuing interventions will be muddied by questions of values related to their choice of sexual preference and the degree to which they act on that preference.

From a consumer point of view (Hall, 1985), one of the most concrete pieces of advice given to homosexuals seeking help is to be sure to choose a therapist who is not in the business of proselytizing for heterosexual behaviors. As expressed by Blair (1975), *good* counseling "can mitigate the effects of oppression and mismanagement of one's life and can facilitate fuller functioning for homosexuals and families" (pp. 94–95). If the client is struggling with wanting to choose a heterosexual lifestyle, then a new series of issues would emerge. However, within the context of this chapter—issues that relate to the choice of a particular lifestyle—it is imperative to begin from the perspective that this lifestyle is viable and not necessarily problem-laden.

The recognition that homosexuals are in many ways an oppressed population demands that the therapist help patients (or clients) strike a balance (Moses & Hawkins, 1982) "between recognizing and validating the person's experience of being oppressed and helping the client move out of the role of victim . . . which essentially abdicates responsibility to the oppressor" (p. 67). The task is to help people separate the issues that are related to the environment and demand environmental manipulation as well as personal adaptation from those that stem from their own dysfunctional behaviors, so that they can make changes that afford them more fulfillment and successful adaptation within the context of their chosen sexual patterns and lifestyle.

INTRAPSYCHIC AND INTRAPERSONAL ISSUES

Homophobia

Homophobia has been defined in a variety of ways, including "those who have a fear or dread of homosexuals or homosexuality" (MacDonald, 1976; Marmor, 1980). The term allows us to examine, for both homosexuals and heterosexuals, irrational fears, attitudes, and resulting behavior centered around their negative associations with homosexuality. It is the client's issue when his or her own homophobic attitudes prevent him or her from living without a constant accompaniment of guilt and shame about the homosexual lifestyle. Intervention must then deal with an exploration of these fears and attitudes, with the goal of self-acceptance, so that the client can react in a more constructive way to the homophobic behavior of others.

Woodman (1982) suggests in a discussion of working with clients in lesbian relationships that "growth in self-appraisal can help the partners reassess the validity of their choice of lifestyle and minimize their perception of lesbianism as 'second best to marriage' or as crazy or sinful" (p. 119). That same concept is valid for working with gay male couples or, for that matter, gay individuals. When people accept their choice of lifestyle as valid, they can move toward accepting themselves and as a result are better able to increase their effectiveness in interrelating with other people.

Homophobic behavior on the part of therapists may be manifested in feelings of fear, disgust, or discomfort about the lifestyle of the client. Some therapists may be frightened or uncomfortable around homosexuals because of their ignorance or inexperience. According to theories expressed by Moses and Hawkins (1982) such therapists are unsure what homosexuality means, how to act around it, and what to do about it. They may think they should ignore it, although at the same time it is salient to them in developing a relationship with this person. This kind of homophobia may be reduced by a willingness on the part of the therapist to be self-aware and to learn from the people who are in treatment with him or her.

Homosexuals need to deal with issues of homophobia with people in the community as well as with therapists. If individuals do not react defensively or hostilely to initial homophobic reactions, they are sometimes able to educate and subsequently include others (gay and nongay) in their support network who might otherwise be excluded because of negative reactions. The kind of homophobic behavior that is seemingly more malicious may also be based on fear, but it is a level of fear that is less readily reduced. Theoretically some people are homophobic because of their own concerns about their personal sexual identity and some because they fear tolerance will lead to lack of control and chaos in their world.

Other causes of homophobia are the kind of socialization, religious training, and instillation of values that people are given. Such "socialized" homophobes are better left alone by members of the gay community, but this cannot be done until gays and lesbians accept that the problem is in the homophobic person rather than within themselves. Other oppressed groups have recognized that there is a time and place for fighting institutional discrimination and a time and place for ignoring bigoted individuals, not allowing them to dissipate one's personal energy.

It is important for practitioners to examine the homophobic attitudes they may unconsciously have that interfere with effective intervention. The practitioner's commitment to supervision and resolving areas that are problematic for him or her is important. It has been suggested (Cummerton, 1982) that there are three areas where the therapeutic work with lesbian clients is undermined: underestimation of the daily stress that lesbians undergo; encouraging superhuman expectations in their ability to deal with conflicting roles; and ignoring the problems or issues peculiar to lesbian relationships. These areas apply to work with gay males as well.

Daily stress is related to the fact that gay males and lesbians must make constant, moment-to-moment decisions every day about being "out of the closet," regardless of how they interact in their private lives. Because there is always a potential risk involved in being open in the job, career, and public world, the safest bet is conservatism in the area of publicly avowing one's sexual preference. This forces people to pay a price in terms of their own self-esteem and self-acceptance.

The second area deals with the therapist's conscious or unconscious encouragement of extraordinary expectations for the client. It is true, as Cummerton (1982) observes, that the ideal is that "self-esteem should be independent of what others think and of what type of work one does, but as therapists, there needs to be a recognition that such independence is difficult to achieve, and it is unrealistic to expect lesbian clients to be impervious to what others think of them" (p. 109). It is also unrealistic to think that gay clients will feel no need to share their personal life with heterosexual friends and co-workers or will never resent the limits that secrecy places even on casual conversations.

Last, therapists are sometimes guilty of ignoring the issues that are specific to homosexuality, in particular for those who have not participated in or had children in heterosexual relationship before becoming committed to a gay or lesbian lifestyle. A woman who chooses to live as a lesbian gives up the fantasies of being taken care of by a man, having children, and being a member of a nuclear family, fantasies that are all part of female socialization in our culture. It is true that lesbians often group together and take care of each other, but there is nevertheless a loss that must be addressed. Men give up the fantasy of taking care of someone weaker and needier, which, in the fantasy, allows men to define themselves as "men." They, too, must give up the fantasy of being fathers. For both men and women there are issues related to power, decision making, and sexual exclusivity, to be discussed later, that are very specifically affected by sexual choice. To ignore these is to lessen one's therapeutic effectiveness.

Signification and Coming Out Process

Theoretically the signification and coming out process describes a more-or-less extended period during which the individual puts together feelings, thoughts, and sometimes sexual experiences with a learned definition of what a gay man or lesbian is (Lee, 1977). "The end result may be a sudden 'aha' of recognition, or it may be a slower occurrence as the individual accumulates evidence about her or his sexual preference. The actual act of self-labeling is technically the act of signification" (Moses & Hawkins, 1982, p. 80).

While dealing with the signification process can be a time of great turmoil for clients, it can also be a period of growth. However, as Moses and Hawkins (1982) caution, "Professionals must use discretion and sensitivity in helping clients choose and define the meaning of the label they believe best fits them. . . . Concern about the possibility of being gay, or thoughts or fantasies about members of the same gender do not necessarily mean that it is appropriate for a person to think of herself or himself as gay" (p. 84).

For a woman, self-admitted lesbianism "may result in the realization that one no longer fits into the expected female role" (Groves, 1985). Furthermore, "lesbianism can be seen as a political statement, as it may be dangerous and powerful for a woman in our society to define herself as independent of men" (Rawlings & Carter, 1977, p. 20), although that danger is perhaps lessened in our current social climate. It is interesting to speculate on the opinion (Groves, 1985) that most lesbians have much more in common with heterosexual women than with gay men and that therefore the coming out process means different things to gay men and lesbian women. The greater social opprobrium against homosexual men than against lesbians, with the resulting fear by heterosexual men that they might be labeled gay through association, probably explains a good part of this often-observed phenomenon.

Once there is a recognition of who one is in terms of sexual preference, the gay/lesbian community can be a place where people can usually find strong support. An often-neglected aspect of intervention related to this issue may include assisting homosexuals to find networks within the gay community. In a study of the coming out process for male homosexuals (Dank, 1971) the conclusion is drawn that as the homosexuality-as-a-way-of-life philosophy is increasingly accepted by gays and nongays (as compared to the homosexuality-as-mental-illness philosophy), the gay community more and more will become a place in which one's sex life is less fragmented from the rest of one's social life, and hence homosexuals can form a stronger, more integrated social network.

An additional complication in dealing with the signification and coming out process relates to conflict in a relationship in which one partner wants to come out publicly (or to a greater degree) and one wants to remain "in the closet." Even if both partners are completely in the closet, the existence of a relationship makes problematic issues of "passing," or concealment of one's sexual identity, such as explaining to family members and work associates who the "roommate" is. In a study of 200 lesbians (Woodman, 1982) a variety of fears surfaced related to coming out, including fear of exposure to their families, fear of the impact that other publicly gay cohorts or activist gays might have on an established way of life, and fear of losing the partner to new persons and associations. Even those who wanted to come out but felt restrained from doing so for practical or economic reasons felt that their conflict over coming out lessened their potential for growth and their ability to communicate meaningfully with their partners.

Social Relationships and Sexual Exclusivity

Issues related to finding social/sexual relationships and then maintaining them are affected by some problems specific to homosexual relationships. For example, fusion (Krestan & Bepko, 1980) is a common problem in lesbian relationships, affecting both their quality and longevity. Fusion refers to a process of undifferentiation between people within relationships. Theoretically, it occurs if the lesbian pair finds social rejection of their relationship as a couple. This creates a tendency to rigidify tight partner boundaries further and turn in on themselves in a fused relationship, adopting what has been termed a "two against a threatening world" posture.

It makes sense that a subsystem (the couple) trying to relate to a larger system (their outside environment) that either ignores them or criticizes them will lead to an attempt on the part of the subsystem to become as independent as possible. However, the fused relationship is subject to an inordinate amount of pressure, just as a fused heterosexual relationship would be.

In cases of fusion the therapeutic task becomes one of understanding and intervening in the cycle of one partner distancing; the partners alternating the distance between them; fusion; and unrelatedness—in short, continual conflict and impairment of one or both partners (Karpel, 1976). The partners become more fused with each other as they attempt to distance themselves from the outside world, and then the cycle is reversed when that does not lead to a satisfactory reduction in tension. Therapeutic intervention with couples suggests that an important issue involves "acknowledging and facing aloneness. . . . The partners often need reassurance that continually alternating between being in a relationship and being alone is not the only way to balance closeness and separation. This balance can be achieved within a relationship" (McCandlish, 1985) which allows each person to have her or his own separate identity but also involves commitment to each other as a couple.

The expectation that any relationship will provide unconditional and unlimited love (especially needed to replace the feelings of loss generated by actual or implied rejection from the family of origin and the larger environment) requires "reality testing of the implications of loving and being loved. The couple probably needs to develop skills in communicating with each other so they can send messages of esteem and express their differences." (Woodman, 1982, p. 121)

It has also been shown, however (Krestan & Bepko, 1980), that there is a greater attempt among lesbian couples to "triangulate" either outside issues or other people into the relationship to a dysfunctional degree. For example, other lovers or a symptom such as alcoholism are brought into the relationship as an attempt to minimize the intolerability of the fusion/unrelatedness cycle. The anxiety that is generated by being part of a relationship that ricochets from intense closeness to complete withdrawal is relieved, albeit in an unhealthy manner, by outside stimulation such as other lovers or alcohol.

When dealing with the issue of fusion/unrelatedness, it is suggested that the task is a multifaceted one, including subtasks of first sanctioning the validity of the relationship and then helping the clients understand some basic systems principles, such as boundaries, triangulation, and distancing. "For the couple, this process leads to a reframing of their relationship as a system that is inherently capable of being maintained as opposed to one that is pathological in nature" (Krestan & Bepko, 1980, p. 288). The third step revolves around helping each partner become more differentiated within the relationship, allowing him or her to tolerate the discomfort of distancing while setting internal boundaries.

These issues are common in many couple and parent-child relationships. However, a large part of the special problem for homosexuals results from the intensity of the environmental pressures in conjunction with the isolation of a hostile world. However, essential for effective intervention is a recognition that the survival of their own couplehood depends on a more functional reaction to those pressures in a way that does not promote fusion.

Another area that appears to be a more common issue in maintaining significant relationships for people living a homosexual lifestyle is that of sexual exclusivity. Statistics support the notion that the pattern among homosexual couples follows that of heterosexual couples in that gay male couples are much less sexually exclusive than are lesbian couples. Explanations of this phenomenon (Blasband & Peplau, 1985) include the fact that gay male sex-role socialization, similar to heterosexual male sex-role socialization, often promotes frequent, casual, and multipartnered sexual activity. Additionally, the presence of children, which is more common in lesbian couples, promotes sexual exclusivity as a way to protect the family setting for the children. Whatever the reason, the issue that emerges for homosexuals is whether or not the decisions they make regarding sexual exclusivity affect the quality of their relationship.

Blasband and Peplau (1985) studied 40 gay male couples in regard to those decisions and the effect on the relationship. The results showed that "on measures of duration and commitment, open and closed relationships were indistinguishable," indicating that what is important therapeutically is for the couple to understand the meaning of sexual exclusivity related to their feelings about the need for sexual variety, concerns about independence and jealousy, and basic definitions of monogamous and nonmonogamous relationships. Some couples felt that time-limited sexual contacts would not damage a relationship, whereas longer-term affairs would.

It has also been found that lesbian couples (again, socialized similarly to heterosexual females) are more likely to engage in long-term affairs than short-term, casual sexual activity. This could lead to sexual nonexclusivity being more damaging for lesbian couples, not because of the sexual activity but because of the meaning of exclusivity for them.

Decision Making and Power

The area of power and decision making is considered to be important in relationships in general, and it needs to be considered specifically related to the dynamics of homosexual coupling. In all relationships decision making and other kinds of power are closely associated with economic clout. Harry (1987) discusses the fact that since men in our society routinely earn more than women, this leads to fairly predictable statistical patterns of power and dominance, with the males being dominant and females being less so. In homosexual relationships the economic factors are usually more equal, and therefore power is distributed on a different basis.

For men money is more of a way of defining oneself. It was found (Cavan, 1966; Hoffman, 1968) that pairings of gay men are often troubled by the question of who is to be dominant, while in lesbian relationships the concern is more about the need for egalitarianism. In male relationships the partners are more likely to maintain separate apartments or develop bookkeeping systems that allow each to live according to his own scale of income, while in female relationships there is much more likelihood of combining incomes.

In terms of intervention it is important to recognize that status differentials are not related to gender roles but rather to other factors such as health or age. Additionally, the therapist cannot assume that differences in status are or are not problematic. If the differences are problematic, however, they may be damaging to an otherwise well-functioning partnership (Moses & Hawkins, 1982). Intervention needs to focus on the specific problem the couple is facing; they need to determine not only what they do not like about their current situation but also what it is they would like to achieve.

Foremost in establishing goals for achievement is that the partners need to establish good communication, which then becomes an important aspect of therapeutic intervention. Women may have learned that it is not appropriate to express their desires or to be assertive about what they want. Men may have never learned the art of compromise without a concomitant feeling that their self-esteem has been lessened. Although the problem of status differentials means different things to a gay couple, the skills a couple needs to clarify those differences are similar to those used with heterosexual couples—cognitive skills, communication skills, and an ability to affectively express their needs and desires.

Adolescent and Aging Populations

Adolescents and older people have certain additional issues to deal with that must be included in the therapist's assessment of the situation. Theoretically, adolescents are dealing with the developmental issue of identity versus role confusion (Erikson, 1950). Their primary concern relates to what they appear to be in the eyes of others as compared to what they feel they are. Adolescents have "love" relationships with others primarily as a way to arrive at a definition of their own identity, by projecting their diffused ego image onto another. Also, young people can be "remarkably cruel in their exclusion of all those who are 'different' . . . as a defense against a sense of identity confusion" (Erikson, 1950). Therefore, coming out for an adolescent can be especially traumatic, as it often means that the young gay man or woman learns to think of him- or herself as sick or bad and then feels isolated and trapped (Adair & Adair, 1978).

Older gay men, moreso than older lesbians, also face special problems in relationships, because of the double burden of growing old in our society and being part of an oppressed minority group. Berger and Kelly (1986) suggest, however, that there are advantages as well as disadvantages to homosexual aging.

The disadvantages include the fact that older homosexuals are subject to inaccurate stereotypes and myths, including a misconception that they have a propensity for child molestation, that they go through an accelerated aging process, and that they exist in a situation of social isolation. Research has demonstrated these conceptions to be untrue, but the "buying" of the myths by older people themselves and/or the rest of their social world has negative effects on their ability to maintain a positive self-image.

The issue of "passing" for an older person has direct impact on the ability to resolve the final developmental dilemma of "ego integrity versus despair" (Erikson, 1950) in a positive way. Ego integrity is described as "the acceptance of one's one-and-only life cycle as something that had to be and that, by necessity, permitted of no substitutions. . . . Although aware of all the various life styles which have given meaning to human striving, the possessor of integrity is ready to defend the dignity of his own life against all threats" (Erikson, 1950, p. 268).

How can people reach that state of ego integrity when they have denied such important aspects of themselves? On the other hand, however, older homosexuals have had to possess the strength and fortitude to engage in what has been called "mastery of stigma" (Francher & Henkin, 1973, p. 673). Older homosexuals have come to terms with a stigmatized identity earlier in life and have developed the inner resources to achieve some modicum of self-acceptance in the face of overwhelming societal disapproval. Clearly this degree of self-acceptance depends on their adaptation all through life and would range from unhealthy to healthy degrees. This mastery, however, perhaps allows older people to retain their ego integrity more easily than their heterosexual counterparts, who begin the struggle at a later date and with fewer resources than they had previously.

Additionally, older homosexuals are more likely to have developed role flexibility by having to be self-reliant and independent, which enables them to care for themselves and adapt more effectively than their heterosexual counterparts. In terms of intervention, it is important to facilitate people's continued integration into an active support network while recognizing the intrapsychic strengths that they may have developed over time.

It is also important to recognize that there are healthy, non-neurotic reasons for relationships ending. Although much of this discussion has centered on maintaining relationships, Moses and Hawkins (1982) suggest that there are many mitigating circumstances, including the fact that gay and heterosexual long-term relationships have different functions. "The counselor should be willing to explore with the client both the positive and negative consequences of termination of a given relationship. Clients need to learn that ending a relationship is not a sign of failure either on the part of the individuals or the couple as a whole" (p. 130).

ENVIRONMENTAL ISSUES

The second group of practice issues are those that emerge by virtue of people choosing a homosexual lifestyle in the context of an environment that is predominantly heterosexual in its beliefs and attitudes. Specifically, the issues of relating to one's parents, being parents and dealing with custodial arrangements, dealing with the work environment, facing one's religious conflicts, and understanding the context of cultural mores are issues that gay men and lesbians bring to the therapeutic situation. These issues stem directly from their choice of lifestyle and cannot be dealt with without putting them into the context of the larger environment.

Relations with Families of Origin

Relationships with parents are a universal issue, regardless of whether the parents are physically or emotionally present or absent. Relationship to one's family of origin has been found to be important in present-day functioning and is considered by many to be an integral part of any therapeutic intervention (Hartman & Laird, 1983).

Obviously, one of the first considerations related to people's relationships with their parents is whether or not they have "come out" to their parents. It is not, however, the therapist's role to decide for people whether or not being open makes sense given the context of their relationship with their parents. Rather, it is the therapist's job to help people explore that relationship and to support the decision to be public or private. Often therapeutic intervention will include either family sessions or "rehearsals" in which clients practice discussing their sexuality with their families.

It is important to recognize that there is a coming out process for recipients of such information as well as for homosexuals (Silverstein, 1977). Parents need support to know that their child is the same person as he or she was "before," that the child is being honest with them out of caring rather than anger, and that the choice of lifestyle is a separate entity from his or her relationship with the parents.

However, once that piece of information is out in the open or the decision has been made for it to remain private, the therapeutic intervention then focuses on the overall quality of the relationship and improvement, if it is a source of conflict, in those general areas. For people who choose to keep their sexual identities separate from their relationship with their parents, there needs to be a great deal of understanding of the difficulties in compartmentalization in order to avoid those difficulties becoming dysfunctional in any communication with their parents. If parents are overwhelmingly negative and unaccepting and the process of time does not change their attitudes, then clients will need assistance in emotionally separating, in allowing their self-esteem and self-identity to come from within rather than from their parents.

Many therapists urge family counseling (Silverstein, 1977; Berzon, & Leighton, 1979) as a means of providing support for parents by allowing them opportunities for catharsis, explanation, reassurance, confrontation, suggestion, guidance, and recommendations. Together these reaffirm "basic parental responsibilities, such as to supply their [child's] . . . need for their continued caring, love, understanding, support, and respect" (Myers, 1985, p. 140).

Parenting Issues

Most often discussions that focus on children and homosexuals center on lesbian mothers, since our culture still promotes the idea that the mother is the predominant parent. However, gay men who have fathered children also struggle with paternity and parenting issues and perhaps with more anguish because they feel so alone. A major category of "problems" associated with homosexuality and parenting concerns custody issues. It is common for gays and lesbians to be discriminated against in this area (Potter & Darty, 1981) based on the grounds that their sexual preference automatically makes them "unfit" parents. An additional group of people who are concerned with these issues are those who have not had children and would like to care for foster children or adopt children.

The mental health professional's role in the parenting issue often becomes that of a consultant for recommendations to the court regarding custody. The issue for intervention involves exploring guidelines for a decision that includes but does not focus only on the sexual lifestyle chosen by the parent. Hoorwitz and Burchardt (1984), suggest a series of questions to be explored, including the following:

1. Are there compelling reasons to change the current custody situation?
2. What obstacles exist to joint custody?
3. Who is the major parenting person?
4. What can be said about the adequacy of parenting capacities of each parent?
5. How well are the child's needs being met judging from his or her development?
6. What is the child's preference, and is the child competent to make an objective judgment about custody?

Seeking answers to these questions can help people make a more nearly accurate determination of what is best for the child without focusing solely on issues of sexual preference. At times the therapeutic task involves helping people recognize that they may not be able to care adequately for their child (or do so "better" than the other parent), while at other times it involves the clinician becoming a strong advocate for lesbian/gay parenting rights, both for the people in specific cases and in general. For example, the American Psychological Association adopted the following resolution: "The sex, gender identity, or sexual orientation of natural or prospective adoptive or foster parents should not be the sole or primary variable considered in child custody or placement cases" (Slovenko, 1980, p. 215, note 50). Such a statement suggests a stance for therapists to adopt in their practice.

The issues in counseling for parents who have custody often relate to their relationships with their children. Issues to explore may include an assessment of the potential for the child's becoming a homosexual like the parent (Russotto, 1980). However, since some scholars (Boggan et al., 1975) believe that sexual orientation is determined by age 6 or so, the parent's sexual lifestyle should probably not be a factor on that ground in most custody decisions. Since this is not as yet proven, however, and many custody cases do involve children under 6, the area is one that arouses controversial and contradictory opinions.

More central is an understanding of the issues that the children of lesbians and gays must cope with and to assist them with that coping process. One study (Lewis, 1980) identified early family discord as a factor that made subsequent coping with family problems more difficult. The mother's lesbianism "became another problem around which the children's feelings were blocked since they could not express freely both sides of their ambivalence" (p. 203). Therefore, the intervention effort needs to be directed at clearer communication and encouragement of open discussion of feelings rather than just the issue of homosexuality. Parents also need to understand and deal with the specific homosexual issues their children are apt to be struggling with, such as feeling alienated from their peers as well as being uncomfortable about possible sexual activities in the home.

However, it has also been found in a few small studies that the children of single lesbian mothers had the same degrees of severity and numbers of problems as did those of single heterosexual mothers, and these problems related to divorce issues rather than parental homosexuality (Maddox, 1982). Children were concerned about whether they had caused their parents to break up and whether they would lose either parent in the future. The two groups could not be differentiated by degrees of disturbed gender development.

A study of gay fathers (Miller, 1976) suggests that successful gay fathering is strongly affected by acceptance on the part of the larger society that gay parenting is a viable alternative. When the stigma imposed from without lifts, then individual parents are helped to become more effective. Within the therapeutic situation it becomes important to separate the problems imposed from without from those that arise within the context of the family.

With homosexual as well as heterosexual couples children's behavior is often a symptom of marital dysfunction. It cannot be assumed that the issues the children are dealing with are related to their parents' homosexuality, as it is also possible that their symptoms might be an enactment of a relationship problem between the two adults in the home. It is suggested (Russotto, 1980) that "relationship counseling for the homosexual couple is indicated if the children's behavior can be traced to some dysfunction in the system, if the relationship has lasted over a period of time, or if there is sufficient motivation and potential for growth."

Employment Issues

The work situation for adults who have chosen a homosexual lifestyle can also cause problems specifically related to that choice. Tensions related to the work environment often emerge in therapeutic situations. How "open" the client is at work has ramifications for his or her career and also for self-esteem. A examination of current legal theory (Rivera, 1982) suggests that private employers in the United States have an absolute right to hire and fire as they please for whatever reasons they choose. The only limit on private employment actions is federal law. Title VII of the Civil Rights Act of 1964 forbids private employers from discriminating on the basis of sex and race but *not* on the basis of sexual preference. At least three major court cases have sought to include homosexual persons among those protected by Title VII, and all have failed.

The task of therapists is to help people explore and resolve for themselves an acceptable balance between honesty and security, between the tension of concealment and the tension of hostility directed at them.

Religious and Cultural Conflict

Religious and cultural conflicts are difficult to separate since culture is so greatly affected by religious ideas. In a discussion of the basis of attitudes toward homosexuality in our culture. Bullough (1978) suggests that the concept of the sinful nature of sex in general, and particularly of homosexuality, lies deep in the Jewish tradition. This was reinforced in Christian theology, which, among other things, emphasized that the pleasures of the mind were to be preferred to those of the body. Christianity emphasized that sexuality, except within marriage and for reproductive purposes, was sinful and that those who departed from societal norms should be punished. That tradition has little application to an overpopulated modern world, but it leaves many people who have internalized these tenets in their religious upbringing in the throes of inner conflict.

Treatment needs to deal with the issues of helping homosexuals come to an understanding of the religious beliefs that are important to them. Many, for example, speak of the notion of following their own "conscience" in making moral decisions. Referrals to sources such as Dignity (Rueda, 1982), which is the best known of all Catholic homosexual organizations, can allow people to struggle with this issue in a supportive atmosphere. Their purpose is to unite gay Catholics, develop leadership, and allow the gay Catholic to be heard by the Church and society.

The Problem of AIDS

Since the AIDS (Acquired Immune Deficiency Syndrome) crisis has exploded, the work place has become the stage on which the larger society's fears of homosexuality has been particularly enacted. Although most experts agree (Gong, 1985) that AIDS cannot be transmitted by nonsexual contact, even of an intimate nature such as between household members who share eating utensils, there have been instances of people being fired because of the disease or even because of the potential danger of the disease.

AIDS is not only a disease that destroys the body's immune system and leaves it powerless against infection. It has also intensified homophobia in our society, which has dramatically and drastically affected homosexuals whether or not they have the disease. Much is being written about how to prevent the spread of this disease, how to promote "safe sex," and how to reduce sexual promiscuity and drug use, both of which are associated with the contraction of the disease (NASW, 1985). It is important for therapists to understand that AIDS is passed to other people only through an exchange of blood (as in transfusions from an infected person or sharing the same needle for drug injections) or through contact with the semen of an infected person. The consistent and careful use of high-quality condoms at the time of intercourse is basic to "safe sex."

In terms of working with people who have AIDS, it has been recognized that "more than any other population of cancer patients, this one suffers a dramatic change in self-esteem, daily habits, and general life style in response to the onset of the illness. Psychological and social interventions are an integral part of treatment, for without adequate coping strategies and environmental supports, patients are easily lost from follow-up care" (Barbuto, 1983).

The general counseling issues for people with AIDS are related to those dealing with death and dying but with the added burden of having a disease that has "branded" one as homosexual. Some guidelines offered at a National Association of Social Workers International Conference on AIDS (Wein & Lopez, 1985) included encouraging people to be vocal and expressive about the disease, as significant others in patients' lives often shrink away from such topics, and, as long as it does not interfere with medical care, permitting denial. Denial often reduces stress and keeps people intact, coping, and maintaining a positive quality of life. Encouraging participation in peer support groups is highly recommended, as this allows AIDS patients to see examples of effective coping philosophies in other group participants.

Clearly, this is a complex and difficult issue and is an area that needs (and is receiving) much further study.

CONCLUSION

There are therapeutic issues that have not been addressed in this chapter. Sexuality, for example, may be better dealt with in the context of sexual counseling: the symptoms may be different, but the task of assisting gay men and lesbians to achieve their full sexual potential would be similar to the task in working with heterosexual couples in which ignorance, guilt, anxiety, underlying anger, or medical problems tend to play important roles to a variable extent for different individuals.

The issue of dealing with AIDS has been only very briefly addressed. The difficulty of dealing with such an illness is greatly exacerbated by a self- and societally inflicted viewpoint that one's sexuality is perverse and that the illness is a punishment for one's socially rejected behavior. This fear complicates the primary concerns in a therapeutic setting—involving the person in a regimen of medical care and dealing with the multitude of social and emotional losses that are part of the grieving process.

In general, effective human services treatment of the issues related to the choice of a gay/lesbian lifestyle requires the same skills as the treatment of other people. Dulaney and Kelly (1982) suggest a number of principles to focus on, including that of accepting the person as a total human being, accepting his or her sexual orientation, and accepting that the therapist does not have all the answers. Being clear that you, the therapist, do not have a hidden agenda—that of changing the person's sexual orientation—and that sexual preference is only one part of a person's functioning can help a person become engaged in the therapeutic process.

Achieving self-acceptance is a primary task of clinical treatment in the majority of people who come to our attention. The subgroup of people who have chosen a homosexual lifestyle is no exception. Recognizing that the environment we live in makes the process of self-acceptance difficult, our goal is to enable people to be content with themselves, their functioning, and the choices they have made.

It becomes important for therapists to examine their own attitudes and thoughts about health and pathology, in order to assess accurately whether treatment issues are related to people's sexual choices, and ultimately to assist people to become the most they can be, within themselves and in relation to the larger environment.

7

Widows and Their Families

HELENA Z. LOPATA

This chapter examines our knowledge of the problems faced by widows and their families. The effect of a man's death on his immediate family depends on a variety of factors, including very importantly the society and culture in which the unit is embedded. The consequences of the death of a spouse and father are very different if the nuclear family is part of a larger extended kin unit that works and lives together than if the family lives alone with only one adult male and one female dividing the economic, service, social, and emotional supports. Patriarchal and patrilineal family systems, especially when accompanied by patrilocal residence, bring the wife into an already existing unit that is traditionally responsible for her and the children should the husband die. That is part of the rights she acquires in marriage, accompanying the rights of the husband, as studied by Bohannan (1963).

The husband's rights include the right to share a domicile, to sexual access, and to filliation of the children to the male line; also included are various economic rights to objects the wife brings with her, they create together, or she produces through her own efforts. In societies in which these rights are strictly enforced, the wife gains shared work in the domicile and right to have children and to have them and her cared for following the death of the husband/father.

What becomes immediately apparent from this brief anthropological description of marital rights is that American society is very different in the relationship of the husband and wife to each other and to his family line. All the features of social development, such as industrialization; urbanization; mass education; mobility, including immigration; and the changing roles of men and women have increased the importance of the marriage partners to each other and of each parent to the children. No longer do whole kin or village networks raise the children or supply social and emotional supports to all. In addition, much work has been transformed into jobs, with bureaucratically defined criteria for entrance, duties and rights, and established social circles. Thus, work organized into jobs has been built into social roles as sets of patterned relations between a social person and a social circle and involving duties and rights (see Znaniecki, 1965; also Lopata 1971b; Lopata, Miller, & Barnewolt,

1984; Lopata, Barnewolt, & Miller, 1985). The world in which people live and work also became divided in the last century or so and has only recently melded. The divisions are the public sphere, assigned to men, and the private sphere, assigned to women (Welter, 1966; Lopata & Brehm, 1986; and numerous others).

These two major changes, the breaking away of the nuclear unit from the power but also from the supports of the extended family and the division of the world into public and private spheres, have made partners in the marital unit highly interdependent. Until very recently the woman, though educated and usually employed in the public sphere in youth, left it upon marriage or with entrance into motherhood, becoming economically dependent on the husband. He remained in the public sphere when not at home, which means for many hours a day. The husband, in turn, became highly dependent on the wife to maintain the household, raise their children, and provide the back-up to a two-person career of which he was the public member (Papanek, 1973, 1979; Lopata, 1988a).

Because of social and geographical mobility, few husbands or wives have an automatically engrossing network that can supply not only social but, even more importantly, emotional supports, so they must turn to each other for these. This is one of the reasons why there is such a high divorce, separation, and desertion rate in this society. The demands placed on marriage are tremendous. People who fail to separate voluntarily are assumed to define their marriage as at least adequate. Thus, they are expected to feel deeply the death of the spouse. Of course, the burden placed on parenthood is also enormous in the absence of other people caring about and responsible for the children.

The importance of each member of the nuclear unit to all the other members becomes apparent when one of them dies. This is true of the death of children as well as of the spouse and parent.

DYING, DEATH, AND MOURNING

The problems of widows and their families begin even before the death of the spouse in the case of any but sudden death. Unanticipated sudden death, of course, has its own negative consequences. There is no opportunity to complete "unfinished business" in that the victim and the family cannot settle accounts, prepare for the death, and "say goodbyes" (Glick, Weiss, & Parkes, 1974). Survivors are unable to go through "anticipatory grief," although there is some debate among the researchers as to its beneficial effect in decreasing grief after the death (Clayton 1973, 1974; Neugarten, 1973). Illness, too, can be very disruptive to the family, whether short or prolonged, known to be fatal or not, experienced at home or in a hospital.

Each of these situations results in a different set of problems, and there is little agreement about the degree of grief and personal disorganization faced by family survivors according to the length of the illness. Clayton and associates (Clayton et al., 1971) claim that the differences disappear after the first year of bereavement. There is some agreement, however, on two very important factors in how the dying process affects all involved: the degree of open awareness as to the fatal nature of the illness, and where the dying takes place (Charmaz, 1980; Glick, Weiss, & Parkes, 1974). Prolonged dying at home can require a great deal of personal care by the wife and sometimes other family members, which contributes to social isolation, both physical and psychological; exhaustion; and numerous occasions for irritation and anger followed by guilt. Dying patients are not easy to live with or even to visit.

In addition, other problems do not go away. Children demand attention or act out their anxiety and other feelings that they do not themselves understand. The mother may be so involved in her own feelings and providing care that she cannot respond adequately. Nonetheless, other aspects of living must be carried forth. Often there are other relatives who are also experiencing problems in connection with the dying process of the patient, and they must be responded to.

As time goes on everyone, sometimes even the patient, may have gone through all the stages of dying and dealing with the death to the extent of having completed anticipatory grief. The result is the social death of the patient, who becomes increasingly ignored or withdrawn (Charmaz, 1980). Another problem connected with fatal illness is the frequently uncertain time of death. The patient appears to be dying, the family is alerted, and then the crisis passes. This process is often quite expensive, as adult children and others may have to come great distances to be at the bedside at the time of the expected death. The burden on the spouse can be heavy if these people must be taken care of, housed, fed, and "entertained."

Death of the spouse/parent in the hospital, which is becoming much more common than dying at home, has its own problems, although the physical care is turned over to the staff. One of the major difficulties is the modern American attitude toward death, especially as reflected in the education of medical personnel. Trained to heal rather than to simply care for a dying person, physicians tend either to withdraw when they feel they cannot cure or fail to admit that the patient is dying. Glaser and Strauss (1965) analyzed these various contexts in their book *Awareness of Dying*, pointing out that hospital staffs often do not want the patient or the family to be aware that the patient is going to die. One reason is that the staff fears the patient may become unduly disturbed upon being deprived of hope of recovery and that this might hasten the death or create problems for the nurses and physicians. Hospital staffs do not want their system to become disrupted, other families and patients to be disturbed, rules broken, or demands for special attention constantly made.

Kubler-Ross (1969) concludes from the study of many patients that they are aware they are dying anyway, so that the failure to share this awareness makes for serious artificiality of interaction and a failure of communication. The "unfinished business" on the part of the patient in going through the stages of dying (if there really are such stages) openly and with cooperation from others is not made possible.

The denial of impending death can be very difficult for the spouse who is left in limbo, not knowing what is happening, never receiving an adequate answer, not able to prepare for the death, or having to pretend in all interactions with the patient. In addition, the family faces a loss of power in the situation and feels helpless to do anything directly for the patient. All in all, this is an enormously traumatic time for everyone involved.

The death itself may come as an anticlimax after all the caring and waiting. However, it must be followed by decision making and new forms of behavior. Most people hear of the death by telephone and are often not told very empathetically. If the death was sudden and away from home, a coroner's deputy may come to the home with this information (Charmaz, 1980). Hospital staffs usually turn to the family member they judge best able to take the news and make the necessary arrangements. This is rarely the spouse, who is assumed to be much too emotionally upset, even in shock, to make the necessary decisions about disposal of the body, funeral arrangements, and notification of all those for whom the death is important, including the newspapers.

The next stage experienced by the widow surrounds the funeral, which according to Gorer (1967) has been deprived of many of its beneficial rituals. The whole subject of funerals has been negatively described in the literature, especially after Mitford's (1963) exposé of funeral directors as mercenary and capitalizing on the grief of survivors. The directors themselves defend their part in the funeral, insisting that they perform an important function in making the reality of the death apparent. They point to the open casket, the wake, and internment in the cemetery as beneficial to the survivors (Raether, 1971).

Many social psychologists find the Jewish rituals of sitting "shiva" helpful to those in mourning. According to this custom, relatives and friends of the main survivors visit them in their home and allow them to relive the past life with the deceased and the circumstances of death. But even the grieving involved in this process is often not fully allowed in modern America because of our dislike of showing emotions such as crying and because of reluctance to discuss death.

After the funeral rituals are over, other people return to their own homes and lives, leaving the surviving family to its own devices to work out its grief. This period is difficult for the widow and her children. Unfortunately, little is done to help them because society generally does not provide outreach programs to help educate the survivors about resources, solutions to problems, and emotional supports. We will come back to this subject later.

One immediate problem is the solution of day-by-day and special problems such as finances. Situations that were ignored during the period of illness and immediately after the death rise up, often with unpleasant consequences. The house and yard have been neglected and neighbors indicate dissatisfaction; bills must be paid, even if the remaining spouse did not manage the finances before. Children are still upset, regardless of age. It is currently believed that children as young as 3 years are affected by all these events, as well as by the traumatic absence of the parent. My studies of widows in the Chicago area indicate that mothers are unable to deal with the grief of their children (Lopata, 1973, 1979) and obtain little help from others, including the schools, church groups, or other societal resources (Lopata, 1978a).

GRIEF

One of the first psychologists to undertake an intensive examination of grief was Eric Lindemann (1944). Basing his analysis on

Freud's "Mourning and Melancholia," he defined the process of "grief work" as requiring the following:

> A widow is faced with two concurrent tasks; she is required, through the processes of mourning, to detach herself sufficiently from the lost object to permit the continuation of other relationships and the development of new ones; at the same time, she has to establish for herself a new role conception as an adult woman without a partner. (Lindemann, 1944, pp. 144)

The process of detachment from the love object is accompanied, at least among the Chicago widows, by what I (Lopata, 1981) have called "husband sanctification." We were not able to get our respondents to recall the time before the husband's fatal illness or accident without running constantly into an image of him as the supplier of all supports, even when in other places in the interview he appeared less supportive. The scale that I finally developed to determine the extent of sanctification and the factors influencing it had as its bottom line the statement: "My husband had no irritating habits." Analysis of the items of the scale and of the characteristics of women who were extreme at either ends in their score is published elsewhere (Lopata, 1981).

The sanctification process performs several important functions. In the first place, it makes the widow feel better. After all, if such a saintly man married her, she must not be as worthless as her depressive days indicate. In addition, the process "cleans" the late husband of all mortal jealousies and removes his presence from hovering over her. He becomes a benign spirit. Finally, it helps her to dissociate herself from him as a love object without the guilt of cutting herself off from him.

There is a growing literature on grief, some of which has disfunctional effects on many grieving persons in that a timetable has been disseminated in the mass media and appears to be known by many. Caine (1974) worried that she was not moving from stage to stage at a "normal" rate and even questioned her sanity. People in the social circle may also push the widow toward the "next stage" and watch her for abnormal sequences of symptoms. Grieving is a painful process, and there appears to be no way of avoiding it if a person is attached to the deceased.

LONELINESS

Most people who are widowed and remain in that marital status are of an age in which the household consisted of only themselves and their spouse. Children are already grown and have formed their own households, and in modern urban America servants and other family members or friends seldom share a residence with the nuclear family. Most widows who are able financially and physically to remain in their own homes do so. The historical and even current custom of the oldest, or any, son remaining in the ancestral home as the parents age and become widowed is no longer in existence (Lopata, 1986). Widowed parents do not wish to give up the household over which they have control in order to move into the home of a married offspring (Chevan & Korson, 1975).

I (Lopata 1971, 1973) found that widows have several reasons for not moving in with their children. One is the matter of control. They like having the right to decide what goes where, what to eat and when to eat it, and what activities to schedule. They like feeling that they are in control. Another is the felt undesirability of being a peripheral member of someone else's household. A third is the fear of conflict or even disagreements. Visits quickly show the possibility of a clash of lifestyles or childrearing ideas. Also present is the unwillingness to undertake the work of helping maintain a home and a family, which could fall on the widow if the woman of the household holds or is planning to hold a job.

Social Security and other sources of income have given widows relative independence, and they like the freedom that accompanies it, even if they have to live in a more restricted life space than was true in the past or that could be available in the home of an offspring. Finally, many older widows are accustomed to a very different lifestyle and support network than would be available to them in the home and neighborhood of the next generation.

One problem with this form of independence can be loneliness, defined broadly as a wish for a level and form of social relations that is currently absent (Lopata, 1969). Loneliness is a sentiment of relative deprivation. The lonely person compares the present to the past or to an imagined life of other people. Loneliness can also be experienced as anxiety about the future, when desired relationships will no longer be available.

Weiss (1973) writes of both emotional and social loneliness. Some of its forms cannot be resolved by living with or even just being with other people. The subject of loneliness has received increased attention in recent years, to the extent that Gordon (1976) concludes in her book *Lonely in America* that such a feeling is devastating, with its undertones of hopelessness and worthlessness, and also quite prevalent in our society. Two anthologies have been devoted to this subject (Peplau & Perlman, 1982; Hartog, Audry, & Cohen, 1980). and Weiss (1973) integrated and analyzed results of prior work. Our studies of widows brought out the complexity of the forms of loneliness (Lopata, 1969; see also Lopata, 1980). A widow can experience loneliness for any or all of the following: the very person of her husband; being a love object; having an immediately available love object; a sexual companion; someone who thought her important enough to even argue with; an escort to social events and public places; a companion in activities (even watching television); and the half of a couple in couple-companionate relations, someone around whom work and life scheduling is organized and simply another presence in the home.

In addition, the widow can miss the whole lifestyle that the presence and activities of the husband made possible. Most of the women in our sample were widowed while the husband was still working, so loss of income and loss of status from being attached vicariously to an employing organization were often experienced simultaneously. Widows often feel like a "fifth wheel" or "second-rate citizen" because our society is very couple-oriented after the youth years. In addition, women obtain much of their status vicariously, from fathers and then from husbands. Sons are less often now a source of status for the mother unless they are famous, since the mother does not share their lives (Lipman-Blumen & Leavitt, 1976).

Many traditional widows do not like to go to public places of entertainment, even to eat, without a male escort—and definitely not alone. Associated with the feelings of loneliness and dissociation from past life is the tension felt in relationships with married friends. Middle-and upper-class urban women in America are accustomed to couple-companionate relations of a social nature. Most report that they are no longer included in such events (Caine, 1974; Lopata, 1973, 1979). Friends explain that it is awkward to have new widows during "fun times" because of the fear that they will break down or talk of the deceased.

The asymmetry of social interactions is also bothersome. The widows themselves often report that their married women friends are protectively jealous of their husbands and therefore avoid the unmarried women except during all-female events. Widows often move, not being able to afford the marital home, and give up the car, which is foreign to them since it is traditionally seen as male-controlled object. This makes getting around difficult.

Then there is the matter of payment for social events. Men have traditionally been expected to pay for restaurants, movies, taxis, and related expenses since they earn the money or generally earn more than women. This means that a friend's husband may be seen as responsible for paying the widow's costs, which is often resented. All in all, almost all studies of widows report tension in their relations with married friends, a readjustment of interaction to hours when the friends' husbands are not present, or complete severance of contact. Many of the Chicago widows still count the married friends whom they saw when the husband was alive as close friends, but they do not see them very often (Lopata, 1979).

One solution to some forms of loneliness is male companionship, which provides an escort to public places and the opportunity to rejoin couple-companionate events. However, the demographic distribution of widows and widowers makes women much more available to men than the other way around. In the United States in the early 1980s there were over 10 million widows and only 1.8 million widowers, and the older the woman, the less the probability of her finding a close male companion. Also, men in this society are typically able to attract younger women which is not true of most women. According to Hunt (1966), divorced men do not like to date widows because they cannot compete against the sanctified image of the deceased husband.

Of course, the experience of loneliness may be different for widows who are left with children still in the home, and the age of these children can influence feelings of loneliness. Women who have small children and are not employed outside the home often find themselves restricted, with no other adult to relieve them or to share their problems and be a companion.

FACTORS INFLUENCING GRIEF AND LONELINESS

Many factors contribute to the depth of grief and the sentiment of loneliness. The major one is the closeness to and emotional dependence on the deceased. Since modern marriages involve such intensive interdependence, especially among the middle classes, the widow can be expected to experience intense grief. Of course, not all marriages involve both partners to such an extent or symmetrically. My first study of widows (Lopata, 1973) found that the higher the education level of the woman and the more middle-class a lifestyle she and her husband developed during his life, the more disorganized her self-concept and life became and the more she expressed grief. One of the reasons may be the greater verbalization by such women, who are accustomed also to reconstructing their reality with each major life event. Working-class wives tend to be more involved in the role of mother than that of wife and tend to live in quite sex-segregated worlds.

Husbands and wives with major commitments outside the marriage appear not to have been as dependent on the spouse as those who focused on home roles, and they are more able to work through their grief with the help of those distractions. In addition, the presence of other sources of social and emotional support is an important factor in easing the grieving process. However, we must keep in mind the need to go through grief work rather than suppress it. Lindemann (1944) and all others who have worked with grieving persons stress the importance of survivors' being able to really grieve. (See also Charmaz, 1980; Glick, Weiss, & Parkes, 1974; Kubler-Ross, 1969; Lynch, 1977.) Very frequently what happens is that one person becomes singled out as the main griever, and the grief of other members of the family and of nonrelatives is ignored. Before starting my studies of widows I ran a story about the research in the campus paper, asking students to come and talk about their widowed mothers (Lopata, 1979). What I heard, however, was the pain felt by the students. For example, the young men complained that they lost not only their fathers but also the rest of the family, since the grieving mother turned to the daughter, leaving the son out. The young men also felt they should not express grief but should help carry out the father's role in the family.

Grief and loneliness are also affected by the degree of disorganization in the whole life pattern experienced by the survivors. Family conflict can occur over the inheritance and division of personal property, for example. A very disturbing event can be the need to sell the home and move into less expensive quarters (Lopata, 1979). As in the case of divorce in no-fault states (Weitzman, 1985), the breakup of a marriage can have serious economic consequences. The need to move, often to a less desirable neighborhood, reduces social status, but any move cuts off social relationships. Children who must change schools lose friends. Attempts are made to continue contact, but such efforts are difficult, and the movers gradually fade from the consciousness of their former neighbors. As stated before, married friends often remove the widow from their circle of couple companions, hurting egos and decreasing life space. This is most likely to happen when the survivor is still grieving and thus rather immobilized from being able to form new relationships. It takes time before the enormity of the change in the self and in the life patterns of survivors is fully understood.

An important factor in this set of experiences is the degree to which the identity of the survivors was dependent on the deceased. According to Berger and Kellner (1970), upon marriage middle-class American couples go through a process of reconstructing their world. This involves redefining the self vis-à-vis the partner and all significant others. It is my hypothesis that the American wife undergoes more of a change in self-concept than does the husband, because the whole socialization process pushes the man toward identification with an occupation and the woman toward commitment to family roles.

This may be changing now, but most of the widows who have been studied are of generations when the "feminine mystique" was very strong (Friedan, 1963). With the help of a wedding ring and a name change from Mary Smith to Mrs. John Brown, the woman must redefine her view of herself and her relationships with others. Her life change becomes even more dramatic if she withdraws from a job and becomes a full-time homemaker, especially if this move results in her becoming the back-up person in a two-person career in which the husband is the main partner and her association with others is vicarious through him.

Widowhood can result, then, in the need for the woman to change her self-concept. This change becomes, according to my research, a major component of the grief work process (Lopata, 1984). American society does not provide a role of "widow" with distinctive functions and a social circle. She cannot return to being a never-married woman, so the marital role must recede into the background of the role hierarchy, and other identities must move forward. Luckily, from one point of view, this society is highly individualistic, and it is possible for someone to identify herself only by a personal name rather than a status. New relationships provide opportunities for new self-images. The question, still unanswered because no one has tried to answer it, is whether men go through as strong a reconstruction of the self in marriage and in widowhood as do many middle-class, American widows. The ease with which a surviving spouse can restructure the self and the reality of the world around affects the complexity of the grief work.

There are many factors that influence how these processes are experienced by widows. Age is an important one because each stage of the life course has its own stage of marriage and life patterns. Death at a young age is not expected, so the survivors may feel doubly cheated and that they have been treated unfairly compared to others. Unfinished business may still hang over the marriage. Young widows report feeling highly stigmatized in relation to their married friends and, in fact, in relations with everyone (Lopata, 1971). They are much more deviant than are older widows, who are more the norm.

Allegedly race makes a difference in marital relations, and thus in widowhood, but, unfortunately, not enough is known about the experiences of nonwhites. Hyman (1983) had to remove both black widows and black widowers from the combined samples from which he did secondary analysis. Black men die younger than white men, so that the average age of the black widows is younger. These widows are also more disadvantaged economically, since the husbands often did not hold jobs covered by Social Security or pension programs, and the wives worked in low-paying jobs.

In addition, I found that black widows did not have any advantage over white ones in terms of sharing households at any one time (Lopata, 1973). At the time of the interviews, black widows in Chicago were just as likely as were the whites to be living alone, although they and other people had moved in and out of each other's homes in the past more frequently than was true for the whites. Black widows are often lonely because of high mobility and crime in their neighborhoods. Health and financial problems restrict their movement and social life space. Many are, however, much more active in church affairs, and this role has greater salience for them than for many white widows (Lopata, 1979).

All in all, the most important factors influencing the grieving process and loneliness were the length of time since the death, closeness of the relationship, amount of disorganization of self and life patterns, health and financial situation, social support networks, and social class. The social class factor combines many elements of self and life patterns. As alluded to before, the higher the education of the woman (and among all but the young, only about 12% of women have a college education) and the more middle-class a lifestyle the couple developed, the more disorganized the woman's life becomes with her husband's death because of the higher interdependence between them. However, the more education she has, the more personal resources she can command to reorganize the self and life patterns once the period of heavy grief is over. I will deal in greater detail with this point in the next section.

LIFE PATTERNS IN WIDOWHOOD

There are many directions a woman's life can take after she becomes a widow, as American urban society has created innumerable resources for social engagement available through the life course. However, these resources must be used voluntaristically. A widow must decide what she wants to do for the rest of her life, analyze the resources available, and obtain the necessary tools for taking advantage of them. In order to do so she must be able to plan ahead, learn what needs to be known, and feel competent and independent. She must restructure a full support network and life space. She must also take the initiative, since few of the helping or involving groups or people have adequate outreach programs. We found that the Chicago-area widows with more education and middle-class lifestyles, the very same women who were so disorganized by the death of their husbands, were the ones who were best able to re-engage in social roles and relations once the period of heavy grief was over, barring any complications. They were accustomed to solving problems and had the self-confidence to try new roles or to modify old ones. One can assume that as Americans gain more education and competence at modern urban living, the proportion of such self-sufficient widows will increase dramatically. This is especially true of women who are decreasingly limiting themselves to family roles and thus increasingly competent to build new support networks in adulthood.

At the other extreme are widows who are isolated and/or very unhappy. The Chicago samples included such women, some of whom had always been peripheral to social networks, others of whom are the "disengaged" as studied by Cumming and Henry (1961). They do not have the resources to replace social roles and social relations that disappeared or were broken by retirement, mobility, death, or disagreement. Thus, their social life space withers until the final break with society through their own death. In between these two extremes are widows involved in a variety of social networks of a great range of complexity. Some are very active in neighborhoods, social organizations, or volunteer or paid work. They develop a variety of schedules to handle problems of time or energy. (See Rubenstein, 1986, and Burgess [the next chapter in this volume] for comparable information on how widowers organize their lives.)

Many widows are deeply involved in their family roles at all age levels but especially in old age (Shanas, 1979, 1980). Some are highly dependent on one person, usually a daughter, for most supports (Lopata, 1979; see also the various chapters in Shanas and Sussman, 1977). We have yet to establish why one of the children, usually one of the daughters, is selected or selects herself to live a convenient time/distance from the mother and provide the majority of supports, but an asymmetric relation with children definitely occurs.

There are widows who are relieved by the death of their husbands, not only because they may have required long-term and draining care but also because of their characteristics. Our Chicago samples contain many a woman who could not sanctify her husband, remembering full well his irritating habits or even worse behavior (Lopata, 1979, 1981). They and their children, if they were involved, can now live in peace, no longer frightened. They often have a steady income from Social Security, while in the past they never knew what money the husband/father would bring home.

The families of widows can go through a variety of problems and create a variety of lifestyles. Children grow up lacking a father, and the uniqueness of their situation can often result in deviant behavior or strain within the family unit. Sons may not know how to relate to the mother, or she to them. "Being a father and mother to the children" was defined by the Chicago widows as a major problem. In addition, "normal" strains and difficulties are often taken by the mother very personally. Finally, however, the offspring move away, leaving the widow to live alone. This process changes relations between the mother and the adult child, especially as in-laws and grandchildren are added.

Of course, studies of widows do not cover everyone who has been in that marital situation (Hyman, 1983). Two categories are missed: those women who have died and those who have remarried. Lynch (1977), Clayton (1974), Parkes (1964, 1976), and others have documented the actuality of the "broken heart" (Lynch, 1977; Parkes, 1976) and the disproportionally high mortality rate among the widowed. The men are especially prone to illnesses, alcoholism, accidents, and other behavior resulting in death.

The other category of widowed people that is often neglected in social research is that of the remarried. We purposely included women who had lost Social Security because of remarriage in our sample described in *Women as Widows: Support Systems* (Lopata, 1979). We found them feeling the benefits of companionship and security as well as of having a father for their children, if young. On the other hand, they experienced a loss of independence. Those women who did not remarry although they had the opportunity to because they dated or had close relationships with men explained their failure to reenter marriage as an unwillingness to give up this independence, fear of having to care for another ill husband, objections by children, and concern over depriving children of the father's inheritance. Many women claimed not to be at all interested in remarriage, mainly because "there are no good men" equivalent to the sanctified husband. However, most older widows are well aware of the statistics and the lack of opportunity to meet an eligible unmarried male, so that the explanations may be simply "sour grapes." Widowers are much more likely to remarry, and to do so relatively soon after the death of the wife.

HELPING WITH PROBLEMS RELATING TO WIDOWHOOD

Families faced with the terminal illness of the husband/father usually need all kinds of supports to help them through the process of his dying and death. Instrumental help includes transportation to and from the hospital, baby-sitting, shopping, and even cooking. Those families that care for the ill in the home need "release time," help with nursing, and homemaking aid as well as all the previously mentioned services. The hospice movement has been of great help to many families, although there are too few organizations as of now, and the continued denial of death and unwillingness to seek help has limited the number of families that use this resource (Charmaz, 1980). The emotional supports needed are similar to those needed by any family going through a traumatic crisis: companionship and the opportunity to talk about feelings, fears, angers, guilt, and hope. Very frequently none of these supports is readily available from the community.

Absent also from the support systems of newly widowed families are community groups and the "helping professions" (Lopata, 1978). This fact was apparent in the study of the Chicago-area widows. Although church groups were helpful during and immediately after the funeral, the group members, religious personnel, club members, and others in the community soon returned to their own lives and functions so that the widow felt let down and neglected. And there are many areas of need facing these women during bereavement and as they try to build a new life:

1. *Financial advice and training.* Many widows had not handled the family's finances when their husbands were alive and are bewildered by this area of life, although their problems vary from management of property to finding sources of income (Bowling & Cartwright, 1982; Lopata, 1978; Silverman, 1986). Financial advice may be needed very soon after the spouse's death, but training in these matters is also important so that the widow does not become dependent on another person in these matters.
2. *Job training and job search.* In the American past many women withdrew from the labor force, if they had been in it in the first place, during the years of marriage and now do not know how to go about preparing for and getting a job (Steinhart, 1977). Most assume that job training programs are very expensive or feel that they must take the first job that comes along rather than spending time in training. One of our recommendations to the Social Security Administration is that widows who are not eligible for benefits because of their own or their children's age be economically supported for job training (see Lopata and Brehm, 1986). Their job search methods are inefficient, so intervention is needed here, too.
3. *Housing.* Widows may have two types of problems with housing. One is that of maintaining the home they shared with their late husbands. Sometimes the financial part of remaining in the home can be solved with house-sharing, roomers, or boarders, but women are often leery of having someone else living with them. Housemate matching services would be of help here. The second problem is that of selling the home and finding another dwelling. This is often an overwhelming process, especially if the woman does not know the housing market or neighborhoods. Silverman (1986) reports that widows often end up in lower socioeconomic neighborhoods than they had been accustomed to, so that they fear crime, reject friendships with neighbors, and become quite secluded. They can become increasingly lonely and withdrawn, and are often unaware of the resources of the new area.
4. *Other problems.* The widowed family may be facing other problems, such as behavior difficulties of children, conflict within the family unit, health difficulties of the widow or others, and so forth.
5. *Social supports.* All the constraints discussed above can lead to the need for regular and personal social supports. Not knowing new neighbors, lacking the self-confidence to join a religious organization or voluntary association, being geographically distant from relatives and former friends all can leave the widow needing new relationships. Outreach programs, discussed below, are necessary.
6. *Emotional supports.* Widows need to continue grieving even as they are forging a new life; they also need a variety of social contacts, confidantes, and companions who are interested in them and help

provide a positive self-image. Casual social contacts cannot meet these needs.

Following my two studies of widows in metropolitan Chicago (Lopata, 1978a, 1978b, 1979) I recommended the creation of "neighborhood networks" consisting of representatives of existing voluntary associations, especially religious ones.[1] The network can learn of crisis situations among local families, provide immediate support, and refer people to resources. Members can keep in contact with the families as long as needed and serve as a link between the families and whatever sources of support are available or even create their own. Neighborhood networks would provide such services to people in all kinds of crisis situations, not just to widows and their families. An organization devoted specifically to widows has been recommended and a model created by Phyllis Silverman (1986). Based on research at the Harvard Medical School that found that grief work involved a transition to a new life and that this transition can best be made with the help of other widows, Silverman organized a Widow-to-Widow program. In talking with the widowed she found, as we did, that professional mental health workers, funeral directors, clergy, and other caregivers simply could not meet their major needs. The program used as helpers women who had been widowed and had worked through most of the problems facing new widows. An outreach program was established in which all new widows in selected areas of metropolitan Boston were contacted and offered assistance by a Widowed Service Line that people could call to talk out their immediate concerns. The helpers were knowledgeable about solutions of immediate, practical problems and served as both companions and providers of emotional support. Sometimes this merely involved empathetic listening, which people who have not gone through the widowhood experience are allegedly unable to do.

NOTE

1. The first study of widows, focusing on role modification and published as *Widowhood in an American City,* was funded by the Administration on Aging. The second, focusing on support systems and published as *Women as Widows: Support Systems,* was funded by the Social Security Administration.

8

Widowers

JANE K. BURGESS

This chapter will be written in two parts. The first section examines our knowledge of the problems faced by widowers and their families. The second section examines the issue of helping with problems related to widowhood. Much of the material is drawn from the author's own clinical studies of a small group of widowers. No large formal investigation of this topic appears in the literature.

THE EXPERIENCE OF WIDOWHOOD

Studies on widows abound, but few focus on the problems and needs of widowers (Burgess, J. J., 1985). The few studies that have considered the problems of men related to widowhood indicate that while the bereavement of losing a spouse is traumatic for women, it is more so for men. Hyman's nationwise study (1983) of the enduring effects of widowhood clearly illustrates the relatively good adjustment widows make as time passes in contrast to the relatively poor adjustment widowers make over time. Hyman, using a secondary analysis of national sample surveys, presents evidence based on a comparison of 2,000 married women with 650 widows and a comparison of 585 married men with 90 widowers. Berardo (1973) obtained empirical evidence that agrees with Hyman's nationwide findings and supports his speculations.

Widowhood awaits millions of men and women, usually when they are older, but death in any family relationship can cause severe problems. While there are about 250,000 new widowers each year and a total of approximately 2 million widowers each year in our society at any given time, knowledge about them is scarce. To find answers to such questions as how a man reacts when his wife dies, what his immediate reactions are to his loss, and what some long-term consequences are of the loss, I interviewed, with the use of tapes, 25 widowers using an in-depth structured instrument as a guide. The interviews were largely with middle-class and upper-middle-class whites. These findings were broadened through the use of responses to a pencil-paper questionnaire administered to 100 widowers using a sample of convenience. The total range in occupational status in my sample is from professional men to skilled laborers, but the majority of respondents were middle-class white men. The average age of the men was 56, and they ranged in age from 45 to 77.

Reactions to the Death of a Wife

How the death occurs will influence the reactions and coping skills used to recover from the trauma of losing a spouse (Burgess, J. J. 1985). Whether the death of a loved one comes suddenly and without warning, as it did for William, or after months of knowing the inevitable, as David experienced, one is unprepared to face the many resulting emotions. David was 77 when his wife died of cancer after an illness of 6 months. "We knew she had an inoperable tumor, and I felt so helpless being a physician and not being able to do anything for my wife," he said tearfully, as we discussed his wife's death. "I felt so alone and sad. I thought, given the news that my wife was going to die, I would be prepared, but you are never prepared."

Whether a man is aware that his wife is going to die or death happens unexpectedly, he is likely to have feelings of shock, denial, helplessness, loneliness, self-pity, confusion, and numbness. But the men who told me about the sudden loss of their wives seemed to express a much more intense feeling of shock, some with intense feelings of anger and others with deep-seated guilt.

William, 51, whose wife Betty committed suicide, felt deep shock as well as intense guilt. "The impact of my wife's suicide was so great that I needed immediate psychiatric help," he said. "She hung herself in the garage, which was a terrible blow to me. At the moment I found her, I felt anger—terrible anger. Why?

"I thought, 'God dammit, you put me here in this psychiatrist's office.' I was emotionally drained. I felt nothing. Nothing. Things that were previously important to me were now unimportant. I had to reckon with my feelings of guilt before all this buried anger could come out."

The literature suggests, as does my research, that persons whose spouses die after a very short illness with little warning of death or who die as a result of suicide have the most difficulty in coping with their loss (Parkes, 1976).

Several authors have discussed grief responses, Simos. 1987, for example, has distinguished qualitative differences in the grief response by categorizing death as either high-grief death or low-grief death. The basic difference in the level of grief experienced relates to the period of time prior to death in which the bereaved were able to experience anticipatory grief. In the case of a high-grief death such as suicide, the bereaved would have no time to prepare socially or psychologically for the impending death. In the case of low-grief death such as attending a terminal illness, the bereaved would have opportunity to prepare psychologically as well as socially and begin to develop new social roles and responsibilities. Glick and colleagues (1974) disagree with these views, saying that anticipating a death does not diminish the grief experience. Probably there is no simple resolution of this question, but it appears that emotions are more intense when death is unexpected and sudden.

Among the several authors who have discussed the anticipatory grief process, the most well-known author is Kubler-Ross (1969). On the basis of her clinical experience she suggests that the bereaved who are "working through" the grief process prior to the actual death have a shorter duration of grief following the death.

Literature on the grief of persons who have lost a loved one suggests that there are many adverse effects on the grieving person (Simos, 1987; Bowlby, 1980). The metaphor of the broken heart appears to have a strong basis in reality. A British study of widowers over the age of 54 found an increase in their death rate in the 6 months following bereavement, with a high proportion of the deaths due to heart disease (Parkes, Benhamin, & Fitzgerald, 1969). As a result of depression or hopelessness bereaved persons often develop physical symptoms that are thought to have a direct effect on body chemistry, altering resistance to disease (Kalish, 1981). The literature as well as my research suggests that widowers often display nervousness, fear of "going crazy," insomnia, fatigue, indigestion, chest pains, and depression. In addition, I have noted feelings of dejection, self-recrimination, and worthlessness. It seems that the sense of loss involved more how these men felt about themselves in relation to their loss than feelings about their dead wives.

Death is apt to be a traumatic, stressful situation for anyone but particularly so for the widower because of his inability to get his deep feelings out in the open. Jack, for example, a 35-year-old physician, told me, "The way my friends and colleagues treated me, it was as though I was expected to bury Anne on Saturday, return to work in a week, and then in another week be out looking for a date. My practice is in a moderately large city where I am quite well known, particularly in the medical profession. Yet, no one mentioned Anne to me, and if it appeared as though I might want to bring up her death, the conversation was changed or my colleagues would excuse themselves and walk away. It was as if my wife had never existed. My friends couldn't handle talking about my wife either. I might cry, and they wouldn't like that. They couldn't face the reality that Anne was dead."

Social Isolation and Loneliness

Family, friends, and, yes, professionals seem to believe the myths perpetrated in the literature on widowhood about how well men handle their grief and other problems such as social isolation (Lopata, 1973). Society gives the widow the right to cry, but when a man hurts inside, he is expected to hide his real feelings, or he may not even recognize what his emotions are. My research indicates that men suffer more problems of loneliness and social isolation than do women during all periods of grief. Most men tend to lack social skills because it is usually the wife who makes social arrangements. Thus, when a widower desires some social life, he is often at a loss as to how to go about making social contact (Berardo, 1973).

Unlike women, men have few if any confidantes other than their wives with whom they can feel free to "bare their souls." And when a wife is gone, a man is usually alone in coping with his grief. Furthermore, it appears that the frequency of interaction with friends and family usually declines more rapidly for the widower than it does for the widow (Hyman, 1983).

Not only is this a paired society, but no clear-cut traditions or customs have been developed on how to behave toward the formerly married. A widower is perceived differently by different people. Married men may look at him as the debonair, man-about-town whose freedom they envy. Married women may see him as someone who is so lonely for female companionship that they attempt to arrange dates for him.

Others see widowers as men half-crazy for sex. Bert, a widower in his 70s, remembered the remarks passed his way: "What do you do to take care of yourself—or do you get so every woman looks good to you?" He went on to say, "And some women, too, get pretty aggressive. These women aren't ashamed to let you know they would like to spend time with you in your bedroom. Maybe some men pursue this stuff; I don't know. I didn't go for it. Sex without love isn't much."

What can a widower do to escape his aloneness, both emotionally and socially? The need for companionship appears to be the most urgent need of widowers. Some found new friends through work. Several younger widowers reported finding that the single women in their office seemed quite willing to offer them companionship. Others turned to matchmaking friends and relatives for dates.

The Presence of Children

Having children in their care may provide widowers with a sense of involvement that alleviates their concentration on their own grieving process. The literature suggests that men who have their children readily available to them or whose children are in a position to be supportive to them seem to cope better with their feelings of loneliness and despair than those without children.

In my study of widowers I found that during the early stages of bereavement, fathers had some difficulty dealing with the emotional problems of their children. However, most of them eventually learned to do this for a variety of reasons. First, in most instances the wives had died after a terminal illness, which had drawn the children closer to the surviving parent. Then, too, most of the widowers described their marriage and family life as having been generally happy, which suggests a closeness between both parents and their children prior to the death. In addition, the parents shared their feelings with their children about the impending loss. As a family they talked over what would happen in the future. They talked about life, about death, about love. They said their farewells. The children began their anticipatory grief process together with their father prior to their mother's death. They felt the assurance of their parents' love.

With few exceptions the widowers said they felt that their relationship with their children had improved and that they were closer to them than they had been when their wives were alive. However, this depended somewhat upon the age of the children. Men with very young children found that the relationships became more strained. A father of 3-year-old son said, "It is very difficult to explain to a small child what these changes are all about. Timmy is hostile to me and seems to think I am in some way responsible for his feeling abandoned by his mother."

Widowers with children between the ages of 8 through 13 said they found their relationship became much closer than it had been prior to being a single parent. The widowers expressed great satisfaction with how well their children and they themselves were becoming socialized into their new lifestyle as a single-parent family. They enjoyed taking over the tasks involved in looking after their children and were proud of their accomplishments. One widower offered this advice as the best way to make the transition from a two-parent family to a single-parent family: "You have to go on pretty much as though it was the way it was before—the children have to go to school, the house has to be kept up, you have your work—and it all seems insurmountable for a few months. That's normal. I told myself that I would give myself at least a year to just keep things running tolerably well. I am reaching the end of that year, and feel that I have done fairly well."

When a man finds that he can meet the practical as well as the emotional needs of his children, he is apt to feel far more confident in himself not only as a parent but as a person. However, because of the traditional view of women as being "naturally" competent in filling the parenting role, a custodial father is likely to question his ability. He is apt to have had little experience dealing with the emotional problems of his children. In addition, during their married lives men are likely to expect their families to adjust to the demands of their work. Career performance is considered to be one of the outstanding features of a male's sense of identity (Nye & Berardo, 1973). Given the general importance of work as a major source of well-being for men, learning to overcome feelings of inadequacy in the fathering role is very difficult for some men. However, given the opportunity many males can learn to be more involved in parenting and can find great satisfaction in it.

A Widower's Coping Skills

One of the widower's critical problems is the emotional stress of dealing with the immediate and later stages of grief. With family and friends around, arrangements to be made, and perhaps a sedative and a few extra highballs, a man might feel that he is handling the situation quite well. But then he suddenly realizes he is alone. There are so many things that he misses from the relationship he had with his wife. The memories of their love, the happy moments, the birth of their children, all the ups and downs, the decisions they shared together—and now everything is changed for this man whose wife has died.

"The first few months after my wife's death were almost unbearable—the loneliness, the emptiness" is a typical statement made by men who have lost a wife. "The reality of it all came when people stopped helping," Tom explained. "The first month our friends brought supper over every night. They offered to baby-sit. Then suddenly this all stopped and I had to carry the whole burden of grief myself. Lots of crazy things would go through my mind, like how was I ever going to get over the loneliness? I woke up in the morning and the other side of the bed was still perfectly smooth, and I would realize again she wasn't there, and the emptiness was very depressing."

Widowers may use a variety of ways to cope with their grief. Some adopt a rational approach. For example, Richard, whose wife died of a stroke, seemed to recover well, helped by his philosophy toward life. "Even after four years," he said, "I miss her every day, but I understand what happened, and the pain is not so poignant now. I feel if she had to go, this was the best way for her to die—suddenly, and without prolonged suffering. And I know she would not have been happy had she survived to be a helpless vegetable."

William reported that he managed to get control of his emotions so that he could cope with his grief. He said, "I would tell a person to believe that things will get better, but it takes time. No one can rid you of your grief. There is no timetable that will suit everyone."

It is clear that many factors influence the ability of the bereaved to cope with their losses. These influences pertain to the earlier life experiences of both husband and wife, including those in their family of origin, personality characteristics of each family member, the dyanmics of the entire multigenerational family system, religious beliefs, cultural patterns, age of each family member, occupational responsibilities, satisfactions and goals, and social and economic resources.

The Need for Companionship, Love, and Sex

It appears that most widowers begin dating to fill a void in their lives. Most say they miss the company of a woman. And eventually sex becomes an important issue for most of them. When the need for a sexual relationship is felt, many men develop conflicts in their minds about their sexuality. It is one thing to date, but the desire for intimacy, for sexual release, is something else, and it is here that severe guilt feelings may arise. How a man resolves his need for sex is related, among other things, to his perception of his previous relationship (Burgess, J. J., 1985). Men who endured an unhappy marriage prior to widowhood were less likely to experience guilt over their needs for a new love/sex relationship than men who perceived their marriage as having been satisfying.

Then too, many men, because of guilt mixed with feelings of loyalty, have trouble separating themselves emotionally from their deceased wives. Some widowers who believe there is no replacement for their "one-and-only love" hesitate to form new relationships, preferring to adjust as a "formerly married," now single, man.

HELPING WITH PROBLEMS RELATING TO WIDOWHOOD FOR THE WHITE MIDDLE-CLASS MALE

As discussed in the first section, the stresses that accompany dying and death are intense. This is true for the person who is dying, for family members and friends, and for people in the health-related professions. At one time or another most people need emotional support, and this is especially true for those who are dealing with the stresses of death. This discussion should provide further understanding of what may help a widower cope with his grief and other life problems.

Psychotherapy and Counseling with the Bereaved

According to many clinical specialists, there appear to be four stages in bereavement, each of which calls for different kinds of support (Kalish, 1981). In the first stage, prior to the death of a spouse, emotional stress is high and often unrelenting. At this point a relaxed dinner, a weekend away, or entertainment may be more valuable than any kind of therapy. The role of the psychotherapist in this stage of bereavement is to help people handle their feelings of guilt and the unresolved, distressing aspects of the relationship with the dying mate. Spouses in this situation need help sorting out their responsibility taking on those that only they can handle but turning over lesser ones to others. They need to recognize and accept their own limitations and begin to think about what life will be like after the death occurs.

During the second stage, at the time of the death, feelings are usually intense, and depression is apt to be constant. The role of the psychotherapist then is to provide the bereaved with an opportunity to reminisce and also to begin to think of the future.

For some bereaved persons the third stage, the weeks following the death, is often still filled with acute grief and intense mourning.

Some, however, display few signs of grief. According to some theories for those men who have played the role of "brave soldier," the task of the psychotherapist is to give them permission to cry or express their feelings in some way that provides relief.

For those who may continue on for years without completing the grief process, psychotherapy may be needed to help them through this fourth stage of bereavement. According to some therapists, the bereaved person needs to be encouraged to "let go" and then to accept that life is for the living.

Of the widowers I have worked with, the majority were able to work through the grief process with the help of family, physicians, friends, clergy, and self-help support groups. In the early stages of grief counseling may be needed. Contact for grief counseling services can be obtained through one's religious affiliation, local mental health association, or individual and family counseling services.

During the early stages some people need medical assistance such as tranquilizers to cope with their grief. Some need group activities to help with loneliness. Self-help groups are sponsored nationally and locally by various church and community groups. Relatives and friends can be very helpful if they give "permission" to the person to grieve and if they express empathy and provide support.

Each person is unique in the time required to cope with grief. In the early stages most widowed persons show an increase in physical and emotional problems. Their complaints include loneliness, sexual frustration, gaining or losing unusual amounts of weight, drinking problems, vague pains, nausea, sleeping problems, headaches, digestive problems, and difficulty in dealing with their emotions. They can be assured that these reactions are normal, not signs they are "going crazy," and that these reactions will become less intense over time.

Depression is almost inevitable for the person who has lost a spouse, but many widowers do not know this. They may need reassurance that depressive feelings and behavior are normal in their situation and that they should not try to hurry through their mourning. They can be assured that the intensity of their sorrow will diminish over a period of 2 or 3 years, but periodically—and temporarily—they will re-experience the sense of loss with great intensity, particularly around major holidays, birthdays, and other occasions that had special meaning for the couple. At these times especially, widowers may need permission from a counselor or therapist to be depressed. Without this they may feel ashamed of acting depressed and thus become even more depressed. Friends and family often are not tolerant of depressive behavior for long, and widowers usually feel socially constrained to hide their sadness and may feel embarrassed when found out.

When a widower is having trouble managing his depressive feelings, it sometimes helps to have him schedule a time and place each day when he will totally focus on his loss and his sorrow. Then usually for the remainder of the day he is able to focus on other things.

Eventually widowers find that they are able for periods of time to forget about the loss and enjoy themselves. They may then feel guilty about this and fear to enjoy. It may help to reassure them that it is normal to again relish life and that there is nothing disloyal in this.

If depression seems to persist overly long (e.g., symptoms such as insomnia, loss of appetitie, fatigue, and apathy evident a year or two after the death) it may help to tell the widower that he has made clear his love and loyalty to his wife and that he now needs to find other ways of cherishing her memory. Rituals that express loyalty can be encouraged, such as memorial announcements in the newspaper on the anniversary of death, flowers to the cemetery on special occasions, and so forth.

Careful inquiry should be made about time, place, and circumstance in which the widower does *not* feel or act depressed or is less depressed than usual. These data offer clues as to what can alleviate the depression and what needs to be encouraged by the counselor.

In particular during the first year after the death widowers should be encouraged to make a few changes as possible in their life situation and postpone major decisions if they can. This is even more crucial if there are dependent children. Having undergone a drastic change in their lives, the children are likely to be further stressed by additional changes. Of course, practical and pressing circumstances sometimes make additional changes unavoidable. The widower may benefit from the opportunity to talk over his pressures, needs, and options with a counselor in reaching decisions, since during the first year the widower's problem-solving abilities are usually "below par." Some help may be needed in thinking things through logically.

Widowers are often helped by a relationship with a therapist who provides opportunities for ventilation of feelings, encouragement to face the reality of the present and future, and "permission" to handle guilt, anger, and depression with the recognition that these are common, normal reactions.

Anger, a frequent reaction to loss, seems to be an especially difficult feeling to cope with. A man may be able to swear and hit his fist into the wall, but he usually is not able to get his feelings of anger out verbally. Many people have been taught they should not talk about their hostile feelings. This may be why anger sometimes contributes to deep feelings of guilt and anxiety. Thus, one approach to helping a grieving widower is to find ways for him to cope realistically with his anger. If the problem is not resolved, the anger generated can be turned inward, causing intense physical and mental pain, possibly leading to masochistic behavior or even suicide. "I get these pains in my throat and way down into my stomach whenever I think of that drunk driver who killed my wife," explained a 22-year-old widower. "I hurt. I resent the fact that he is still out driving his car and my wife is dead." Rudy had attempted suicide a few days before coming for help. He was feeling guilty because he had sent his wife on the errand she was on when the accident occurred and because he felt murderous thoughts toward the man responsible for her death. I, the counselor, explained to him that feelings, whether positive or negative, are neither right nor wrong. Anger and resentment or love and tenderness are emotions that surface when we are aware of what we are feeling. When Rudy was able to get in touch with his feelings and talk about them openly in an accepting atmosphere, he was able to let go of his desire for revenge and for self-destructive behavior.

Not all cases are readily helped through grief counseling. Some widowers have long-standing, complex problems that go beyond strategies of ventilation, reassurance, support, understanding, and acceptance. They may need referrals for more intensive psychotherapy or other forms of specialized help.

Family System Effects

According to Simos (1987) bereavement is a family matter. Since bereavement through the death of a family member evokes intense stress, it can break families apart. The strong emotions of grief, often not acceptable in our individualistic, achievement-oriented society, may be denied by some or all family members expressed in indirect, often disruptive ways such as blaming others, sexual acting out, retreating into illness, and fighting with other family members. Although it is often claimed that the death of a family member brings families together and reunites their bonds, clinicians working with the bereaved generally find that individuals who are seriously stressed with grief find it difficult to be truly empathetic with the mourning of others.

Children and adolescents who lose a parent may act out their grief rather than deal with it directly. Their resulting problematic behavior may be overwhelming to the parent who is unable to deal with their grief because of his or her own stress. Children may be put in the parenting position and in effect asked to nurture their parent rather than the other way around. This can lead to the pseudomaturity of children and delay their normal development (Bowlby, 1980).

Bereavement for adults is apt to be especially stressful if they had earlier losses that they were unable to handle directly and realistically. Thus, the new loss in effect resurrects old problems that were not resolved. The multiplicity of losses becomes almost normative, though still painful, for elderly members of the family who need to deal with the stresses of their own old age plus a series of bereavements.

Thus, therapy with a widower may well include assistance in understanding and dealing with the reactive problems of the members of his family. Clearly, the more he can be helped to handle his own grief, the more he will be able to respond appropriately to his mourning children and other relatives. Mobilization of community resources, such as support groups for various family members; help from friends and relatives with child care; and perhaps direct therapy with particularly distressed family members, are strategies that may be useful.

It is important to recognize the family system effects of the death of a family member, in this case a wife who is perhaps also a mother and grandmother. The effect may be especially adverse if the widower continues to grieve deeply over a long period of time and shows little evidence of recovery. If he becomes "stuck" in this way over the coming months and years, other family members, such as children, parents, and in-laws, may also become "stuck" in their own developmental processes of coping with loss and moving on. Thus, successful therapeutic efforts to help the bereaved widower are apt to be useful not only to him but to the entire family system to which he belongs.

Health

Although coping with grief and depression are the primary problems of the newly widowed man, it is important that he be reminded that emotional stress may manifest itself in physical malfunctions as well. Although he may resist, as men are especially apt to do, he should be encouraged to have a thorough physical exam.

The widower may need encouragement to exercise and follow a nutritious diet. Often, because of despair, loneliness, or plain lack of knowledge, widowers neglect their nutritional needs. The same comments apply to members of his family, especially if he still has children at home. Their health, too, may suffer from the situation and of course requires careful attention.

Dependency on alcohol to dull the pain associated with grief is also common among both men and women. A constant round of taverns, tranquilizers, junk food, sugar, and inactivity is obviously unhealthy. It is far better for the widower to learn about the benefits of good nutrition and exercise and to become involved with living a healthy, rewarding life. Whether he accepts this regimen or not and whether or not he can finance medical care are of course other matters.

Dating and Sexuality

It is important for a man to become involved in some kind of social life, because isolation may deepen his depression. However, prior to his getting out into the world again, he should be made aware that as his thoughts turn to dating or his desire for sexual intimacy returns, guilt feelings and anxiety may arise, as discussed in the first part of this chapter.

The counselor/therapist can often help a widower with these feelings should they occur. It is clearly normal for most widowers to want to form love/sex relationships with new mates. Reassurance and acceptance from the counselor should be useful here. Men who are interested in dating might well be encouraged to join an organization for singles or formerly married persons. Developing a new hobby such as attending dancing classes or skiing will bring persons into contact with group activities. For the older widower many communities have activities established for senior citizens. In addition to group activities that provide opportunities for dating, many women make their availability known to men. As Dick said, "Accepting that invitation for dinner from a woman I met at a church party was not difficult at all."

Most men find that for a time after their wife's death they have no desire or need for sex, but slowly this need returns. Some widowers develop anxiety about their capacity to engage in sexual intercourse and may experience erectile failure or inability to achieve orgasm. If careful review of his earlier activities reveals that a widower was sexually competent earlier and that he is currently still mourning his mate, it may help to reassure him about the normality of his present symptoms and to caution him against rushing things. It simply takes time to fully recover from the loss of a spouse. It may be helpful for him to masturbate, and some men, socialized against this behavior, may need the permission of their therapist or physician to do so.

If his concern about possible impotence continues, it may be important for the widower to see a physician in order to learn whether or not he has related physical problems. (See also Kaplan, 1983; Wagner & Green, 1981). Depression is a common cause of temporary impotence. Unrealistic expectations of the self may also be an important factor.

In sum, sexual frustration is one of the most difficult and sensitive problems faced by the widower. As might be expected, this varies with individual characteristics such as age, self-esteem, skills in social relationships, religious values, experiences, knowledge, acceptance of sexuality, the nature of the former marital relationship, attitudes of peers, and self-confidence as a heterosexual partner. Counseling that is reassuring, accepting, and informative can be very helpful to most widowers; in other instances more intense therapy may be indicated.

Remarriage

Each widower finds a slightly different path toward rebuilding his life. Some remarry. Some remain single. Some live with family members or friends. The younger man will probably have extreme pressures placed on him to marry, and if he has children in his care, he may be told that he should provide a mother for them.

The older the widower is, the more likely the pressure is on him not to remarry. A "dirty old man" should not be interested in sex, so goes the myth. A counselor can be useful to both young and old widowers in helping them stand up to societal pressure and make decisions that are best for themselves. Before a man is ready to remarry, grief should be well over so that the new marriage is not a quick attempt to replace the lost loved one, an impossible goal that is almost sure to lead to an unhappy second marriage. It is crucial that a widowed person develop a new self-identity as a "me" instead of the "we" of his former marriage. Until this change in identity takes place, he is not ready for a new wife. A counselor may assist a widower in this selection process as well, helping him review his options and make a well-reasoned decision. (See also the chapters on remarriage in this volume.)

Financial Problems

As mentioned earlier, widowers are seldom considered in the few available studies on widowhood and therefore little is known about the financial problems faced by them. Hyman (1983) reports that white widowed men between the ages of 60 and 79 are apt to be poorer than their married counterparts, and the great majority of them live alone. Children are less likely to provide economic and psychic support for widowers than for widows.

Generally the financial problems of widowers tend to vary according to their educational and occupational levels. Research indicates that men from lower socioeconomic backgrounds have the most difficulty in coping with their loss (Parkes, 1975). The U.S. Bureau of Census (1985) reports that 49% of widowers in the United States are living at or near the poverty level, with an annual income ranging from $1,000 to $9,999. This level is probably due to the demographic fact that men who are widowed relatively early in life tend to come from a lower educational/occupational status, a status that is characterized by higher rates of severe illness and early death.

Then, too, widowers do not have the advantage of belonging to a two-earner, husband-wife family. The majority of widowers in my study were financially secure, but this did not preclude financial problems. William, age 79, for example, had turned over management of the family finances to his wife because of his diminished eyesight and mobility. When she died suddenly, he felt incapable of managing his finances and so obtained the services of a financial planner.

Many people in the helping professions underestimate the importance of financial problems as they focus on the problems of bereavement. It should be remembered that having to cope simultaneously with the emotional pain of losing a spouse and meeting the costs of a final illness can present financial problems that seem overwhelming.

9

Adoptive Families

JUDITH SCHAFFER AND RON KRAL

INTRODUCTION

Adoption has long been the victim of the commonsense dictum "If it is different, there must be something wrong with it." Although much has been written about the potential pitfalls of building families through adoption, unfortunately much of the literature in this field is based on anecdotal reports and authors' "hunches." This chapter will present research-based information that calls some of the previous thinking into question. Certainly, more needs to be learned about adoptive families before a more authoritative final chapter can be written.

HISTORY OF TRADITIONAL ADOPTION

Since ancient times couples have turned to the adoption of unrelated infants as a remedy for infertility. References to this method of continuing a family's lineage have been found in the ancient codes of Babylon, Egypt, Greece, and Rome. In the United States early statutes regulating adoption specified that the adopted child was to be considered the property of the father (Schwartz, 1984). In the contemporary Western world traditional adoption was concerned with finding a healthy infant of good genetic background and social class for a couple that was unable to give birth. Attempts were made to match the characteristics of the child and family in order to simulate a birth family. It was thought that if the couple adopted when the infant was young enough and if their characteristics were similar enough, the resulting family would be just like a birth family.

In the past the traditional adoptive family was usually middle- or upper-class in status. The husband worked and the wife stayed at home with the children. They were unable to have a live birth and were required to prove this with medical reports. Because there were usually fewer infants than prospective adoptive parents, agencies developed strict standards for applicants to meet. Now these standards are being relaxed, and adoptive families can be of all income levels, be unmarried, have birth children, and even be handicapped themselves.

HISTORY OF SPECIAL-NEEDS ADOPTION

Foster care is substitute care for a child who cannot be cared for in his or her own home, a state-mandated service used primarily by families whose incomes are below the poverty level (Mayor's Task Force on Foster Care, 1980). It is a generic term that includes foster family and institutional care and it is intended to be temporary—the child is expected to return home. In fact, foster care has become a permanent way of life for nearly half of all foster children (The Foster Care Monitoring Committee, 1984). When foster children do not return home, it is likely that they will spend their childhoods moving from home to home and institution to institution until discharged as adults. Until only recently adoption was rarely considered for such children because of their "inferior" backgrounds of age, race, handicaps, or membership in sibling groups that should be placed together. Foster care was seen as a service for poor children and adoption as a service for middle- and upper-class couples.

As a result of the efforts of citizen advocacy organizations and enlightened professionals over the past two decades, adoption has undergone a revolution. In earlier periods adoption served to meet the needs of adults. Today public support requires that adoption be primarily concerned with meeting the needs of children without parents. Foster children who cannot be promptly returned to their families and whom their biological parents are willing to legally relinquish for adoption, as well as children who are involuntarily removed and legally severed from their birth families, are entitled to have adoptive families sought for them, regardless of the individual characteristics of these children. Foster families are often encouraged to adopt the children who are in their homes, and income and medical subsidies are provided as needed to help them do so. Recruitment of adoptive homes for the remaining youngsters is now a priority at many departments of social services. Although most foster children who are adopted are adopted by their foster parents, this review will focus on those families for whom adoption was the prime motivating factor in originally seeking a child's placement in their homes.

CURRENT PRACTICES IN ADOPTION

Nobody knows how many adoptions take place in the United States each year or even what proportion of individuals are adopted, since the federal government stopped collecting this information in 1973. Estimates of the numbers of nonrelative adoptions have ranged from 2 to 4.5% of live births (Brinich & Brinich, 1982). Kirk (1985) hypothesizes that one in every five persons has a family member who is adopted. Adoptions of nonrelatives come about in three ways: child welfare agency adoptions; private or independent adoptions in which an individual, often a lawyer or physician, acts as an intermediary between two sets of parents; and "black market" adoption in which a middleperson charges a "babyfinding" fee and earns a profit. Adoption is a legal process; it must be finalized in court where custody of the child is transferred to the adoptive family and he or she becomes the legal child of the family. Black market adoption, often referred to as "babyselling," is illegal in all states. Many states have also made private or independent adoptions illegal.

Although it is common for departments of social services to place children of all ages for adoption, the number of infants being surrendered to them by their mothers has been decreasing. The number of black children placed for adoption through social agencies has always been low for a variety of reasons, including less opprobrium usually attached by black families to children born outside the marriage, high fealty values, child care provided by the extended family, a dearth of social agencies focusing on adoption for black children, and the desire by black people that black children not be placed in racially different families.

The primary source of white infants available for adoption has been those born out of wedlock and surrendered at birth. The availability of abortion, the widespread use of contraception, and the lessened stigma associated by white people as well as black ones with unmarried parenthood are all thought to be related to the decrease in the numbers of infants being surrendered to agencies. Individuals who want to adopt healthy infants, especially white ones, are therefore likely to find it difficult to do so. As a result, few applications are accepted by child welfare agencies for such babies, and the wait for placement is said to be from 3 to 5 years.

Because there is such intense competition for the few infants available at public agencies, some individuals who want to adopt healthy infants and who have adequate financial resources choose independent, nonagency adoption for a baby born in the United States. Although there are no accurate statistics available, the number of independent adoptions is said to be increasing. It is thought that at least as many if not more adoptions of nonrelatives occur independently through lawyers, doctors, and other intermediaries as through social agencies. An additional option for those who want infants is foreign adoption. Infants from other countries can be adopted both privately and through child welfare agencies. Feigelman and Silverman (1979) report that between 1968 and 1977 the Immigration and Naturalization Service reported a 400% rise in the numbers of "transcultural" adoptions by American citizens.

There is and will continue to be a great need for more adoptive families for children with special needs, both for the backlog of these children who have been abandoned by their parents and have been in foster care for many years as well as for the increasing numbers of children coming into foster care. Foster care case rolls were declining in the late 1970s, but this trend appears to have reversed. The Reagan administration's economic policies and the cuts in social programs such as day care and low-cost public housing have resulted in an increased number of families who live below the poverty level and need public services that are no longer available or are strained to capacity. In New York City, for example, children from female-headed households receiving public assistance constitute the great majority of foster children (Mayor's Task Force on Foster Care, 1980). The major factors related to the placement of children in foster care are poverty-related problems such as inadequate housing and homelessness. The numbers of poor and homeless families are increasing, and the increase in foster care populations reflects this.

Because foster children are predominantly the children of the poor, the racial and religious backgrounds of the children available for adoption at public agencies are often similar to those of families on local Aid for Families with Dependent Children (AFDC) rolls. In New York 87% of children in foster care are black, Hispanic, or other minority (The Foster Care Monitoring Committee, 1984). Therefore, the children who need adoption services are more likely to be black or Hispanic infants, toddlers, school-aged children, children who are part of sibling groups who should be placed together, and children who suffer from a range of handicaps. Following are descriptions of two children who exemplify those currently available for adoption.

Karen is a 12-year-old white girl who has lived in four different foster homes since her mother placed her in foster care when she was 2 years old. Although her mother never visited her or made plans for her to return, Karen was only legally freed for adoption recently. She is attractive but rude and defensive when confronted with authority. She is performing below grade level in school. The agency would prefer to place her with her 11-year-old foster brother Tom who is not her biological brother but with whom she has always lived.

Jim is 4 years old. His mother is white and his father black. A healthy, responsive, and intelligent infant, he was abandoned at birth and spent his first 3 years moving from foster family to foster family. At first the moves had nothing to do with Jim. Later the moves were caused by his own deteriorating behavior. He was placed for adoption, but the couple found him too difficult to handle. Next he was placed in a residential treatment center. A childless professional couple who had initially requested a white infant were told about Jim. They visited him for a while, but the father suspected that Jim's early experiences would leave him with permanent scars that the couple would find difficult to deal with. A new family is being sought for him.

Some adoptive applicants have found that they are able to consider children like Karen or Jim once they hear about them or see their photographs. In her study of 177 families who had legally adopted children who were (a) part of a sibling group of three or more; (b) at least 8 years old at the time of placement; or (c) with physical, intellectual, and/or emotional impairments, Nelson (1985) discussed a practice called "stretching." This practice is used by agencies to promote the adoption of children with special needs. Nelson reports that 57% of study families took children who were older, more impaired, or in some other way different from their initial preference. This "stretching" beyond their original expectations enabled these study families to consider children like Karen or Jim. Most of the families report that they were satisfied. Six percent of the study sample were, however, dissatisfied with their adoptions, and the major reason cited by them was such "stretching" beyond their original requests (Nelson, 1985).

The characteristics of families who adopt children with special needs can be very different from those of the more traditional adopters. Fiegelman and Silverman (1979) use the term "preferential adopters" to characterize a group that has birth children or the capacity to give birth and chooses to adopt for ideological reasons. Since these families are not seeking to reproduce birth families, they are often interested in children with characteristics that are different from their own.

Many parents have adopted youngsters who have different racial, ethnic, and cultural backgrounds. The ability to choose the age and sex of a child is often given as a major reason for the adoption. In an effort to understand how these parents compare to more traditional adopters, a number of studies have been undertaken to determine their characteristics (Feigelman & Silverman, 1979; Simon & Alstein, 1977; Grow & Shapiro, 1974; Fanshel, 1972). The studies indicate that these families are characterized by less-extended family affiliations, individualism, political liberalism, and higher education, occupational, and income levels.

Unmarried individuals are increasingly turning to adoption as a way of creating or expanding a family. Fiegelman and Silverman (1977) report that single adoptive parents who responded to their questionnaire were likely to be urban, older, nonwhite, highly educated, and employed as teachers or social workers. Even though they had adopted special-needs children, they reported that these children were doing quite well. However, more research is needed on this topic. Some agencies even consider single-parent households to be the placement of choice for certain children. The following paragraphs give examples of preferential adopters who could become families for special-needs children.

Ralph and Jane have been married for 10 years. They have a 6-year-old birth daughter, Ann. Ralph works part time, and he cares for Ann and the household in the afternoon. Jane is a full-time administrator, earning more in salary and benefits than Ralph. They are both in their late 30s. They would like a school-aged son. Ralph is of Hispanic background, and he would like his son to share his background. They are willing to consider a youngster with mild handicaps as a potential addition to their family.

Betty and Bob would like to adopt a child who could not live in a family otherwise. They are fertile and would like to give birth to a child at some later time. They would like the child to be younger than school age and of a different cultural and racial background from their own. They would prefer a child without handicaps. Since they are firm in their preference for a young, healthy child, they will be placed on a waiting list until one becomes available.

Frank, a 40-year-old divorced black man, is the administrator of a youth program. He sees his 12-year-old daughter regularly, but she now prefers to do things with her friends in her home town on weekends. Frank suspects that he will not marry again. He wants very much to be a parent full time and do homework with a child, cook for him or her, and so forth. He is interested in a black boy, older than 8, who has the potential for independent living in the future. He can accept correctable learning and behavior problems.

Janet is a woman in her 50s who was disabled many years ago and has always stayed home to care for her children. They are now grown, and her husband is dead. She would like to continue doing the thing she believes she does best—be a parent. She would be willing to accept a youngster older than 12 and to consider a sibling group as well. She enjoys working with children and would consider a child who requires a great deal of attention because of medical or developmental problems. She does not want a child with serious behavior problems.

The growing need for adoptive parents for children with special needs coincidently corresponds to a greater demand for adoptable infants. According to analysis of data from the 1976 National Study of Family Growth, infertility has been increasing among married couples in the United States for a variety of reasons, including voluntary sterilization (Bachrach, 1983). She suggests that the upward trends in sterility point to the potential for an increased demand for adoption. The couple described in the following paragraph exemplifies current trends.

Mike and Liz are both professionals. They postponed having children until both were established in their careers and had achieved a certain standard of living. Now in their late 30s they are unable to conceive. Three years of intensive infertility treatment have yielded no positive results, and they are beginning to consider adoption. Adoption agencies they have contacted are unwilling to consider them because of the length of current waiting lists for babies. By the time they reach the top of the list, they will be, by agency standards, too old to adopt an infant.

It is likely that there will be an increase in the numbers of adoptive families both as a result of the increased efforts to place special-needs children and the demand for adoption by infertile couples and unmarried individuals. Adoptive families, both those who adopt special-needs children and those who adopt more traditionally, face some unique complications and challenges. Nelson (1985) reports that 80% of her study families who had adopted special-needs children cited as their greatest unmet need mental health services that were timely, specialized, sensitive, and competent. Fifty percent claimed they had received no counseling services or that the services they had received were too superficial. Because these families are different in so many ways from the norm, the clinician who treats such families should be familiar with research-based information on the outcomes of these adoptions. A therapeutic model that is family-focused, is present- and future-directed, and assumes that positive change in context can be healing is likely to be most helpful (see Chapter 10 of this volume).

Families who adopt infants are reported to be somewhat more likely than natural parents to seek professional help for parent/child difficulties. It is important for the clinician treating adoptees and their families to be able to distinguish between adoption-related difficulties, many of which need to be seen as normal and accepted as such, and problems that may not be related to adoption. Here again a knowledge of adoption-related difficulties will assist the therapist in addressing the needs of the family and child.

COMPLICATIONS OF ADOPTIVE FAMILY LIFE

Because it is different from the norm, membership in an adoptive family may make life more complicated than life in a birth family. Through analysis of a small sample Kirk (1964) proposed a theory of role handicap suffered by adoptive families that has been referred to and evaluated by researchers over the years. Kirk suggests that adoptive families may be forced to reject their adoptive status, denying it to others and perhaps even to themselves and their children, because American culture tends to denigrate adoption. In addition, Kirk contends that an infertile couple may have to cope with a sense of inadequacy related to the failure to bear biological offspring, with the need to depend on outsiders to obtain a child, and with the adopted child's illegitimacy and "inferior" heredity. Families are exposed to subtle and blatant examples of the stigma attached to adoption: press reports that stress the adoptive status of certain criminals or mass murderers; comments on how much nicer it will be for an adoptive family when they can give birth to a child of their own; obvious favoritism by grandparents of birth grandchildren; and even our language, which refers to the birth parents as "real" and, by implication, adoptive parents as unreal.

Feigelman and Silverman (1979) investigated these aspects of role handicap in their nationwide sample of adoptive parents, using a mailed questionnaire. The sample was drawn from membership lists of adoptive parent organizations. Their analysis of data reports evidence of self-perceived role handicap among infertile adopters especially as it relates to being dependent on the assistance of outsiders in getting a child. These families are also reported to suffer a greater measure of role distress associated with the transition to adoptive parenthood. In addition, 32% of the traditional adopters and 28% of the preferential adopters said that they were frequently subjected to "subtle and obvious disparaging remarks" related to adoptive parenthood.

•

Complications for Adoptive Parents

A variety of experiences relating to parenthood are unique for adoptive parents. These include evaluation by a social agency and/or the court with the power to deny them the opportunity to be parents; not having the experience of a completed pregnancy and live birth; having no control over when the child will come into the family; the trial period before court finalization, during which time the child could be removed from the adoptive parents; and contending with the stigma of adoption and responding to some of the unique aspects of raising an adopted child. All of these are thought by some to add to the conflicts and problems associated with being adoptive parents. Hartman (1984) suggests that these experiences pose a difficulty in what she calls "entitlement." Birth parents rarely question their right or "entitlement" to be the parents of their children. Adoptive parents may do so. Entitlement for Hartman includes the right to be firm with children. She suggests that this may be especially difficult for parents of adopted children and may be related to the higher reported incidence at certain ages of acting out behaviors in adopted children (Brodzinsky et al., 1984; Bohman & Sigvardsson, 1982).

The difficulties sometimes faced by couples who find they are infertile have been enumerated by Kraft and associates (1980). In the authors' observation of clinical cases of couples wishing to adopt babies from St. Mary's Services, a psychodynamically-oriented child welfare agency in Chicago, they found that many of the individuals had experienced difficulties regarding their infertility. These included feelings such as anger, guilt, denial, projection of blame, and humiliation. The couples had also been challenged with marital conflicts and crises.

Based on clinical observations, Kraft and associates have proposed theoretical formulations concerning infertility and adoption, in particular the ways couples were found to have confronted infertility. Some of them were judged to be good candidates for adoption, and others were judged otherwise. For example, unresolved feelings that one is defective because of infertility were associated with negative fantasies about the birth mother and concerns with the child being the "bad seed." As a result of this analysis, these clinicians suggest that adoptive parent functioning may be related in part to how they continue to adapt to, compensate for, and resolve infertility issues throughout their lifetimes.

Complications for the Adoptee

Adoptees who are adopted in infancy are faced with a full range of unanswered and perhaps unanswerable questions about their birth backgrounds and their birth parents. Children understand different aspects of adoption at different stages of their development. Brodzinsky and colleages (1984) studied 200 youngsters between the ages of 4 and 13 years, half of whom were adopted prior to age 2 years and 6 months and half of whom were birth children. An open-ended interview and an Adoption Motivation Q-Sort with items derived from earlier adoption research were used. The authors found little difference in the related knowledge of adopted and nonadopted children.

They did find, however, that understanding adoption was a process of cognitive conceptualization and not merely a gradual accumulation of facts. Because of their early stage of cognitive development, few children younger than 6 were able to differentiate between family membership through adoption and through birth to their biological parents. It was not until midadolescence that a sophisticated, abstract understanding of these differences and of the legal bonds in adoption were developed. As a result of these findings, the authors recommend that adoptive parents not overestimate their children's understanding of and knowledge about adoption (Brodzinsky et al., 1984). Thus, it is appropriate for these parents to discuss this issue with their children at many stages of their development.

Adoptees can have more complicated lives because of unresolved curiosity about their roots and because they must further accept the possibility of never knowing their birth parents. When adoptees are young, it is not unusual for them to wonder if they were given up for adoption because of something naughty they did. A group of healthy, well-functioning adopted adolescents were interviewed at the Center for Adoptive Families in New York City in 1984. The 13- and 14-year-olds spoke of their fantasies about their birth parents—they were either rich and famous or poor and destitute. These young people were concerned about what they would do if their birth parents suddenly appeared—how it would complicate their lives and to whom they would belong.

The 15- and 16-year-olds had mastered the concept of adoption and had a more realistic interpretation of their birth parents. A 15-year-old girl said, "When I was younger, I used to think my mother was someone famous like Diana Ross. Now I know that she was just someone who made a mistake and needed to do something about it."

All the adolescents in this study group spoke about wondering, especially on birthdays, what their birth mothers were doing and whether or not they were thinking of them. As one girl put it, "Am I a memory or something she just threw away?" It is frequently observed that adopted adolescents are curious and want more information about their birth parents, but they tend not to be ready to search them out. Those adoptees who search usually do so as young adults. It is thought that marriage, the birth of a child, and the death of an adoptive parent appear to be related to the decision to search (Melina, 1986). However, the experiences of adult adoptees and birth parents are beyond the scope of this chapter. Some clinicians have suggested that because most adoptees are illegitimate and because this is difficult for them to resolve in adolescence, they are more likely to have births out of wedlock themselves. There is no evidence in the literature to confirm this hypothesis; however, the issue has not been systematically studied with adequate control groups.

Some psychoanalysts have long been concerned with problems they see as inherent in the adoptive family and that they believe influence not only the parent-child relationship but also the developing personality of the adopted child. These concerns, based on clinical theory, revolve around the fantasy system of the adopted child (Blum, 1983). It is suggested that classical issues such as the resolution of the Oedipal complex, family romance fantasies, and relaxation of the incest taboo are especially complicated in adoptive families. Blum further hypothesizes that the denial of adoption can promote certain shared fantasies and collusive denials between parents and children.

Children who have been adopted following removal from their birth homes and who have experienced a series of impermanent placements often have many additional burdens to overcome that are unrelated to adoption per se. Based on clinical experience and a review of the clinical literature, Hartman (1984) describes the many difficulties for these children regarding the losses they have suffered, the abuse and neglect they may have experienced, and the problems they therefore have in trusting new family relationships. Issues of loyalty to one's birth family, no matter how abusive, are a major concern for many of these children. Relationships with former foster families and birth siblings may complicate the relationship with a new family. A further difficulty for many of these children is that they have never experienced what it means to be nurtured and cared for by any parents. It is something that they do not know cognitively and will learn only gradually as they begin to trust in the permanence of their adoptive homes.

(The child whose adoptive family comes in for treatment prior to legalization of the adoption, within a few months after placement of the child, is a topic beyond the scope of this chapter.)

RESEARCH: ADOPTION OUTCOMES

There is little quality research on the development of the adopted child and his or her family over time. A major difficulty is the fact that following the legal adoption of the child, adoption records are sealed by the courts. It is therefore difficult to obtain an unbiased sample for research, and studies must rely on volunteers imperfectly recruited. The greatest amount of adoption research has little to do with adoption in that it emphasizes the study of certain supposedly inherited conditions. A substantial body of literature is based on clinical populations of adoptees and their families and therefore seeks connections between certain pathological conditions and adoption. Most adoptees and their families do not seek mental health services; therefore, these hypotheses may have limited application. A smaller and newer body of literature using longitudinal designs and more representative populations is much more promising, but many questions will remain unanswered until more research, preferably using a longitudinal design, is undertaken

Inherited Conditions

One body of literature does not address adoption per se but rather the role of genetic inheritance in certain kinds of disturbances such as schizophrenia and criminality in children who did not grow up in their biological families (Bohman, 1980, & Sigvardsson, 1982; Bohman, Sigvardsson, & Cloninger, 1981; Kendler, Gruenberg, & Strauss, 1981a; 1981b; 1981c). This research suggests a genetic component in the transmission of certain mental illnesses and kinds of antisocial behavior such as petty criminality (Bohman et al., 1982). For example, research suggests that 10% of close relatives of those with schizophrenia and manic depressive psychosis run the risk of developing these mental illnesses compared to 1% of the general population (Melina, 1986). These studies have not, however, evaluated the functioning of the adoptive families.

A more recent study by Tienari et al. (1987) examines the relationship between genetic inheritance, the adoptive rearing environment, and serious mental disturbances in adopted children. A nationwide sample of all women in Finland who had been hospitalized for schizophrenia and had relinquished children for adoption was collected. Because schizophrenic symptomatology is usually not visible until an individual has reached late adolescence, the study sample was composed of 196 children born in 1970 or earlier and adopted by nonrelatives before the age of 5 years. These subjects, their birth mothers, and their adoptive parents were compared to a matched control group of adopted children who were born to mothers not hospitalized for psychosis.

Tienari and associates (1987), using sophisticated research methods and interviews and established measures, evaluated the birth mothers, children, and adoptive couples. The mental health of the adopted children (index and control) was blindly rated and compared. Family functioning was evaluated and blindly rated using interview material, the Beavers-Timberlawn family evaluation scales, and the Couple Consensus Rorschach. Five global classes of family functioning were established: healthy; mildly disturbed; neurotic; rigid syntonic; and severely disturbed.

The authors (Tienari et al., 1987) caution that the findings they report are preliminary ones, since only a portion of the sample was interviewed at the time of this paper (102 of 196 matched pairs). Of the investigated cases and their matched controls, seven of the psychotic children were the offspring of schizophrenics and only one was a control offspring. The total number of severe diagnoses was 31.4% in the index group and 15.7% in the control group.

When family evaluations were included in the analysis, Tienari and associates report that thus far not one seriously disturbed child has been found in a healthy or mildly disturbed adoptive family.

Seriously disturbed children were nearly all reared in seriously disturbed adoptive families. Based on these preliminary findings, the authors suggest that while heredity and rearing environment appear to interact in the development of serious mental disturbances, healthy family rearing may protect a child with a genetic vulnerability from developing psychosis (Tienari et al., 1987).

Studies of the inheritance factor as an aspect of intelligence indicate that the adopted children who were studied had I.Q. scores that had a closer correlation with their birth mothers than with their adoptive parents. This has led to the assumption by some that a complication for adoptees and their families might be that adoptees are less intelligent than their new families in ways measured by these tests.

However, Walker and Emory (1985) computed the I.Q. scores of the adoptees in their correlational studies and found the scores to be virtually the same as those of biological children born into the adoptive families. Thus, they question the role of genetics in intelligence at least as it pertains to adoptive families.

In France, Schiff and associates (1982) reported on a group of youngsters born to lower-class mothers and adopted by families in the top socioprofessional class. These children's I.Q. scores were a mean of 14 points higher than their biological siblings who had been reared in the birth homes. The authors conclude that the I.Q. and academic achievement of upper-middle-class children are less reflective of the genes transmitted from parents to children and more reflective of the conditions in which they are raised.

In summary, as a large number of studies have shown over the years, intelligence is strongly affected by both inheritance and environment, with the latter component being somewhat stronger. Thus, children born to parents with dull adult intelligence may do considerably better than their natural mothers, fathers, and siblings if they are placed in their early years with adoptive parents with higher measured intelligence.

Longitudinal Research

It is necessary for the clinician to have knowledge of nonclinical adoptees and their families to determine whether adoptive family life is likely to result in severe problems. Bohman and Sigvardsson (1982) have followed a group of 624 Swedish youngsters who at the time of their birth were candidates for adoption. Their report describes these youngsters at 15 years. The study is especially interesting since only 28% of this group were in fact adopted. Thirty-seven percent were raised by their own mothers who had originally intended to surrender them for adoption and then changed their minds. An additional 35% were raised in foster homes. These groups were followed and also compared to matched controls. The authors conclude that "the risks concerning the subsequent development of adopted children are in no way greater than the risks for children in the general population. . . . The prospects for these children are very good, irrespective of the social or genetic background" (1982, p. 354). They further report that the children who returned to their birth mothers as well as those raised in foster family care were at greater risk of developing problems. This sample of adopted youngsters continued to do as well as the nonadopted controls at 18 and 22 or 23 years old. The findings from this study need to be viewed with caution, however, because the culture and conditions of life in Sweden may be quite different from those in the United States; one cannot assume highly similar outcomes in this country.

Adjustment in Nonclinical Adoptees Adopted as Infants

A group of papers published during the 1950s and 1960s reported that adopted children were more frequently treated at psychiatric facilities for psychological problems (Simon & Senturia, 1966; Tousseing, 1962; Schechter, 1960). Although these studies are old and methodologically flawed, they are often referred to in articles concerning the possible psychological vulnerability of adopted children and their families. They have influenced the ways in which mental health professionals, teachers, and physicians have viewed adoptees and their families for decades. A number of studies have been undertaken to determine whether adoptees in fact have a greater incidence of emotional problems.

A team of researchers at Rutgers University, led by David Brodzinsky, studied academic and psychological adjustment in a sample of 260 adopted and nonadopted children ranging in age from 6 to 11 years. The adopted children had been placed for adoption when younger than 3.5 years. Psychological adjustment was measured using maternal ratings and academic adjustment by teacher ratings. The children were reported to be well within the range of normal behavior and were not manifesting severe pathology (Brodzinksy et al., 1984). It was reported in the Rutgers University study that while these youngsters as a group were rated as being somewhat more poorly adjusted on the average than nonadopted children in terms of acting out behavior, they were in fact doing especially well taking into account the SES background of their birth parents and the stress and poorer prenatal care during gestation. These findings, as well as those of Bohman and Sigvardsson (1982). suggest the need for more longitudinal studies of adoptees so that we can learn more about the nature of difficulties experienced at certain ages and stages of development.

Stein and Hoopes (1985) have been interested in the issue of identity formation in adolescents who were adopted by nonrelatives in infancy. Hypothesizing that this process would be more difficult for adoptees than other youngsters, they studied a group of teenagers who had been adopted in infancy. They used interviews and questionnaires, with norms already established for nonadopted adolescents, to measure self-concept and self-esteem. Although they expected the adoptees to score somewhat lower on these items, their findings were in fact the opposite of their expectations. Stein and Hoopes reported that the adoptees were doing quite well based on their performance on standardized measures. The authors concluded, "Adoptees as a group perceived their status rather positively, noting few ill effects emanating from adoption per se" (1985, p. 63). They further found that the adolescents who were the most well adjusted, regardless of birth status, came from families in which the parents provided a source of intimacy and guidance and in which parental values and influence were in balance with those of the adolescents' peers. (This is a finding similar to results of research with nonadopted children and adolescents: see Volume 3 in this series.)

A number of studies have been undertaken to determine whether adoptees are at greater risk for psychological difficulties in young adulthood and later. Brinich and Brinich (1982) reviewed the records of 5,145 patients registered for their first psychiatric service between 1969 and 1978 at Langley Porter Psychiatric Institute. While adopted children were patients at a somewhat higher level than expected, 5% as against an expected 2.2%, adult adoptees were represented at a lower-than-expected rate, 1.6%. The authors suggest that the overrepresentation of children may be explained by the following: Adoptive families are from higher socioeconomic strata, and these families tend to use psychiatric services more frequently; and the act of adoption through an agency connects a family to and encourages them to use a range of support services including psychiatric services more readily than others would.

This latter hypothesis appears to account for an interesting phenomenon at both The Center for Adoptive Families, Inc., in New York City and Brief Family Therapy Center Adoptive Family Project in Milwaukee, Wisconsin, both family treatment centers focusing on adoptive families. At both treatment facilities the authors of this chapter have noted that 25% of the families coming for therapy come for problems that are not psychological in nature and do not require treatment in any conventional sense. They reflect, instead, a need for education and information about certain behaviors and difficulties that are unique to adoption (see Chapter 10 for a fuller discussion of this).

Marquis and Detweiler (1985) were interested in the differences between adopted and nonadopted persons in their attributional judgments and in how they experienced their parents. They studied 121 nonadopted and 46 adopted persons using attributional stories, a Locus of Control Scale, and a Perceived Parenting Questionnaire. They reported that compared to the controls the adoptees in this study were "significantly more confident, viewed others more positively, had a greater sense of internal locus of control and experienced their adoptive parents as significantly more nurturant, comforting, predictable, protectively concerned and helpful" (1985, p. 1054) than the nonadoptees. Norvell and Guy (1977) compared self-concept scores of 38 adoptees and 38 nonadopted persons between the ages of 18 and 25 years. No significant differences were found between the two groups.

Aumend and Barrett (1984) were interested in differences in the self-concepts, attitudes toward adoptive parents, and experiences with adoption revelation in searching and nonsearching adult adoptees. The sample was drawn from search groups and adoption agencies. They report on the results of 131 responses to a self-concept scale, a parental attitude scale, and an adoption questionnaire. Although nonsearchers scored significantly higher on the scales, the authors note that the majority of the adult adoptees scored above the 60th percentile on the self-concept scale and had positive scores on the Attitude Toward Parents Scales. Furthermore, the majority of adoptees stated they were happy growing up, with only 12% reporting being unhappy (Aumend & Barrett, 1984).

Adjustment and Special-Needs Adoptions

Children with poor genetic and prenatal histories and those who have suffered abuse, neglect, and deprivation of consistent nurturing by one caregiver are frequently considered to be at risk for a wide variety of psychological problems. The foster child is likely to have lived under conditions that do not promote stable emotional development and may have developed negative attitudes and feelings about caregivers. It is also held that lack of consistent nuturing can make it difficult for such children to develop normal ties to other people, especially in close family relationships (Goldstein, Freud, & Solnit, 1973).

Clinicians will therefore be interested in how children fare when they experience a positive change in context through adoption. Kadushin (1979) studied a group of parents who adopted white, older, special-needs children during a 10-year period from 1952 to 1962 in Wisconsin. These families were interviewed several years after adoptive placement and court finalization. Kadushin hypothesized that parental satisfaction was a logical way to determine the success of these placements since it was unlikely that they would be satisfied if the youngsters and they had not formed a close family attachment. Interviews and measurement devices demonstrated that between 82 and 87% of these parents expressed satisfaction with their adoptions. He indicates that this rate of satisfaction equals and sometimes exceeds the rate of satisfaction reported by families who have adopted healthy infants.

A more recent study conducted by Nelson (1985) also showed a high rate of satisfaction. She reported that 73% of the parents who had adopted children described as having special needs said that their experience with the adoption was excellent or good. Another 20% reported satisfaction with their experience. These parents not only described the ways in which the children had changed, but they also spoke of the ways the parents had grown as individuals (Nelson, 1985, pp. 66–67): "We don't take things for granted anymore"; "We've become more tolerant"; "It has made me more compassionate"; "Our other children are more responsible now."

Other researchers have measured the impact of adoption on children who have experienced early deprivation of consistent nurturing by one caregiver, to determine whether the effects are devastating and permanent. Tizard and Rees (1977) report that children who were adopted from infant institutions, considered by some to be depriving by their very nature, scored higher on I.Q. and other measures of adjustment and well within normal ranges compared to a matched sample of their peers who remained in the institutions or returned to their birth mothers. They suggest that adoption can have a healing effect on children deprived of early nurturing.

Children from Different Racial, Ethnic, and Cultural Backgrounds

An attempt has been made to answer the question of adoption outcome for those families who adopt children from racial, ethnic, or cultural backgrounds different from their own. Researchers have interviewed the parents and tested the youngsters at intervals following adoption. The children were found to be doing well at home, at school, and with their peers (Feigelman & Silverman, 1979; Simon & Altstein, 1977; Grow & Shapiro, 1974; Fanshel, 1972). However, further research is needed to determine how these families and children do when they become adolescents and adults.

Clinical Treatment

Although a number of articles refer to the adoptee in clinical treatment, few say anything specific about special treatment approaches. Based on clinical theory and analysis of clinical cases, Blum (1983) reports that psychoanalyses of adopted children are usually characterized by a focus on their fantasy systems. These fantasy systems are especially complicated because they are based in part on the reality of having birth parents who "may still be alive and who may be found or who may choose to find and even reclaim their own natural child" (p. 142).

Systemic family therapy journals have been remarkably barren of articles that report on special treatment needs of adoptive families. Those who have written about adoptive families and their children (Hartman, 1984; Talen & Lehr, 1984; Kramer, 1982) discuss the difficulties that appear to be adoption-related in clinical families. Through analysis of a small number of cases Hartman (1984) and Kramer (1982) suggest that the issue of "belonging" can be especially complicated in adoptive families. The child appears to struggle with issues of loyalty and to which family he or she belongs. At the same time the parents in treatment struggle with whether or not they are entitled to be the parents of this child. For Kramer the question may be to which family tree is the child attached—the biological family's, the adoptive, both, or neither (Kramer, 1982)? In their analysis of a small number of clinical cases Talen and Lehr (1984) discuss issues with which they think adoptive families must cope and with which birth families do not. They contend that there is additional adoption-related stress connected with the usual developmental stages in the family life cycle. These authors report that an important aspect of their treatment of adoptive families has been to clarify with them the difference between adoption and birth. In fact,

Kramer suggests that the child cannot truly become a member of the family until denial of these differences is challenged and more realistic bonds between the youngster and family are established. Further research using a normal population is necessary to confirm this suggestion and similar clinical hypotheses briefly summarized here.

Research Conclusions

The research on nonclinical adopted children and their families shows that on the average both children and parents express considerable satisfaction with one another. Although the lives of these family members are complicated by the fact of adoption, and some of the normal developmental stages have added tasks associated, it appears that this in and of itself does not create severe problems. It appears that most adopted children who have been studied do as well as matched controls in the long run and better than their own siblings who grow up in their birth families. Most adoptees studied as adults appear to be positive, optimistic, stable, and well adjusted.

Most adoptive parents, including those who have adopted special-needs children, say they are satisfied with their adoptions. Most adult adoptees also report being satisfied with their adoptions. All in all, however, only a few small studies are available on the topic of adoption as it affects both adoptees and their adoptive parents. Many more investigations are needed with a greater variety of adoptive parents and adopted children over longer periods of time. Moreover, greater research sophistication is needed, including improved instruments and complex statistical analyses. Then, too, the study of life outcomes for parents who release their children for adoption is an important topic that has been seriously neglected by both researchers and clinicians and therefore has not been covered here.

10

Treating the Adoptive Family

RON KRAL AND JUDITH SCHAFFER

INTRODUCTION

Theories about adoptive families are a lot like ice cream stores; you have a lot to choose from, and everybody seems to have his or her own favorites. The previous chapter's discussion of the historical background and research findings on adoption underscored the complexities of the issues around adoption. Similar to the menu at an ice cream parlor, each issue has some validity and attraction for therapists who are presented with an adoptive family in their practice. This chapter will provide direction in terms of useful concepts and techniques for therapists in this situation, with case examples that demonstrate the effectiveness of the Brief Therapy Model.

In a group estimated to make up 2 to 4% of the population, adopted children and adolescents are thought to account for a disproportionate number of referrals for mental health services. Estimates suggest that adoptive families represent from 3 to 13% of the clients at child guidance and psychiatric facilities. On the other hand, there are statistics that suggest that the rate of service for adult adoptees is below the national rate for nonadopted adults (Brinich & Brinich, 1984). It appears that during the time between finalization of the adoption and when the adoptee leaves home, the possibility of involvement in some form of mental health treatment is higher than it is for the adopted child's nonadopted friends. Therefore, clinical social workers, psychologists, psychiatrists, mental health counselors, nurses, and school personnel need to develop a greater understanding of the needs of adopted individuals and their families along with ideas about how to help them effectively. Unfortunately, research offers the helping professional little in this regard, including the fact that it is not known whether or not reported higher rates of requests for service are accurate and whether or not this reflects a higher incidence of problems among adopted children. If the service requests are indeed higher, this may reflect a somewhat greater readiness to ask for help among adoptive compared to biological parents.

THE SYSTEMIC PERSPECTIVE

Adoption is a family issue. It can affect both the way parents view their role (Kirk, 1964) and how adoptees see themselves (Lifton, 1979). It can also color the interactional, systemic pattern of relationships within the family unit and with other systems such as schools, health care facilities, extended families, and social institutions. Society as a whole does not know how to deal with the idea of adoption. Adoptive parents complain about the responses they encounter in stores, on the street, or in school conferences. The Caucasian couple with an Asian daughter is often asked, "Did you adopt her?" and "How much did it cost?" Families with both adopted and birth children are asked, "Which is your *real* child?" These types of responses put additional burdens on parents and their children and may in fact be contributory factors to the higher rate of service.

However, things are not much better once service is sought. Professionals in their desire to be helpful are sometimes insensitive to the needs of adoptive families (Nelson, 1985). Parents may be told that they must first "deal with their infertility" before they can get help managing their child's temper outbursts. Well-meaning physicians are known to have encouraged parents of hyperactive, adopted children to send them back to the agency rather than live with them. The adoptive family can feel stigmatized due to the lack of highly respected and accepted role models of adoptive parents within society (Kirk, 1964). Members of the family are often prone to internalize this stigma and thus fulfill negative expectations.

It is, therefore, clear that treating the adoptive family requires sensitivity to more than the psychology of an individual adoptee. It requires discussions with parents about the normal course of child development and the unique features of the adopted child. It also necessitates actively encouraging and supporting the parents as people who possess the necessary skills, attitudes, and abilities to raise a child successfully. Consideration must also be given to the family as a system.

Examples of psychodynamic approaches to the treatment of adoptees underscore the relationship factors inherent in clinical cases (Eiduson & Livermore, 1953; Schechter, 1960; Tousseing, 1962; Sorosky, Baron & Pannor, 1975). These authors discuss the adoption-related complications that act upon the mother-child dyad and in emotional problems. Such classic concerns as the resolution of the Oedipal conflict, family romance fantasies, and the child's identification with a parent have been discussed. These potential pitfalls to normal development can be viewed from a family systems perspective and treated through the use of family therapy.

As early as 1953, for example, Eiduson and Livermore describe the necessity of including parents in treatment. Hartman (1984) advocates the use of a systems treatment approach in the provision of postplacement services for adoptive families with or without problems. She believes that families need to be consciously aware of the interrelatedness of their members along with the quality of relationships among them. Hartman discusses the use of family therapy techniques to establish clearly defined boundaries between parents and children along with an understanding of the adopted child's continuing sense of connectedness with the previous foster parents or unfinished business related to birth parents.

Kramer (1982), in discussing the treatment of the adopted child in family therapy, presents the concept of extrusion. To Kramer extrusion involves the adoptive parents' denial of the early maternal-infant experiences, which can be different than those of a birth child, and of the reality of the adoption itself. His thinking closely parallels Kirk's (1964), which emphasizes that the acceptance of difference is at the core of successful infant adoptions. Kramer suggests that without this acceptance the adoptee's sense of belonging to the family is negatively affected.

In biological families the issue of belonging is usually not problematic. When a birth child misbehaves, his or her mother is apt either to accept it as something that children do or to blame it on "genes from the father's side." With the adopted child, however, worries such as bonding problems or unknown genetic defects negatively color the misbehavior and tend to limit the effectiveness of the parental response. In this fashion a pattern of misbehavior/anxious speculation/indecisive action/continued misbehavior can develop. Family systems therapy is an appropriate and successful method of intervening in this pattern by working with parents as well as children to change both the behavior and faulty perceptions that maintain the sequence.

Talen and Lehr (1984) discuss the use of structural and strategic family therapy with adoptive families. In their sample many of the families presented conflicts connected with developmental or life cycle crises. For example, several cases involved parental difficulties in coping with an adolescent's growing sense of independence. Similar to Kramer's cases, Talen and Lehr's families found themselves blocked from interacting with their children in useful parental ways as a result of factors in the parent-child relationship. Caution is necessary to avoid the temptation to attribute these dynamics solely to adoption. Biological parents also respond to life-cycle crises with distorted perspectives. Adoption, however, is more complex, with more room for fantasizing that can increase the probability of this type of difficulty.

From the systemic view adoptees, as part of the family system, affect the level of stress in the parent-child relationship. Brodzinsky and colleagues (1984) investigated the psychological adjustment of adopted children. In their comparison of adoptees and nonadopted, matched controls, they found both similarities and differences. The adoptees who were not involved in treatment were rated by parents and teachers as within the normal range on standardized behavior rating scales. However, as a group they tended to act out more than their nonadopted peers. The severity of this acting out was seen as nonpathological. This finding may reflect the quality of the parent-child relationship already discussed, or it may suggest that for some other reason adopted children tend to act out slightly more than controls.

Hoopes and associates (1969) reported a similar finding, suggesting that the prevalent disorders in the adopted children of their sample were antisocial in nature. One possible interpretation of this data was: "If the adoptive parents are characterized as rigid and defensive and fearful of aggression and sexuality (as some studies have indicated), the adopted child will be in conflict with his parents throughout childhood" (1969, p. 4). Again the message that interactional factors affect the success or failure of adoptive families' adjustment is clear.

EARLY DECISION-MAKING IN TREATMENT

Studies of adoptive families that seek help have produced some interesting distinctions. Some families are simply looking for advice and information. These families are unlike the traditional client population seen in treatment agencies, even though they show up at the counselor's door. They simply find it very difficult to recognize the difference between normal hassles with kids and significant problems. Common folklore in part has led these parents to believe that adopted children are more vulnerable to problems. Although there are some unique complications with adoption, adoptive children and adolescents go through the same developmental stages as nonadopted youngsters. They test limits, they have temper tantrums, and they make mistakes in school. In addition, most adopted children check what their parents will do with statements like, "You're not my *real* mother!"

The therapist must determine whether education or therapy is required. Rather than psychotherapy the proper course of treatment may be to normalize behavior, provide bibliographies, and make referrals to adoptive parents' groups. In order to make this decision, however, the clinician needs to understand the unique situation of the adoptive family as well as the stages of child and family development. It is important to help these families avoid developing a perception of pathology. After all, their experience has included significant involvement with social service agencies during the adoption study process, and they have been encouraged to seek help. In many cases workers have predicted future problems, so there is a much greater danger for these families than for nonadoptive families to see normal concerns as major difficulties.

Another group of families presents primarily adoption-related issues. These families, then, err on the other side of the same coin. As mentioned previously, Kirk (1964) discusses the potential difficulties of families who deny the realities of adoption. This group is often made up of families who adopted infants and who have striven to avoid the sense of difference inherent in acknowledging adoption. They may avoid telling the child about the adoption or deal with the question in awkward, anxiety-producing ways. In Kramer's terminology the sense of a child's belonging to the family is weak. These parents may feel that this child is not really theirs, so they are unable or unwilling to effectively set limits or actively share affection. Under stress they can turn to the other position, the "insistence on difference."

Schaffer and Lindstrom (1984) and Kral (1985) discuss the other end of the denial-of-difference continuum, the "insistence of difference." Families with this frame consider that a child's adopted status is the root of all problems. Faced with this seemingly unalterable fact, these parents experience a sense of hopelessness and panic in dealing with their children. Behavior problems are viewed as signs of deeper problems that the parents are unable to resolve. Adoption is seen as the cause of difficulty. Often the only way to solve the problem appears to be to "fix the child" or "unadopt," (i.e., terminate the adoption). In view of this dynamic it is not surprising that adopted children are overrepresented in residential treatment centers (New York Spaulding for Children, 1986).

With either case, the denial of or insistence on difference, therapy is indicated. The clinical experience of the authors, however, suggests that neither position is useful in determining specific treatment approaches. In fact, some families have been observed to vacillate between these positions. What is important is that these two "types" of positions on the part of the adoptive family be distinguished from two other groups: those who accept adoption and simply need education and/or support and those who accept adoption but still need therapy. This final group represents a population of families who face the same types of problems as those seen in nonadoptive, clinical groups and should be treated as any distressed family.

BRIEF THERAPY WITH ADOPTIVE FAMILIES

It is beyond the scope of this chapter to cover all the components of treating families with problematic children. The reader is encouraged to consult Lipchik's (1987) chapter in Volume 3 of this series. The family systems approach to therapy she describes, based on the Brief Therapy Model (de Shazer, 1985; de Shazer et al., 1986), has proven to be very effective in treating adoptive families. Data collected at the Center for Adoptive Families in New York and the Brief Family Therapy Center in Milwaukee parallel the outcome-positive results based on a 6-month follow-up as described with nonadopted families in the articles reported above. The success of this model appears to relate to several specific factors: focus on human interaction, focus on solutions, acceptance of the client's point of view, understanding of the possibility of multitudinal points of view, and searching for exceptions to problem occurrences.

Factors in Success of the Model

Human interaction is the basis for most complaints brought to a family counselor. As described above, adoption is a family issue, and many of the problems with adopted children appear to be maintained as a result of ineffective patterns of relating based on the myths and/or complexities inherent in the adoptive relationship. Therefore, by changing the patterns of interaction and/or perceptions that maintain these patterns, in many cases problems relating to adoption can be treated successfully.

Therapy is more likely to be successful when its focus is on solutions rather than problems. The Brief Therapy Model promotes the concept that "an intervention only needs to open the way to a solution, which can be done without knowing all of the details of the complaint" (de Shazer et al., 1986, pp. 208–209). Due to the complexity of issues associated with adoption, it may be virtually impossible to define clearly the multitude of background variables at play in the complaint. Therefore by using a future focus, therapy can proceed despite the lack of accurate historical information. For example, a couple may take their infertility to mean that they are inadequate as parents. In this model parental adequacy can be enhanced by interventions that both prove the couple's skill as parents and increase their abilities to parent their child.

Another important concept is that clients cooperate with the therapist in their own unique ways. This premise requires that the therapist understand and accept the client's point of view regarding the complaint. Nelson (1985), in her study of special-need adoptions, reported that dissatisfaction with postplacement services was a significant problem. One hypothesis to explain this phenomenon is that adoptive families were viewed in prejudicial ways by therapists. It has been a common experience of the authors that many families have been in treatment in a variety of other settings prior to seeking "adoption-specific" therapy. This observation underscores the need for therapists to have factual, research-based information regarding adoption issues so that they can understand and join with the family's world view.

The Brief Therapy Model further proposes that "any behavior can be seen from a multitude of points of view" (de Shazer et al., 1986, p. 209). This position is especially relevant in the treatment of adoptive families. As suggested previously, much of what makes the adoptive family appear different from other clinical families are the fantasies they may hold about adoption and its perceived role in the complaint. These fantasies or attributions serve both to develop and to maintain dysfunctional patterns within the family system. It is not uncommon that simple reframing or normalizing can result in useful and lasting changes, as demonstrated in the following example.

Miles and Joan brought their 10-year-old adopted son, James, for therapy because he "had not bonded with his father." James would taunt his dad, who worked part time as a teacher and maintained the household. He would ask his father to make a special supper and then refuse to eat it. At other times James would request a special favor and then refuse to accept it. The boy had been in numerous foster homes prior to the adoption, a fact that added to his father's concern about attachment. The therapy team told the family that James's behavior was quite understandable based on his history. He had little if any experience in a permanent family and was raised primarily by his foster mothers. Miles needed to "teach" James how to be a son to a father. Miles understood this new interpretation of James's behavior and eagerly undertook the task. Within several weeks the boy's relationship with his father had improved to the point where further treatment was unnecessary.

A final consideration in the Brief model is that clients act as if their problem occurs *all* of the time; they perceive that there is never a situation in which it could have or would have occurred but did not. Yet in the vast majority of complaints there are exceptions to the rule, times when the problem was not present. Clients must be helped to describe these exceptions, which provide valuable information about what is already working and what should be increased. Data about these exceptions also enhance the therapist's ability to cooperate with the family, as the tasks for family members can be designed around what they not only can do but are doing. This model promotes the idea of "simple ideas," the process of approaching problems from the common sense angle first before developing more complex interpretations. In this way "a wet bed is a wet bed . . . and nothing more" (de Shazer, 1986, p. 7). If a simple conceptualization of the road to solution fails to result in positive movement, then small doses of complexity can be added. This implies, of course, an experimental approach to therapy in which an intervention is tried and the subsequent results are evaluated before doing anything else. The following example illustrates rather dramatically the utility of this approach.

Patrick was a 9-year-old adoptee brought in for lying and stealing. His parents, John and Ella, were both successful professionals who worked long hours away from home. When asked the question about when Patrick did not steal or lie even when he had the opportunity, his parents were unable to respond. Patrick, however, stated that he never lied or stole when he stayed with his grandparents. Upon further inquiry Patrick said that his grandparents spent a lot more time with him playing games and watching TV than his parents did. John and Ella were assigned the task of each alternately putting aside one half hour per day to just be with Patrick. This intervention was followed by a marked decrease in the frequency of the problem behaviors. Patrick's description of the exception to the pattern was accepted and utilized. So instead of anticipating problems, each parent began to look forward to spending a generally enjoyable half hour with him. Therapy was completed in three sessions without focusing on adoption in any significant manner.

The Procedure of Brief Therapy

While several excellent descriptions of the procedure of Brief Therapy are available (de Shazer, 1985; de Shazer et al., 1986), a short description will help the reader understand how it is done. Generally, each case is seen by a team of therapists using a one-way mirror, although a therapist working alone can successfully employ this model. The family is interviewed for 30 to 40 minutes, during which time the therapist elicits the family's view of the problem, any patterns of behavior around the complaint, useful exceptions to the pattern, and a definition of what will be an acceptable solution. Following this, a ten-minute consulting break is taken. The therapist leaves the room to consult with the team or to work alone. During the break, a series of positive compliments about the family is designed and an intervention, typically in the form of a task, is composed. The therapist then returns to the family and delivers the message. Another appointment is then scheduled if necessary.

At the start of the next session the therapist inquires about the completion of the assigned task or asks a general question about what the family has done or observed that has been "good for them." Further questioning regarding any differences noted is then conducted, with the therapist underscoring changes in the direction toward solution. The consulting break is taken in every session.

Sessions are initially scheduled at weekly intervals until positive changes occur. At this point, sessions are scheduled at intervals of several weeks. At times, particularly in child-focused cases, parents and children can be seen separately for one or more sessions. This helps to strengthen the boundary around the parental subsystem and provides for the use of more strategic interventions.

While one of the strengths of Brief Therapy is the individualization of tasks and messages for each case, the use of standard or invariant tasks has also proven effective. De Shazer and Molnar (1984) describe several useful interventions, one of which is the "Fixed, First Session Task." This task is particularly helpful when the family has not been able to clearly define a solution and/or exceptions in relation to the presenting complaint. The task is:

> Between now and the next time we meet, we (I) want you to observe, so that you can tell us (me) next time, what happens in your (life, marriage, family or relationship) that you want to continue to have happen (de Shazer and Molnar, 1984, p. 298).

Research has shown that most clients notice positive things, and a majority of those report something new or different that can often be used to facilitate movement toward solution. The thrust, then, of Brief Therapy is not to start change but to increase positive differences that are already occurring unnoticed.

PROBLEM DEVELOPMENT AND DIFFERENT SOLUTIONS

Doing Something Different

The commonality among all the clinical groups—those that deny difference, those that insist on difference, and those that need therapy for nonadoption-related concerns—lies in the pattern of problem development. The family perceives a difficulty, something that they want to stop from happening, to have happen differently, or to begin to happen. In response to this felt need they attempt to do something about it. When the attempted solution is effective, the difficulty goes away, and the family continues on. When, however, the attempted solution fails to work as desired, they either attempt another or apply the same, unsuccessful solution again.

The latter case is the beginning of a pattern in which the solution becomes the problem (Watzlawick, Weakland, & Fisch, 1974). This pattern then continues because family members either have failed to recognize the changes as a result of the solution or because the attempted solution is the only thing that makes sense from their world view. A common example is the parent who spanks the child in an effort to stop his or her crying. The more the parent spanks, the more the child cries. This pattern can escalate to physically abusive or even lethal proportions. When something different is done, such as removing the child from the situation or providing reassurance, the crying will eventually stop.

Many adoptive parents become stuck in the same type of pattern when faced with the accusation "You're not my *real* parent!" Their initial response is to try convincing the child that they care for and love the child just like a real one. This serves to either increase the child's anxiety due to the parent's perceived need to reassure the child, or to provide the child with a handy way to "change the subject" when being disciplined. It is often more useful for the parent to agree, "Yes, you are adopted, and we will talk about that after you pick up your toys." In this manner the child's concern is heard and put into proper perspective.

For example, Ms. Davis brought her adopted daughter, Sheila, in for therapy. The presenting complaint was that Sheila, age 6, was having severe school problems to the point of impending removal from a private school. Her mother indicated that Sheila was generally well mannered and compliant at home. Ms. Davis felt that she had established a positive relationship with Sheila. Beyond this information both mother and daughter were quite closed during the initial interview. The therapist, who had previously been trained to do music therapy, discovered that Sheila enjoyed singing. She asked Sheila to sing with her. They began improvising little tunes, and the therapist asked her to sing about what was bothering her. The little girl immediately sang about how her mother was very happy to adopt her, but Sheila was very sad about leaving her foster parents. Her mother then joined in and sang about her joy at having a daughter. She added that she had not even considered Sheila's feelings. The two left the session with a new understanding and cancelled the next appointment since Sheila's school behavior was improving enough that further therapy was not desired. This case dramatically demonstrates the power of doing something different in the parent-child interaction. Through her new understanding of Sheila's feelings, Ms. Davis was able to treat her daughter differently, as a unique person instead of "her adopted daughter."

Education

For some families more education is necessary—accepting difference may not be enough. It sometimes becomes the task of the therapist to teach parents how to successfully parent their children. One major area of education, of course, is about adoption. Lois Ruskai Melina's book *Raising Adopted Children* (1986) is an excellent resource for therapists and parents alike. Many parents need to realize that it is perfectly normal for their adopted children to be curious about their backgrounds and that this does not imply that the child is rejecting them.

Parents also need to know that telling children at age 3 that they are adopted does not mean that they will never have to deal with the subject again. Adoption is a life issue. Like sexuality, a child's understanding of the implications and facts of adoption changes with increased cognitive development (Brodzinsky, Singer, & Braff, 1984). Young children may be satisfied to know that they were "chosen" by these parents. Older children, however, regardless of the age at which they were adopted, begin to realize that if they were chosen, then someone must have given them up. Should this issue arise, parents need to be prepared and coached on possible responses.

At the same time many adoptive parents seem to lack confidence in their understanding of normal child development. Cognitively they understand that adolescence can be a time of conflict for all teens, but acting out or rude behavior in an adopted teen is somehow different to them. The techniques of normalizing and reframing are often necessary at these times, as shown in the following example.

Mr. and Mrs. Stein brought Sarah in because of a marked change in her behavior. Sarah was 15 and had been "Daddy's little girl." Bright, happy, and compliant, she had been doing well in school and was popular with both peers and her parents' friends. She suddenly became verbally combative with her parents and started to miss school. The Steins feared that her behavior reflected some genetic defect, since her birth mother had conceived Sarah at 16 and was known to be "wild."

An evaluation of the family revealed that Sarah was an only child, and the Steins had limited contact with other parents of teens. Mr. Stein had a long history of depression to the point of being unable to work. He was dependent on Sarah and his wife, since there were times when he was unable even to get out of bed. The therapist normalized Sarah's behavior by telling the family:

> It is very difficult and complicated for parents to help their daughter to grow from a "good little girl" to an independent young woman. And it is particularly tough to let her learn the lessons of life on her own. But this is a process we all have gone through and need to experience. For Sarah it appears to be especially tough, since she obviously cares for both of you a lot. She was happy to be your little girl and now is confused about her growing sense of separation and independence, just as you, Mr. and Mrs. Stein, are confused about how to help her do it.

This message resulted in a rapid change in Sarah's behavior, although her parents needed several additional sessions to learn how to live with a teenager and to address the father's depression.

Education about issues specific to adoption is often necessary as a part of therapy. In many ways the model of therapy we propose for adoptive families is educational. The difference is in the client's style of learning. Some families, such as the Davises and the Steins, learn by being told. Others need to discover for themselves, through the course of therapy, the new behaviors and/or perceptions that will lead to the solution of their complaints. The unalterable assumption is, however, that clients come into therapy with resources and strengths that can be used by the therapist to promote a useful solution.

Therapy

The following case examples will demonstrate the use of this model with adoptive families. The first is an example of a child adopted at birth and seen in therapy as an adolescent. The second describes the treatment of an adolescent adopted as an older child. One case was seen at the Adoptive Family Program, Brief Family Therapy Center, Milwaukee, and the other at the Center for Adoptive Families, New York City. Each case was seen by a team using a one-way mirror. Both are similar in that the identified patient is an adolescent boy presenting concerns about lying and stealing. These cases were chosen because they reflect the authors' experience with a majority of adoptive family cases.

The Case of "He Done It"

Fred and Rita Palmer brought their 13-year-old adopted son Frank in for therapy on the recommendation of the school social worker. Frank had been found in possession of his teacher's grade book after it had been missing for several weeks. The Palmers also had an 18-year-old birth son who was living at home but attending college.

When asked if the fact that Frank was adopted at 8 weeks old played any role in the problem, they denied it. When Frank was asked why he thought his parents adopted him, he stated, "They wanted someone for my brother to play with." His parents had no reply to this other than to add that Frank had inherited great musical talent from his birth parents as neither of the Palmers could carry a tune.

Upon further questioning it became clear that the incident with the grade book was not an isolated one. Fred had noticed a change in Frank over the past 3 months, with Frank becoming less open with his father. In addition, there was a growing concern about

Frank's dishonesty. He was doing poorly in school, even though he contended that he did his homework every night. He also was in trouble with his part-time job because he was calling in sick yet telling his folks that he was at work. Finally, Frank was "finding" things, such as money and small personal items, that did not belong to him.

His parents grounded him for these problems by making him stay home at night. However, he could still use the phone, have friends over, and go to special occasions at school. The Palmers felt that the problems with Frank would be solved when he showed progress in school and when he was where he said he would be. Frank added that when his parents let him do things without extensive questioning, he would know they trusted him. The family was given the following intervention message from the team:

> Fred and Rita, we are impressed with your willingness to come in quickly in response to the school's concern. While Frank's behavior has many elements of typical boyish pranks, we are concerned that unless something is done, this could grow into a serious problem. So it is best to nip it in the bud.
>
> We are also impressed that you have been open to discovering Frank's individuality and his special talents, for nobody wants to see them go to waste.
>
> Frank, we are impressed that you realize it will take some doing to regain your parents' trust. We don't know doing what—but doing.
>
> Grounding is grounding, and that should apply across the board—after-school activities, the phone, and so on, so Frank knows that you mean business.
>
> We expect that Frank will test whether you can tell if he has been trustworthy, so you need to plan together what you will do, other than grounding and talking, when he is trustworthy or untrustworthy. Be prepared for both!
>
> Frank, you need to figure out what you are going to need to do to convince your mom and dad and the school that you are trustworthy.

The Palmers were seen one week later. Fred and Rita were seen together without Frank for the first part of the interview. They had developed a lengthy list of positive things to do when he was trustworthy and negative things when he was not. Fred stated that he had been firmer on the rules for grounding and had noted some small improvements. Frank was working harder on schoolwork, and he had spent more time just talking with his father. Rita was worried because she had discovered more things missing that Frank had taken. She was "tense and nervous" and did not want to spend time with Frank at all.

Frank was seen alone. He, too, had compiled a list of things he needed to do.

The team message to all three was:

> We are impressed with the thorough lists you prepared for tonight. It is refreshing to find parents who know they have options. Kids Frank's age are in a tough spot. On the one hand they want to be grown-ups, while on the other they want to be little kids without responsibilities. Frank is no different, but to him being trusted as a grown-up means you love him enough to keep control.
>
> We think that his behavior is a way he has tried to test your commitment to him. It is not uncommon for adopted teens to wonder if their folks really care, and we think you have responded as committed, caring parents with faith when he asks for it maturely, through his behavior, and with control when he asks for it as a little kid. But being afraid that you might not be committed, he asks for your commitment indirectly.
>
> We suspect that Frank will need to continue to talk about this without words—by what he does. So when he asks maturely, you have a list of responses. When he asks like a little boy, you also know what to say—without words.
>
> Frank, it is important for you to keep this conversation up until you are convinced of their caring.

The family was seen two weeks later. During this time Frank continued to show improvement along the lines of the family's initial goals. Early on in this period Fred and Rita planned to go out for the evening, and Frank's brother was also out. Frank had grilled his mother intensely about when they planned to return. Rita simply refused to answer him until they were at the door. She then said he could listen when they "told the baby-sitter." Frank was beside himself, since he had not had a baby-sitter for nearly 3 years. The parents were congratulated on this clever move and the message of caring it expressed to Frank. The couple was then helped to define signs of continued improvement and how they could distinguish childish pranks from a reoccurrence of the problem. The family was told:

> The team was impressed with the solid signs of improvement that you've all been able to list—asking before leaving, doing things to-

gether, Frank's initiative at school, and the two of you seeing it happen. Things are certainly going in the right direction. As we've said before, sometimes things go two steps forward and one back, so be prepared for mistakes and have a plan ready for backsliding.

Frank, while it may seem like your folks are calling the shots, just remember, it is you who tells them when you are ready to be grounded.

Rita and Fred, if it seems like time to come back, try one more thing, for one more week, and then call for another appointment. We'll be happy to see you then.

With this message therapy was concluded, and the Palmers have not seen the need to return. Contacts with the referral source confirm Frank's progress and his parents' satisfaction with his behavior.

This case is in many ways prototypic for infant adoptions. The Palmers suggested that Frank had always lied, yet they felt helpless and impotent in disciplining him. Their feeble attempts at talking to him and grounding him had understandably proven ineffective. The therapy team goals were twofold: to help Fred and Rita learn more effective ways of responding to problem behaviors and to overtly make positive connections with this boy, who defined his family role as his brother's "toy." The two goals were combined in the reframe that Frank was in need of the reassurance of their commitment, which they could provide through firm discipline. The family view that adoption was not an issue here was overtly accepted, but adoption issues were considered by the team as they were explored with the family and normalized in the intervention message.

"Three Coins"

The Whites came into therapy with their 12-year-old adopted son, Billy. He was one of four children living at home and one of 14 children in the White family. Ten children had been adopted by the Whites as older or special-needs placements. Mrs. White wanted therapy for Billy because he had recently stolen $65 from her purse. This was the fourth incident of stealing since he was adopted 3 years ago. Each of the previous incidents involved large sums of money as well, including a portion of the rent money a year ago. She told the therapist that Billy always denied that he stole the money even when it was found on him or in his things. When he had money he would buy things for other kids such as candy or small toys.

Mrs. White appeared to be distraught, as "none of the other children had ever stolen anything." She said she had been warned by

Billy's foster mother that he stole things and that his birth father had been a thief. "People inherit things like that, you know!" Attempts to elicit exceptions to the rule by discussing what occurred between the stealing incidents or by reframing the behavior were met with references back to Billy's past and his inheritance. When Mr. White stated that they would know the problem was solved when money could be safely left out, his wife scolded him for saying this in front of the boy.

Throughout the session Billy sat rather passively and responded to his mother's direct question, "Why did you take the money?" with, "I don't know."

The team sent the following message to the family after the break:

> We are impressed with your ability, Mr. and Mrs. White, to successfully raise so many children. Obviously you are good and caring parents. We also are impressed with how clearly you were able to describe the problem with Billy; that was helpful to us.
>
> Billy, we were impressed by how polite and attentive you were during this session. Most other teenagers would not have been able to do that. It seems to us that you do care about your parents.
>
> We need more information about this complex and serious problem so that we can be helpful to you. What we would like each of you to do, privately, is to pay attention to the good things that happen in your family over the next week so we can be careful not to change any of them.

Upon hearing this intervention, Mrs. White spontaneously described Billy as a kind, helpful boy who was good most of the time.

The second session began with a list of many positives about Billy and some perceived changes. Billy's sister said that he had helped with the dishes without being asked, something new for him. Mrs. White appeared more relaxed and less upset about the presenting incident. She again asked Billy why he stole. This time he stated that he had a "little voice" in his head that told him not to steal and he usually listened to it. The therapist observed that it probably was like a little transistor radio, which sometimes needed to be turned up a little louder so Billy could listen to it. The remainder of this session revolved around the many good things Billy was doing at home.

The Whites were told by the team:

> We are impressed with the many good things that are going on in your family. That was useful for us to know. We also are convinced that Billy has developed a conscience, the little transistor radio. We are

> concerned, however, that he is not able to hear it as often as he would like to. We need just a bit more information about his conscience before we can decide what needs to be done, so we would like you to get two jars. One should be empty and the other should be filled with 100 pennies. Every night, before he goes to bed, Billy should move 1 penny from the full jar to the other one for every time he listened to his conscience.

Both Billy and his parents seemed pleased with this idea and left the session discussing where they could find the jars.

The next session was 2 weeks later. Billy came in carrying a jar containing only a few pennies. The therapist asked Billy about the jar. He said that these were the times he listened to his conscience. Upon counting them, the therapist remarked that there were only three pennies in there. Mrs. White immediately responded, "He was only tempted three times." Billy agreed that indeed he was only tempted three times and that he had listened to his conscience each time. Mrs. White indicated that the positive behaviors that she had said last time she had noted in Billy had continued and that she was beginning to trust the boy more. These changes were acknowledged by the therapist.

The team's message complimented the family on the continued positive changes and noted what a powerful conscience Billy had. It supported Mrs. White's increasing trust and cautioned that progress can slip sometimes, but things certainly seemed to be going in the right direction, a statement she immediately agreed with. They were told that there did not seem to be anything else that the team could do for them at this time, but if further help was needed, they should make another appointment. A follow-up call several months later indicated that Billy was still listening to his conscience, and money was safe at the Whites.

The White case demonstrates a rather common problem with older adoptions, the possibility of inherited or background problems. Using the Brief Therapy Model, the team avoided addressing this as the problem while at the same time listening to the family's concern. Instead, therapy focused on a solution—Billy's conscience and how he used it. Even with "bad blood," Billy had a conscience that for the most part was working. Therapy simply needed to increase its efficiency while pointing out the existence of the conscience to Mr. and Mrs. White. In this case the simplicity of this approach resulted in positive results.

SUMMARY

This chapter presented a number of important considerations and approaches in the treatment of adoptive families. Research in this area is quite limited, although there is some evidence to suggest that adopted children are overrepresented in mental health care during the time that they are living with their adoptive parents. A search of current literature has failed to produce data on outcomes with specific therapeutic approaches. The focus of this work has been on viewing the complications of adoption systemically, from a family perspective. Methods of treatment include both education and therapeutic intervention. It is the position of the authors that the complications of adoption result in parental feelings of incompetence, so therapy that is both positive and enhances parental strengths has proved to be most effective. The Brief Therapy Model was presented as meeting these requirements. In addition, the model's future focus makes it uniquely suitable to this population, as it can successfully resolve the presenting complaints and distorted parent-child relationships without unnecessary speculation about hypothesized causal factors. As the need for postplacement adoptive services increases (Hartman, 1984; Nelson, 1985), therapists will need more information and training in proven methods of treating adoptive families. Therefore, further clinical research in this area will be necessary.

11

Remarriage and Stepfamilies

KAY PASLEY AND MARILYN IHINGER-TALLMAN

INTRODUCTION

Americans have one of the highest marriage rates in the world and have always been a "marrying" people. A unique change has occurred, however, in that about 43% of all marriages contracted now are remarriages for one or both spouses. While remarriage is not a new phenomenon in the United States, the condition under which it now occurs is new. That is, remarriage today typically follows a divorce rather than the death of a spouse (see Ihinger-Tallman & Pasley, 1987b). As has been suggested in the literature, the process of divorce and remarriage presents families with more complicated kinship patterns and unclear rules and conventions regarding appropriate social behavior (Cherlin, 1978; Furstenberg, 1987; Pasley & Ihinger-Tallman, 1982; Visher & Visher, 1985).

Recent estimates suggest that about 50% of all first marriages will end in divorce, with about half terminating by the eighth anniversary. Furthermore, between 70 and 75% of persons who divorce will elect to marry again within a relatively short period of time (median length of time between marriages is 3.2 years); males remarry more quickly than females (Glick, 1980, 1984).[1] Evidence suggests that several factors influence the probability of remarriage, including age, employment status, education and income levels, number of children, and manner in which the prior marriage ended (death versus divorce). (See as examples Chilman, 1983; Glick, 1980, 1984; Price-Bonham & Balswick, 1980.) For example, 50% of the women who remarry following divorce can be characterized in this way: She married the first time at 22 and had one child, typically a daughter. She completed high school and worked until the birth of her child. She was not employed at the time of her divorce at age 27. She maintained a single-parent household for almost 3 years before remarrying before age 30 (Glick, 1984).

About 65% of remarriages involve children from a prior marriage, which suggests that many remarriages result in the establishment of a stepfamily (Cherlin & McCarthy, 1985; Glick, 1984). Various types of stepfamilies exist, categorized by the degree of structural complexity. Because mothers continue to be awarded custody of children about 90% of the time (Weitzman, 1981, 1985), stepfather families are the most prevalent type of residential stepfamily. Males involved in remarriages either do not have children from their prior marriage, or, when they do, the majority do not continue to have contact with them.[2]

When these men remarry, a "simple" stepfather family structure develops—one in which only the wife's children from her prior marriage are residential family members. Cherlin and McCarthy (1985) suggest that "complex" residential stepfamily structures are less common than the literature on remarriage and stepparenting suggests. A complex stepfamily structure is one in which children from both spouses (whether residential or nonresidential) are considered to be and are treated as members of the family. Estimates show that 30% of remarriages do not involve children at all. Another 49 to 56% include children from one spouse's prior marriage, and 7 to 12% include children from both prior marriages. Three percent of remarriages are the most complex stepfamily structure of all—they involve his children, her children, and children in common. It is imperative to note that the figures used to calculate the incidence of stepfamilies admittedly underrepresent the population. It has been suggested that by 1990 16% of all children under 18 years will reside within a stepfamily (Glick, 1984).

Since the majority of divorces occur early in marriage, those that involve children tend to involve children under the age of 18. Thus, estimates indicate that the average age of children at the time of parental remarriage is 2 to 5 years for about one-third of the children in remarriage. About one-sixth of the children in remarriage are 12 years or older (Norton & Glick, 1985). Because about 60% of remarriages eventually terminate and half of these do so within 5.5 years (Glick, 1980, 1984), we can conclude that both adults and children will encounter a series of changes in family structure within a brief period of time. That is, by the time a child reaches the teen years, he or she could have been part of an original, first-marriage family, then spent time in a single-parent household, resided in a stepfamily, and finally lives again in a single-parent household (Bumpass, 1984; Hill, 1986).

Glick (1984) projects that children whose parents married in 1980 and divorced sometime thereafter will experience the following changes in their family structures by the time they reach their 17th birthdays: (a) 24% of white children will be living in their second stepfamily as compared to 19% of black children; (b) 8% of white children and 5% of black children will be living with a lone father; and (c) 24% of white children and 19% of black children will be living with their mother. While many children currently live with two biological parents, this status is clearly a tenuous one for many.

The events of divorce and remarriage are touching the lives of many Americans, which may explain why it has become an increasingly important area of investigation for scholars who study the family. We have witnessed a great increase in the number of publications on these topics in the empirical, clinical, and lay literatures in the past 40 years. Reviewers of these literatures conclude that the quality of empirical investigations has improved over time, resulting in a larger body of knowledge about these family structures (Ganong & Coleman, 1987; Pasley & Ihinger-Tallman, 1985, 1987).

In this chapter, we summarize what is currently known about remarriage and stepfamily living and examine the influence of this family form on children and family relationships. We have elected to discuss the findings from the most recent research on remarrieds and stepfamilies rather than provide a comprehensive review of all studies. We selected those studies that are examples of quality research, limited primarily by the issues facing family research in general. In addition, we summarize studies that provide valuable descriptive information and that can serve as the basis for future research attempts. We conclude this chapter with a discussion of the limitations of this knowledge and the implications for future investigations.

WHAT IS KNOWN ABOUT THIS FAMILY FORM

Because of the burgeoning information on remarriage and stepfamilies and the number of fine reviews available to the reader,[3] this section will only briefly summarize the literature. However, one word of caution is in order. There are two primary literature bases, one of which is empirically based and a second that is clinically based. The findings reported in empirical studies and by clinicians about remarriage and stepfamilies differ (Ganong & Coleman, 1986, 1987). In addition, there is also variation in the research questions asked; the samples, methods, and instruments used; and the extent to which theory guides research. What we offer here is an extrapolation of the common themes from the diverse findings.

Remarried Family Life

The findings from several studies suggest that remarrieds are as happy or happier than their first-married counterparts (Albrecht, 1979; Albrecht & Bahr, 1983; Furstenberg, 1987; Hetherington, 1987; White & Booth, 1985). Although stepfamilies face unique problems and experience greater stress in daily living (see as examples Visher & Visher, 1978; Pasley & Ihinger-Tallman, 1982), they are found to have a general sense of well-being equivalent to that of first-marrieds (Weingarten, 1980, 1985). The findings from a recent longitudinal study of children (Furstenberg, 1987) found few differences between first-marrieds and remarrieds regarding their conjugal beliefs and expectations or the daily character of family life (e.g., household expectations, rules, and responsibilities). Other studies have found no differences between these groups on anxiety and worry, self-esteem, self-acceptance, or the propensity to cohabit (Pasley, 1986).

These findings should not suggest that there are no differences between first-marrieds and remarrieds. Differences between the two groups have been found on: (a) the ranking of problem areas (for remarrieds children and finances rank highest while for first-marrieds infidelity and emotional immaturity rank highest [Albrecht, 1979; Duberman, 1975; Visher & Visher, 1978]); (b) level of income (remarried women report lower overall income than women in first marriages—less than one third of remarried women receive any financial support from a prior spouse [Furstenberg, 1987]); (c) marital quality as a predictor of family adjustment (in stepfamilies the quality of the stepparent-stepchild relationship is generally a better predictor of family adjustment than is the quality of the marital relationship [Crosbie-Burnett, 1984; Clingempeel, Ievoli, & Brand, 1984]); (d) parenting competence and parenting styles (stepfathers tend to see themselves as less competent than biological fathers and less competent than either their spouse or stepchild see them), and stepparents employ a more detached parenting style [Bohannan & Yahreas, 1979; Hetherington, 1987; Anderson & White, 1986]); and (e) negative stereotypes (stepfamilies and stepfamily members are usually perceived as less positive than other family structures [Bryan et al., 1986; Coleman & Ganong, 1987]).

A recent study of 63 family triads (mother, father/stepfather, and child or mother's child) compared functional and dysfunctional first-marriage families with functional and dysfunctional stepfather families (Anderson & White, 1986). Families were placed in groups based on their Family Adjustment score on the Family Concept Test. The results indicated that functional first-marriage families and stepfather families are similar in that they both reported: (a) good marital adjustment, (b) strong, positive bonds between biological parent and child, (c) a disinclination to exclude family members, and (d) the ability to make mutually compromised family decisions. The key differences were (a) less intense interpersonal involvement between stepfather and child and (b) a stronger tendency toward the existence of parent-child coalitions in stepfamilies. Similarities between the two dysfunctional groups included stronger parent-child coalitions than found in the functional groups and lack of mutual decision-making. Interestingly, the relationship patterns in functional and dysfunctional stepfamilies were similar except that they were more extreme in dysfunctional stepfamilies.

Researchers have examined various aspects of remarriage without using first-married families as a comparison group. Instead, they have compared remarrieds without children or remarriages with children born to that remarriage in order to assess the impact of children on stepfamily adjustment. These studies provide further insights into the nature of stepfamily living. For example, findings indicate that the structural complexity of a remarried family influences marital quality and family satisfaction, with quality and satisfaction generally being less in complex family structures (Pasley & Ihinger-Tallman, 1983; Clingempeel, 1981). Further, certain "types" of remarriages show more ambiguity about who holds membership in the family, and there is less agreement about who actually resides in the household (Furstenberg, 1987; Pasley, 1987). Remarried couples who only have children born to the current union and simple stepfather families (only his spouse has children from the prior marriage) seem to share similar perceptions about family membership, and they agree about who resides in the home. Stepfamilies in which couples do not share the same perception about family memberships or the residence of family members are most commonly stepmother families and stepfamilies in which both adults are stepparents. It seems that biological fathers in stepfamilies and stepmothers tend to underreport the existence of children from a prior marriage.

Recently scholars have begun to examine racial and ethnic differences in remarriage. The primary emphasis of these investigations has been to examine differences in the rates of divorce and remarriage with some attention to demographic variables (e.g. education and income). For example, the rates of remarriage for blacks and whites indicate that although divorce is more prevalent among blacks, the remarriage rate is lower for this group (see Ihinger-Tallman & Pasley, 1987a, for a brief summary of these data).

Recently, other racial and ethnic groups have been examined. Frisbie (1986) reported the findings from a nationwide sample regarding marital instability among Mexican Americans. Although he found that Hispanics had a low prevalence of instability, there was, however, a substantial amount of variation across the racial-ethnic groups such that marital disruption is lowest among Mexican Americans, Cuban, and Anglo women and comparatively high among Puerto Rican and black women. Brodbar-Nemzer (1986) examined the relationship between divorce and religious group commitment in a large sample of Jews. He found that the preexisting level of group commitment had an effect on marital stability in that higher commitment was related to lower marital dissolution. Remarriages were also related positively to group commitment; that is, for remarried Jews (regardless of whether the remarriage followed divorce or the death of a spouse), group commitment (as measured by ritual observance and proportion of friends who are Jewish) was significantly higher than for those who were currently divorced yet lower than for those who were ever married.

The Role of the Stepparent

The nature of the stepparent role and different parenting styles has been the focus of some research. Not surprisingly, studies suggest that the stepparent role is more difficult and less clearly defined than the parental role (Duberman, 1975; Fast & Cain, 1966; Furstenberg, 1987; Giles-Sims, 1984). This generalization is supported by several research studies that found that stepfathers often feel inadequate in their role (Bohannan & Yahreas, 1979) and that they tend not to perceive mutual love or mutual respect between themselves and their stepchildren (Duberman, 1975). Stepfathers often feel inadequate in their ability to maintain close physical and/or emotional contact with their stepchildren (Weingarten, 1980).

Findings from another study of remarried adults (all biological parents or stepparents themselves) that examines the role of the stepparent suggest that stepparents are expected to be less involved in the "parenting" of their stepchildren and are given positive sanctions for less involvement (Giles-Sims, 1984). However, another study reports that biological parents tend to complain that the stepparent is inadequately involved in rearing children (Furstenberg, 1987; Furstenberg et al., 1983).

It has been suggested that the stepmother role is a more difficult one than that of stepfather. The findings from some studies suggest that stepmothers emit more negative behaviors toward their stepchildren than do stepfathers (Clingempeel, Ievoli, & Brand, 1984; Clingempeel, Brand, & Segal, 1987; Hetherington, 1987; Santrock & Sitterle, 1987). Stepchildren raised in stepmother families show significantly more negative behaviors, for example inappropriate school behavior, truancy, delinquency, and acting out, than those raised in stepfather families (Furstenberg, 1987; Peterson & Zill, 1986). Stepmothers have been found to exhibit higher levels of stress and greater dissatisfaction with their role than either biological mothers, fathers, or stepfathers (Ahrons & Wallisch, 1987; Nadler, 1976). Adams (1982) found that having all female stepchildren was the best predictor of discontentment and dissatisfaction among stepmothers, regardless of whether the children were residential or nonresidential.

Recent research using small, select samples suggests that stepparents tend to use a parenting style characterized as detached and distant (Hetherington, 1987). This research corroborates the findings from Giles-Sims (1984) about expectations and sanctions for less involvement. It has been suggested by clinicians that such detached parenting behaviors are essential for improved relationships between stepparent and stepchild, especially during the early years of remarriage (Stern, 1978; Mills, 1984). Findings from a study by Hetherington (1987) identifying the parenting styles of stepparents support this contention, especially where stepfathers are concerned. She found that stepfathers who were detached or authoritative in their parenting style had fewer negative encounters with their stepchildren and their relationships improved over time, while stepfathers who used permissive or authoritarian styles[4] had stepchildren who exhibited negative behaviors that continued over time. The same did not hold true for stepmother families. Regardless of the parenting style of the stepmother, positive stepmother-stepchild relationships did not develop over time—a finding particularly strong for stepmother-stepdaughter relationships.

Custody Issues Following Remarriage

Recently several studies reported on custody issues that follow the remarriage of spouses. Giles-Sims (1985) examined changes in child custody (not necessarily legal custody) of a small sample of stepfamilies ($n = 14$). Paternal custody (residential change) occurred either at the time of divorce or sometime following the remarriage of one or both parents. Giles-Sims identifed five circumstances that led to paternal custody of the children: (1) father obtained custody at divorce, (2) overstressed mother relinquished custody, (3) neither parent wanted the responsibility, (4) children could not get along with the mother, and (5) children sought residence with the father. Giles-Sims describes the characteristics of these various types of custody shifts and suggests that types 1, 2, and 3 tend to occur under the following circumstances: when the child is preteen, when there is moderate to high conflict between ex-spouses, when the children's relationship with their mother is either "mixed" or poor, and when the parent desires the change. In types 4 and 5 the child initiates the change in residence. In these cases the children were at least 12 years of age, the conflict between former spouses was moderate to low, and the change often resulted in positive effects on the integration of the stepfamily with which the child began to reside.

Ihinger-Tallman (1985) reports similar findings from a small exploratory study of stepsibling perception of custody changes in their families. She conducted in-depth interviews with 12 college-aged children raised in stepfamilies in which they lived with at least one stepsibling. Several of her case studies involved a legal change in custody from maternal to paternal custody, and more than a few of these children did not welcome the change, particularly female children who changed residence from their mother's to their stepmother's home. Her interviewees commented that their stepsibling relationship both before and after custody shifts were influenced by perceived differences in treatment of the children in the stepfamily by parents and stepparents. Differential treatment sometimes negatively and sometimes positively influenced the relationships between stepsiblings.

In a sample of 87 mother-stepfather households with adolescent children Crosbie-Burnett (1985) examined parental participation in decision-making concerning the child after divorce and remarriage, financial support of the child, visitation, and the quality of the step relationship on stepfamily adjustment. She found that joint custody was associated with more involvement by the father when involvement was measured in terms of decision making and visitation but not for financial support. This finding held regardless of the father's current marital status. Stepfathers who had no biological children but whose wives had joint custody of their children from a prior marriage were found to make the lowest financial contribution to their stepchildren. Those stepfathers with no biological children and whose wife had sole custody of her children from the prior marriage made the greatest financial contribution to their stepchildren. Mothers also reported that stepfathers contributed more when they had no biological children, although significant differences between custody statuses were not found. These findings suggest that custody alone may be less influential than the parenting status of the stepfather. Finally, the findings from this study suggest that joint custody may inhibit quality step relationships. That is, step relations may be better when the stepfather does not have biological children and worse when there is joint custody between ex-spouses. These findings were even more pronounced when the stepchildren were older adolescents.

Admittedly the findings on custody shifts and the influence of custody arrangements on stepfamily integration reported here are derived from small, select samples. While such samples limit our ability to generalize findings to the larger remarried population, their findings offer us new ideas for investigation. For example, the typology that Giles-Sims (1985) offers regarding custody change stimulates a variety of research questions. Are there other reasons that parents or children use to initiate change in residence? Are there other conditions under which such changes are made, who initiates them, and what is the outcome for the remarried couples? While Ihinger-Tallman (1985) suggests that differential treatment of stepsiblings influences their relationship negatively, several questions arise: Are there areas in which differential treatment is beneficial to the quality of the stepsibling relationship and to overall stepfamily adjustment? In what ways is differential treatment demonstrated? What strategies do stepsiblings use to cope with perceived injustice?

Relationships with Ex-spouse and Kin

Research on the relationship between ex-spouses following the remarriage of one or both suggests that between 50 and 75% of noncustodial parents (usually the father) do not continue to see their children by 5 years postdivorce (Furstenberg, 1983, 1987; Jacobson, 1987). Furstenberg believes that the co-parenting relationship occurs in fewer families than might be expected, and even then he suggests that what tends to occur in divorced families is parallel parenting relationships in which there is little, if any, meaningful joint decision making between former spouses regarding childrearing issues. Furstenberg (1983) reports that the typical pattern of a noncustodial parent's relationship with his or her child when contact with that child is maintained is a relationship characterized as primarily recreational. The custodial parent, on the other hand, has primary responsibility for general care and decisions that revolve around the needs of the child.

One longitudinal study of children who continue to have contact with both parents following divorce and remarriage reports a high degree of contact. Jacobson (1987) found that noncustodial fathers saw their children on the average of between 27 and 41 hours per 2-week period. A child's time spent with the nonresidential parent, however, varied depending on the family structure of each parent. For example, in cases in which children lived with a remarried father and visited a single mother, the children spent an average of 27 hours during a 2-week period with the mother. However, if the children lived with a remarried mother and visited a single father, the average time spent with the father during a 2-week period averaged 32 hours. If the child lived with a single mother and visited a remarried father, the time spent with the father during the same period averaged 36 hours. The most time spent with a nonresidential parent was 41 hours; this occurred in "linked" families in which both parents had remarried. These findings might suggest that a remarried father may believe he can offer his children a more stable or "normal" environment and, therefore, maintains greater contact with his children. Or he may feel more supported by his new wife to regain and maintain regular contact with his children. She may in fact prompt his continued contact with comments regarding his "rights" to his children, thus empowering him as a father.

Estimates at the national level suggest that few fathers pay child support consistently following divorce (Weitzman, 1985). In a study of 101 divorced men, Troph (1984) found that voluntary support increased following the remarriage of the father and decreased following the remarriage of the mother. Further, he found that many biological fathers expect a new stepfather to assume financial responsibility for the biological father's children. The study by Crosbie-Burnett (1985) reported earlier suggests also that joint custody of children from their prior marriage may inhibit the willingness of the stepfather to assume financial responsibility for his stepchildren.

Recently Bowman and Ahrons (1985) reported the results from a study that compared the parenting one year after divorce of 28 joint-custody fathers and 54 noncustodial fathers. They found joint-custody fathers to be more involved on two indicators: contact and activities with the children, and shared responsibility and decision making. Moreover, the researchers examined the ability of a series of variables, of which remarriage was one, to predict father-child contact, parental involvement, and parental interaction. Examples of these variables included income, job, age of youngest child, education, number of children, attachment to ex-spouse, quality of co-parental communication, and degree of guilt regarding divorce. Only custody status had a statistically significant effect on parental involvement.

Some research has examined the nature of the relationship between former spouses in light of a remarriage of one or both of them. Although much of the writing implies that the relationship between former spouses is characterized by conflict, little empirical evidence supports such allegations. For example, Furstenberg (1983) found that this relationship was not generally characterized by high levels of conflict. Ahrons and Wallisch (1987) found that for their small sample the contact between former spouses decreased when the father remarried but not when the mother remarried.

Further, recent research suggests that relationships between same-sex biological parents and stepparents are characterized by detachment or ambivalence. Ahrons and Wallisch (1987) suggest that the relationships between mother and stepmother and father and stepfather are generally characterized by distant, detached feelings rather than hostile ones. They also found that the relationship between mother and stepmother was usually a more difficult one than between father and stepfather, with women reporting more differences of opinion and less satisfaction with their interactions. These findings suggest that women, whether they are biological mothers or stepmothers, may be more invested in the parenting role and thus may be more critical of their same-sex counterparts.

Few have investigated the influence of remarriage on other kin such as grandparents. Furstenberg and associates (1983) report that 80% of parents in a national study of children indicated that the grandparents had no difficulty accepting stepchildren as grandchildren. In fact, findings suggest that contact with stepgrandparents is as frequent as it is with grandparents and that grandparents are likely to shower attention on their new stepgrandchildren (Furstenberg & Spanier, 1984). At the same time Cherlin and Furstenberg (1986) suggest that grandparents usually see their relationship with stepgrandchildren as "emotionally thin"; they believe that their interaction and "acceptance" of the stepgrandchildren help to maintain their tie to their own adult children, which may be a primary motivation for their frequent contact with stepgrandchildren.

Little research has focused on the nature of the interaction between remarrieds and the broader community. Pasley and Ihinger-Tallman (1983) examined the reported use of "inner" and "outer" core support systems. They found that remarrieds tended to report more frequent contact with inner core support systems (e.g., friends, relatives) than outer core support systems (e.g., schools, social service agencies, the legal system), a finding that is reported for other samples as well. The use of the two different categories of support systems was influenced by the structural complexity of the remarried family, with more complex remarried families (e.g., with resident children who are his and hers or his, hers, and "theirs") using more outer core support systems than childless remarried couples or those remarrieds whose children are joint (in common) biological children.

Recently Ihinger-Tallman and Pasley (1986) examined the relationship between several social characteristics of remarried persons and community integration. The findings from this study of 784 remarried husbands and wives suggest that age, education level, and presence of children are correlated with greater community involvement. That is, younger, more highly educated husbands and wives and remarriages with children tended to be more connected within the community. Further, in comparing differences between remarrieds whose marriage represented a remarriage for one of the spouses and a first marriage for the other and remarrieds whose marriage was a remarriage for both spouses, the latter were not significantly less connected to an extended kin network.

Effects of Remarriage on Children

Ganong and Coleman (1984) provide a thorough review of the available literature on the effects of remarriage on children. This review suggests that on the average few differences exist between children reared in stepfamilies and those reared in first-marriage families when the following characteristics are measured: psychological functioning (e.g., self-sufficiency, dominance, psychosomatic complaints, self-esteem, self-acceptance, and well-being), behavioral measures (e.g., church attendance, delinquent behavior, delinquent companionship, crime involvement, drug use, number of days absent from school), cognitive measures (e.g., school grades, academic achievement, field dependence, I.Q. scores), social measures (e.g., relationships with friends, school and community activities, social adaptation), and general mental health (e.g., positive attitudes toward parents, school attitude, attitude toward marital roles). Differences have been reported on measures of overall adjustment (using instruments to measure general psychological well-being), although family structure alone is an inadequate predictor of adjustment. Also, significant differences have been reported regarding feelings of closeness to parent/stepparent (i.e., stepchildren usually do not feel close to their stepparent, they tend to perceive more rejection and discrimination from their stepparent, and they do not aspire to be like their stepparent).

The findings from a recent study using a national sample of children (Peterson & Zill, 1986) suggest that having a stepparent, particularly if the stepchild is male, ameliorates the negative outcomes of divorce (i.e., depression/withdrawal, antisocial behavior, and impulsive/hyperactive behavior). That is, the measured level of depression and withdrawal tends to decrease with the remarriage of the mother for both male and female children. Also, while antisocial behavior decreases for male children following parental remarriage, such is not the case for female children in stepfamilies.

Research studies on the effects of remarriage on children that do not include comparative data on children from first-marriage families offer additional information regarding the nature of remarried family life. For example, the responses of 103 adolescents residing in stepfather and stepmother families suggest that many experience loyalty conflicts that they define as stressful (Lutz, 1983). While the clinical literature consistently suggests that loyalty conflicts are problematic in stepfamilies, this was the first study to attempt to empirically test this clinical impression.

Another study of 63 adolescents examined stressful aspects of stepfamily life and reported discipline to be the most stressful, more so than other areas measured such as pseudomutuality, unrealistic expectations, or parental/stepparental understanding of the adolescent's feelings about the stepfamily (Strothers & Jacobs, 1984). Some clinical literature also suggests that adolescents have a more difficult time adjusting to parental remarriage than do younger children (Visher & Visher, 1979).

The frequency of contact between a stepchild and his or her nonresidential parent influences the quality of the relationship with the stepparent, particularly the stepmother. That is, it has been reported that frequency of contact with the noncustodial biological mother tends to negatively influence the quality of interaction between the stepmother and child (Clingempeel & Segal, 1986; Furstenberg, 1987). Also, the quality of the stepparent-stepchild relationship may be the best indicator of child outcomes (e.g., antisocial behavior, depression, aggressive behavior). For example, in a study of 40 stepfather and 20 stepmother families with a 9- to 12-year-old target child, Clingempeel and Segal (1986) found that positive stepparent-child relationships (as measured by scores derived from a modified version of Schaefer and Finkelskin's [1975] inventory with love-hostility and detachment dimensions) were associated with lower inhibition and aggression ratings for male and female stepchildren and with higher self-esteem scores for females. Inhibition, aggression, and self-esteem were measured with reliable instruments where national norms had been established.

One finding that appears consistently in the recent literature suggests that residential stepmother families, particularly those with female children, may be at greater risk of dissolution than other stepfamilies (residential stepfather, nonresidential stepmother, and stepfather families) and may foster more negative outcomes for children. Jacobson (1987) reports that while on the average children in stepfamilies were not significantly different in their adjustment level than children in first-marriage families, children in stepmother families reported higher degrees of stress. Further, several studies found the interaction between stepdaughters and stepparents to be more negative than the interaction between stepsons and stepparents. This was particularly true when examining the child's behavior toward the adult, and, in the case of the stepmother, her behavior toward the child. This contrasts to more positive interaction between stepsons and both stepfathers and stepmothers (Clingemepeel, Ievoli, & Brand, 1985; Clingempeel & Segal, 1986; Furstenberg, 1987; Hetherington, 1987; Santrock & Sitterle, 1987).

The results are contradictory regarding changes in negative outcomes over time. That is, while Furstenberg (1987) suggests that they tend not to dissipate over time, particularly for females in stepmother families, Clingempeel and Segal (1986) found that the longer stepdaughters lived in a biological father-stepmother household, the more positive stepmother-stepdaughter relationships tended to be and the lower the stepdaughters' aggression (measured on infantile aggression, hyperactivity, and antisocial behavior scales) and inhibition (measured on social withdrawal, sensitivity, and fear scales).

CONTINUING CONCERNS AND ISSUES IN RESEARCH

Research on remarriage and stepparenting has made major advancements in the last 5 years, with an increased commitment on the part of scholars to incorporate theory into their research. We are beginning to move beyond what has been called the "deficit model" approach (Marotz-Baden et al., 1979) to the study of nonnuclear families (Ganong & Coleman, 1987). That is, researchers are no longer implying that differences in outcomes from distinct types of families are attributable to family structure alone. Instead, we are seeing the application of other perspectives in an attempt to explain the findings from research studies. For example, Clingempeel, Brand, & Segal (1987) have incorporated both Brofenbrenner's (1979) ecological framework with Hill and Rodgers (1964) family development conceptualization to identify voids in current research.[5] Similarly, Ihinger-Tallman (1987) has used the ecological framework to conceptualize stepsibling bonding and to develop propositions for future investigation. Still other examples of the use of existing theory include the work by Giles-Sims' (1987) using exchange theory to examine mate selection and power in remarriage and Roberts's (1980) use of role theory to examine the stepparent role. Others have extrapolated research propositions from psychology, sociology, and social psychology[6] (e.g., Ihinger-Tallman, 1984, 1986; Rodgers, 1983).

The issues that plague research on remarriage and stepparenting also pertain to the study of the family in general. While much of the remarriage research to date has used small, white, middle-class samples, self-report methods, and single-source data (e.g., information is obtained from only one member in a stepfamily), changes are evident in current studies. A growing number of studies on this topic have obtained data from large, random samples, collected from more than one source, and used a combination of data-gathering techniques such as questionnaire, interview, and observation.

While the quality of research on remarriage is improving, the

involved in adjusting to remarriage and stepfamily life. Too, the quality of research demonstrates a commitment on the part of investigators to eliminate the weaknesses and attend to the methodological complications that accompany the investigation of complex family structures resulting from divorce and remarriage.

While the two primary bodies of literature (clinical and empirical) offer somewhat conflicting pictures of stepfamily life (Ganong & Coleman, 1986, 1987), it has been suggested that there is much that these two groups can learn from one another. Clearly, both groups of professionals can and will profit from ongoing dialogue. (See as an example the following chapter by Visher and Visher.)

NOTES

1. Estimates suggest that 60% of the children born in the 1980s will live for a portion of their childhood in a single-parent household (mean length of 5 years) at two different time intervals and that 35% of these children will reside in a stepfamily sometime before their 18th birthday (Glick, 1984; Norton & Glick, 1986).

2. See as examples the findings from Hetherington (1987), Furstenberg (1987), Furstenberg and associates (1983), and Jacobson (1987).

3. See as examples those literature reviews by Chilman (1983); Clingempeel, Brand, and Segal (1987); Ganong and Coleman (1984); Macklin (1980); Pasley (1985); and Price-Bonham and Balswick (1980).

4. Editor's note: It is appropriate here to clarify the difference between authoritarian and authoritative styles of parenting. The term "authoritarian" implies a dominating, undemocratic style of behavior, whereas "authoritative" implies a self-confident parent behavior in which the parent recognizes that she or he knows more about what children need and how they should behave than children know themselves.

5. Editor's note: An ecological framework for this research would include attention given to the impact of factors in the environment on the effects of various stepfamily forms; a family development framework would include measurement of stepfamily functioning at differing stages of the family development cycle.

6. Editor's note: Exchange theory would include measurement of the perceived costs and benefits of various stepfamily forms as seen by the adults and children involved.

12

Treating Families with Problems Associated with Remarriage and Step Relationships

EMILY B. VISHER AND JOHN S. VISHER

"We need someone who knows about stepfamilies to help us because our present therapist keeps trying to make us fit a nuclear family model, and it isn't working."

—upset stepmother to family doctor

Stepfamilies differ from biological families in many significant ways. Because of this it is important that therapists become knowledgeable about the differences and familiar with present information on ways to be helpful to stepfamilies seeking therapeutic assistance.

In the stepfamily therapy literature, aside from expected variations in therapeutic techniques used by individual therapists, we have noticed two major areas in which theoretical differences appear to exist: (a) the classification of problem areas for stepfamilies, and (b) the question of whom to see in therapy.

Isaacs (1982) states that stepfamilies get stuck in their development primarily because of the following:

1. A family acts like an instant family; the space of the absent parent is invaded, forced blending occurs, and the new woman takes over parental functions for the father.
2. An adversarial relationship between the new partner and the child's other parent is established.
3. The family hierarchy is reversed, with the new partner lower in the hierarchy than the child.

Following from this framework, Isaacs sees "turf" as the therapeutic focus. Isaacs (1986) sees the adults first. During the initial assessment stage she meets with the couple together and then individually. If the adults are focused on child problems and an agreement is made to proceed with therapy, the children are then seen to assess the situation from their point of view. Other suprafamily individuals are added later if appropriate.

Wald (1981) sees the fundamental goal of therapy with stepfamilies as that of assisting them with their task of "blending and becoming" so that they "will learn to perceive the remarried family as different from the idealized nuclear family, but nevertheless as a 'real' family that has dignity, worth, and value in its own right." (p. 193). She conceptualizes her thinking in a schema that includes the structural, legal, cultural, and developmental characteristics of the stepfamily together with a "Problem-Process Profile" (p. 178) that focuses first on who is involved (the locus of the difficulty) and second on the content of the problem. Determination of the locus indicates whom to see in the therapeutic sessions, while the type of difficulty suggests the content of the therapy.

Wald (1981) summarizes problems as follows:

I. Environmental Problems
   Space Time Money
II. Individual Adjustment Problems
   Reactive emotional responses and behavior Self-esteem School
III. Intrafamilial-Interpersonal Adjustment Problems
   Adoption of prior lifestyles Establishing an identity and becoming a family unit Roles Bonding
IV. Interfamilial Problems
   Extended family Absent parent

Another formulation is given by Sager and colleagues (1983), who dedicated their book "to the courageous families who worked with us to fulfill individual, marital, and family life-cycle needs." To them the focus is on conflicts generated by the necessity of operating on "multiple tracks" as they deal with incongruent individual, marital, and family life cycles. A major issue for the adults is a loyalty conflict between love for one's child and love for one's new partner. For the children there are also loyalty issues, the pressure of relating to stepsiblings, and sometimes a change in ordinal position in the family. When the problem is viewed as a couple issue, the couple is seen in therapy. If, however, a child is presented as having the problem, an attempt is made to involve all the individuals "connected" to the child.

The focus for Sager and associates is on the "suprafamily system," made up of functionally related subsystems; for example, marital couple, former spouse and new partner, children, aunts, uncles, grandparents. While the Sager team remains flexible, its goal is to work initially with all the relevant members of the suprasystem, seeing important subgroups later as seems advisable. They point out that it is difficult to include new people later after forming a therapeutic relationship with those seen initially. Therefore, the clinic devotes much telephone or personal interview time to the contact person in an attempt to persuade the initial caller to invite those involved in the suprasystem to meet together and explore their perceptions of the situation. If the initial contact person is unsuccessful in obtaining the cooperation of the group, the therapist asks permission to call the other members directly. The therapist meets with those willing to come, even if some suprasystem members refuse to participate.

THE SEARCH FOR FAMILY IDENTITY

As we conceptualize it, the basic struggle for a stepfamily is the search for its identity as a family unit. This is an emotionally charged task, not only because of the overwhelming number of possible interactions between the people that make up the stepfamily suprasystem but also because of conflicting internal and external pulls and continual shifts in the configuration of the household (Visher & Visher, 1978, 1979). From this foundation it follows then that the basic therapeutic task becomes one of validation of the stepfamily unit and helping with the steps that are necessary for the family to attain an acceptable and comfortable identity.

There are many factors, both internal and external, that can assist or hamper the integration process. A major external force is the interface between society and stepfamilies, a force that is not generally positive. While external pulls do not usually lead stepfamilies to seek therapeutic help, they do directly affect the basic sense of "family selfhood" experienced by members of the stepfamily. There is a sense of discomfort, because at the same time that stepfamilies are working to validate their type of family, society tends to ignore the differences between stepfamilies and first-marriage families.

Although such negative societal interactions are upsetting, what sends stepfamilies to therapists for help is the debilitating effect of a myriad of internal pulls, each of which can pose a threat to the security of one or more subgroup or suprasystem members. When working to help stepfamilies in their search for a satisfactory adjustment and sense of adequacy, the major factors for us to consider are: (a) presenting difficulties and which subgroups appear to be most affected; (b) whom to include initially in the therapy sessions based on the particular stage of stepfamily development the family has reached, as defined by Papernow (1984); and (c) individual stepfamily characteristics such as family constellation, custody agreements, age of children, and length of remarriage.

AREAS OF THERAPEUTIC CONCERN

As with all families, the difficulties encountered by stepfamilies are varied and interrelated. We feel, however, that it is helpful to organize the major stepfamily difficulties into eight general areas that occupy the majority of time and attention of stepfamily members. These eight problem areas are discussed in detail in the following sections.

Change and Loss

Stepfamilies are formed after a loss due to death or divorce. First-marriage dreams no longer exist for the adults whose marriages have ended in divorce nor for those who have never been married before and did not expect to marry a person with a former spouse and three children. Children and parents have frequently lost contact, as have grandparents and grandchildren.

Any change involves losses as well as gains, and for stepfamily individuals there are many changes. Children may be leaving their schools and friends, moving to new neighborhoods, sharing rooms, becoming middle rather than only children, or leaving a sibling in their other household. Adults may have moved, changed jobs, relinquished activities and associates formerly enjoyed, sold cherished furniture and possessions, and given up their freedom from responsibility for daily contact and concern with children or stepchildren.

Often those involved with these changes have not acknowledged their losses or sadness. The adults interpret their children's depression as a failure to accept their new situation rather than the need to work through feelings connected with the changes. With help a family can disengage psychologically from the past and move toward an appreciation of the present. For children the working through is usually a much longer and more involved process than for the adults. As they go back and forth between households, there are reminders of the past, so to be able to accept the present situation children need to be allowed to retain memories of the past. Contrary to public opinion, children can accept a stepparent more readily when they are not asked to give up contact with the biological parent of the same sex (Crosbie-Burnett, 1984).

The following paragraphs give two case examples illustrating the need to work out difficulties of change and loss.

When she married, Marie gave up her job as chief librarian of a public library so that she could care for her two stepchildren, aged 9 and 11. Marie cooked and cleaned and turned herself into a tour director for the children and their friends. Her husband beamed with satisfaction, but the children did not respond appreciatively. Within 3 months Marie was angry and resentful, and the couple's relationship was becoming strained. Marie had traded the appreciation and satisfactions of her work at the library for a life with little satisfaction and appreciation for her stepmother role. With the help of a therapist, she decided to return to work and share the homemaking tasks with her husband. Her need for approval from her stepchildren lessened, and the couple relationship developed more positively.

In another situation, Derek's parents had divorced when he was 2. Derek spent equal time in each household, both before and after each of his parents had remarried. When Derek became 6 a major difficulty arose over a decision about which of two schools he should attend. Each parent feared loss of time with the child, and for the first time they began to fight and talked of going into court and letting a judge decide. At this point Derek's mother telephoned a therapist. With her permission the therapist then called Derek's father, who was also willing to talk with the therapist.

Derek's mother and stepfather were seen together once, and Derek's father and stepmother were seen on another occasion. Then all four came together for two appointments. The therapist helped the adults talk about their love for Derek and their sense of impending loss. Between the first and second sessions the couples decided between themselves that Derek was to enter the school in his mother and stepfather's neighborhood. During the second session the adults worked on the details and accepted the father and stepmother's need to have something special for Derek at their house. Baseball with the Little League team in his father and stepmother's location was suggested as an alternative activity, and the stepparents as well as the two parents reaffirmed their interest in maintaining an active parenting role with Derek.

As seen in the preceding examples, a therapist's acknowledgment of losses, acceptance of the related feelings, and eventual validation of the existing situation can be most valuable. These adults in Derek's case were faced with the necessity of giving up some of the closeness they all had enjoyed with him during the preschool years. If Derek had been having difficulty going from one household to the other or was 16 years old instead of 6, it could have been important to include him in the discussions. As it was, a decision was made to deal exclusively with the four parenting adults, since they were the ones who needed to make the final decisions and Derek had no investment in which school he attended since friends in his private nursery school were from a wide geographic area.

Unrealistic Belief Systems

There are many unrealistic expectations about stepfamilies because our concept of family is predicated on our image of the traditional nuclear family. As a result, adults attempt to fit their own stepfamilies into a nuclear family mold. They may believe that close step relationships will form immediately, that children ought to call a stepparent Mom or Dad, that the children's contact with the other household is upsetting and suspect, or that a stepparent can function immediately as a parent in the household. The negative effects of such unrealistic beliefs are apparent in the following case example.

Ginger became distraught and sought therapy because of her relationship with a 12-year-old stepdaughter, Jill. Ginger and her husband Bob had a total of three children from a previous marriage, but the two younger children were quite young and had fit rather quickly into the new household where they lived with Ginger and Bob. Jill, however, was refusing to relate warmly with her stepmother. When Ginger came for help, she was angry about an article she had read that said there were fundamental differences between nuclear families and stepfamilies. When the therapist asked her to describe her "ideal" family, Ginger talked about her aunt's family, which she had known quite well when she was a child. Her first-marriage family had not replicated her ideal family, and "I'm determined this one will."

In therapy Ginger began slowly to accept a new reality. She experienced a week of sadness and tears as she gave up her old beliefs about stepfamilies and began to embrace new and more realistic ideas about stepfamily dynamics and structure. As Ginger relaxed and stopped pushing Jill to relate, to her surprise Jill began to approach her. In time the family moved much closer to the family of Ginger's dreams, even though retaining its stepfamily characteristics.

Education about stepfamily structure and dynamics can sometimes do much to shift unrealistic beliefs, but when this is met with resistance, even a tacit recognition by the therapist of the difficulty inherent in stepfamily integration will often produce relaxation and increased feelings of self-esteem. This in turn paves the way for a gradual shift toward realistic expectations. In Ginger's case as her frustration was accepted by the therapist and her hopes for the family explored, she began to recognize the validity of the article she had read. Her tears gave way to acceptance. She "backed off" from Jill, and soon important and satisfying changes took place.

From the children's point of view, when they are young they often do not have a clear conception of what a family is; when they are older they become aware that nuclear families and stepfamilies are not the same. Unfortunately, the conflicting, confusing messages they often receive are that it is not acceptable *not* to love their stepparent, or to love their stepparent, or to be angry at one or both of their parents. Reassurance that these are realistic and expectable reactions to their situation is, of course, supportive.

Outsiders and Insiders

When a stepfamily begins, there are both outsiders and insiders. A stepparent without children who joins a parent with children, a 14-year-old girl who comes to live with her father and stepmother after they have been married for 5 years, or a mother and her two children who move into her new husband's former home are all outsiders in the family system, and outsider status can give rise to difficulties.

For example, Betty called because she was growing increasingly unhappy with her 2-year-old marriage to Paul, who was the father of three young children. He spent several hours each week talking to the children's mother in person or on the telephone, and Betty was feeling totally outside the family circle. Paul was willing to come with her for a first appointment. Paul said that he did not wish to have Betty accompany him when he picked up his children or went to their school events. He was afraid to take his new wife and children to places where his former wife might see them.

Paul and Betty were seen individually several times and then together for a few more sessions. During their individual appointments Betty began to consider that her feelings of alienation were valid and that changes were in order. Paul, however, needed time alone to deal with his anger about all the pressures he was feeling before he showed any willingness to explore his reactions. When they again came together, Betty was clear about her needs, and Paul shared his fear that the children would experience the same feelings he had when he was 15 and his parents divorced. Together they looked at their present situation and agreed to make changes slowly. Betty began to feel that she was a part of the unit, and both were surprised that positive rather than the negative repercussions Paul had anticipated began to reverberate through the larger family system.

Power Issues

Power has been defined as the ability to implement one's decisions, and the distribution and sharing of power is an important aspect of any family. The picture that emerges from a careful study of healthy families is one in which the couple is in control of the household and the children have input (with the amount increasing as they mature) into the way the family operates. The relationships with the children's grandparents are important ones, but the grandparents do not interfere in the household (Lewis et al, 1976).

Within a stepfamily the issue of power or control is very complex and often disturbing (Isaacs, 1982; Lutz, 1983; Visher & Visher, 1978, 1979). Legally stepparents have little power, and psychologically they usually never achieve the same position with the children as that occupied by the parent. The relative power hierarchy of adults in the suprasystem vis-à-vis the children is in general the following:

1. Custodial parent
2. Noncustodial parent
3. Spouse of custodial parent
4. Spouse of noncustodial parent.

Joint custody situations are more complex. The power hierarchy will also depend on specific elements such as personal factors, living arrangements, and age of children. The order given appears to be the most common one, both legally and psychologically.

In any household situations arise in which children are more powerful than the adults. In stepfamilies the structure allows more opportunity for this to happen, because the parent/child relationship precedes the new couple relationship; also, parents fear the loss of the parent/child relationship. Another power variation for stepfamilies is that having a nonresident parent creates a very different external power structure. The family system is influenced by a powerful person who is outside the household.

A sense of helplessness, which is often realistic, pervades many stepfamily households—a 12-year-old cannot be with both parents at once; a mother and stepfather cannot control the time when her children are returned to their household by their father; a new stepfather has little power asking stepchildren to obey the house rules unless they want to please him; a father and stepmother are helpless when his former wife refuses to let the children visit with them.

Individuals react strongly to feeling helplessness, often in unproductive ways. Therapists can help individuals accept and deal constructively with situations in which they have little control by helping adults to take control of their own households and share power with the children's other household, helping children gain a sense of personal mastery over things they can control, helping remarried parents share and delegate power to their new partners, and helping the suprafamily system work toward an effective balance of power.

Unlike biological families in which nurturing precedes limit setting and both parents theoretically have equal power, stepparents enter a family system in which nurturing and limit setting are needed immediately and yet in which they are not in a position of authority with the children. As mentioned in the previous chapter, research has indicated that a stepparent needs to form a relationship with a stepchild before taking on the role of an "enforcer" of disciplinary rules (Hetherington, 1984; Stern, 1978). While the couple needs to work together from the first on household rules and priorities (input into these decisions by the children can be extremely beneficial), the parents may need help in remaining or in becoming active with his or her children while supporting the stepparent in a *gradual* assumption of the enforcing role. Stern found that it takes an average of one-and-a-half to two years for a stepfather to attain a comanagement position with his spouse.

With older stepchildren a limit-setting function may not be a productive role expectation for a stepparent (Mills, 1984). When a stepparent must care for stepchildren in the absence of the parent, all family members need to hear a clear delegation of authority by the parent: The stepparent will be in charge in the parent's absence. However, specific situations that arise between stepchild and stepparent involving their personal relationship or possessions are best resolved without a third person's intervening. For example, when Sally borrows her stepmother's sweater without asking, the matter needs to be resolved between Sally and her stepmother. The parent needs to stay out of the middle.

Loyalty Conflicts

Children with two households are placed in the untenable position if the adults use them as spies, pawns, or messengers or attempt to influence their loyalty by saying hurtful things about the child's other parent. As one teenager said, "You love both of your parents, and you don't want to hurt them, and there's nothing you can do." Lutz (1983) has shown that teenagers experience the highest degree of stress in such situations.

Even when parents behave civilly toward each other, it is difficult not to fear a loss of children to the other household. As a result, children feel the tension and are caught in a loyalty bind. They often feel they are being disloyal to a parent if they care about the stepparent of the same sex as their parent. The greater the potential for caring between stepparent and stepchild, the more the stepchild may push the stepparent away in an attempt to reduce this sense of guilt and disloyalty. These feelings are particularly strong if the child believes that the stepparent is attempting to displace or to replace the other parent. Helping the adults and children realize that "there is enough love to go around," as one stepmother said, can reduce the tension and bring about a relaxation on the part of all concerned.

Another source of conflict is the guilt that is felt by the parent who has remarried. He or she often feels guilty that the children have been upset by the death or the divorce and wishes to shield the children from further hurt. To form a close relationship with a new spouse may seem a betrayal of the remarried parent's relationship with the children, so that in remaining "loyal" to the children, the parent does not adequately support the stepparent. In actuality, the long-term needs of the children are not being met by a failure of the adults' relationship. If the couple does not stay together, the children may face another disruption of their household. In addition, the children will be deprived of the experience of knowing a functioning couple that acts as a model for their own future relationships. The importance of resolving loyalty conflicts is demonstrated in the following case example.

Helen sought therapy for herself and her husband, Philip, because she continually observed that her feelings were trampled on by her stepdaughter, Julie. Philip was fearful that he would lose his daughter's affection, and he felt guilty if he said "no" to her. As a result, for instance, if Helen wanted a weekend vacation with her husband and Julie said she wanted to come along, Philip would disregard his wife's wishes and tell Julie that she could come too.

The couple had not yet reached the stage at which they could work together on restructuring the family. The therapist saw the couple, at times together and at other times separately. Slowly Philip began to see the advantages to his daughter of seeing him and his wife as a couple who could work together. He also realized that his fear of loss of relationship with his daughter was pushing him to try to placate Julie in ways that were unproductive for Julie and damaging to his marital relationship. Through therapy Helen was able to give up her unrealistic demands, which arose from insecurity about her relationship with Philip. Both became better able to listen and empathize with one another, so that eventually they were able to work together in therapy to meet their own needs. Several sessions with all three gave them the opportunity to understand Julie's needs as well. The household tension diminished markedly, and Philip's guilt and loyalty conflicts subsided to the point where he could ordinarily control himself before acting in an unproductive and disruptive manner. Julie and Helen became more tolerant of one another's needs, and they decided they could work out future situations with the help of a mutual support group for stepfamilies in their area.

Boundary Problems

Developing appropriate subsystem and household boundaries is a difficult task for most stepfamilies. Disengaging from former marital subsystems and forming a boundary around the new couple and around the new household can cause difficulties. Keshet (1980) states, "The stepfamily will always have strongly bounded subsystems to which members remain loyal. The realities of the children's visitation schedules and the existence of the ex-spouses make this inevitable" (p. 530).

For example, Ellen and George sought help when George's former wife Darlene returned after a 3-year absence and wished to again parent the three children who lived with their father and stepmother. Ellen and George had purchased a home of their own. However, when Darlene picked up the children for a visit, she might walk into the house, use the telephone and the bathroom, and take a soft drink from the refrigerator. Ellen was distraught about this behavior, and George felt confused as to whether they had a right to speak to his ex-wife about using their home in this manner.

The couple felt invaded by Darlene. There was no sense of privacy or a space over which they had control. George and Ellen did need to work with Darlene in planning for the children, and the household boundaries, therefore, needed to be "permeable" (Messinger, 1976) so that the children could move easily from one household to the other. However, it was important for there to be a psychological boundary around their household. With therapeutic help George and Ellen took control of the situation and worked out an arrangement with the children so that they would be ready to leave when their mother came for them. In this way the transition period was more structured, and Darlene no longer had a convenient opportunity to leave her car and walk into their home. A clear boundary was established. As a result, it became easier for the adults in the two households to work together on other matters pertaining to the three children.

Establishing a clear couple boundary can create as well as alleviate tension. Children also universally fantasize that their two parents will somehow get back together, and as a result they often impede the efforts of the parent who is attempting to disengage from the former marital subsystem and form a strong bond with the new partner. During the single-parent household phase the children may have had unrestricted access in the household, including to the parent's bedroom, so that after the remarriage the new spouse feels the lack of privacy and the incompleteness of the partner's shift from the former relationship. The adults often find that they have no special time or place for themselves. The need to make time to nourish their couple bond. This is important because the children need a couple subsystem that is in control of the household. In this control lies the children's sense of security.

Discrepant Life Cycles

In a first marriage both individuals are entering the "marriage" phase of their lives, both will become parents at the same time, and both will have experienced having a "family" for the same length of time as the age of their oldest child (Goldner, 1982). It is likely that they will also be at similar career stages and fairly close together in age.

In a remarriage the adults may be dissimilar in a number of ways.

Much more frequently than in first marriages they are apt to be dissimilar in age, length of time they have previously been married, and where they find themselves in their careers. They may have children of very different ages; one may not yet have been a parent; and they may have had very different family experiences.

As far as the children are concerned, their developmental needs may not be syntonic with the needs of the adults. At the same time that the couple is attempting to form close family ties, teenage children are at a time in their lives when their peers rather than their family are of prime importance. They are breaking away from family and becoming increasingly independent at the same time that the adults are asking them to become involved in family activities. Negotiating these incompatible needs and helping the adults understand the developmental pressures on their adolescents is a task that often needs therapeutic assistance. Taking a child development course together can also aid the couple in their understanding of the conflicts they are experiencing. It can enable them to live with a looser structure than they had expected and leave the door open for the children to return as young adults to form a closer relationship with their parent and stepparent.

One of the deepest conflicts in remarriage situations can be whether or not to have children together. A typical situation is one in which a man with children marries a woman considerably younger than himself who has not had children. Sometimes they have made a joint premarital decision not to have children, and then as time passes she realizes that she does want to have a child; or, conversely, they have decided before getting married that they do want to have a child, and then the husband decides that to have another child would be an unwanted additional responsibility; or the wife feels overburdened and discouraged by the difficulty of being a stepmother and becomes increasingly upset and ambivalent about motherhood.

Sager and associates (1983) describe a situation in which a couple spent 3 months in therapy discussing the difference in their needs regarding having a mutual child. (He had two sons, and she had no children.) At the end of therapy they decided to divorce, seeing the "[impasse] in the context of their needs no longer being met *enough* to continue their relationship" (p. 287).

For Susan and Charles the outcome was different. In their case they came to therapy "to decide whether or not to have a mutual child" and then needed a year and a half of therapeutic sessions before they could address this issue with understanding. They first needed to resolve power and intimacy issues before looking at this decision as a dilemma that had arisen because of differences in the life cycle stages of each of them. When it became possible for them to explore and share their feelings about a mutual child, Susan resolved her ambivalence about wanting a child, and Charles decided that many of his fears about becoming a father again were unrealistic. In this situation Susan and Charles made the decision to have a child together.

Often couples do not understand the nature of their difficulties. Helping them recognize natural discrepancies between them in their individual life cycles can remove the feeling that something is "wrong" with their wish either to have a child or to not return to diapers and the PTA. Feeling better about themselves can then free the two adults to talk, frequently with the aid of a counselor, and arrive at a mutually satisfactory resolution.

Closeness and Distance

When a remarriage takes place, the adults often have a need to create an "instant family." To them this means that there will be close relationships between family members, since the concept of "family" is based on the model of a nuclear family with strong family loyalty and deep, loving relationships between family members. No thought is given to the fact that a remarriage brings individuals together who do not yet feel a sense of belonging to this new unit and who have not yet developed a caring relationship. It is no wonder that adults with this unrealistic goal in mind become upset when they perceive distance between individuals in the household. Because of its different structure, a stepfamily tends to have less cohesiveness than a biological family, so that the "distance and closeness" dimension in a functioning stepfamily is usually dissimilar to that of the ideal nuclear family of the adults' dreams. Therapists are often asked to help the family forge a sense of closeness, as in the following case examples.

In one stepfamily a stepfather and stepson had quickly formed a close bond, only to have the boy withdraw and become distant and destructive in the household. The family entered therapy and was helped to understand their unrealistic expectations of instant affection. Slowly a less intense yet very caring relationship developed between the stepson and the stepfather as the 11-year-old worked out the difficult task of coping with two households and two male parenting figures. If the therapist had entered the unrealistic belief system of the adults, it is likely that he would have pushed for a return to the original premature closeness, thus reducing the ability of the stepfamily to work through necessary stages before the family could structure itself in a more satisfactory manner.

In another instance the unrealistic expectations of a large stepfamily led them to be dissatisfied with their progress, although in actuality they had worked through many of the beginning stages very quickly. When the therapist they saw complimented them on their progress, the reframing of their experience brought about a reassessment of their situation and new pride in the work they had done together. They could then move on to other difficulties that needed their attention.

WHOM TO SEE

While the locus of the difficulties, the type of problems, and the specific characteristics of the stepfamily are important to consider, we feel that a major determinant of whom to see in therapy is the emotional stage of development achieved by the couple. Papernow (1984) has studied stepfamily formation and traces stepfamily development through a predictable sequence of seven stages. Building on Papernow's work, the stages are summarized in Table 1.

In our experience stepfamilies do not come to see a therapist while in the Fantasy Stage. With increasing frequency today they are reading helpful literature and seeking educational stepfamily courses, either as a couple or as a household group. This education can be valuable in that it prepares the individuals for the typical situations that may arise and gives them suggestions for ways of handling their challenges.

One detrimental result of self-education that we have noticed, however, is the reaction of some stepparents who then subscribe to a new myth: Knowing what to expect ensures against feeling the usual emotions of jealousy, isolation, resentment, and anger. So when the feelings emerge, they are often followed by a profound sense of "what's wrong with me?" Dispelling this myth then becomes a part of the therapy when further help is sought.

During the next three stages, Pseudo-Assimilation, Awareness, and Mobilization, we observe a growing awareness, primarily on the part of the stepparent, that things are not going well and that changes need to be made. During these phases the household tends to divide

Table 12.1
Determination of Whom To See in Therapy

	Stage	Characteristics	Productive Therapeutic Contacts
I.	Fantasy	Adults expect instant love and adjustment. Children try to ignore stepparent in hopes that he/she will go away and biological parents will be reunited.	1. Couple 2. Stepfamily household (unlikely to see anyone except for education)
II.	Pseudo-Assimilation*	Attempts to realize fantasies. Vague sense that things are not going well. Increasing negativity. Splits along biological lines. Stepparents feel something is wrong with them.	1. Couple seen individually and/or conjointly 2. Children if disturbed
III.	Awareness	Growing awareness of family pressures. Stepparent begins to perceive what changes are needed. Parent feels pulled between needs of children and new spouse. Groups divide along biological lines. Children may observe and exploit differences between couple. Usually takes outside "push"—reading, stepfamily group, support from a friend, therapy—to get to Stage IV.	1. Couple seen individually and/or conjointly. 2. Children if need help urgently
IV.	Mobilization	Strong emotions begin to be expressed, often leading to arguments between couple. Stepparent clear on need for change. Parent fears change will bring loss. Sharp division between biological groups. Stepparent with no children is in isolated position and lacks support.	1. Couple seen individually and/or conjointly. 2. Children if need help urgently
V.	Action	Couple begins working together to find solutions. Family structure changes. Boundaries are clarified. Children may resist changes.	1. Emphasis on couple 2. Appropriate subgroups 3. Suprasystem subgroup combinations
VI.	Contact	Couple working well together. Closer bonding between stepparent-stepchild and other steprelations. Stepparent has definite role with stepchildren. Boundaries clear. More ability to deal with suprasystem issues.	1. Any suprasystem grouping (depends on issues)
VII.	Resolution	Stepfamily identity secure. When difficulties arise family may regress to earlier stages, but move ahead quickly. Usual difficulties are around nodal family events involving the suprasystem.	1. Any suprasystem grouping (unlikely to come in now)

*Papernow uses the term "assimilation." We consider "pseudo-assimilation" to be a more accurate description of this stage.

along former family lines, and for this reason we consider that including more than the couple in the therapeutic sessions tends to divide the groups even further. For us it is essential that the couple relationship become viable before children or other members of the suprasystem are included. Working out the couple relationship often improves household functioning to the extent that the children need not be seen therapeutically. This is particularly true with younger children, since they are especially vulnerable to the psychological functioning of their parent and stepparent.

When children need to be included in therapy so that the couple can be helped to work together as a team, they can be seen by the same therapist at other times or by a separate therapist. The latter plan can be particularly important when children are in the later teen years and are attempting to move toward independence. We almost never see together a biologically related group only (i.e., both ex-spouses or a parent and biologically related children), as this can create still another interaction that breaks the new household along biologically related lines.

For example, Pam and Paul had been married for two and a half years, and Pam felt isolated in the household. She had no children, and Paul's three children lived with them. The children had lived with their father for 3 years before his marriage to Pam, and they and Paul were very close. Paul and Pam had little understanding of one another's feelings. For this reason, the couple was seen together in therapy for several months. When their relationship seemed solid, it was agreed that the children would come with them to the next appointment. On the day of the appointment Pam at first refused to come with the group, only changing her mind when the therapist made it clear that it would not be productive for Paul and his children to come without her and that all needed to be present or no one should come at this time.

In another instance, both adults had children, and until the couple had some "glue" in their relationship, therapy with the group divided the household even more unproductively than when they began to see a therapist. The family had not yet reached the Action Stage, and the structure was still too fragile for the group to deal constructively with needed changes.

Once the couple has formed a functioning subgroup, many therapeutic combinations appear to be productive. This becomes possible during the Action or fifth stage. When parent and stepparent feel supported by each other, reaching the Action Stage comes quickly, but for many couples it takes about 4 years. Many redivorces take place between the Fantasy and the Action stages, particularly during the time of Mobilization when the couple is experiencing great stress as they share conflicting emotions and are not yet able to tolerate their differences, negotiate, and function as a unit.

Once the couple is working well together, there is opportunity for the relationships between steprelatives to deepen (Contact Stage) and for Resolution (Stage VII) to occur as the sense of stepfamily identity becomes secure. "Family" events such as births, deaths, weddings, bar mitzvahs, christenings, and graduations can produce strains that cause regression to earlier stages and may require therapeutic intervention. On the whole the suprasystem members seem to be able to work things out themselves.

Throughout the life of the stepfamily there is, of course, not a steady progression from one discrete stage to the next. Usually, however, one stage is predominant, and it is helpful for the therapist and the family alike to realize that these stages are predictable. As one discouraged stepmother said when she learned that it usually takes 1 to 3 years to progress from the beginning of the Action Stage to the next stage, "I guess I can stick it out and work on it then. We've been in this Action Stage for one and a half years now, and as long as it's not going to go on forever, I can do it."

Where the problems lie will determine which subgroups are appropriate to see therapeutically, and clues as to how to proceed will be provided by the ages of the children, available individuals, and other specific stepfamily characteristics. One important determination will be whether individuals or subgroups need to be seen at once but separately or whether it is effective for them to wait to join the therapy sessions later when the couple has achieved adequate stability.

INTERVENTION STRATEGIES

Whatever the problems and whomever is being seen in therapy, we feel that the following 15 intervention strategies are particularly valuable when working with stepfamilies. While a number have been illustrated in previous examples, we would like to mention all of them briefly.

Enhancing self-esteem needs to underlie every interaction, verbal and nonverbal. This is especially important because stepfamily individuals usually feel that their type of family inherently is "not as good" as a nuclear family.

Drawing a genogram is a neutral task that relaxes the couple or family and allows for discussion of important individuals, often people who cannot be spoken about in a household. It also is often revealing to the family to see the number of people involved and the emotional complexity of the issues everyone faces. This can sometimes reduce the tendency to create an "identified patient" and also reduces feelings of personal inadequacy. For the therapist it supplies information that can produce "hunches" to follow in working with the family members.

Making educational comments is important, especially at the beginning of therapy. Bohannan (1970) stated that "the present situation [no common expectations in stepfamilies] approaches chaos, with each individual set of families having to work out its own destiny without any realistic guidelines" (p. 137). Fortunately, this is no longer the case. Many guidelines are now available in the popular and professional literature,[1] so that comments made by knowledgeable therapists can provide important information to stepfamilies to help them with their structuring process.

Clarifying realistic expectations often takes time and must be done with great sensitivity to the resistance that adults in stepfamilies may have regarding goals for their stepfamily. Pushing too quickly or adamantly against the belief that a stepfamily can be the same as a first-marriage family, for example, will often send the stepparent or parent fleeing from therapy. In many instances being able to let go of this expectation comes slowly and painfully.

Assisting with the recognition and acceptance of losses has been illustrated in some detail previously. When helping an adult explore the losses of the former relationship, it is often necessary to do this in individual sessions. Listening to a spouse of 14 months talk of happy times or satisfactions that were lost at the breakup of a former marriage of 14 years is not something most individuals can manage well.

Filling in past histories becomes important, because a stepfamily comes together from various backgrounds and suddenly is a family "with no history." One therapist spent most of the first session with a large stepfamily household helping them learn about each other. One girl had been separated from her father for 3 years, from the time of her mother's death to her father's remarriage. She had remained aloof from all members of her new stepfamily, and this therapy session marked a beginning of family members sharing their past experiences with one another.

Reducing a sense of helplessness by encouraging stepfamilies to take charge of situations they can control and let go of those they cannot control can be beneficial to most stepfamilies. Within the stepfamily household there is less control than in biological families because the children often have another parent or household that is important to them. While the adults cannot control what time that absent parent picks up the children, for example, they can control whether or not the household activities continue or stop while they wait with mounting impatience and anger.

Teaching negotiation in the therapy session by example and by outlining and perhaps practicing productive steps to take in the negotiation process is also useful. These negotiation steps include:

1. Valuing each persons' feelings and opinions (including one's own)
2. Stating wishes and ideas
3. Brainstorming solutions (no evaluation of ideas allowed!)
4. Evaluating the proposed solutions
5. Choosing the best solution to accommodate the various needs

Since individuals in stepfamilies come together from varied backgrounds and are used to different ways of doing things, they often need help to escape the right/wrong and blame game and concentrate—and perhaps laugh about—the differences. In stepfamilies much negotiation is required.

Separating feelings and behavior is particularly important for individuals in stepfamilies because they are living together as "relatives" at the same time that they may have little "relationship" between them. Often they need to hear the message that it is not hypocritical to bring similar presents for your child and stepchild when you have been away on a business trip even though you do not care about your stepchild the same way you do about your biological child. Being fair does not require feeling the same. Too often stepparents attempt to change their feelings rather than concentrate on behaving in ways that would produce positive interactions.

Relating past family experiences to present situations is also important. The experiences can include losses, couple relationships and parent/child bonding in the family of origin, discipline issues in the family of origin, sibling relationships in the family of origin, and past marriage experiences. These experiences appear to be important historical antecedents that can lead to difficulties in a remarriage. In our experience asking for clarification of these areas when couples are together can give each one much needed understanding of the events and modeling experienced by the other. One common dynamic is the inability of a remarried parent to form a solid relationship with his or her new spouse when the primary relationship in the family of origin was between parent(s) and child rather than between the two parents. Since the remarried parent in this case enters the stepfamily with a strong parent/child bond and this is his or her original model, forming a strong couple bond feels "wrong."

Restructuring and reframing in positive ways can help individuals view their situations in a new light, thus enabling them to cope more effectively. One stepmother felt empathetic rather than antagonistic when she changed her perception of her 5-year-old stepson's behavior. No longer did she see him as attempting to separate her and her husband when he wanted to walk between them, holding a hand of each adult as the three walked together. After a reframing statement she viewed it as the boy's attempt not to be left out now that his father had remarried.

Making specific suggestions supplies needed guidelines when a family is stressed. Anxiety produces an inability to see options, so that creative ideas may need to come from the therapist. It did not occur to a mother that she could ask a friend of her son's to come on the weekend with him so that the child would not feel unhappy and isolated in the new community into which she and her new husband had just moved. Having a special drawer for a child who was in the household on weekends solved the problem of a forgotten toothbrush and nightclothes. The drawer also contained special toys for the weekends.

Encouraging dyadic relationships is of great value in building new stepparent/stepchild bonds and in maintaining older parent/child relationships. It is difficult to get to know a person "in a group," so that short times spent one to one help stepparents and stepchildren develop their relationship. Also, having some direct contact with a parent after a remarriage reduces the loss experienced by children when a parent remarries. Too much one-to-one time, of course, is unproductive, as it becomes divisive.

Reducing therapeutic tension may be necessary with emotionally explosive stepfamilies, since they do not have the family loyalty or basic cohesiveness to be able to handle the same degree of tension as a nuclear family. The tension in many stepfamilies who seek therapeutic assistance is extremely high, and cooling off is often needed. In such cases, having individuals communicate their feelings through the therapist rather than directly to one another allows the therapist to reframe the communication in a more helpful or positive way. Using a tape or video recorder also reduces the tension in highly emotional families by replaying what has been said. Indeed, replay can at times be productive, as it allows people to see themselves as others see them.

Using accurate language helps stepfamily individuals begin to deal with their type of family. Referring to Bob's "stepmother" as his "mother" or Julie's father as her "real" father does little to improve the situation. Inquiring what children call their stepparents acknowledges one difference between stepfamilies and nuclear families, with which such a question would not ordinarily be considered necessary. Unfortunately, present-day language is inadequate for many modern family arrangements. Acknowledging new relationships and situations in as accurate a way as possible is the best that can be done and creates a climate of understanding of stepfamily situations that is important.

SUMMARY

In our view there are many external and internal pulls that make it difficult for stepfamilies to acquire a good self-image and a satisfying identity.

In their search for identity as a family and in their attempt to deal with these challenges, stepfamily adults go through predictable emotional stages, with problems surfacing in one or more of eight general areas.

We believe that the emotional stage the stepfamily has reached is an important consideration in deciding with whom to work in therapy. While there are a number of particularly helpful interventions no matter what the difficulties are or whom is seen, the basic need in therapy is for validation of the stepfamily as a valuable American family. This can enable the stepfamily to gain a clear identity and positive self-image so that its members can experience the benefits of this type of family—many rich interpersonal experiences, a diversity of rewarding situations, flexibility and creativity, and an awareness of the importance of nourishing human relationships.

The experiences of clinicians and the self-reports of many individuals in stepfamilies suggest that therapy with a therapist knowledgeable about working with such families can be extremely helpful in assisting them with the challenges of stepfamily integration.

We are not aware of objective research that has systematically studied the efficacy of stepfamily therapy. Given the large proportion of stepfamilies in the population, however, such a study could be extremely valuable.

NOTE

1. A list of available book titles and an extensive bibliography of stepfamily literature is sold by the Stepfamily Association of America. These may be obtained by writing to 28 Allegheny Avenue, Suite 1307, Baltimore, MD 21204.

13

Public Policies and Families

CATHERINE S. CHILMAN

INTRODUCTION

This chapter briefly discusses some of the salient aspects of public policies and families. It is a prelude to the next chapter, which is concerned with present and needed programs and policies to mitigate the health problems of families. It is very like a similarly-fitted chapter in volume I but is included here for the benefit of readers who do not have that volume.

DEFINITIONS OF FAMILY WELL-BEING

It can be argued that the chief goal of public policies concerning families is the promotion of family well-being. There are a number of conflicting definitions of this term, but many of them include the concept of "strong families." To traditionalists strong families are apt to mean patriarchal ones in which members marry as young adults "until death do us part," have a number of children, refrain from the use of artificial contraceptives and abortion, and follow traditional sex roles with husbands as the only (and adequate) wage earners and wives as full-time homemakers and mothers. Such families are often conceptualized as "stable and strong." They present a united front to the outside world, regardless of the divisions and conflicts that may occur within them.

A more modernist view is that strong families are ones that promote the physical, social, psychological, and economic well-being of each person, both as members of the family and as autonomous individuals. This well-being is viewed in process terms; that is, each family member, young and old, is capable (in fact, needful) of growth and development throughout the life span. The processes of this kind of family system support individual growth through respect for the autonomy of each family member and through the nurturance of each member as an integral part of a caring, interdependent, intimate family group. Following such a definition, family stability is not necessarily seen as desirable if stability means that marriages should be permanent regardless of their quality and that parenthood should be perpetually selfless regardless of the problems that offspring may present in their adult years as well as in their younger ones (Terkelson, 1980).

PUBLIC POLICY PROCESSES

As in the case of "family well-being," the term "policy" has numerous definitions and interpretations. A full discussion of this topic alone could fill many volumes. For the present purposes, however, the term means public (i.e., government) policy and is conceptualized as a series of processes. Moreover, the primary emphasis is on federal public policies as constituting the most general approach. Public policy by itself might be thought of as a guiding principle of government, such as "every child in the United States shall receive a high quality of education," a familiar and enticing principle! However, the principle does not move beyond the enticement (and probably vote-getting) stage unless it is developed into legislative proposals, which then need to be passed by Congress and signed by the President.

The outcome of these processes is affected by highly political forces. Typically, numerous lobbying groups as well as individual citizens become involved. Action by Congress and the President is strongly influenced by these groups and individuals, most especially by strong, well-financed, national lobbies.

The process is far from finished, however, even if legislation is approved and signed. Appropriations that provide adequate funding must be made by Congress, and this funding is strongly influenced by the nature of political support for opposition to the legislation. Then, too, relevant federal departments must be provided with administrative personnel, a step that is affected by political considerations. Following these steps in the process, administrative guidelines must be developed.

The legislation then moves for its further financing and implementation to state levels. In turn, state governments must develop programs to be carried out by local units of government. These units then need to further develop and administer programs so that they actually reach the individuals and families for whom the legislation was intended. The degree to which the legislation is funded and implemented at state and local levels also depends on political considerations within the various units of government and, ultimately, on the views that individual, local staff members may have about the matter. Even more ultimately the ways in which these programs are used or not used by individuals and families are strongly affected by *their* particular attitudes, values, and behaviors in relation to the services offered. (Consider government-supported family planning programs, for instance.)

Furthermore, if it happens that some person or group question the constitutionality of the law and this challenge reaches the Supreme Court, which in turn finds the legislation in violation of the Constitution, the entire process will be moved back to square one. In short, there is a long series of processes that must occur for a policy to have real effect: a study in the many trials and triumphs of a democracy in a federal (national-state-local) system![1]

Although ideally public policy development and implementation is a rational process based on the best scientific knowledge, rational process is only one piece of the much larger policy puzzle. For instance, findings from scientific research are often brought into the policy process to provide a patina of rational respectability to a piece of legislation that more fundamentally has pragmatic political purposes.

The complex, lengthy political processes described above may well be discouraging to those who wish to affect public policies. To be effective, it is often useful for individuals to select a few policy issues that seem to them to be crucial, to affiliate with groups (often representative of one or more of the human services professions) that share their concerns, and to keep informed and politically active with those groups and follow the legislation through its many processes: congressional and presidential legislative actions, budget appropriations, development of administrative guidelines, state and local implementation, and court challenges. It also helps to know one's elected local, state, and federal representatives and to join and contribute to the political party of choice as well as campaign organizations for candidates supporting desired public polices.

In general, it is unproductive to complain, as many do, that public policies are "just a mess of politics." Within the American system of government "politics" is a process of democracy in action. As discussed above the many processes involved are heavily affected by pressures from politically active individuals and groups. Thus, the way for human service professionals to affect policies is to become politically active themselves, especially through knowledgeable, well-organized groups. To simply criticize and stay outside the processes is to pass the power to others who *are* actively involved, often pushing agendas that are not in the best interests of families in trouble, especially poor and minority families who have relatively little power themselves.

A major point to the policy chapters in this series is to provide both a knowledge background and a stimulus to readers to involve themselves, to one extent or another, in political activities to affect public policies that play such a large part in the lives of troubled families. An ecological approach to services for families clearly implies that concerned human service professionals should involve themselves, to one degree or another, in policy- and planning-oriented political activities as well as in the provision of direct services, the major focus of most practitioners serving families today in the late 1980s.[2]

FAMILY RELATED POLICIES

The preceding discourse leads to another definition: family policies or family-related policies. Again, policies referred to here are public—that is, government—policies. Like the concept of "family well-being," the term "family policy" has numerous meanings and involves numerous controversies. By the mid-1980s the term was attracting increased attention, sparking heated debates covering the entire political spectrum from the extreme conservative political right to the extreme liberal left. Virtually everybody appeared to be "pro-family" and in favor of supports for family well-being, including supports for families' economic and occupational well-being. But, as we have seen, definitions of family and family well-being have many interpretations. To some the term "public family policy" may mean that certain kinds of families and family-related behaviors, as determined by government action, should be promoted and other kinds officially opposed.

On the other hand, many others hold that "family public policies" should be defined as including all government policies and programs that have an impact on families; they also tend to believe that government should not impose a particular standard of family roles and functions on its citizens. The concept that family policies consist of all policies affecting families has lead in a number of directions, including that of "family impact analysis," a term that became popular during the Carter-Mondale administration of the late 1970s (Zimmerman, 1982).

Family impact analysis takes a rational planning approach to family policy. It seeks to gather large bodies of data concerning numerous public programs that affect families and to assess their effects through complex statistical analyses of relevant data. Impact is measured by demonstrated or probable effects on birth, marriage, divorce, separation, illegitimacy, employment, and income. These statistics are primarily provided by the U.S. Bureau of the Census, the National Center of Vital Statistics, and the U.S. Department of Labor. Data from these government agencies are reported in most of the chapters of this book. Moreover, numerous studies of various aspects of family well-being and of program effectiveness on family life, broadly defined, have been carried out by many government agencies and universities as well as by public and private human service organizations. Findings from these investigations are also used to supplement the above data. Many of these studies are also discussed in the relevant chapters of this series.

Senator D. Patrick Moynihan, who has long had an interest in family policy, writes that in essence family policy focuses on the outcomes of other policies. He sees family welfare as being the business of numerous social and economic programs at national, state, and local levels and holds that their impact on families can be assessed, at least in part, by analyses of family data (Moynihan, 1986).

Kamerman and Kahn (1978), who have conducted extensive surveys of family policies and programs in this and other countries, define family policies in ways that are close to Moynihan's conceptions. They hold that family policy consists of activities funded and sponsored by government that affect families directly or indirectly, intentionally or unintentionally, whether or not these policies have specific family objectives. They write that family policy is both a perspective and a set of activities. As an activity it includes such family specific programs as family planning services, food stamps, income maintenance, foster care, adoption, homemaker services, day care, child development programs, family counseling and therapy, and employment services.

All of the above views include, or can include, the concept of family impact analysis. As I see it, this analysis has considerable merit primarily because it recognizes the huge network of government programs that impinge on families. This analysis also calls for the application of survey data and of many kinds of research, both basic and applied, to the formation and analysis of public family-related programs and policies. However, family impact analysis by itself cannot be expected to change public policy. Those who apply its methods will have major problems if they fail to recognize and deal with the many political processes that are also necessary to actualize policies, as previously discussed.

Also, family impact analysis is deficient if it merely takes the passive approach of simply analyzing what effects government programs and policies will have or are having on families. An active approach is also needed, in which the needs of families are the primary consideration and planning activities are then directed to formulating what programs and policies, both existing and not yet existing, are needed.

Another far more conservative view of family policy was presented by President Reagan's Working Group on the Family in 1986 (Washington Cofo Memo, 1986). Their report called for less government infringement on the rights and responsibilities of families. State-funded day care, income assistance through public family allowances for children, school feeding programs, and national health care systems were all seen as socialistic evils that undermine American families and the larger society. The report called for local, volunteer assistance to families in lieu of federal state government programs. On the other hand, the report opined that government should take an active stand to affect cultural patterns perceived by the working group as being hostile to families; these patterns included drug use, pornography, and "bigoted" stands against religions.

The group also saw economic expansion as essentially a profamily program. Such expansion could be brought about, the report stated, through such measures as low taxes, control of inflation, and the end of "social spending schemes." The report further posited the need to reaffirm old principles that prevent erosion of family rights and responsibilities through court actions, dominance by public education, and control by social programs.

Senator Moynihan considered the report of the working group on the family to be not so much an analysis of public policies and families as a "conservative tantrum." Indeed, it seemed to reflect some of the main aspects of the extreme conservative position. Furthermore, the report illustrates the principle that *all* aspects of the functioning of society can be viewed as relevant to family policies. It also shows that the field of family policy is highly sensitive and readily politicized.

Family issues deeply engage the heart as well as the mind. They touch on the most intimate, significant aspect of our lives, the central identity each of us derives through our total development from infancy onward. Family issues include our most private and personal attachments, values, and beliefs. For many, probably the majority of Americans, family issues are closely intertwined with religious ones. And a basic principle of the American credo is a separation of church and state. Probably all religions see the guidance and succor of families as being central to their function and sharply different from those of government.

Furthermore, individual and hence family freedom from government interference is also basic to the American tradition. Millions of immigrants from the 1600s to the present have come to this country in search of this freedom. Thus, the very words "family policy" can serve as a red flag to many of our citizens of all political persuasions.

Schorr (1986) writes that it is preferable to plan for a wide range of public policies and programs that families need rather than to advocate family policies per se, since the former concept is less sensitive and controversial than the latter. Moreover, many such programs can be offered as services that can be chosen or not, depending on the values and beliefs of individual families and their members, thus safeguarding principles of freedom.

FAMILIES VERSUS SOCIETAL RESPONSIBILITY

The concept of "family responsibility" is another controversial and complicated one that usually arises in debates about families and policies. It lies at the heart of many issues, including those concerned with poverty and public assistance. Although our traditional cultural patterns hold that it is desirable for families to be self-reliant and self-supporting, responsible toward each of their members, and independent of any public aid, virtually no family in today's highly urbanized, technological society is totally independent of the services provided by large networks of external systems, both private and governmental. Government-aided and/or-regulated systems within the country that are crucial to the well-being of virtually all families include transportation in its many aspects, water supplies, waste disposal, fire and police protection, dependable money supplies and insured savings bank deposits, public education systems, public health services, social security provisions, the court systems, and so on. And international programs aimed at implementation of foreign policy and national defense as well as improved international trade theoretically at least provide important assistance for every individual and family in the country.

Although many of these forms of assistance are more or less taken for granted, sharp arguments quickly arise over such issues as special income, health, employment, housing, child care, and education assistance targeted to the poor and near poor. Such programs are highly visible, are incorrectly seen as inordinately expensive, and are often viewed as replacing family responsibilities—with many of these responsibilities fundamentally being the traditional functions of women, including child care, nursing care of the ill and disabled, and stretching the food, housing, and clothing dollar through home production. Some traditionalists claim that keeping these kinds of responsibilities within the family actually enhances the well-being of families. However, if we return to our earlier definition of family well-being we can see that this well-being is eroded, rather than supported, if the basic survival and developmental needs of families and all their members, including wives and mothers, are not met. An overload of economic adversities or severe illnesses or handicaps may make it impossible for some families to handle problems such as these without the supplementary assistance of public programs. Although conservatives often argue that private, voluntary efforts should provide the assistance needed, our society has become too urbanized, costly, and complex for these activities by themselves to make much of a dent on the host of problems that many families encounter today. Voluntary efforts can be helpful as a supplement to, but not a substitute for, necessary family assistance programs.

Families in our complex, technologically advanced society have only limited control over their own well-being. A careful analysis of the points discussed above can lead to the recognition that many of the problems faced by families today are not solely a result of irresponsible actions on their part; rather, to a large extent they are a result of a combination of factors external to families. These include various kinds of discrimination, unemployment and underemployment, poor educational and health services, and the like. Thus, a number of public policies and programs are needed to promote and support the well-being of many kinds of family forms, as will be discussed in more detail in the next chapter.

NOTES

1. Other legal challenges regarding legislation and its administration may be raised through the courts at various local, state, and regional levels, but a discussion of details concerning this and other issues affecting public policies transcends the space constraints of this chapter.

2. Although the foregoing paragraphs may seem like a high school lesson in civics, it is my experience that the majority of citizens, including graduate students, many academicians, and human service professionals, fail to understand a number of the principles sketched here. These principles grow out of my experience and study as a university professor, as a former staff member of the (then) U.S. Department of Health, Education and Welfare during the 1960s, and as a former staff member of various state governments and private social agencies.

It was my common government experience during the 1960s that both academicians and human service professionals outside the federal government sought to impress me with their views of what policies and programs were needed because they assumed I was an "influential policy-maker." In actuality, the executive branch of government (i.e., the President, his Cabinet, and the staff of the various federal departments) cannot create public domestic policies (with "domestic" referring to policies internal to this country) without supportive legislation and appropriations as provided by Congressional action. Also, any staff actions must be within guidelines provided by the relevant legislation. Furthermore, federal staff members need to be sensitive to the reactions of citizens, as groups and as individuals, at local levels since these citizens may protest to their Congresspeople if they object to any part of federal programs and the way they are administered.

Thus, it seems to me that the term "federal domestic policy makers" tends to be a fallacy if it refers to federal staff personnel, since their options are limited by many factors. In fact, given the constraints it is something of a miracle that federal "bureaucrats" can act at all. Similar comments apply to local and state governments, but our focus here is on the federal government.

14

Public Policies and Variant Family Forms

ROGER H. RUBIN

INTRODUCTION

The past few decades have brought increasing recognition that the policies of both the public and private sectors of society have pervasive effects on families. As discussed in this volume, this includes families with a variety of lifestyles. Because of space constraints, the emphasis in this chapter is on a selected group of federal government policies as well as on some of those established by the courts at various governmental levels. For the same reason policies adopted by the private sectors of society are given little attention. Moreover, only salient policy issues are discussed because so many kinds of lifestyles that may present problems to their participants have been described in the foregoing chapters.

The socially acceptable prototype by which various family forms are often judged is the traditional nuclear arrangement. However, according to Ross and Sawhill (1975), the goal of any public policy should be "neutrality with respect to family organization," not attempting to promote one family living pattern over another. This neutrality would allow more options and flexibility for families as they move from one form to another (Gongla, 1982). Moroney (1979) writes: "The 1980 White House Conference had ended up addressing the subject of 'Families.' Plural. It was to be asserted that no one set of arrangements was to have social priority over alternative lifestyles, as the phrase went." Minuchin (1986), among others, recognizes that nurturance and support can be derived from different family forms.

Katz (1979) writes that present and future definitions of the family are influenced by social policy decisions, while Furstenberg (1979) notes that policy makers can influence the direction and outcomes for various emergent family forms. Most American communities regulate the composition of households, and such power often has most impact on those selecting "nontraditional lifestyles" (Pollak, 1985).

Are nontraditional family forms burdened by the disapproval, prejudice, apathy, or ignorance of policy-makers? Is there a defensible rationale for public policies that support one particular family form or another? Do all family forms suffer from bureaucratic traditionalism? Are policy decisions promoting the existence of particular family forms? If so, is this beneficial or destructive? What kinds of changed public policies are indicated in association with changing family forms? These are among the questions that remain unresolved as policy responses to a variety of family structures evolve.

Using the concept of family ecology, a basic principle of this series, the purpose of the present chapter is to identify issues, assess current public policies, and recommend additional policies for improving the lives of people who encounter problems associated with their particular family lifestyle.

SINGLE-PARENT FAMILIES

Owing to rising rates of divorce, separation, and nonmarital births, the proportion of single-parent families in the population grew rapidly between 1970 and the mid-1980s, as discussed in Chapter 1. As of this writing, in 1987, about half of black families and about one-fifth of white families were headed by only one parent. Over 20 million children lived in such families.

Financial problems are the major policy-related issues affecting single parents and their children. For instance, Espenshade (1979) has noted that by the end of the 1970s female-headed households represented 49% of all families in poverty although they made up only 14% of all family forms. The lower wages of women, especially minority women, is a contributing factor of this poverty, and 35% of single mothers are minorities (Garfinkel & McLanahan (1986). On the average this population also has low educational levels and high mobility rates when compared to other family forms (Norton & Glick, 1986). The economic situation of this group has become worse in recent years. "Between 1972 and 1984 the average total real income of a working, poor single mother of three, including wages, AFDC, Food Stamps and federal tax benefits, declined by over 22 percent to 10,372 dollars in 1984 dollars (House Select Committee on Children, Youth and Families, 1986).

It is not difficult to understand why Thompson and Gongla (1985) conclude from their literature review that "the major problem faced by single-parent families is not the lack of a male's presence, but the lack of a male income" (p. 111). This lack is especially acute because the majority of absent fathers fail to provide child support payments. Thompson and Gongla (1985) cite additional public policy explanations for the economic plight of single-parent mothers. These include child care costs, public assistance policies limiting eligibility and the size of family benefits, the unwillingness or inability of fathers to provide financial support, employment discrimination against women, and the lower wages and greater unemployment of younger women. (See also Volume 1, chapters 5 and 10.)

Thompson and Gongla (1985) also note a rising public concern over the increasing number of single-parent families. They state that the single-parent family is a mainstream family form today and that the ideological characterizing of single-parent families as deviant and incomplete often has negative public policy implications. For example, Gongla (1982) writes that female-headed households confer an untraditional position of authority on women, a fact some oppose. Brandwein, Brown, and Fox (1974) also note the negative social attitudes directed toward single-parent mothers. As examples they cite financial discrimination such as the refusal to rent housing or to provide credit and mortgages.

Many researchers expect to find problems in single-parent families (Gongla, 1982). They pay too little attention to the family as a system affected by the larger environment and place too much emphasis on individual behavior. Thompson and Gongla (1985) maintain that single-parent families are seen as transitional and temporary by program planners and not recognized as "real" families. Policy makers, citing high remarriage rates for single-parent women raising children, tend to do little to accommodate their needs as single parents.

Perhaps the greatest interest and anxiety have been directed at unwed teenage mothers. As shown in Chapter 1, the rate for teenage motherhood peaked in 1957 (96 per 1,000), but by 1985 it was 51 per 1,000 (or 5% in a given year) for women aged 15 to 19. Although the actual rate of childbearing declined, that of pregnancy rose until 1984, declining somewhat in 1985 and 1986. Almost half of the pregnancies to teenagers were terminated by abortion in 1985. There was also a marked rise in *nonmarital* childbearing between 1960 and the mid-1980s.

As shown in Chapter 1, teenage childbearing is most apt to occur among adolescents whose families are poor and of low educational/occupational status. These adolescents have often suffered also from the deprivations associated with racism and ethnocentrism. Moreover, many live in neighborhoods in which the unemployment rate for male and female youth is well over 50%. In effect, the most vulnerable teenagers in the population are particularly apt to become unmarried adolescent parents. The poverty and unemployment that many experience after they became parents may well have occurred in any case, but parenthood usually intensifies their susceptibility to these problems. Somewhat the same might be said of some older single parents, since poverty and racism are known to impose stresses on families that in turn lead to single-parent status; that is, while single-parent status can lead to poverty, the opposite is also true.

Current Policies and Single-Parent Families

Income Maintenance

Given the current state of many single-parent families, what has been the policy response thus far? Aid to Families with Dependent Children (AFDC) is the largest program directed to relieving poor, single-parent families. A means-tested public assistance program, AFDC was established in 1935 as part of the Social Security Act. AFDC plus food stamp and Medicaid programs form the core of "welfare" and government policy toward assisting single mothers and their offspring (Kamerman, 1985; Levitan, 1985).

The administration of AFDC differs from state to state, with wide variations in eligibility determination and size of grants. However, in 1986 in no state was the size of the grant higher than 50% of the poverty line. Because of federal cuts in this and related programs through the Omnibus Budget Reconciliation Act of 1981 (OBRA) and because of inflation, the financial plight of AFDC recipients became increasingly desperate during the early 1980s. Cuts in eligibility for Medicaid, low-income housing, food stamps, and working expenses particularly hurt those employed mothers whose low earnings had previously made them eligible for these forms of assistance. Thus, penalties for working were one effect that OBRA cuts had on low-income single mothers.

There are numerous other problems with the AFDC program, a full discussion of which is beyond the scope of this chapter. Instead, see Schorr (1986) and Danziger and Weinberg (1986) as well as chapters 5 and 10, Volume 1 in this series. However, a few salient AFDC problems are listed here.

1. Administrative regulations of AFDC have escalated over the years, with the result that the program is exceptionally complex and almost impossible to administer fairly and punctually (Schorr, 1986).

2. Families are not eligible for AFDC in over 20 states if the father is in the home, with the result that single parenthood is, in effect, promoted by the program. Somewhat the same result obtains in other states, since it is essentially very difficult for a two-parent family to obtain AFDC.
3. In contrast to other Social Security Act programs for the elderly, disabled, and unemployed, AFDC is particularly singled out by the public and by legislators for criticism and inadequate financing, in the mistaken belief that recipients are lazy, unwilling to work, and perpetually dependent. However, studies have shown that the majority of AFDC recipients are welfare-dependent for less than 2 years and are eager to work if they can obtain steady jobs with adequate pay plus affordable, quality child care.
4. As of 1987 pressure was mounting to move AFDC recipients from welfare to work as a "cure for welfare dependency," but the extreme difficulty of reaching this goal has not been recognized sufficiently. Associated problems include widespread unemployment and underemployment in the total population, the inadequacy of minimum wages to support a family, and the high cost plus shortages of adequate substitute child care for employed parents.

In brief, it is essential to recognize and correct the damaging poverty that affects a large proportion of the nation's single parents and their children. Although the situation in itself is not necessarily harmful to children, single parents are apt to be overloaded with the many tasks of solo parenting plus trying to obtain and hold jobs. When these parents are also poor, their burdens are usually extremely heavy, and both children and parents are likely to suffer (Pearlin & Schooler, 1982). All in all, it is essential that more adequate income maintenance and related services be made available to all poverty-level families, including single-parent families. (See also Volume 1, Chapter 10 of this series.)

The elimination of damaging poverty requires adequate federally funded and administered income maintenance programs for all families, both one-parent and two-parent, who are in economic need and whose needs are not being met by other income-maintenance provisions of public programs such as OAISDB (Old Age Insurance and Survivor and Disability Benefits), Unemployment Insurance, Veteran's Benefits, and the like.

Child Day Care

The issue of child day care exposes a fundamental deficit in American social thinking. In contrast to many other industrialized countries the United States lacks a coherent policy regarding the provision of high-quality, free or low-cost child day care facilities. This presents a serious problem for many families with employed parents, but the issue is particularly critical for single-parent families.

As of this writing little federal funding is available for these centers, partly owing to 1981 OBRA budget cuts for facilities for children of low-income families funded through Title XX of the Social Security Act. Although preschool programs for poor children are fairly well funded through Head Start legislation, these centers are of limited help to employed mothers of young children because many centers do not operate full time throughout the day.

Acceptable standards for high-quality child care include well-trained staff; a small number of young children per each staff member; safe and sanitary housing; a good supply of educational, recreational, and child development materials, and adequate insurance. It is difficult for governments to secure and finance the personnel to inspect and license such facilities, especially for small centers that offer day care in a provider's home. Also, the cost of day care that meets the acceptable standards is so high that only prosperous families, often with two working parents, can afford such care. Thus, public financial assistance to the centers or to low-income user parents is needed in order to make quality child care available to them.

It has been difficult over the years to persuade both the general citizenry and legislators that high-quality substitute day care for young children is extremely important. Partly because of traditional, sexist attitudes, there tends to be a prevalent belief that the care of young children is mainly the business of their mothers and that it is simple work that any mother can do whether or not she is employed outside the home. However, large bodies of research, especially in the past few decades, point to the fundamental importance of enlightened, consistent, committed, and developmentally oriented care of young children in order to provide them with the essential foundation for positive physical, cognitive, social, and emotional development. (See, for example, Field & Widmayer, 1982; Scarr & Weinberg, 1986). This kind of care is especially difficult for low-income employed, single mothers to give on a full-time basis unless they are assisted by supplementary help through "willing and able" friends and relatives, supported and licensed child care facilities, or preferably, both kinds of resources.

Employment

In general, it is exceptionally difficult for single mothers to support themselves and their children through employment because of a number of factors including: (a) inadequate education and training for well-paying jobs; (b) barriers to employment due to institutional racism and sexism, a situation that worsened during the Reagan administration owing to reduced support for enforcement of the civil rights legislation of the 1960s; (c) a rise in the cost of living without a concomitant rise in wages; (d) shortages of affordable, high-quality child care; (e) reductions in AFDC payments, Medicaid, food stamps, and low-income housing for employed parents; and (f) generally high rates of unemployment and underemployment.

These problems call for public policies that not only provide for subsidizied, high-quality child care but also provide for programs for youth and adults, both females and males, in the following areas: (a) support of continuing education and vocational training; (b) job counseling, placement, and development; and (c) an increase in the minimum wage or supplementation of low wages (Danziger & Weinberg, 1986; McAdoo & Parham, 1985; Garfinkel & McLanahan, 1986; Levitan, 1985; Schorr, 1986). (See also Volume 1, Chapter 10 of this series.)

Because in 1987 unemployment and underemployment rates in general were quite high in this country and seemed likely to remain so, the provision of secure jobs at adequate pay for single parents appeared to be but one piece of a larger employment and wage problem, a problem that is multifaceted, complex, and part of an ever-changing worldwide economic puzzle. Finding better approaches to this problem requires intensive studies and recommendations for action by interdisciplinary groups with expertise in such fields as economics, politics, and related areas of government, business, industry, labor relations, and the like.

Child Support by Absent Parents

Further contributing to the financial problems of female-headed families is the inadequacy of the child support system. Only 59% of women are awarded child support when fathers are outside the home because of nonmarriage, separation, or divorce. Nuta (1986), citing 1985 U.S. Bureau of the Census figures, notes that in 1983 only 51% of the fathers ordered to pay support paid in full, 26% made partial payments, and 24% paid nothing. This difficult situation led Congress in 1984 to require states to proceed with ". . . automatic and mandatory wage attachments when child support is more than 30 days late. Additionally, states were ordered to pass state income tax refund intercepts for child support with the federal tax refund intercept program which was opened up to apply to nonwelfare, as well as to welfare parents who owed support payments (P.L. 98-378)" (Nuta, 1986, p. 177). However, since many absent fathers earn little or nothing and since many father other children, the enforcement of child support as a general method of reducing the financial problems of low-income families is unlikely to result in significant improvements in the situation of the majority of single, female parents. Nonetheless, it is important to establish the principle that absent fathers (or mothers) are obligated to provide financial aid to their families to the extent that their resources allow.

Policy Issues Concerning Adolescent, Single Parents

The policy principles cited above also apply to adolescent parents. Further policy issues concerning them are discussed here, partly because they tend to be an especially vulnerable group and partly because there has been such widespread concern about them. However, it appears that ideally all of the recommendations made for assistance to adolescent parents, as discussed later, could be cogently applied to older ones.

As shown in Chapter 1, there are many kinds of adolescents who become single parents. Although they represent many sectors of society, the majority come from low-income families. A larger proportion of black than white teenagers become single, adolescent parents, and many adolescent parents grew up in female-headed families. Chapter 1 also presents research evidence to the effect that teenagers who become pregnant outside marriage often had school problems preceding this event, and many felt hopeless about eventually graduating from high school and getting a good job.

In brief, a complex of disadvantages associated with poverty, racism, and poor educational/vocational opportunities tends to play a large part in the childhood and adolescence of the young people of both sexes who are particularly prone to having early, unprotected coitus and experience a pregnancy, to not resolve the pregnancy through abortion, and to not marry before the birth of the child.

The research evidence also suggests that other teenagers who did not grow up in poverty but who also became pregnant outside marriage when they were very young were likely to have had early school problems and to be in conflict with members of their families.

All in all, research findings point to the need for *primary prevention* policies that provide early assistance to the families in which children and adolescents are growing up and in which the foundations are being laid for their total development. This assistance should be directed most cogently to the structural economic problems of unemployment and underemployment that are the root causes of poverty and frequently of unmarried parenthood and divorce in the adolescent's family of origin.

Adequate income maintenance and employment assistance programs for low-income families through various federal and state governmental mechanisms is also called for so that children and adolescents can grow and develop in families that are able to provide them with essential food, shelter, clothing, health care, and educational opportunities. As shown earlier, serious cuts in these programs occurred during the early 1980s in the Reagan administration. These cuts should be restored, along with further improvements in basic family assistance, income, employment, food, health, housing, and educational programs. (See also Volume 1, Chapter 10.)

Affordable individual and family counseling services should also be available to all who need and want them when family relationship problems first arise, since these problems can escalate into a variety of serious difficulties including nonmarital adolescent pregnancy. Here again there were deep cuts in the early 1980s in federal funding for programs that had made social and psychological counseling services available in at least some of the states under such federal programs as Medicaid, Medicare, and Title XX of the Social Security Act. After 1981 these services were much less well funded, so that poor people who were not employed in organizations with generous health insurance benefits were apt to be deprived of individual and family counseling services. Public funding of these services should be restored so that people with low incomes can have equality of access to high-quality professional aid with family relationship difficulties. This aid should include equal attention to the needs of boys and girls, women and men. Continuous evaluation of service effectiveness is also indicated so that improvements can be made in the field of practice.

Still at the primary prevention level, early assistance through the schools for children's educational problems is suggested for a variety of reasons, including the fact that research indicates a close relationship between a young person's school difficulties as a precipitating cause of early, unprotected coitus. Such assistance calls for an expansion of specialized school personnnel and corrective programs together with continuing research on educational problems and their amelioration.

Further development of employment opportunities for adolescent girls and boys of all races is also indicated. There are many reasons to support such a recommendation, including the fact that young people who feel they have little chance to obtain work that eventually leads to a secure job with adequate pay are more apt than others to have fatalistic attitudes that lead to risking unprotected intercourse. Then, too, if young men cannot obtain jobs with adequate pay, they lack the financial resources for marriage. The financial problems associated with unmarried, adolescent parenthood in such instances are apt to be increased, rather than decreased, by marriage (Furstenberg, 1976; Ross & Sawhill, 1975).

As discussed in Chapters 1 and 2, sexuality education is often recommended as a primary prevention strategy. Some advocates of this education hope that it will prevent early, nonmarital coitus. Others see it more as promoting contraceptive use among sexually active teenagers, while still others see it as supporting "healthy" human relationships in general, including relationships between the sexes. This is a complex topic beyond the scope of the present chapter. Rather, see for instance Chilman (1983) or Gilchrist and Schinke (1983).

In general, sexuality education is recommended as part of a broader curriculum in education and counseling about human development in a changing society that has numerous social and psychological components, including changing sex roles, family structures, and relationships between the sexes. Ideally such a curriculum should be offered to parents as well as to children and adolescents and in a variety of settings: home, school, religious organizations, and the like. (See especially Scales, 1983.) On the public policy level it is recommended that insofar as possible depending on community support, this education should receive state and federal funding so that it can be available without charge to people of all income levels.

At the *secondary prevention* level it is essential that high-quality family planning, both birth control and abortion services, be readily available to both young men and young women. School-based comprehensive health services that include contraceptives appear to be especially effective for adolescents. Beyond these programs, free or low-cost family planning services are important for all low-income people who cannot afford private health care. This often particularly applies to single mothers who are no longer adolescents and thus not eligible for school-based programs. Studies during the 1970s and 1980s showed that the majority of women at all income levels want small families of two children or less. It is important that they be helped to achieve this goal for a number of reasons, including the continuing threat of worldwide overpopulation and the close association between poverty and large family size. (See, for example, Birdsall and Chester, 1987). Here again, Reagan administration–inspired cuts in federal funding of family planning programs caused a 15% cutback in financial support for these services in the early 1980s. These cuts should be restored and the services expanded (Jones, 1985).

Federal funding of abortion services was ended in the late 1970s. Although some states provide support for these services out of their own funds, many do not. As of 1986 the average price of an abortion was about $1,000, a prohibitive amount for people with limited incomes. While abortion remains controversial among a minority of U.S. citizens, freedom of choice for pregnancy resolution is supported by most. This freedom is not present for those who lack the funds to pay for an abortion from a private physician if they choose to end the pregnancy (Chilman, 1987; Rodman & Trost, 1986).

Issues of unwanted pregnancy resolution are complex. Ideally they call for free or low-cost, highly skilled counseling services that help young women and men and, if possible, their parents examine the options of abortion or carrying the pregnancy to term under varying circumstances: placing the baby for adoption; keeping the baby and marrying or not marrying; living with the young woman's or young man's parents; the young mother living alone with the baby; the young couple living alone with the baby; the young father living alone with the baby.

Often the choice of continuing the pregnancy and keeping the baby requires that public assistance such as AFDC be available to both the young couple or to parents with whom they choose to live. In 1987 an unfortunate aspect of AFDC policy is that grandparents are not eligible for AFDC even though they may be poor and caring for a grandchild or grandchildren. This is a policy problem that calls for resolution.

An abortion decision must be made especially quickly, since an abortion after the third month of pregnancy has increased dangers. It is important that the young couple or woman not be rushed into an abortion out of a sense of panic and that they or she alone have an opportunity to examine all possible options in an objective and realistic framework. Of course, the availability of options varies from place to place, with some communities having far more abortion, adoption, and family assistance resources than others (Feldman & Chilman, 1983).

If the decision is made to carry the pregnancy to term, it is essential that the young mother obtain high-quality health care early in her pregnancy and throughout the pregnancy, childbirth, and afterwards. Studies have shown that the higher maternal and infant health problems associated on the average with adolescent child-bearing are more a result of the lack of health care available to low-income adolescents than of the mother's age per se (Baldwin & Cain, 1980). When appropriate, free or low-cost health services are made available to adolescent mothers, higher rates of poor pregnancy outcomes generally disappear. This has obvious policy implications for the public funding of child and maternal health services for poor families, including pregnant adolescents.

A *third level of prevention* of problematic outcomes of adolescent pregnancy consists of comprehensive health, family counseling, child care education, and employment services for adolescent parents, as discussed in Chapter 2. Public funding to support such services comes from a variety of federal, state, and local sources and is supplemented by private funding, including foundation support, in some communities. (See, for example, Quint and Riccio, 1985.) These comprehensive service programs, of which there are a thousand or more in various parts of the country, have yielded promising results in some but not all instances. Essential components appear to include broad-based community support; a complex of high-quality services brought together in one center (a difficult and expensive feat to achieve); concrete services such as outreach to target groups, transportation, child care, income assistance, continuing education, health care (including family planning), and job counseling and placement; inclusion of young fathers; assistance to families of origin; and *long-term* service provisions.

Clearly, high-quality comprehensive services centers for adolescent parents are expensive, and large cuts in social programs during the early 1980s made these programs exceedingly difficult to develop and implement (Weatherley et al., 1985). It is essential that the outcomes of these programs be evaluated carefully (McGee, 1982; Quint & Riccio, 1985; Hofferth, 1985; Mott Foundation, 1986). Moreover, it is essential to bear in mind that a small, intensive, time-limited demonstration project with a well-paid, specially selected, and dedicated staff can show promising results over a short period of time, but when that program is extended to reach a large population and when it becomes part of a general, ongoing community program with the usual staff services and lower levels of funding, positive results may disappear—especially when program outcomes such as prevention of further childbearing, enhanced employment stability, and financial independence are examined over a period of 3 or more years.

In a sense it seems that an overemphasis has been placed on services to prevent *teenage* pregnancy and to assist *teenage* parents and their children as a special group. It should be recalled that the highest teenage birth rates are to 18- and 19-year-old women, women who are not essentially different in many ways from parents in their 20s or beyond.

The basic economic, educational, occupational, and family ecological system problems that often play an important part in *causing* unmarried, unplanned pregnancies usually continue to play an important part in the problems encountered by many low-income parents, more or less regardless of their age. Thus, ideally, to the extent that they prove to be effective, comprehensive services, including job training, job placement, and income assistance, should be available to *all* parents and their children who are in need and wish help. Furthermore, as pointed out earlier, services to families and individuals are only one part of what is needed. A reliance solely on services implies that individual and familial characteristics are the root causes of the economic, employment, health, and educational problems that some families, often single-parent families, including adolescent families, tend to exhibit. However, these problems are more frequently a primary result of the adverse social and economic conditions in which people live rather than of particular individual or family characteristics. Thus, fundamental changes in the basic economic and social structures of society are a more central policy issue than that of services alone, as important as they may also be.

ISSUES, POLICIES, AND RECOMMENDATIONS

Singles and Cohabitors

As the United States entered the decade of the 1980s, over 58 million adults were unmarried. This represented 34% of American men and 40% of American women (Stein, 1985). These individuals were divorced, separated, or widowed, with the greatest number being never married. Historically, this latter category has "been consistently treated as members of an insignificant and deviant group" (Stein, 1985, p. 28). The problem may be worse for some blacks than whites. Staples (1981) has written about the difficulties of middle-class blacks in establishing satisfactory social lives. The U.S. Bureau of the Census (1981) reported that in 1980 in every age group up through 65, never-married black men and women proportionately exceed the number of never-married whites.

Generally, the total singles population is less healthy than the married population and has less longevity, and the lack of a viable support network for singles may be an important explanation for these differences. For example, the lack of care for singles when they become ill is an essential factor in explaining these health statistics. Single people, especially if they are poor, are the most prone to depression. Singles without a support network are the most likely to be institutionalized. Physical illness such as genital herpes and Acquired Immune Deficiency Syndrome (AIDS) impact most heavily on the singles population, yet only recently have they become major public health concerns as the spread of AIDS threatens society. Verbrugge (1979) envisions improved health for singles when society defines them as less deviant and therefore more socially acceptable to people and social institutions.

Housing issues, particularly the great expense of living alone, confront singles. For example, the eligibility of singles who live together in public housing is occasionally challenged by legal definitions of what constitutes a family.

Workplace discrimination against singles can be as subtle as that faced by women and minorities. Primarily this takes the form of exclusion from the informal social contacts that influence occupational advancement. Stein (1978) maintains that "the social service community has not traditionally been oriented toward support services for the nonmarried."

In spite of these attitudes a "singles industry" has developed in the past two decades in response to the needs of the increasing singles population. It caters to the special circumstances of younger, affluent singles who, it is assumed, will marry eventually. This limited focus and bias excludes the recognition of unmarrieds as a permanent component in the population with their own special needs. For example, virtually no attention is given to the life cycle transitions of permanently single people and their economic, social, and psychological needs at different life stages.

Increasing numbers of single individuals are moving in with other singles, and the emergence of nonmarital heterosexual cohabitation over the past 20 years has challenged the most fundamental definitions of family forms. By 1980 the number of couples who have established households without legal or religious sanction was reported to be over 1,500,000, tripling the figures reported in 1970 (Macklin, 1985). If this trend continues, a large number of Americans will experience a period of cohabitation at some time in their lives.

Among the policy issues arising from cohabitation are property and inheritance rights, insurance benefits, bank account claims, the legal inheritance rights of children, custody and alimony decisions, and discrimination.

Judicial decisions regarding cohabitation have received the greatest public attention as courts increasingly recognize nonmarital relationships (Myricks, 1980). Since no legal tradition existed regarding the rights and responsibilities of cohabitors, agreements had to be entered into that began defining the legal parameters of the relationships. Within the last decade cohabitation was illegal in almost half the states, and sexual intercourse between an unmarried man and woman was a criminal act in one-third.

Bernstein (1977), among the first to examine the legal ramifications of cohabitation, found that some laws extend protection to cohabitors, but not all circumstances are covered. In real estate transactions, for example, all parties are likely to be protected if they have invested mutually in their shared homestead. Personal property can be protected by listing what is owned by each individual. Bills of sale in individual names would also serve as protective measures should the relationship end. Insurance policies, however, do not generally protect live-in lovers. "The agent must guarantee that the surviving beneficiary has an insurable interest, and that the insurance contract is not subject to contest by a former spouse, children of a former marriage, parents or other family members" (Berstein, 1977, p. 363). Thus, cohabiting couples must take extra caution to obtain the insurance protection that married people automatically receive. Wills should be drawn to protect the estates of cohabitants; otherwise, blood relatives will receive the property. While when a married partner dies, all or part of inherited property going to the spouse is tax exempt, this is not true for a cohabitant.

The birth of children within a cohabiting relationship raises important personal and legal concerns. Such births are considered illegitimate, although the rights of these children have been expanding. Gifts, wills, insurance, and contracts can protect the property rights of a child growing to majority in the household of cohabiting parents (Bernstein, 1977). Paternity suits and child support battles may be the lot for cohabitors who dissolve their relationship. There is also legal danger for parents who have custody of children from a previous relationship when they enter a cohabitation situation. Many judges are not tolerant of such a nontraditional arrangement and may switch custody to the noncustodial parent who makes such a request.

Housing problems may also confront the unmarried couple, who may be denied the opportunity to purchase or rent property. Upon discovery, these individuals may be evicted, especially in states that outlaw intercourse between unmarried persons. The same type of legal restrictions and personal biases may operate in the employment sphere. Denial of employment or firing may result when an employer discovers a cohabitation arrangement. Most states and the 1964 Civil Rights Act, Title VII, do not protect individuals from discrimination based on marital status or living situation. Considering present court trends regarding not interfering with state laws that outlaw sodomy, the future appears to be uncertain regarding the legal protection of cohabitors. It is also difficult to determine to what degree insurance and credit have been denied to individuals who are living together out of wedlock.

In addition, Macklin (1978) comments that the law does not provide for confidentiality of communication between unmarried partners. Therefore, they may be called upon to testify against one another in court. Consent to medical treatment for each other is not recognized. Macklin (1978) also underscores how federal tax and benefit policies traditionally discriminate against cohabitors:

> Married couples with one income and a joint return pay less taxes on the same income than two single persons (who, in turn, pay less than a two-income, married couple). Moreover, persons who are cohabiting cannot claim each other as dependents. Should the couple remain unmarried and one partner never work outside the home, they will receive less social security benefits upon retirement than if they had

> married. If a partner is injured or dies on the job, the surviving partner will receive workers' compensation only if there was a legal marriage." (p. 10)

In these respects government policy discourages the option of cohabitation. Under the Tax Reform Act of 1986, however, some change has occurred. For example, the two-earner deductible has been eliminated, so that one-earner, two-parent families will no longer pay higher taxes than dual-career families.

In conclusion, for singles, some of whom may be cohabiting, there exists a range of policies that have a negative impact on their lifestyle. Health care problems, housing, work discrimination, biased insurance, unfavorable tax and social security regulations, and punitive laws related to sex, child custody, property, and inheritance are among the many obstacles the courts and legislative bodies must deal with if the goal is to make this lifestyle option a more equitable choice in American society.

Remarriage and Stepfamilies

In almost 43% of all marriages today a remarriage is occurring for at least one of the spouses (Pasley & Ihinger-Tallman, this volume). The majority of those remarrying will bring at least one child into the new marriage, thus creating a stepfamily. It is further predicted that 16% of all children under 18 will live in stepfamilies by 1990 (Glick in Pasley & Ihinger-Tallman, this volume). While the state and federal governments at present pay little attention to stepfamilies, the increasing number of stepfamilies in the United States has led Ramsey (1986) to conclude that new federal laws and policies related to stepfamilies will be passed in the near future. Ramsey further emphasizes the importance of clarifying stepparent obligations regarding support of stepchildren. Traditionally such decisions have been left up to the state. Fourteen states obligate stepparents to support their stepchildren, but to a lesser degree than biological children. The rest of the states make no support requirements.

Ramsey (1986) also raises the following questions. Should stepparent obligations continue if the stepparent divorces the biological parent? Should only stepparents who are living with the stepchild and are married to the custodial parent be responsible for support? Should all stepparents be liable? How should resources be apportioned between biological parent and stepparent and natural children and stepchildren? Must stepchildren be supported by stepparents only when public support is the alternative? If stepchild support is automatic for stepparents, will this have an impact on the remarriage and divorce rates of stepfamilies?

Encroachments by the federal government are beginning to influence state-based domestic relations law. Ramsey (1986) cites as an example AFDC regulations that continued to provide benefits when there was no clear legal obligation between a man in the home (not married to the mother) and the children of a different father. However, in 1981 the Omnibus Budget Reconciliation Act amendments to the AFDC program changed this to an assumption that stepparents are obligated even if the children are not biologically theirs.

Essentially, federal policy toward stepfamilies is designed to lower costs to the government. As mentioned earlier in this chapter, P.L. 93-378 (the Child Support Enforcement Program, Title IV-D of the Social Security Act) has been an effort to collect support money from absent fathers. However, it does not attend to the present needs or circumstances of the father's current family situation. (For further technical details, see Ramsey, 1986.)

Recognizing the stepfamily as a complex and heterogeneous family form leads to the identification of other issues. For example, the need for counseling and therapy services for stepfamilies and the remarried has been identified by Visher and Visher (this volume). Often ignored are emotionally controversial issues and legal dilemmas related to kinship rights following divorce and remarriage. This is especially evident in the increase in grandparent visitation rights granted by the states during the past decade. Furstenberg (1979) is critical that policy makers often do not recognize that children in stepfamilies may have more than two parents and that many parents are dealing with more than one family. Schools, businesses, religious and health organizations, tax laws, welfare regulations, and voluntary associations often do not logistically connect with this reality. What is needed for further policy development is increasing social science data on how different types of stepfamilies operate and how this information can be used to enrich these family forms.

In addition to questions of child support as it relates to stepchildren, a current preoccupation of the federal and state governments, the issues of child custody and visitation rights are also important. (These were discussed in detail in the final chapter of Volume 3 of this series.) The legal adoption of stepchildren changes their status, giving them all the rights of biological children. But short of adoption there are difficult questions about the rights of stepparents to make decisions affecting their stepchildren, including such matters as medical care and education. In general, stepparents have such rights only if they are specifically delegated by biological parents, and the strains between custodial and noncustodial parents in stepfamilies may make such delegation problematic.

Finally, stepchildren do not automatically inherit the estate of their stepparents. A will must specify the share of a stepparent's estate that a stepchild will receive in the event of the stepparent's death, whereas there is a presumption under the law that a biological child will inherit a portion of the biological parent's estate unless a will specifies something else. These are all matters to which legal and family researchers as well as human service practitioners should give their attention so that where necessary public policy can be adjusted to meet the needs of the growing numbers of stepfamilies (Wald, 1987).

Gays and Lesbians

In the past 20 years there has been increased social visibility and activism among gay males and lesbians. Within this period there has also been a substantial increase in the research literature on homosexual relationships, although this research is still considerably less than definitive. According to Harry in Chapter 5 of this volume, gay and lesbian couples are most often dual-worker, dual-career units with rarely a person at home full time. In a sense this lifestyle serves as a prototype for what increasing numbers of heterosexual couples are experiencing. However, gays and lesbians are confronted with a level of societal hostility uncharacteristic of that directed at any other family form. Religious, legal, social, and economic tenets have been used overtly to suppress this lifestyle, condemning it in terms of sinfulness, decadence, and as a threat to the social fabric of the community.

The most recent evidence of this was the 1986 U.S. Supreme Court decision to uphold Georgia's antisodomy law. The court held that the constitutional right of privacy did not extend to homosexual sodomy, a ruling that confirmed the long-standing existence in many states of statutes restricting sexual acts between consenting adults (Myricks & Rubin, 1977). In the rare instances of criminal charges being filed against consenting adults, it is largely gay males who are prosecuted. This situation is apt to become more acute as a result of increased anxiety about AIDS, an illness found most frequently among male homosexuals.

Little attention has been paid to the effects of public policies and programs on the lives of homosexuals. An exception, however, has been gay and lesbian issues focusing on parenthood. Harry (Chapter 5 of this volume) cites figures that 14 to 25% of gay men have been married at some time in their lives, and it is estimated that half of these marriages produced children. About one-third of lesbians have been married, with approximately half bearing children, and some adoptions also add to the number of homosexual parents. Several major metropolitan areas now have gay foster homes to care for gay adolescent runaways and "throwaways." Following a divorce the children of a gay male are usually remanded to the custody of their mother.

Thus, a vast majority of divorced gay males, as is the situation with divorced heterosexual males, do not live full time with their children. This is another reason more children live with lesbians than with gay males. Harry (1985) reports that lesbian mothers retain custody in approximately 15% of divorce proceedings when the sexual orientation of the homosexual parent is known, but gay fathers are less frequently assigned their children.

Clearly, the sexual orientation of parents is a major factor in custody battles. The courts have generally held that the public or child's good is not served by placement with a homosexual parent. The potential for social ostracism and community harassment of children raised by gay males and lesbians, for example, is cited by the judicial system in denying custody. Fears of influencing the child's sexual preference are also a factor in custody decisions. However, although the studies are few and with small, nonrandom samples, findings question the assumption that children raised by homosexuals become homosexual.

As previously mentioned, most homosexual couples live in households with two incomes. Harry (1985) comments that when judges require that lesbians not live with their lovers in order to obtain child custody, the result may be a severe diminution of financial resources. Court denial of custody to males primarily because they are gay denies a child its father and negatively labels the parent.

The inability of homosexual couples to marry prevents "the advantage of symbolic equality, spouse social security benefits, spouse health insurance benefits, lower car insurance, family membership in various organizations, and inheritance rights" (Harry, 1985, p. 231). Also, the lack of major family medical care for live-in gay and lesbian partners has been a recent controversy in California.

In their place of occupation gays must often conceal their sexual orientation. "Public opinion polls report strong support for barring gays from high status occupations; application forms are constructed to weed out gays; there is discrimination even in government licensing and security clearances" (Levine in Stein, 1985, p. 39). Firings, transfers, and low-level employment also exist.

Kelly and Rice write in Chapter 6 of this volume that sex and race discrimination is forbidden in the workplace by Title VII of the Civil Rights Act of 1964, but sexual preference is excluded from this protection. In numerous other spheres policy discrimination and exclusion appear much more tolerated by the public for homosexuals than for other family forms. The unacceptability of homosexuals in the military services is an overt example. Somewhat more subtle is the lack of curriculum material that pertains to homosexuals in family life education programs, a matter of acrimonious debate in the late-1980s pertaining to education about AIDS.

The practice by some communities of barring home ownership by individuals unrelated by blood or marriage (Harry, Chapter 5 of this volume) has obvious adverse consequences for gays and lesbians. It is recommended that civil rights legislation be extended to forbid discrimination against gays and lesbians with respect to employment, housing, and educational opportunities, as discussed in further detail below.

Public concern over homosexuality today is most dramatically shown by fear of AIDS. Over 33,000 cases have been reported in the United States, predominantly among homosexual males. Controversial public policy issues focus on the contraction of the disease, health care, and employment. The position taken by the U.S. Justice Department that employers can fire people with AIDS if they believe they are a threat in the workplace lends little comfort to the homosexual community. However, the 1987 Supreme Court decision protecting individuals with contagious diseases from arbitrary firing may assuage this anxiety. Is AIDS a qualifying handicap for disability programs, and are sufferers subject to state and federal protection from discrimination as handicapped individuals? Antidiscrimination statutes of this type exist in 42 states and the District of Columbia. The potentially high medical expenses of AIDS patients are of concern to companies with extensive health care insurance benefits. Estimates for the average cost of treating an AIDS patient are approximately $140,000, according to the Centers for Disease Control. Increasingly companies will look for alternatives to hospitalization to defray health costs. BankAmerica is exploring the use of hospices as it pioneers a role as one of the first companies to develop an AIDS policy (Abramowitz, 1986). The AIDS crisis presents American business with legal and ethical issues that it has not customarily addressed. How these will affect the high-risk population of gay male employees is difficult to discern.

The policy issues and possible solutions to problems consequent to being homosexual are not fundamentally dissimilar to those of being single, especially a cohabitor. The issues relate to repressive laws and to discrimination in occupation, housing, health care, Social Security, insurance, taxes, inheritance, and child custody. But solutions will be more difficult to achieve because of the powerful social taboos against this form of interpersonal lifestyle. However, the recent opening of a school for gay and lesbian children in New York City may portend a shift in public thinking toward the problems of homosexuals.

Widows and Widowers

Widowhood has been described as a "roleless role," as Lopata discusses in Chapter 7. Although women are socialized to become wives and mothers, they receive virtually no preparation for widowhood. Ironically, it is a situation in which almost all married women will eventually find themselves. Hiltz (1978) describes widowhood as "a negatively evaluated social category where the individual loses the central source of identity, financial support, and social relationships" (p. 1). In Chapter 8 Burgess emphasizes that widowers are a seriously neglected and often highly needy group of men.

There are many indications that imply the need for policies and programs to assist those whose lives and identities have been damaged by the loss of a spouse through death. Yet little attention has been paid to the specific needs of widows and widowers as they attempt to adjust to their losses. For example, medical needs following the death of a spouse are only now being recognized. Emotional problems related to grief and bereavement are increasingly being understood. A literature review by Goddard (1979) documents the frequently found physical and mental deterioration of widows and widowers, and Seperberg (1975) found their death rates to be excessively high in the year following the loss of a spouse.

In general, the medical needs of the elderly tend to be both extensive and costly. This is apt to be especially true of aging widows and widowers, since spouses are the chief providers of care for their ailing mates. In fact, loss of spouse is a major reason for moving a frail older person to a nursing home. This is particularly apt to occur for older women, since so many more women than men become widowed. (The health care needs of younger widows and widowers are not discussed here largely because older people tend to have so many more serious health problems than younger ones.)

The cost of medical care is a severe problem for many of the elderly. Medical expenses are covered at a considerable, but far from total, extent through Social Security Act provisions for Medicare (Title XVIII) or Medicaid (Title XIX). Generally speaking, Medicare pays medical benefits for people and their spouses who were employed for 10 years or more in occupations covered by the Social Security Act; Medicaid is a program for poor people not eligible for Medicare. A thorough discussion of these programs is far beyond the scope of this chapter. Instead, see Volume 2, Chapter 10 and Brody and Brody (1987), Starr (1986), and Schorr (1986).

In the late 1980s there are a number of central, critical issues surrounding Medicare, Medicaid, and the health needs of the elderly. These include the rising numbers of the elderly, the stronger tendency of the aging to have serious and long-term medical problems, escalating costs of medical (including hospital) care; lack of assurance of a high quality of care; methods of financing this care (government or private insurance) and problems of long-term care of the chronically ill or disabled.

Contrary to widespread assumptions, only about 5% of the elderly live in institutions, but it is estimated that another 10% are so disabled as to need home nursing care. Although it has been thought that such care is less expensive than the costs of nursing homes, recent studies show that this is not the case (Fox & Clauser, 1980; Palmer, H., 1983; U.S. Comptroller General, 1977).

As discussed above, frail widows and widowers are especially apt to need help that was formerly provided by their spouses. In recent years there have been insistent calls for the family to provide care for elderly relatives in need of nursing services. Although these calls are often pitched in idealized, pro-family tones, the basic agenda tends to be one of saving money from public coffers.

Studies show that in actuality family members, especially daughters and daughters-in-law, do provide many services for their ailing elders. They also show that the needs of older relatives often outstrip what their younger relatives can handle, especially since so many women as well as men are employed outside the home today.

Using a family systems perspective, it becomes clear that the multiple physical, social, and psychological needs of the frail elderly can cause numerous stresses throughout a multigenerational family system. For example, Brody and Brody (1987) write that unresolved family relationship problems may become reactivated so that the older person becomes the focus of exacerbated latent or overt conflicts. Family conflicts erupt over such issues as how to share caregiving responsibilities fairly or where the older person is going to live. The burden of providing care to the elderly can create stresses in the marriage relationships of their children and in the parenting of their grandchildren and can create struggles between siblings. Thus, advocacy for outside assistance for the elderly can be advocacy for the well-being of the entire extended family.

A true pro-family stance on meeting the health requirements of the elderly is a stance that recognizes that families may need supplemental supportive services from public and private agencies if they are to adequately meet the sometimes overwhelming health needs of their senior members as well as the multiple needs of other members of the total family system. This is especially true in the complex, predominantly urban society of the present, a society in which the majority of able-bodied, younger woman and men are employed outside the home; in which more and more people are living to advanced age and developing chronic illnesses and disabilities; in which the cost of medical, hospital, and nursing home care is skyrocketing; and in which community life tends to be impersonal and bureaucratic.

Widows and widowers also are apt to encounter social and economic problems, with the problems being more common for women. For instance, far more women than men are widowed (Lopata, this volume). This raises numerous policy and program issues concerning the economic and social well-being of widows as an at-risk population. It has been estimated (Cleveland & Gianturco, 1976) that few widows past the age of 55 will remarry. One reason is that there are approximately 2 million widowers and 10 million widows in the United States, and the widowers tend to marry younger women. However, even though widows are more numerous than widowers and even though they may be more likely to have serious economic problems, widowers are not immune from such difficulties.

Old Age, Survivors, and Disability Insurance (OASDI) through the Social Security Act is the federal government program most Americans associate with relieving the economic plight of widows as well as other older people. OASDI benefits increased during the

1970s, and this helped poverty decline among the elderly. However, widows without young children must be 65 years of age to be eligible. For young widows with children, a rather small group, mother's benefits stop when the last child reaches age 16. There is no transition period for a mother to retrain or gain economic skills, a time that has been called the "blackout period." Since young widows share the child care problems of other single-parent families, young widows who are receiving substantial survivors benefits for themselves and their children may have a disincentive to remarry.

Older widows receive 50% of a former husband's OASDI benefits that would be paid to a couple. This is also true for men whose wives have died if they choose to receive the wife's benefits rather than their own. These comments apply to workers who have been employed for 10 years or more in occupations covered by the Social Security Act. The size of OASDI benefits is largely determined by the amount of salary the worker had received. Thus, the widows of men who earned low wages are apt to have meager benefits unless these benefits are supplemented by the deceased husband's retirement payments from employment, insurance, and/or savings. This, of course, presumes that the husband left his money and property to his widow. In general, the widows who are especially apt to be poor are those whose husbands had not been covered by OASDI and who had no other sources of retirement income.

An increasing number of women are covered by OASDI themselves because of their own employment. However, their benefits are apt to be particularly small because of their shorter periods of employment and their lower average earnings. Moreover, they do not receive benefits from their own employment if they opt to receive them from their husband's work, a choice they frequently make because they often receive a larger amount from their husband's payments than they would from their own. The foregoing remarks also apply to widowers if their wives had been the chief wage earner.

Widows and widowers, like other elderly people who receive little or nothing from OASDI, are apt to be eligible for assistance from another part of the Social Security Act—SSI (Supplemental Security Income). As in the case of OASDI, payments under this act increase if the overall cost of living rises. These payments average about 75% of the so-called poverty line and, though small, are more generous than payments made to needy, divorced, or unmarried mothers of young children who are assisted by AFDC. (See an earlier section of this chapter and also Volume 1, Chapters 5, 6, and 10.)

Older black widows and widowers are more likely than white ones to draw smaller amounts from the OASDI system due to the legacy of lower wages resulting from segregation and racially discriminatory hiring practices.

The entire topic of income maintenance as provided by the Social Security Act is highly technical and complex, both in terms of its present provisions and those that are recommended for the future. For further references see Schorr (1986), Garfinkel and McLanahan (1986), and Brody and Brody (1987).

In 1974 the Retirement Income Security Equity Act (ERISA) was passed. Among other things it set up a nonprofit government corporation to guarantee approved pension plans and survivor provisions to protect spouses. Elderly low-income persons, both as singles and as couples, can also obtain income supplements through the federal food stamp program, Medicaid, and income-assisted housing. Then, too, more and more war veterans as they age become eligible for veteran's benefits, an important source of income. According to Brody and Brody (1987), a wide range of benefits is needed for the elderly, since loss of assistance from any one program could create losses that would have serious effects for people on marginal incomes. (See also the previous discussion of this chapter on Medicare and Medicaid.) Proposed cuts in the funding of these programs should be resisted since elderly people, especially widows and widowers, tend to be a highly vulnerable population group. This is particularly apt to be true as they reach age 75 or so. Surviving spouses may be required to rebuild their social, emotional, and financial lives at a time when their resources may be diminishing dramatically. Although members of their extended families may try to help them resolve their numerous problems, the elderly may find it almost impossible to do so without established outside assistance.

In brief, many families need supplementary help from outside organizations, both public and private, in order to provide assistance to their aging relatives, so that their task does not become an overly heavy burden. Many elderly people themselves might also prefer added assistance from the community so that they will feel less of a problem to their families. This help might include home health services, personal and family counseling, housekeeping assistance, respite care, and income maintenance programs as discussed above. Public policy should be directed toward ensuring that such services and programs are equally available on a nationwide basis as a supplement to the effort of families and as a means of preventing severe stress on both the elderly and their kin.

As noted earlier with respect to teenage parents, there is also a critical need to improve the organization of comprehensive services. Many elements of services needed by the elderly exist in communities, although the services are often uneven in quantity and quality and, in addition, their funding varies in adequacy and availability. Overlap often occurs between programs for community mental health, vocational rehabilitation, senior low-cost housing, services to the aging, services to families, veteran's services, meals-on-wheels, and so on. Like many of the other health and human service programs in this country, these organizations have evolved over the years through various pieces of local, state, and federal legislation as well as through voluntary efforts in the private sector. Although it might seem desirable to bring all these services together under one piece of federal legislation and one administrative organization, such a development is unlikely and might even be unwise for a number of reasons, including the heterogeneous nature of American society and its enormous array of both advocacy and consumer groups. Therefore, rather than pushing for a radical reorganization and streamlining of services, it might be wiser to ensure the training and deployment of a large-enough body of informed, skilled human services professionals to help elderly people locate and obtain the services they need and, if requisite services are lacking, to join with other advocacy groups in pushing for service development.

Foster Families

Unlike other family forms discussed in this chapter, the foster and adoptive families discussed in this section owe their existence primarily to policies and programs of public and private organizations. In a word, they are bureaucratic creations rather than spontaneous adaptations to changing values and living conditions. The focus of sponsoring organizations is on the best interests of the children, but it can be argued that the children's interests are inextricable from those of their families and the systems with which families interact.

Substitute care for children includes both group care and foster care. Group care is defined as 24-hour care in a residential facility designed to be therapeutic and includes treatment, education, and group living and is based on an individual plan for each child who cannot be helped in his or her own home or in a substitute family (Whittaker, 1987). Foster family care is 24-hour care with a family other than a child's biological parents, mostly by people unrelated to the child.

Although the data are far from complete and reliable, the best estimate is that in the mid-1980s there are about one-quarter million children in foster family care, down from about twice that many in 1977. However, since 1983 the numbers have been creeping up somewhat. The median age of foster children has increased by nearly 2 years between 1977 and 1983, from 10.8 to 12.6 years. Males and females are found in nearly equal numbers, and this has not changed over these years. About half are white (down from 62% in 1977), about one-third are black (up from 28% in 1977), and about 7% are Hispanic; these percentages are unchanged over these years.

Over one-fifth of the children in foster family care are disabled, and some of them are considered "hard to place" or "special-needs" children, a category that is increasing dramatically and has received more attention in recent years. Almost all children going into foster care now are either special-needs children or have serious behavior problems. Over half of all foster children experience more than one placement, but the length of time they spend in foster care decreased from a median of about 29 months in 1977 to about 10 months in 1983. Fifty-six percent of the children were in foster care to protect them from abuse or neglect, and an additional 22% were there because of various parental conditions such as illness or absence. In 1977 case plans for foster children existed in nearly 70% of the cases, rising to nearly 90% of cases by 1983 (largely owing to new requirements of federal legislation). Nearly half the plans envisioned return to parents, relatives, or other caretakers; nearly 20% envisioned long-term foster care; nearly 15% aimed at adoption; and 10% pointed toward independent living (Stein, 1987).

The major current legislation in this field is the Adoption Assistance and Child Welfare Act of 1980, P.L. 96-272. Prior to its enactment over half of the funding for foster care was from state, local, and private sources. In 1961 Title IV-A of the Social Security Act authorized the Aid to Families with Dependent Children program, commonly known as "welfare," to provide federal funds in support of foster care in cases where the courts ordered placement. Just prior to the enactment of the 1980 law, about 20% of the children were supported by this source of federal funds (Knitzer & McGowan, 1978). This caused a built-in disincentive to move children thus supported out of foster care because the states thereby lost federal funding.

From 1967 forward, Title IV-B of the Social Security Act was designed to provide for social services for all children, not just those in foster care. However, it was never well funded, providing only about 5% of the states' funds for child welfare services in 1982. Title XX of the Social Security Act, passed in 1976, did a bit better, providing about 30% of the funds for child welfare services in 1982. Unfortunately, cuts in Title XX funding in 1981 seriously reduced the financing of these services.

A series of studies, beginning with Maas and Engler's seminal study published in 1959 and summarized by Stein, Gambrill, and Wiltse in 1978 found that, contrary to legislative intent, foster care programs were not placing children for temporary periods while plans for their permanent care were completed. There were few efforts to provide services that might have permitted these children to remain in or return to their own homes. Over one-third of these children remained in foster care for 4 years or more (Shyne & Schroeder, 1978). Although required, by and large case plans for these children were not being made.

Further, the biological parents were not being provided with services that might have made it possible to return their children to them, and parental visiting was not encouraged. States often did not know how many foster children there were under their care or where the children were placed. In-depth case reviews were the exception. Termination of parental rights so that permanent plans could be made for children who could not be returned to their biological parents was difficult or impossible to arrange in most states. A series of related studies showed that it was impossible to develop effective strategies to promote permanent plans for many foster children (Stein, 1987).

The Adoption Assistance and Child Welfare Act of 1980 was enacted to give legislative support to planning for the permanent care of children. It abolishes Title IV-A, described above, and replaces it with Title IV-E, which provides not only foster care for AFDC-eligible children but also for adoption subsidies for these children as well as for SSI-eligible (Supplemental Security Income) children, who are mainly severely handicapped children. The act makes such children eligible for Medicaid, and for the first time funds are made available for preventive services. In order to receive Title IV-E funds states must make reasonable efforts to prevent placement and arrange for reunification.

Title IV-B funds, authorized for general child welfare services, were actually used prior to 1980 primarily to pay for foster care. To constrain this practice, P.L. 96-272 provides that additional appropriations above the then-existing amounts be used for preventive and reunification services. Other incentives are also provided to encourage states to spend more for prevention and reunification with parents rather than expanding the number of children in foster care (Stein, 1987).

This legislation appears to be a step in the right direction. However, it is not clear in mid 1987 how effective P.L. 96-272 has been or what negative consequences it may be having. One major outcome has been increased efforts to promote the adoption of special-needs children. On the negative side, some concerns have been expressed that an increase in child fatalities may be connected with incentives to keep children with their biological parents in child abuse cases. It is not clear whether there is any basis for such a concern, but the outcome of P.L. 96-272 certainly merits a most careful, research-based assessment on this and other grounds.

Beyond a few pilot projects that have shown it is possible to mount successful efforts at permanency planning for children in foster families, is it possible to replicate these results nationally and on a routine basis. Evaluation research of the state programs put into place by this legislation should be able to supply the answers and suggest further changes, if necessary. Is it possible to intervene early, before a crisis makes a placement inevitable, and to work effectively with families toward children remaining with their biological parents or other close relatives in improved situations that promote the overall well-being of both children and other family members?

Once a placement occurs, is it possible to implement within a relatively short period plans for children to move into benign permanent living arrangements, whether with their biological parents, close relatives, family friends, foster families, adoptive families or, in the case of older children, independent living arrangements? Can these objectives be reached with children presenting special problems, the children often considered hard to place? This includes children who are "status offenders" (school truants, runaways, "behavior problems," and so forth) or delinquents, have physical or mental handicaps, are older, or are minorities.

An early concern with the quality of care offered by both biological parents and foster families has been eclipsed or greatly reduced since 1980 by the current preoccupation with permanency planning. There are both research and operational issues: Can sufficient numbers of high-quality foster homes be found and licensed? This has become increasingly difficult in recent years as more women move into employment outside the home and as more marriages end in divorce. Can methods be developed for valid and reliable measures of foster home quality, preparing foster parents for dealing with the problems of foster parenthood, and sustaining their interest in continuing as foster parents over extended periods of time? Can biological parents' interest in their children be sustained while their children are in substitute care? To what extent have parents whose children were removed from the home because of abuse or neglect actually been effectively "rehabilitated" or retrained so that they become competent, satisfactory mothers and fathers for their children?

Research on the outcomes of the other form of substitute care, group care, suggests that a focus on treating the child and modifying his or her behavior in the group setting (and by extension, in a foster family) and treating the family through education, counseling and/or psychotherapy will not carry over after the child leaves group care unless attention is paid to the broader social context and to the concrete problems faced by so many parents whose children are in foster care. These include difficulties with income, housing, employment, educational opportunities, and medical care. Can a significant-enough impact be made on these concrete problems so that any positive changes in the child brought about during the period of substitute care are carried over into the post–foster family environment? It needs to be determined whether legislative policy and administrative rules as well as sufficient funding can be developed to support the requirements for successful outcomes (Whittaker, 1987; also see Whittaker & Maluccio, this volume).

Among the recommendations for improved public policy found or implied in the literature are the following: (a) Provide more preventive services designed to maintain children in the homes of their biological parents, such as family income maintenance as needed, day care, homemaker services, housing assistance, employment assistance for parents, and family treatment, as indicated; (b) make relatives of children in foster homes eligible for AFDC so that those who might otherwise provide competent parenting can afford to take on the care of foster children who are their kin; (c) maintain communication between children and their biological parents during foster care, especially if the plan is to reunite children with their parents; (d) reduce legal and other barriers to terminating parental rights so that when return to the biological parents is not appropriate other plans can be made, such as adoption; (e) provide financial assistance to families willing to adopt hard-to-place children; (f) develop criteria for decisions about removing children from the care of their parents to reduce the variability of decision-making and ensure that children are removed only when it is not in the best interests of children for them to remain with their parents; and (g) employ sufficient numbers of well-prepared human service professionals to make sure that services needed by biological, foster, and adoptive families and children are both coordinated and of high quality (Burt & Pittman, 1985; Cox & Cox, 1984).

The last point needs special emphasis. There has been a strong tendency over the years to lodge child welfare protective services (including foster care and adoption) in public welfare agencies where, more and more, standards for trained personnel have become relatively low and salaries have been meager. The majority of agencies require only a bachelor's degree in any field. However, child welfare services is a complex, demanding, and stressful field; this is especially true since the passage of the 1980 legislation that requires more effective work with vulnerable children and their families along with better permanency planning. Better-trained and better-paid child protection workers are strongly indicated for this especially troubled group of children and parents at risk of further problematic development.

There is also an urgent need for a number of well-designed and implemented studies to carefully assess the long-term developmental outcomes of a variety of the intervention programs discussed above, as these outcomes apply to children, biological parents, adoptive parents, and foster parents. Although a strong humanitarian case can be made for permanency planning that assures children the security of living in one family rather than a number of them and that emphasizes keeping them with their biological parents, it is also essential to recognize that enthusiasm for cutting the costs of foster and residential care has inspired many of the backers of permanency planning policies. Although economic considerations are important, the lives of endangered children are of more crucial value. Thus, studies that bear both economic and human values in mind are needed to provide guidance on what approaches are most broadly effective with what kinds of children and families.

Adoptive Families

Adoption is defined by the Child Welfare League of America (1978) as "the method provided by law to establish the legal relationship of parent and child between persons who are not so related by birth." It was first recognized in law in the United States in the mid19th century. Although detailed, accurate information about trends in adoption is lacking, there is reason to believe that the earlier focus on the adoption of white infants has shifted to older and handicapped children. The increasing prevalence of birth control and abortion services and the willingness of many mothers to keep their children because of the decreasing stigma of unmarried parenthood have contributed to this result. Thus, very few healthy infants born in this country are available for adoption today. Moreover, as a result of the emphasis on permanency planning, older and special-needs children in foster care have increasingly been considered as candidates for adoption.

Most adoptions, roughly 62% in 1975, are stepparent adoptions. Seventy-seven percent of the children placed that year with unrelated adoptive parents were placed by licensed agencies, a number which has probably declined since that time with an increase in adoptions arranged by other intermediaries (Meezan, Katz, & Russo, 1978). Some nonagency adoptions are arranged by lawyers and physicians on a nonprofit basis; other so-called "black market" adoptions are arranged for high fees by intermediaries. Black market adoptions are illegal in all 50 states and the District of Columbia.

Adoptive applicants are probably older than in the past because more couples are postponing childbearing and discover their infertility later in life. Due to the extreme shortage of healthy, young children available for adoption in this country, there is a current tendency for prospective adoptive parents to try to adopt children from other countries, adopt independently of social agencies, explore the adoption of older children or children with handicaps, and seek new remedies for infertility such as in vitro fertilization and embryo transplant.

Although a high proportion of prospective adoptive couples wish to adopt infants and preschool children (Cole, 1987) there is at the same time a shortage of these kinds of youngsters along with a growing pool of older, minority, and handicapped children who are awaiting adoptive placement.

Policy-relevant studies of adoption are few. Nevertheless, certain issues and recommendations can be identified from a review of the literature. They include the following:

1. It is often recommended that further special efforts be made to recruit adoptive families, including minority families, for hard-to-place chil-

dren, including raising adoptive parent age limits; allowing single people and fertile couples with their own children to adopt; and subsidizing adoptive parents when necessary to reduce the financial burden, such as in the case of a severely handicapped child or of a poor but otherwise suitable adoptive family. The outcomes of these policies, however, need to be assessed carefully.

2. Further consideration needs to be given to the suggestion that more hard-to-place children be adopted across racial lines. This is also an approach that requires evaluative outcome research.
3. The legal process for relinquishing parental rights should be studied and further consideration given to the use of legal procedures and rules of evidence that provide a better balance between the needs of children for the security of a permanent home and the rights of parents to decide what they wish to do with youngsters. One important issue here is the extent to which unmarried biological fathers should be involved in adoption planning. Another is that some parents fail to provide adequate care for their children but hesitate, often for a long period, to make the decision of legally relinquishing them for adoption.
4. Careful outcome research and further consideration should be given to requests from older adoptive children, adoptive families, and biological families for contact between the birth and adoptive families and their children. Further consideration and assessment should also be given to requests from older adoptive children to open their adoptive records and learn the identity of birth parents.
5. Further studies should be conducted to determine whether or not independent adoptions produce results that are different from agency adoptions, as some have contended.
6. Studies should be conducted of ways to fund adoption services so that more low- and middle-income prospective adoptive parents can afford to pay the costs of adoption as well as the care of special-needs children.

CONCLUSION

This chapter has discussed major public policy issues arising from problems encountered by some families who are involved in variant family forms: single parents, singles, cohabitants, gays or lesbians, stepparents, widows, widowers, foster families, and adoptive families. Although none of these family forms is new, many are increasing in number (single parents, singles, cohabitants, stepparents, widows), and/or openness (cohabitants, gays and lesbians) or variety (foster and adoptive families). Although each family form has its particular characteristics, needs, and related public policy issues, all share some universal aspects.

For example, each family form is especially likely to present problems when income, employment, health, and housing needs are not met. The same can be said of all families, but these survival issues often become more prevalent and acute in variant family forms. This is particularly true when children are involved.

Fundamental debates arise over the rights and responsibilities of those youth and adults who apparently choose such family forms as unmarried, divorced or remarried, or adoptive parenthood, or gay or lesbian cohabiting relationships. Also open to debate is the issue of rights and responsibilities of needy widows and widowers to self-help, family help, and help from public and private services outside the home. Also, what are the rights and responsibilities of parents who are found to be abusive and neglectful of their children?

These issues are thorny ones, indeed. As we have seen, individual and family behavior is far from entirely self-determined; rather, it is highly affected by both interpersonal dynamics within families and by environmental forces such as employment opportunities, costs of living, availability of community services, and the like.

Rapid social, economic, and demographic changes since the 1960s have played a forceful part in creating both the necessity and opportunity for variant family forms. People have not only taken advantage of opportunities for greater personal freedom but in many cases have had changed family structures forced upon them. These include divorced persons, widows and widowers, and, especially, the children.

We have pointed out many of the emergent policy issues associated with changed family forms. It is becoming increasingly clear that the traditional family structures—two married parents and their children—have endured for strong economic and social reasons, especially in terms of child care. On the other hand, this form often created severe problems for those persons who were in effect imprisoned in mutually destructive relationships.

Although the debate will continue regarding private versus family and individual rights and responsibilities, at the most basic level it can be recommended that public programs be strengthened so that members of all kinds of families have equal access to such survival mechanisms as education, job training, employment, health services, housing, and income supports. Beyond this, specialized services and legal adjustments are needed to deal with critical issues that arise in association with changed family forms, for example, child custody and support.

At the risk of sounding overly moralistic and conservative, it is suggested that it is important to devise new social norms in response to the changed conditions of our posttechnological society that provide clearer guidance to individuals and family members as and if they make choices regarding their lifestyles. Such guidance can help people understand the probable impact that choices such as unmarried parenthood, divorce, cohabitation, and remarriage may have not only on themselves but on other family members, particularly on present and future children. Just what these new cultural norms may be, how they might be achieved, and what effects they might have remain open to debate.

References

Abel, R., Jackson, J. L., Fein, E., Al-Safag, E. L., & Schuster, D. (1982). Pregnant adolescents: Cost-benefit options. *Social Casework, 63*, 286–290.

Abramowitz, M. (1986, March 16). Workers with AIDS may have legally protected handicap. *Washington Post*, F1, F10.

Adair, N., & Adair, C., (1978). *Word is out: Stories of some of our lives*. New York: Dell.

Adams, B., Brownstein, C. A., Rennalls, I. M., & Schmitt, M. H. (1976). The pregnant adolescent—a group approach. *Adolescence, 11*, 467–485.

Adams, D. J. (1982). *A comparison of confidence and degree of contentment in parental role of custodial and noncustodial stepmothers*. Unpublished doctoral dissertation, Florida State University, Tallahassee.

Ahrons, C. R., and Wallisch, K. (1987). Parenting in the binuclear family: Relationships between biological and stepparents. In K. Pasley & M. Ihinger-Tallman (Eds.), *Remarriage and stepparenting today: Research and theory*. New York: Guilford Press.

Aires, N., & Klerman, L. V. (1982). Evaluating service delivery models for pregnant adolescents. *Women and Health, 6*, 91–107.

Albrecht, S. L. (1979). Correlates of marital happiness among the remarried. *Journal of Marriage and the Family, 41*, 857–867.

Albrecht, S. L., & Bahr, H. M. (1983). *Divorce and remarriage: Problems, adaptations and adjustments*. Westport, CT: Greenwood.

Allen-Meares, P. (1984). Adolescent pregnancy and parenting: The forgotten adolescent father and his parents. *Journal of Social Work and Human Sexuality, 3*, 27–37.

Anderson, J. Z., & White, G. (1986). An empirical investigation of interaction and relationship patterns in functional and dysfunctional nuclear families and stepfamilies. *Family Process, 25*, 407–422.

Aumend, S. A., & Barrett M. C. (1984). Self-concept and attitudes towards adoption: A comparison of searching and nonsearching adult adoptees. *Child Welfare, LXIII*, 251–259.

Authier, K., & Authier, J. (1980). Intervention with families of pregnant adolescents. In I. R. Stuart & C. F. Wells (Eds.), *Pregnancy in adolescence: needs, problems, and management* (pp. 290–311). New York: Van Nostrand Reinhold.

Bachrach, C. A. (1983, November). Adoption as a means of family formation: Data from the national survey of family growth. *Journal of Marriage and the Family*, (November), 859–865.

Bacon, L. (1974). Early motherhood, accelerated role transition and social pathologies. *Social Forces, 52*, 331–341.

Bader, E., & Sinclair, C. (1983). The first critical year of marriage. In D. R. Mace, Ed., *Prevention in family services: Approaches to family wellness*. Beverly Hills, CA: Sage.

Badger, E. (1982). Effects of parent education programs on teenage mothers and their offspring. In G. Scott & T. Field, (Eds.), *Teenage parents and their offspring* (pp. 283–310). New York: Grune & Stratton.

Baldwin, W. (1980). Adolescent pregnancy and childbearing—growing concerns for Americans. *Population Reference Bureau, 31*(2), Washington, DC.

Baldwin, W., & Cain, V. (1980). The children of teenage parents. *Family Planning Perspectives, 12,* 34–43.

Baldwin, W., & Cain, V. (1980). *Adolescent pregnancy and childbearing: Growing concern for Americans.* Washington, DC: Population Defense Bureau.

Bane, M. 1986. Household composition and poverty. In S. Danziger & D. Weinberg (Eds.), *Fighting poverty.* Cambridge, MA: Harvard University Press.

Barbuto, J. (1983, March 27). Letter reprinted from *The New York Times Magazine.*

Barett, C. (1978). *Strategies for preventing the stresses of widowhood.* Presentation of the Southwestern Psychological Association, New Orleans.

Barrera, M., Jr. (1981). Social support in the adjustment of pregnant adolescents: Assessment issues. In B. H. Gottlieb (Ed.), *Social networks and social support* (pp. 69–96). Beverly Hills, CA: Sage.

Barret, R. L., & Robinson, B. E. (1982a). Teenage fathers: Neglected to long. *Social Work,* 27(6), 484–488.

Barret, R. L., & Robinson, B. C. (1982b). A descriptive study of teenage expectant fathers. *Family Relations, 31,* 349–352.

Barth, R. P., & Schinke, J. P. (1984). Enhancing the social supports of teenage mothers. *Social Casework, 65,* 523–531.

Bassoff, E. S. (1983). The pregnant client: Understanding and counseling her. *The Personnel and Guidance Journal, 62,* 20–23.

Bell, A., & Weinberg, M. (1978). *Homosexualities.* New York: Simon & Schuster.

Bell, A., Weinberg, M., & Hammersmith, S. (1981). *Sexual preference.* Bloomington, IN: Indiana University Press.

Bell, C., Casto, G., & Daniels, D. S. (1983). Ameliorating the impact of teen-age pregnancy on parent and child. *Child Welfare, 62,* 167–173.

Berardo, F. (1970). Survivorship and social isolation: The case of the aged widower. *Family Coordinator, 19,* 11–24.

Berardo, F. (1973). Survivorship and social isolation: The case of the aged widower. *Family Coordinator, 19,* 11–25.

Berg, M., Taylor, B., Edwards, L. E., & Hakanson, E. Y. (1979). Prenatal care for pregnant adolescents in a public high school. *Journal of School Health, 49,* 32–35.

Berger, M. E. (1974). *Trial marriage followup.* Unpublished.

Berger, P., & Kellner, H. (1970). Marriage and the construction of reality: An exercise in the microsociology of knowledge. In H. Dreitzel (Ed.), *Patterns of communicative behavior* (pp. 50–73). London: Collier-Macmillan.

Berger, R., & Kelly, J. (1986). Working with homosexuals of the older population. *Social Casework, 67*(4), 203–210.

Berman, E. M., & Goldberg, M. (1986). Therapy with unmarried couples. In N. Jacobson and A. Gurman (Eds.), *Clinical handbook of marital therapy.* New York: Guilford Press.

Bernstein, B. E. (1977). Legal problems of cohabitation. *Family coordinator, 26*(4), 361–366.

Berzon, B., & Leighton, R. (Eds.) (1979). *Positively gay.* Millbrae, CA: Celestial Arts.

Bierman, B. R., & Street, R. (1982). Adolescent girls as mothers: Problems in parenting. In I. R. Stuart & C. F. Wells (Eds.), *Pregnancy in adolescence: Needs, problems and management* (pp. 407–426). New York: Van Nostrand Reinhold.

Birdsall, N., & Chester, L. (1987). Contraception and the status of women: What is the link? *Family Planning Perspectives, 19*(1), 14–23.

Blair, R. (1975). Counseling and homosexuality. *Homosexual Counseling Journal, 2*(3), 94–106.

Blanc, A. K. (1987). The formation and dissolution of second unions: Marriage and cohabitation in Sweden and Norway. *Journal of Marriage and the Family, 49*, 391–400.

Blasband, D., & Peplau, L. A. (1985). Sexual exclusivity versus openness in gay male couples. *Archives of Sexual Behavior, 14*(5), 395–412.

Block, J. (1980). *Friendship.* New York: Macmillan.

Blood, R. (1972). *The family.* New York: Macmillan.

Blum, H. P. (1983). Adoptive parents. Generative conflict and generational continuity. *Psychoanalytic Study of the Child, 38*, 141–163.

Blumstein, A. (1982). On the racial disproportionality of United States prison populations. *Journal of Criminal Law and Criminology, 73*, 1259–1281.

Blumstein, P., & Schwartz, S. (1983). *American couples.* New York: Morrow.

Boggan, E., Carrington, et al. (1975). *The rights of gay people: Basic American Civil Liberties Union guide to a gay person's rights.* New York: Avon Books.

Bohannan, P. J. (1963). *Social anthropology.* New York: Holt, Rinehart & Winston.

Bohannan, P. J. (1970). Divorce chains, households of remarriage, and multiple divorcers. In P. Bohannan (Ed.), *Divorce and after.* Garden City, NY: Doubleday.

Bohannan, P., & Yahreas, H. (1979). Stepfathers as parents. In E. Corfamn (Ed.), *Families today: A research sampler on families and children* (pp. 347–362). Washington, DC: U.S. Government Printing Office.

Bohman, M., & Sigvardsson S. (1980). A prospective longitudinal study of children registered for adoptions: A 15-year follow-up. *Acta Psychiatrica Scandinavica, 61*, 339–355.

Bohman, M., & Sigvardsson S. (1982). Adoption and fostering as preventive measures. In E. J. Anthon & C. Chiland (Eds.), *The child in his family* (Vol. 7). New York: Wiley.

Bohman, M., Sigvardsson, S., & Cloninger, R. (1981). Maternal inheritance of alcohol abuse. *Archives of General Psychiatry, 38*, 965–969.

Bohman, M., Cloninger, R., Sigvardsson, S., & Von Knorring, A. L. (1982). Predisposition to petty criminality in Swedish adoptees. *Archives of General Psychiatry, 39*, 1233–1241.

Boszormenyi-Nagy, I., & Spark, G. (1973). *Invisible loyalties: Reciprocity in intergenerational family therapy.* New York: Harper & Row.

Bowen, M. (1978). *Family therapy in clinical practice.* New York: Jason Arron.

Bowerman, C., Irish, D., & Pope, H. (1966). *Unwed motherhood: Personal and Social consequences.* Chapel Hill, NC: Institute for Research in Social Sciences, University of North Carolina.

Bowlby, J. (1980). *Attachment and loss: Volume 3. Loss, sadness and depression.* New York: Basic Books.

Bowling, A., & Cartwright, A. (1982). *Life after death.* New York: Tavistock.

Bowman, M. E., & Ahrons, C. R. (1985). Impact of legal custody status on fathers' parenting postdivorce. *Journal of Marriage and the Family, 47*, 481–488.

Bozett, F. (1980). Gay fathers: How and why they disclose their homosexuality to their children. *Family Relations, 29*, 173–179.

Bozette, F. (1985a). Gay men as fathers. In S. Hanson & F. Bozett (Eds.), *Dimensions of fatherhood* (pp. 327–352). Beverly Hills, CA: Sage.

Bozett, F. (1985b, April). *Identity management: Social control of identity by children of gay fathers when they know their father is a homosexual.* Paper presented at the 9th Annual Midwest Nursing Research Society Conference, Chicago, IL.

Brandwein, R. A., Brown, C. A., & Fox, E. M. (1974). Women and children last: The social situation of divorced mothers and their families. *Journal of Marriage and the Family, 36*(3), 498–514.

Brindis, C., Barth, R. P., & Williams, A. (1985). *Continuous counseling: Case management in a comprehensive teenage pregnancy and parenting project.* Unpublished manuscript, Teenage Pregnancy Program, San Francisco.

Brinich, P. M., & Brinich, E. B. (1982). Adoption and adaptation. *Journal of Nervous and Mental Disease, 170*(8), 489–493.

Brodbar-Nemzer, J. Y. (1986). Divorce and group commitment: The case of the Jews. *Journal of Marriage and the Family, 48*, 329–340.

Brody, E., & Brody, S. (1987). Aged services. In *Encyclopedia of social work* (Vol I, pp. 106–126). Silver Spring, MD: National Association of Social Workers.

Brodzinsky, D., Schechter, D., Braff, A., & Singer, L. (1984). Psychological and academic adjustment in adopted children. *Journal of Consulting and Clinical Psychology, 52*(4), 582–590.

Brodzinsky, D. M., Singer, L. M., & Braff, A. M. (1984). Children's understanding of adoption. *Child Development, 55*, 869–878.

Broderick, C., & Schrader, S. (1981). The history of professional marriage and family therapy. In A. Gurman & D. Kniskern (Eds.), *Handbook of family therapy*. New York: Brunner/Mazel.

Broman, S. (1981). Longterm development of children born to teenagers. In K. Scott, T. Field, & E. Robertson (Eds.), *Teenage parents and their offspring* (pp. 195–234). New York: Grune and Stratton.

Bronfenbrenner, Vrie. (1979). The ecology of human development: Experiments by nature and design. Cambridge, MA: Harvard University Press.

Brooks-Gunn, I., & Furstenberg, F. (in press). Antecedents and consequences of parenting: The case of adolescent parenting. In A. Fogel & G. Melson (Eds.), *The origins of nurturance*. Hillsdale, NJ: Elboum.

Brooks-Gunn, J., & Furstenburg, I. (1985). *The feminization of poverty: Adolescent mothers and their children*. Paper given at meetings of the American Psychological Association, Los Angeles.

Brown, S., Lieberman, J., & Miller, W. (1975). *Young adults as partners and planners: A preliminary report of the antecedents of responsible family formation*. Paper presented at 103rd annual meeting of the American Public Health Association, Chicago.

Bryan, L., Coleman, M., Ganong, L., & Bryan, H. (1986). Person perception: Family structure as a cue for stereotyping. *Journal of Marriage and the Family, 48*, 169–174.

Budd, L. S. (1976). *Problems, disclosure, and commitment of cohabiting and married students.* Doctoral dissertation, University of Minnesota, Minneapolis.

Bullough, V. (1978). Variant life styles: Homosexuality. In B. Murstein, (Ed.), *Exploring intimate lifestyles.* New York: Springer.

Bumpass, L. (1984). Some characteristics of children's second families. *American Journal of Sociology, 90*, 608–623.

Burchinal, L. (1965). Trends and prospects for young marriages in the U.S. *Journal of Marriage and the Family, 27*(2), 243–254.

Burden, D., & Klerman, L. (1984). Teenage parenthood: Factors that lessen economic dependence *Social Work, 29*(1), 11–16.

Burgess, J. J. (1985). A comparative evaluation of the pain and coping skills of widowed or divorced men. In R. Williams et al. (Eds.), *Family strengths Vol. 6, Enhancement of interaction*. Lincoln, NE: Department of Human Development and the Family, University of Nebraska-Lincoln.

Burgess, J. K. (1985). The widower as father. In S. Hanson & F. W. Bozett (Eds.), *Dimensions of fatherhood* (pp. 416–434). Beverly Hills: Sage.

Burgess, J. K., & Kohn, W. (1978). *The widower*. Boston: Beacon Press.

Burt, M. R., & Pittman, K. J. (1985). *Testing the social safety net: The impact of changes in support programs during the Reagan administration*. Washington, DC: Urban Institute.

Burt, M. R., & Sonenstein, F. L. (1985). Planning programs for pregnant teenagers. *Public Welfare, 49*, 29–36.

Burt, M. R., Kimmuch, M. H., Goldmuntz, J., & Sonenstein, F. L. (1984). *Helping pregnant adolescents: Outcomes and costs of service delivery*. Washington, DC: Urban Institute.

Caine, L. (1974). *Widow*. New York: Morrow.

Cannon-Bonaventure, K., & Kahn, J. (1979). *The ecology of help-seeking behavior among adolescent parents* [Mimeo]. Cambridge, MA: American Institutes for Research.

Card, J. (1978). *Long-term consequences for children born to adolescent parents*. Palo Alto, CA: American Institute of Research.

Carter, E., & McGoldrick, M. (1980). *The family life cycle*. New York: Gardner Press.

Cartoof, V. (1978). Postpartum services for adolescent mothers. *Child Welfare, 57*, 660–666.

Cartoof, V. (1982). The negative effects of AFDC policies on teenage mothers. *Child Welfare, 61*, 269–278.

Cavan, S. (1966). *Liquor license*. Chicago: Aldine.

Center for Population Options. (1985). *School-based health clinics: An emerging approach to improving adolescent health and addressing teenage pregnancy*. Washington, DC.

Chamie, M., Eisman, S., Forrest, J. D., Orr, M. T., & Torres A. (1982). Factors affecting adolescents' use of family planning clinics. *Family Planning Perspectives, 14*, 126–139.

Charmaz, K. (1980). *The social reality of death*. Reading, MA: Addison-Wesley.

Cherlin, A. (1978). Remarriage as an incomplete institution. *American Journal of Sociology, 84*, 634–650.

Cherlin, A., & Furstenberg, F. F., Jr. (1986). *The new American grandparent*. New York: Basic Books.

Cherlin, A., & McCarthy, J. (1985). Remarried couple households: Data from the June 1980 Current Population Survey. *Journal of Marriage and the Family, 47*, 23–30.

Chevan, A., & Korson, H. (1975). Living arrangements of widows in the United States and Israel, 1960 and 1961. *Demography, 12*(3), 505–518.

Child Welfare League of America. (1978). *Standards for adoption service* (rev. ed.). New York: Child Welfare League of America.

Chilman, C. S. (1980). Areas of parent satisfaction and dissatisfaction. *Family Coordinator, 29*, 339–346.

Chilman, C. S. (1983a). *Adolescent sexuality in a changing American society*, 2nd ed. New York: Wiley.

Chilman, C. S. (1983b). Remarriage and stepfamilies: Research results and implications. In E. D. Macklin & R. H. Rubin (Eds.), *Contemporary families and alternative lifestyles* (pp. 147–163). Beverly Hills: Sage.

Chilman, C. S. (1987a). Abortion. *Encyclopedia of social work*, 18th ed. (pp. 1–7). Silver Spring, MD: National Association of Social Workers.

Chilman, C. S. (1987b). Reproductive norms and the social control of women. In R. Sarri & J. Figueira-McDonough (Eds.), *The trapped woman*. Beverly Hills: Sage.

Clapp, D. F., & Raab, R. S. (1978). Follow-up of unmarried adolescent mothers. *Social Work, 23*, 149–153.

Clatworthy, N., & Scheid, L. A. (1977). *A comparison of married couples: Premarital cohabitants with non-premarital cohabitants*. Unpublished paper. Ohio State University.

Clayton, P. J. (1971). The bereavement of the widowed. *Diseases of the Nervous System, 32*, 597–604.

Clayton, P. J. (1974). Mortality and morbidity in the first year of widowhood. *Archives of General Psychiatry, 30*, 747–750.

Cleveland, W. P., & Gianturco, D. T. (1976). Remarriage probability after widowhood: A retrospective method. *Journal of Gerontology, 31*, 99–103.

Clingempeel, W. G. (1981). Quasi-kin relationships and marital quality. *Journal of Personality and Social Psychology, 41*, 890–901.

Clingempeel, W. G., Brand, E., & Segal, S. (1987). A multi-level/multivariable/developmental perspective for future research on stepfamilies. In K. Pasley & M. Ihinger-Tallman (Eds.), *Remarriage and stepparenting today: Research and theory*. New York: Guilford Press.

Clingempeel, W. G., Flescher, M., & Brand, E. (1987). Research on stepfamilies: Paradigmatic constraints and alternative proposals. In J. P. Vincent (Ed.), *Advances in family intervention, assessment theory*, Vol. 4. Greenwich, CT: Jai Press.

Clingempeel, W. G., Ievoli, R., & Brand, E. (1984). Structural complexity and the quality of stepfather-stepchild relationships. *Family Process, 23*, 547–560.

Clingempeel, W. G., & Segal, S. (1986). Stepparent-stepchild relationships and the psychological adjustment of children in stepfather and stepmother families. *Child Development, 57*, 474–484.

Cole, C. L. (1976). *Living together as an alternative life style*. Unpublished. Iowa State University.

Cole, C. L. (1977). Cohabitation in social context. In R. Libby & R. Whitehurst (Eds.), *Marriage and alternatives*. Glenview, IL: Scott Foresman.

Cole, C. L., & Cole, A. L. (1985). Husbands and wives should have an equal share in making the marriage work. In H. Feldman & M. Feldman (Eds.), *Current controversies in marriage and family*. Beverly Hills: Sage.

Cole, C. L., & Goettsch, S. L. (1981). Self-disclosure and relationship quality: A study among nonmarital cohabiting couples. *Alternative Lifestyles, 4*(4), 428–466.

Cole, C. M., & Vincent, J. P. (1975). Cover letter to *Cognitive and behavioral patterns in cohabitative and marital dyads*. (Personal communication)

Cole, E. S. (1987). Adoption. In *Encyclopedia of social work*, 18th ed. (pp. 67–75). Silver Spring, MD: National Association of Social Workers.

Coleman, M., & Ganong, L. (1987). The cultural stereotyping of stepfamilies. In K. Pasley & M. Ihinger-Tallman (Eds.), *Remarriage and stepparenting today: Research and theory*. New York: Guilford Press.

Colletta, N. D. (1981). Social support and the risk of maternal rejection by adolescent mothers. *Journal of Psychology, 109*, 191–197.

Colletta, N. D., & Gregg, C. H. (1981). Adolescent mothers' vulnerability to stress. *Journal of Nervous and Mental Disease, 169*, 50–54.

Colletta, N. D., & Lee, D. (1983). The impact of support for black adolescent mothers. *Journal of Family Issues, 4*, 127–143.

Colletta, N. D., Hadler, S., & Hunter, C. (1981). How adolescents cope with the problems of early motherhood. *Adolescence, 16*, 499–512.

Connolly, L. (1978). Boy fathers. *Human Behavior*, (January), 40–43.

Cooper, E. (1982). Parental care for the pregnant adolescent. In I. R. Stuart & C. F. Wells (Eds.), *Pregnancy in adolescence: Needs, problems, and management*. New York: Van Nostrand Reinhold.

Cotton, W. (1975). Social and sexual relationships of lesbians. *Journal of Sex Research, 11*, 139–148.

Cox, M. J., & Cox, R. D. (1984). Foster care and public policy. *Journal of Family Issues, 5*(2), 182–199.

Crosbie-Burnett, M. (1984). The centrality of the step relationship: A challenge to family theory and practice. *Family Relations, 33*, 459–463.

Crosbie-Burnett, M. (1985, November). *Type of custody and involvement with children by father and stepfather.* Paper presented at the annual meeting of the National Council on Family Relations, Dallas, TX.

Cummerton, J. (1982). Homophobia and social work practice with lesbians. In A. Weick & S. Vandiver (Eds.), *Women, power, and change*. Washington, DC: NASW.

Cumming, E., & Henry, W. (1961). *Growing old*. New York: Basic Books.

Cvetkovich, G., & Grote, B. (1975). *Antecedents of responsible family formation.* Progress report paper presented at a conference sponsored by the Population Division, National Institute of Child Health and Human Development, Bethesda, MD.

Cvetkovich, G., & Grote, B. (1976). *Psychological factors associated with adolescent premarital coitus.* Paper presented at the National Institute of Child Health and Human Development, Bethesda, MD.

Dank, B. (1971). Coming out in the gay world. *Psychiatry, 34*, 180–197.

Danziger, S., & Weinberg, D. (1986). *Fighting poverty*. Cambridge, MA: Harvard University Press.

Darrity, W. & Meyers. (1984). Does welfare dependency cause female headship? The case of the black family. *Journal of Marriage and the Family, 46*(4), 765–779.

Davidoff, I. F. (1977). Living together as a developmental phase: A holistic view. *Journal of Marriage and Family Counseling, 3*, 67–76.

Dawson, P., Robinson, J. L., & Johanson, C. B. (1982). Informal social support as an intervention. *Zero to Three, 3*, 1–5.

DeLameter, J., & Mac Corquodale, M. (1979). *Premarital sexuality: Attitudes, relationships, behaviors.* Madison, WI: University of Wisconsin Press.

DeMaris, A., & Leslie, G R. (1984). Cohabitation with the future spouse: Its influence upon marital satisfaction and communication. *Journal of Marriage and the Family, 46*(1), 77–84.

de Shazer, S. (1982). *Patterns of brief family therapy: An ecosystemic approach.* New York:Guilford Press.

de Shazer, S. (1985). *Keys to solution in brief therapy*. New York: Norton.

de Shazer, S. (1986). *Simple ideas.* Unpublished manuscript.

de Shazer, S., & Molnar, A. (1984). Four useful interventions in brief family therapy. *Journal of Marital and Family Therapy, 10*(3), 297–304.

de Shazer, S., Berg, I., Lipchik, E., Nunnally, E., Molnar, A., Gingerich, W., & Weiner-Davis, M. (1986). Brief therapy: Focused solution development. *Family Process, 25*(2), 207–221.

DeVall, W. (1979). Leisure and lifestyles among gay men. *International Review of Modern Sociology, 9*, 179–195.

Deykin, E. Y., Campbell, L., & Patti, P. (1984). The postadoption experience of surrendering parents. *American Journal of Orthopsychiatry, 54*, 271–280.

Douthwaite, G. (1979). *Unmarried couples and the law*. Indianapolis: Smith.

Dryfoos, J. G. (1985). School-based health clinics: A new approach to preventing adolescent pregnancy. *Family Planning Perspectives, 17*, 70–73.

Dryfoos, J. G., & Heisler, T. (1978). Contraceptive services for adolescents: An overview. *Family Planning Perspectives, 10*, 223–233.

Duberman, L. (1975). *The reconstituted family*. Chicago: Nelson Hall.

Dulaney, D., & Kelly, J. (1982). Improving services to gay and lesbian clients. *Social Work, 27*(2), 178–183.

Duvall, E., & Hills, R. (1984). *Report of the committee on the Dynamics of Family Interaction*. Prepared at the request of the National Conference on Family Life. Washington, DC.

Earls, F., & Siegel, B. (1980). Precocious fathers. *American Journal of Orthopsychiatry, 50*, 469–480.

Edwards, L. E., Steenman, M., & Hakanson, E. (1977). An experimental comprehensive high school clinic. *American Journal of Public Health, 67*, 765–766.

Eiduson, B., & Livermore, J. (1953). Complications in therapy with adopted children. *American Journal of Orthopsychiatry, 22*, 795–802.

Eisen, M., Zellman, G., Leibowitz, A., Chow, W., & Evans, J. (1983). Factors discriminating pregnancy resolution decisions of unmarried adolescents. *Genetic Psychology Monographs, 108*, 69–95.

Ellwood, D. & Bane, M. J. (1986). Family structure and poverty. In S. Danziger & D. Weinberg (Eds.), *Fighting poverty. Cambridge, MA: Harvard University Press.*

Elster, A., & Lamb, M. (1986). Adolescent fathers: The understudied side of adolescent pregnancy. In J. Lancaster & B. Hamburg (Eds.), *School-age pregnancy and parenthood: Biosocial dimensions*. New York: Aldine DeGruyter.

Elster, A. B., & Panzarine, S. (1983). Teenage fathers: Stresses during gestation and early parenthood. *Clinical Pediatrics, 22*, 700–703.

Erf, L. A. (1981). A moratorium for growth: Groupwork with adolescent mothers. *Clinical Social Work Journal, 9*, 44–46.

Erikson, E. (1950). *Childhood and society*. New York: Norton.

Erikson, E. (1956). Problems of ego-identity. *Journal of American Psychological Association, 4*, 56–121.

Espenshade, T. J. (1979). The economic consequences of divorce. *Journal of Marriage and the Family, 41*(3), 615–625.

Fanshel, D. (1972). *Far from the reservation. The transracial adoption of American Indian children*. New Jersey: Scarecrow Press.

Farley, R. (1980). Homocide trends in the United States. *Demography, 17*, 177–188.

Fast, I., & Cain, A. C. (1966). The stepparent role: Potential for disturbances in family functioning. *American Journal of Orthopsychiatry, 36*, 485–491.

Feigelman, W., & Silverman, A. R. (1977). Single parent adoptions. *Social Casework, 58*(8), 418–425.

Feigelman, W., & Silverman, A. R. (1979). Preferential adoption: A new mode of family formation. *Journal of Contemporary Social Work, 60*, 296–305.

Feldman, M., & Chilman, C. (1983). Contraceptive and abortion services for adolescents. In C. Chilman (Ed.), *Adolescent sexuality in a changing American society*, 2nd ed. (pp. 230–250). New York: Wiley.

Feldman, R., (1985). Training and support services for female-headed families. In H. McAdoo & T. Parham (Eds.), *Services to young families* (pp. 39–74). Washington, DC: American Public Welfare Association

Felice, M. E., Granados, J. L., Ances, I. G., Hebel, R., Reider, L. M., & Heald, F. (1981). The young pregnant teenager: Impact of comprehensive prenatal care. *Journal of Adolescent Health Care, 1*, 193–197.

Field, T. (1980). Teenage, lower class, black mothers. *Child Development, 51*, 425–436.

Field, T., & Widmayer, S. (1982). Motherhood. In B. Wolman (Ed.), *Handbook of developmental psychology* (pp. 681–701). Englewood Cliffs, NJ: Prentice-Hall.

Field, T. M., Widmayer, S. M., Stringer, S., & Ignatoff, E. (1980). Teenage, lower-class, black mothers and their preterm infants: An intervention and developmental follow-up. *Child Development, 51*, 426–436.

Field, T., Widmayer, S., Greenberg, R., & Stoller, S. (1982). Effects of parent training on teenage mothers and their infants. *Pediatrics, 69*, 703–707.

Fine, P., & Pape, M. (1982). Pregnant teenagers in need of social networks: Diagnostic parameters. In I. R. Stuart & C. F. Wells (Eds.), *Pregnancy in adolescence: Needs, problems, and management* (pp. 80–103). New York: Van Nostrand Reinhold.

Finkel, M., & Finkel, D. (1975). Sexual and contraceptive knowledge, attitudes and behaviors of male adolescents. *Family Planning Perspectives, 7*(6), 256–260.

Forbush, J. B. (1979). Adolescent parent programs and family involvement. In T. Ooms (Ed.), *Teenage pregnancy in a family context: Implications for policy* (pp. 254–276). Philadelphia: Temple University Press.

The Foster Care Monitoring Committee. (1984, September 7). *Foster care 1984. A report on the implementation of the recommendations of the Mayor's Task Force on Foster Care*.

Fox, G., & Inazu, J. (1980). Patterns and outcomes of mother-daughter communication about sexuality. *Journal of Social Issues, 36*, 7–29.

Fox, P., & Clauser, S. (1980). Trends in nursing home expenditures: Implications for aging policy. *Health Care Financing Review*, Fall, 65–70.

Francher, J., & Henkin, J. (1973). The menopausal queen: Adjustment to aging and the male homosexual. *American Journal of Orthopsychiatry, 43*, 670–674.

Freedman, M. (1971). *Homosexuality and psychological functioning*. Belmont, CA: Brooks Cole.

Freud, S. (1959). Mourning and melancholia (J. Traviere, Trans.). In *Collected Papers* (Vol. 4). New York: Basic Books.

Friedan, B. (1963). *The feminine mystique*. New York: Norton.

Frisbie, W. P. (1986). Variations in patterns of marital instability among Hispanics. *Journal of Marriage and the Family, 48*, 99–106.

Furstenberg, F. (1981). Implicating the family: Teenage parenthood and kinship involvement. In T. Ooms (Ed.), *Teenage pregnancy in a family context*. Philadelphia: Temple University Press.

Furstenberg, F., & Brooks-Gunn, J. (in press). Teenage childbearing: Causes, consequences, and remedies. In L. Aiken & D. Mechanic (Eds.), *Applications of social science to clinical medicine and health policy*. Rutgers, NY: Rutgers University Press.

Furstenberg, F., & Crawford, A. (1978). Family support: Helping teenage mothers to cope. *Family Planning Perspectives, 10*, 322–333.

Furstenberg, F., Jr. (1976). *Unplanned parenthood: The social consequences of teenage childbearing.* New York: Free Press.

Furstenberg, F., Jr. (1979). Recycling the family: Perspectives for a neglected family form. *Marriage and Family Review, 2*(3), 1, 12–22.

Furstenberg, F., Jr. (1980). Burdens and benefits: The impact of early childbearing on the family. *Journal of Social Issues, 36*, 64–87.

Furstenberg, F., Jr. (1983). *Marital disruption and childcare*. Unpublished manuscript.

Furstenberg, F., Jr. (1987). The new extended family: The experience of parents and children after remarriage. In K. Pasley & M. Ihinger-Tallman (Eds.), *Remarriage and stepparenting today: Research and theory*. New York: Guilford Press.

Furstenberg, F. F., Jr., & Allison, S. (1985, April). *How divorce affects children: Variations by age and sex*. Paper presented at the biennial meeting of the Society for Research in Child Development, Toronto, Canada.

Furstenberg, F. F., Jr., & Crawford, A. G. (1978). Family support: Helping teenage fathers to cope. *Family Planning Perspective, 10*, 322–333.

Furstenberg, F. F., Jr., & Spanier, G. B. (1984). *Recycling the family: Remarriage after divorce*. Beverly Hills: Sage.

Furstenberg, F. F., Jr., Nort, C. W., Peterson, J. L., & Zill, N. (1983). The life course of children of divorce: Marital disruption and parental conflict. *American Sociological Review, 48*, 656–668.

Furstenberg, G., Morgan, K., & Peterson, J. (1985). *Explaining race differences in the timing of first intercourse* [Mimeo] Philadelphia: University of Pennsylvania.

Gagnon, J., & Simon, W. (1973). *Sexual conduct*. Chicago: Aldine.

Ganong, L. H., & Coleman, M. (1984). Effects of remarriage on children: A review of the empirical literature. *Family Relations, 33*, 389–406.

Ganong, L. H., & Coleman, M. (1987). Effects of parental remarriage on children: An updated comparison of theories, methods, and findings from clinical and empirical research. In K. Pasley & M. Ihinger-Tallman (Eds.), *Remarriage and stepparenting today: Research and theory*. New York: Guilford Press.

Ganong, L. H., & Coleman, M. (1986). A comparison of clinical and empirical literature on children in stepfamilies. *Journal of Marriage and the Family, 48*, 309–318.

Ganson, H. C. (1975). *Cohabitation: The antecedents of dissolution of formerly cohabitating individuals.* Master's thesis, Ohio State University, Columbus.

Garfinkel, I., & McLanahan, S. (1986). *Single mothers and their children*. Washington, DC: Urban Institute Press.

Gelles, R. (1985). School-age parents and child abuse. In J. Lancaster & B. Hamburg (Eds.), *School-age pregnancy and parenthood: Biosocial dimensions* (pp. 347–360). New York: Aldine De Gruyter.

Gershenson, H. (1983). Redefining fatherhood in families with white adolescent mothers. *Journal of Marriage and the Family, 45*(31), 591–599.

Gilchrist, L., & Schinke, S. P. (1983). Counseling with adolescents about their sexuality. In C. S. Chilman (Ed.), *Adolescent sexuality in a changing American society* (pp. 230–250). New York: Wiley.

Giles-Sims, J. (1984). The stepparent role: Expectations, behavior and sanctions. *Journal of Family Issues, 5*, 116–130.

Giles-Sims, Jr. (1985, November). *Paternal custody and remarriage*. Paper presented at the annual meeting of the National Council on Family Relations, Dallas, TX.

Giles-Sims, Jr. (1987). Social exchange in remarried families. In K. Pasley. & M. Ihinger-Tallman (Eds.), *Remarriage and stepparenting today: Research and theory*. New York: Guilford Press.

Glaser, B., & Strauss, A. L. (1965). *Awareness of dying*. Chicago: Aldine.

Glick, I. O., Weiss, R. S., & Parkes, C. M. (1974). *The first year of bereavement*. New York: Wiley.

Glick, P., & Mills, K. (1974, October). *Black families: Marriage patterns and living arrangements*. Paper presented at W. E. B. Du Bois Conference on American Blacks, Atlanta, GA.

Glick, P. C. (1980). Remarriage: Some recent changes and variations. *Journal of Family Issues, 1*, 455–478.

Glick, P. C. (1984). Marriage, divorce and living arrangements: Prospective changes. *Journal of Family Issues, 5*, 7–26.

Goddard, H. R. L. (1979). *Coping with widowhood: An exploratory-descriptive study*. Unpublished master's thesis, University of Maryland, College Park.

Goldner, V. (1982). Remarriage family: Structure, system, future. In J. C. Hansen and L. Messinger, Eds., *Therapy with remarriage families*. Rockville, MD: Aspen Publications.

Goldstein, J., Freud, A., & Solnit, A. (1973). *Beyond the best interests of the child*. New York: Free Press.

Gong, V., Ed. (1985). *Understanding AIDS: A comprehensive guide*. New Brunswick, NJ: Rutgers University Press.

Gongla, P. A. (1982). Single-parent families: A look at families of mothers and children. *Marriage and Family Review*, 5(2), 5–27.

Gonsiorek, J. (1977). Psychological adjustment and homosexuality. *JSAS Catalog of Selected Documents in Psychology, 7*.

Gordon, S. (1978). *Lonely in America*. New York: Simon & Schuster.

Gorer, G. (1967). *Death, grief and mourning*. Garden City, NY: Doubleday.

Gramick, J. (1975). Questions and answers. *Homosexual Counseling Journal*, 2(3), 93.

Green, R. (1976). One hundred ten feminine and masculine boys. *Archives of Sexual Behavior, 5*, 425–446.

Green, R. (1978). Sexual identity of 37 children raised by homosexual or transsexual parents. *American Journal of Psychiatry, 135*, 692–697.

Greer, J. G. (1982). Adoptive placement: Developmental and psychotherapeutic issues. In I. R. Stuart & C. F. Wells (Eds.), *Pregnancy in adolescence: Needs, problems and management*. New York: Van Nostrand Reinhold.

Groves, P. (1985). Coming out: Issues for the therapist working with women in the process of lesbian identity formation. *Women and Therapy*, 4(2), 17–22.

Grow, L. J. (1979). *Early childrearing by young mothers*. New York: Child Welfare League of America.

Grow, L. J., & Shapiro, D. (1974). *Black children—white parents—a study of transracial adoption*. New York: Child Welfare League of America.

Guldner, C. (1971). The post-marital: An alternative to premarital counseling. *Family Coordinator, 20*, 115–119.

———. (1983). Growth-promoting family therapy. In D. R. Mace (Ed.), *Prevention in family services: Approaches to family wellness*. Beverly Hills, CA: Sage.

Gwartney-Gibbs, P. A. (1986). The institutionalization of premarital cohabitation: Estimates from marriage license applicants, 1970 to 1980. *Journal of Marriage and the Family*, 48(2), 423–434.

Hagan, D., Astone, N., and Kitagawa, E. 1985. Social and environmental factors influencing contraceptive use among black adolescents. *Family Planning Perspectives, 17*(4), 165–168.

Haley, J. (1976). *Problem solving therapy.* San Francisco: Jossey-Bass.

Hall, M. (1978). Lesbian families: Cultural and clinical issues. *Social Work, 23*(5), 380–385.

Hall, M. (1985). *The lavender couch: A consumers guide to psychotherapy for lesbians and gay men.* Boston: Alyson.

Hamburg, B. (1986). Subsets of adolescent mothers: Developmental, biomedical and psychosocial issues. In J. Lancaster & B. Hamburg (Eds.), *Schoolage pregnancy and parenthood: Biosocial dimensions* (pp. 115–146). New York: Aldine DeGruyter.

Hanna, S. L., & Knaub, P. K. (1981). Cohabitation before remarriage: Its relationship to family strengths. *Alternative Lifestyles, 4*(4), 507–522.

Hardy, J. B., Welcher, D., Stanley, J., & Dallas, J. R. (1978). Long-range outcome of adolescent pregnancy. *Clinical Obstetrics and Gynecology, 21,* 1215–1232.

Harry, J. (1979). The "marital" liaisons of gay men. *Family Coordinator, 28,* 622–629.

Harry, J. (1982). *Gay children grow up.* New York: Praeger.

Harry, J. (1984). *Gay couples.* New York: Praeger.

Harry, J. (1985). Gay male and lesbian relationships. In E. M. Macklin & R. H. Rubin (Eds.), *Contemporary families and alternative lifestyles: Handbook on research and theory,* 2nd ed. (pp. 216–234). Beverly Hills, CA: Sage.

Harry,, J. (1987). Some problems of gay/lesbian families. In C. Chilman, F. Cox, & E. Nunnally (Eds.), *Families in trouble.* Beverly Hills, CA: Sage.

Harry, J., & DeVall, W. (1978). *The social organization of gay males.* New York: Praeger.

Harry, J., & Lovely, R. (1979). Gay marriages and communities of sexual orientation. *Alternative Lifestyles, 2,* 177–200.

Hartman, A. (1984). *Working with adoptive families beyond placement.* New York: Child Welfare League of America.

Hartman, A., & Laird, J. (1983). *Family-centered social work practice.* New York: Free Press.

Hartog, J., Audry, J. R., & Cohen, Y. A., Eds. (1980). *The anatomy of loneliness.* New York: International Universities Press.

Heger, D. T. (1977). A supportive service to single mothers and their children. *Children Today* (Sep./Oct.).

Hendricks, L. E. (1983). Suggestions for reaching unmarried black adolescent fathers. *Child Welfare, 62,* 141–146.

Hennon, C. B. (1981). Conflict management within cohabitation relationships. *Alternative Lifestyles, 4*(4), 467–486.

Henshaw, S., & O'Reilly, K. (1983). Characteristics of abortion patients in the United States, 1979 and (1980). *Family Planning Perspectives, 15*(1), 5–16.

Hetherington, E. M. (1984). Personal communication.

Hetherington, E. M. (1987). Family relations six years after divorce. In K. Pasley & M. Ihinger-Tallman (Eds.), *Remarriage and stepparenting today: Research and theory.* New York: Guilford Press.

Hill, R. (1986). Life cycle stages for types of single parent families: Of family development theory. *Family Relations, 35,* 19–29.

Hill, R., & Rogers, R. H. (1964). The developmental approach. In H. T. Christensen (Ed.), Handbook of Marriage and the family. (Chicago: Rand McNally.

Hiltz, S. R. (1978). Widowhood: A roleless role. *Marriage and Family Review, 1*(6), 1, 3–10.
Hirsch, B. B. (1976). *Living together: A guide to the law for unmarried couples.* Boston: Houghton Mifflin.
Hochschild, A. R. (1973). *The unexpected community.* Englewood Cliffs, NJ: Prentice-Hall.
Hoffer, B. (1981). Children's acquisition of sex-role behavior in lesbian-mother families. *American Journal of Orthopsychiatry, 51*, 536–544.
Hofferth, S. (1985). *Adolescent pregnancy and childbearing.* Bethesda, MD: Center for Population Research. N.I.C.H.D.
Hoffman, M. (1968). *The gay world.* New York: Bantam.
Hoopes, J., Sherman, E., Lawder, E., Andrews, R., & Lower, K. (1969). *A follow-up study of adoptions, Vol. II: Post-placement functioning of adopted children.* New York: Child Welfare League of America.
Hoorwitz, A., & Burchardt, C. (1984). Procedures for court consultations on child custody issues. *Social Casework, 65*(5), 259–266.
Hornick, J., Doran, L., & Crawford, S. (1979). Premarital contraceptive usage among male and female adolescents. *The Family Coordinator, 27*, 181–190.
Hotvedt, M., & Mandel, J. (1982). Children of lesbian mothers. In W. Paul, J. Weinrich, J. Gonsiorek, & M. Hotvedt (Eds.), *Homosexuality: Social, psychological and biological issues* (pp. 275–285). Beverly Hills, CA: Sage.
House Select Committee on Children, Youth, and Families. (1986). *Committee Report, 17.* Washington, DC: U.S. Government Printing Office.
Hughes, E. C. (1971). The study of occupations. In E. C. Hughes (Ed.), *The sociological eye: Selected papers on work, self and the study of society.* Chicago: Aldine.
Humphreys, L. (1979). Exodus and identity. In M. Levine (Ed.), *Gay men* (pp. 134–137). New York: Harper & Row.
Hunt, M. (1966). *The world of the formerly married.* New York: McGraw-Hill.
Hunt, M. (1974). *Sexual behavior in the 1970s.* New York: Dell.
Hyman, H. (1983). *Of time and widowhood: Nationwide studies of enduring effects.* Durham, NC: Duke University Policy Studies.
Ihinger-Tallman, M. (1984). Epilogue. *Family Relations, 33*, 483–487.
Hyman, H. (1983). (1985, November). *Perspectives on change of custody among stepsiblings.* Paper presented at the annual meeting of the National Council on Family Relations, Dallas, TX.
Hyman, H. (1987). Sibling and stepsibling bonding in stepfamilies. In K. Pasley & M. Ihinger-Tallman (Eds.), *Remarriage and stepparenting today: Research and theory.* New York: Guilford Press.
Ihinger-Tallman, M., & Pasley, K. (1986). Remarriage and integration within the community. *Journal of Marriage and the Family, 48*, 395–405.
Ihinger-Tallman, M., & Pasley, K. (1987a). *Remarriage.* Beverly Hills, CA: Sage.
Ihinger-Tallman, M., & Pasley, K. (1987b). Divorce and remarriage in the American family: An historical review. In K. Pasley & M. Ihinger-Tallman (Eds.), *Remarriage and stepparenting today: Research and theory.* New York: Guilford Press.
Institute for Social Research. (1984, Autumn). *Newsletter.* Ann Arbor, MI: University of Michigan.
Irle, R. (1979). Minority ministry: A definition of territory. *International Review of Modern Sociology, 9*, 197–213.

Isaacs, M. B. (1982). Facilitating family restructuring and relinkage. In J. C. Hansen & L. Messinger (Eds.), *Therapy with remarriage families*. Rockville, MD: Aspen.

Isaacs, M. B. (1986). Personal communication.

Jackson, P. G. (1983). On living together unmarried: Awareness contexts and social interaction. *Journal of Social Issues, 4*(1), 35–59.

Jacobson, D. S. (1987). Family types, visiting patterns, and children's behavior in the stepfamily: A linked family system. In K. Pasley & M. Ihinger-Tallman (Eds.), *Remarriage and stepparenting today: Research and theory*. New York: Guilford Press.

Jacques, J. M., & Chason, K. J. (1979). Cohabitation: Its impact on marital success. *Family Coordinator, 28*(1), 35–39.

Jekel, J. F., & Klerman, L. V. (1982). Comprehensive service programs for pregnant and parenting adolescents. In E. R. McAnarney (Ed.), *Premature adolescent pregnancy and parenthood*. New York: Grune & Stratton.

Jessor, S., & Jessor, R. (1975). Transition from virginity to nonvirginity among youth: A social-psychological study over time. *Developmental Psychology, 11*, 473–484.

Johnson, M. P. (1973). Commitment: A conceptual structure and empirical application. *Sociological Quarterly, 14*, 395–406.

Jones, J. (1985). Fertility-related care. In H. McAdoo & T. Parham (Eds.), *Services to young families* (pp. 167–206). Washington, D.C.: American Public Welfare Association.

Jorgensen, S. (1981). Sex education and the reduction of adolescent pregnancies: Prospects for the 1980s. *Journal of Early Adolescence, 1*, 38–52.

Kadushin, A. (1977). Adopting older children: Summary and implications. In A. M. Clark & A. D. B. Clarke (Eds.), *Early experience, Myth and evidence*. New York: Free Press.

Kalish, R. H. (1981). *Death, grief and caring relationships*. Monterey, CA: Brooks/Cole.

Kamerman, S. (1985). Young, poor and a mother alone: Problems and possible solutions. In H. McAdoo & T. Parham (Eds.), *Service to young families* (pp. 1–38). Washington, DC: American Public Welfare Association.

Kamerman, S., & Kahn, A. (1978). *Family policy: Government and family in fourteen countries*. New York: Columbia University Press.

Kantner, J., & Zelnik, M. (1972). Sexual experiences of young unmarried women in the U.S. *Family Planning Perspectives, 4*(4), 9–17.

Kantor, D., & Lehr, W. (1975). *Inside the family*. San Francisco: Jossey-Bass.

Kaplan, H. (1983). *The evaluation of sexual disorders: Psychological and medical aspects*. New York: Brunner/Mazel.

Karpel, M. (1976). Individuation: From fusion to dialogue. *Family Process, 15*, 65–82.

Kaslow, F. W. (1985). To marry or not: Treating a living-together couple in mid-life. In A. Gurman (Ed.), *Casebook of marital therapy*. New York: Guilford Press.

Katz, A. J. (1979). Lone fathers: Perspectives and implications for family policy. *Family Coordinator, 28*(4), 521–528.

Kellam, S. (1979). *Consequences of teenage motherhood for mother, child and family in an urban black community*. Progress report to Center for Population Research, National Institutes of Health, Bethesda, MD.

Kellam, S., Adams, R., Brown, C., & Ensminger, M. (1982). The long-term evolution of the family structure of teenage and older mothers. *Journal of Marriage and the Family, 44*, 539–554.

Kendler, K. S., Gruenberg, A. M., & Strauss, J. S. (1981a). An independent analysis of the Copenhagen sample of the Danish adoption study of schizophrenia. I. *Archives of General Psychiatry, 38*, 979–981.

Kendler, K. S., Gruenberg, A. M., & Strauss, J. S. (1981b). An independent analysis of the Copenhagen sample of the Danish adoption study of schizophrenia. II. *Archives of General Psychiatry, 38*, 982–984.

Kendler, K. S., Gruenberg, A. M., & Strauss, J. S. (1981c). An independent analysis of the Copenhagen sample of the Danish adoption study of schizophrenia. III. *Archives of General Psychiatry, 38*, 985–987.

Kenney, A. M. (1986). School-based clinics: A national conference. *Family Planning Perspectives, 18*, 44–46.

Keshet, J. K. (1980). From separation to stepfamily. *Journal of Family Issues, 1*, 517–531.

Kieffer, C. M. (1972). *Consensual cohabitation: A descriptive study of the relationships and sociocultural characteristics of eighty couples in settings of two Florida universities.* Master's thesis, Florida State University, Tallahassee.

Kilburn, L. H. (1983). An educational/supportive group model for intervention with school-age parents and their children. *Social Work with Groups, 6*, 53–63.

King, M. D. (1975). *Cohabitation handbook: Living together and the law.* Berkeley, CA: Ten Speed Press.

Kinsey, A., Pomeroy, W., & Martin, C. (1948). *Sexual behavior in the human male.* Philadelphia: Saunders.

Kirby, D., Alter, J., & Scales, P. (1979, July). *An analysis of U.S. sex education programs and evaluation methods* (Contract No. 200-78-0804) (Report No. CDC-2021-79-DK-FR). Washington, DC: U.S. Department of Health, Education, and Welfare, National Institute of Education.

Kirk, H. D. (1964). *Shared fate.* New York: Free Press.

Kirk, H. D. (1984). *Shared fate: A theory and method of adoptive relationships.* Canada: Ben-Simon.

Kirk, H. D. (1985). *Adoptive kinship: A modern institution in need of reform.* Canada: Ben-Simon.

Kirkpatrick, M., Smith, C., & Roy, R. (1981). Lesbian mothers and their children. *American Journal of Orthopsychiatry, 51*, 545–551.

Klerman, L. (1983). Adolescent mothers and their children: Another population that requires family care. In R. Perlman (Ed.), *Family home care* (pp. 111–128). New York: Haworth Press.

Klerman, L. (1985). The economic impact of school-age child rearing. In J. Lancaster, & B. Hamburg (Eds.), *School-age pregnancy and parenthood: Biosocial dimensions* (pp. 363–378). New York: Aldine De Gruyter.

Klerman, L., Bracken, M., Jekel, J., & Bracken, M. (1982). The delivery abortion decision among adolescents. In I. Stuart & C. Wells (Eds.), *Pregnancy in adolescence.* New York: Van Nostrand Reinhold.

Klerman, L. V. (1979). Evaluating service programs for school-age parents: Design problems. *Evaluation and the Health Professions, 2*, 55–70.

Klerman, L. V. (1982). Programs for pregnant adolescents and young parents: Their development and assessment. In K. Scott, T. Field, & E. Robertson (Eds.), *Teenage parents and their offspring* (pp. 227–248). New York: Grune & Stratton.

Klerman, L. V. (1985). School-age pregnancy: Stresses and supports. In M. W. Yogman & T. B. Brazelton, (Eds.), *Stresses and supports for families.* Cambridge, MA: Harvard University.

Klerman, L. V., Jekel, J .F., & Chilman, C .S. (1983). The service needs of pregnant and parenting adolescents. In C. S. Chilman (Ed.), *Adolescent sexuality in a changing American society* (Chapter 11). New York: Wiley.

Klinman, B., Sander, J., Rosen, J., Longo, K., & Martinez, L. (1985, September). The teen parent collaboration: Reaching and serving the teenage father [Mimeo]. New York.

Knitzer, A. M., & McGowan, B. (1978). *Children without homes*. Washington, DC: Children's Defense Fund.

Kraft, A. D., Palombo, J., Mitchell, D., Dean, C., Meyers, S., & Schmidt, A.W. (1980). The psychological dimensions of infertility. *American Journal of Family Therapy, 50*(4), 6118–6628.

Kral, R. (1984). Research in progress: Adoptive families. *Morphogensis* (March). Wisconsin Association for Marriage and Family Therapy.

Kramer, D. (1982). The adopted child in family therapy. *American Journal of Family Therapy, 10*, 70–73.

Kramer, J. (1985). *The family interface*. New York: Brunner/Mazel.

Kreis, B., & Pattie, A. (1969). *Up from grief.* New York: Seabury Press.

Krestan, J., & Bepko, C. (1980). The problem of fusion in the lesbian relationship. *Family Process, 19*, 277–289.

Kubler-Ross, E. (1969). *On death and dying*. New York: Macmillan.

La Barre, M. (1972). Emotional crises of school-age girls during pregnancy and early motherhood. *Journal of the American Academy of Child Psychiatry, 11*, 537–557.

Ladner, J. (1971). *Tomorrow's tomorrow: The black women*. Garden City, NJ: Doubleday.

Lavori, N. (1976). *Living together, married or single: Your legal rights*. New York: Harper & Row.

Lee, J. A. (1977). Going public: A study in the sociology of homosexual liberation. *Journal of Homosexuality, 3*(1), 49–78.

Leibowitz, A., Eisen, M., & Chow, W. (1980). *Decisionmaking in teenage pregnancy: An analysis of choice*. Santa Monica, CA: Rand Corporation.

Leishman, K. (1980, June). Teenage mothers are keeping their babies—with the help of their own mothers. *MS.*, 61–67.

Leublum, S., & Perian, L. (1980). *Principles and practices of sex therapy*. New York: Guilford Press.

Leupnitz, D. A. (1984). Child custody: A study of families after divorce. In S. P. McCary & J. L. McCary (Eds.), *Human sexuality*, 3rd ed. Belmont, CA: Wadsworth.

Levitan, S. (1985). *Programs in aid of the poor*. 5th ed. Baltimore, MD: Johns Hopkins University Press.

Lewin, E., & Lyons, T. (1982). Everything in its place: The coexistence of lesbianism and motherhood. In W. Paul, J. Weinrich, J. Gonsiorek, & M. Hotvedt (Eds.), *Homosexuality: Social, psychological and biological issues* (pp. 249–273). Beverly Hills, CA: Sage.

Lewis, J. M. (1979). *How's your family?* New York: Brunner/Mazel.

Lewis, J. M., Beavers, W. R., Gossett, J. T., & Phillips, V.A. (1976). *No single thread: Psychological health in family systems*. New York: Brunner/Mazel.

Lewis, K. (1980). Children of lesbians: Their point of view. *Social Work, 25*(3), 198–203.

Lewis, R. A., Spanier, G. B., Atkinson, V. L., & LeHecka, C. B. (1977). Commitment in married and unmarried cohabitation. *Social Focus, 10*, 367–374.

Lewis, S. (1979). *Sunday's women.* Boston: Beacon Press.

Liebow, E. (1967). *Tally's corner.* Boston: Little, Brown.

Lifton, F. (1979). *Lost and found: The adoption experience.* New York: Dial Press.

Lindeman, E. (1944). Symptomatology and management of acute grief. *American Journal of Psychiatry, 101,* 141–148.

Lindemann, C. (1974). *Birth control and unmarried young women.* New York: Springer.

Lindsey, B. B., and Evans, W. (1927). *The companionate marriage.* Garden City, NY: Boni & Liveright.

Lipchik, E. (1987). The treatment of troubled relationships between parents and children. In E. Nunnally, C. Chilman, & F. Cox (Eds.), *Families in trouble: Knowledge and practice perspectives for professionals in the human services,* Vol. III. Beverly Hills, CA: Sage.

Lipman-Blumen, J., & Leavitt, H.J. (1976). Vicarious and direct achievement patterns in adulthood. *Counseling Psychologist, 6*(1), 26–32.

Lopata, H. Z. (1969). Loneliness: Forms and components. *Social Problems, 17*(2), 248–262.

Lopata, H. Z. (1971a). Widows as a minority group. *The Gerontologist, 11*(1), Part 2, 66–77.

Lopata, H. Z. (1971b). *Occupation: Housewife.* New York: Oxford University Press.

Lopata, H. Z. (1971c). Living arrangements of urban widows and their married children. *Sociological Focus, 5*(1), 41–61.

Lopata, H. Z. (1973). Social relations of black and white widowed women in a northern metropolis. *American Journal of Sociology, 78*(4), 241–248.

Lopata, H. Z. (1973). *Widowhood in an American city.* Cambridge, MA: Schenkman.

Lopata, H. Z. (1975). Grief work and identity reconstruction. *Journal of Geriatric Psychiatry, 8*(1), 41–55.

Lopata, H. Z. (1977). Widows and widowers. *The Humanist,* (July/August).

Lopata, H. Z. (1978a). The absence of community resources in support systems of urban widows. *Family Coordinator,* (Oct.), 383, 388.

Lopata, H. Z. (1978b). Changing roles, projections for the future and policy implication. In *Women in midlife—security and fulfillment* (Part 1). Washington, DC: U.S. Government Printing Office.

Lopata, H. Z. (1979). *Women as widows: Support systems.* New York: Elsevior North Holland.

Lopata, H. Z. (1980). Loneliness in widowhood. In J. Hartog, J. R. Audry, & Y. A. Cohen (Eds.), *The anatomy of loneliness* (pp. 237–258). New York: International Universities Press.

Lopata, H. Z. (1984). Widowhood and husband sanctification. *Journal of Marriage and the Family, 43*(2), 439–450.

Lopata, H. Z. (1984, July). *The self-concept, identities and traumatic events: The death of a husband.* Paper presented at the International Conference on Self and Identity, Cardiff, Wales.

Lopata, H. Z. (1986). Time in anticipated future and events in memory. *American Behavioral Scientist,* 29(6), 695–709.

Lopata, H. Z. (1988a) *Volume I: Widows: The Middle East, Asia, and the Pacific. Volume II: Widows: North America* Durham, NC: Duke University Press.

Lopata, H. Z. Ed. (1988b). Women's Contemporary family roles in life course perspective. In B. Hess & M. M. Ferree (Eds.), *Women in society,* (pp. 381–407) Beverly Hills, CA: Sage.

Lopata, H. Z., & Brehm, H. (1986). *Widows and dependent wives: From social problems to federal policy.* New York: Praeger.

Lopata, H. Z., Barnewolt, D., & Miller, C. A. (1985). *City women: Work, jobs, occupations, careers, Vol. 2. Chicago.* New York: Praeger.

Lopata, H. Z., Miller, C. A. & Barnewolt, D. (1984). *City women: Work, jobs, occupations, careers. Vol. 1. America.* New York: Praeger.

Luker, K. (1975). *Taking chances: Abortion and the decision not to contracept.* Berkeley, CA: University of California Press.

Lutz, P. (1983). The stepfamily: An adolescent perspective. *Family Relations, 32,* 367–376.

Lynch, J. (1977). *The broken heart: The medical consequences of loneliness.* New York: Basic Books.

Lyness, J. F., Lipetz, M. E., & Davis, K. E. (1972). Living together: An alternative to marriage. *Journal of Marriage and the Family, 34*(2), 17–20.

Maas, H., & Engler, R. (1959). *Children in need of parents.* New York: Columbia University Press.

MacDonald, A., Jr. (1976). Homphobia: Its roots and meanings. *Homosexual Counseling Journal, 3*(1), 23–33.

Mace, D., & Mace, V. (1981). What is marriage beyond living together? Some Quaker reactions to cohabitation. *Family Relations, 30*(1), 17–20.

Mace, D. R. (1982). *Close companions.* New York: Continuum.

Macklin, E. D. (1974). *Comparison of parent and student attitudes toward non-marital cohabitation.* Paper presented at the annual meeting of the National Council on Family Relations, St. Louis, MO.

Macklin, E. D. (1978a). Non-marital heterosexual cohabitation: A review of research. *Marriage & Family Review, 1,* 1–12.

Macklin, E. D. (1978b). Review of research on non-marital cohabitation in the United States. In B. I. Murstein (Ed.), *Exploring intimate life styles* (pp. 197–243). New York: Springer.

Macklin, E. D. (1980). Nontraditional family forms: A decade review. *Journal of Marriage and the Family, 42,* 905–922.

Macklin, E. D. (1985). Nonmarital heterosexual cohabitation: An overview. In E. M. Macklin & R. H. Rubin (Eds.), *Contemporary families and alternative lifestyles: Handbook on research and theory,* 2nd ed. (pp. 49–74). Beverly Hills, CA: Sage.

Macklin, E. D. In press. Heterosexual couples who cohabit nonmaritally: Common problems and issues. In C. Chilman, E. Nunnally, & F. Cox (Eds.), *Families in trouble* Vol. 5. Beverly Hills, CA: Sage.

Maddox, B. (1982). Homosexual parents. *Psychology Today, 16*(2), 62–69.

Maracek, J. (1979). *Economic, social and psychological consequences of adolescent childbearing.* Report to Center for Population Research, National Institutes of Health, Bethesda, MD.

Markman, H. S., Floyd, F. J., Standley, S. M., & Lewis, H. C. (1986). Prevention. In N. Jacobson & A. Gurman (Eds.), *Clinical handbook of marital therapy.* New York: Guilford Press.

Marmor, J. (1980). Overview: The multiple roots of homosexual behavior. In J. Marmor (Ed.), *Homosexual behavior: A modern reappraisal.* New York: Basic Books.

Marotz-Baden, R., Adams, G. R., Bueche, N., Munro, B., & Munro, G. (1979). Family form or family process? Reconsidering the deficit family model approach. *Family Coordinator, 28,* 5–14.

Marquis, K.S., & Detweiler, R. A. (1985). Does adopted mean different? An attributional analysis. *Journal of Personality and Social Psychology, 48*(4), 1054–1066.

Marvin v. Marvin. (1976). 18 Cal. 3d 660, 134 Cal. Reptr. 815, 557 P.2d 106.

Massey, C., & Warner, R. (1974). *Sex, living together, and the law: A legal guide for unmarried couples and groups.* Berkeley, CA: Nolo.

Mayor's Task Force on Foster Care. (1980, June). *Redirecting foster care. A report to the Mayor of the City of New York.*

McAdoo, H., & Parham, T. (1985). *Services to young families.* Washington, DC: American Public Welfare Association.

McAnarney, E. R. (1985). Adolescent pregnancy and childbearing: New data, new challenges. *Pediatrics, 75*, 973–975.

McCandlish, B. (1985). Therapeutic issues with lesbian couples. In J. Gonsiorek (Ed.), *A guide to psychotherapy with gay and lesbian clients.* New York: Basic Books.

McCarthy, J., & Menken, J. (1979). Marriage, remarriage, marital disruption and age at first birth. *Family Planning Perspective, 11*(Jan./Feb.), 32–40.

McGee, E. (1982). *Too little, too late: Services for teenage parents.* (Available from Ford Foundation Office of Reports, 2310 E. 43rd St., New York, NY 10017.)

McLaughlin, S., & Micklin, M. (1983). The timing of the first birth and changes in personal efficiency. *Journal of Marriage and the Family, 45*, 47–55.

McWhirter, D., & Mattison, A. (1984). *The male couple.* Englewood Cliffs, NJ: Prentice-Hall.

MDRC. (1986). *Fact sheet: New chance—a new initiative for teenage mothers* [Mimeo]. New York.

Mech, E. V. (1986, June). *Applying adoption research findings* [Mimeo]. Paper presented at the Office of Adolescent Pregnancy Programs Technical Assistance Workshop. Washington, DC: U.S. Department of Health and Human Services.

Meezan, W., Katz, S., & Russo (Ed.). (1978). *Adoption without agencies.* New York: Child Welfare League of America.

Melina, L. R. (1986). *Raising adopted children: A manual for adoptive parents.* New York: Harper & Row.

Mendola, M. (1980). *The Mendola report.* New York: Crown.

Mercer, R. T. (1979). *The adolescent parent.* Philadelphia: Lippincott.

Messinger, L. (1976). Remarriage between divorced people with children from previous marriages: A proposal for preparation for remarriage. *Journal of Marriage and Family Counseling, 2*, 193–200.

Messinger, L., Walker, K. N., & Freeman, S. J. (1978). Preparation for remarriage following divorce: The use of group techniques. *American Journal of Orthopsychiatry, 78*, 263–272.

Miller, B. (1979). Unpromised paternity: The life-styles of gay fathers. In M. Levine (Ed.), *Gay men* (pp. 239–252). New York: Harper & Row.

Miller, E. K., & Miller, K. A. (1983). Adolescent pregnancy: A model for intervention. *The Personnel and Guidance Journal, 62*, 15–20.

Miller, S. (1983). *Children as parents.* (Available from Child-Welfare League of America, 67 Irving Pl. New York, NY 10003.)

Miller, W. (1976). *Some psychological factors predictive of undergraduate sexual and contraceptive behavior.* Paper presented at the 84th Annual Convention of the American Psychological Association, Washington, DC.

Millman, S., & Hendershot, G. (1980). Early fertility, and lifetime fertility. *Family Planning Perspectives, 12*, 139–149.

Mills, D. M. (1984). A model for stepfamily development. *Family Relations, 33* 365–372.

Minuchin, S. (1974). *Families and family therapy*. Cambridge, MA: Harvard University Press.

Minuchin, S. (1986, February 25). Statement before House Select Committee on Children, Youth, and Families. *The diversity and strengths of American families* (pp. 107–110). Washington, DC: U.S. Government Printing Office.

Mitford, J. (1963). *The American way of death*. New York: Simon & Schuster.

Montgomery, J. P. (1973). *Commitment and cohabitation cohesion*. Paper presented at the annual meetings of the National Council on Family Relations, Toronto, Canada.

Moore, K., & Hofferth, S. (1978). *Consequences of age at first childbirth: Final research summary*. Washington, DC: Urban Institute.

Moore, K., & Wertheim, R. (1984). Teenage childbearing and welfare: Preventive and protective strategies. *Family Planning Perspectives, 16*(6), 285–289.

Moore, K. A., Simms, M. C., & Betsey, C. L. (1986). *Choice and circumstance: Racial differences in adolescent sexuality and fertility*. Brunswick, NJ: Transaction Books.

Moroney, R. M. (1979). The issue of family policy: Do you know enough to take action? *Journal of Marriage and the Family, 41*(3), 461–463.

Moses, A., & Hawkins, R., Jr. (1982). *Counseling lesbian women and gay men: A life-issues approach*. St. Louis: Mosby.

Mott Foundation. (1986). *Teenage pregnancy: An update and guide to Mott Foundation resources*. (Available from Charles Stewart Mott Foundation, Flint, MI 48502-851.)

Mott, F. (1986). The pace of repeated childbearing among young American mothers. *Family Planning Perspectives, 18*, 5–18.

Mott, F. L., & Marsiglio, W. (1985). Early childbearing and completion of high school. *Family Planning Perspectives, 17*, 234–237.

Mott, F., & Maxwell, N. (1981). School age mothers: 1968 and 1979. *Family Planning Perspectives, 13*, 287–292.

Moynihan, D. P. (1986). *Family and nation*. San Diego, CA: Harcourt Brace Jovanovich.

Myers, M. (1985). Counseling the parents of young homosexual male patients. In J. Gonsiorek (Ed.), *A guide to psychotherapy with gay and lesbian clients*. New York: Basic Books.

Myricks, N. (1980). "Palimony": The impact of *Marvin v. Marvin*. *Family Coordinator, 29*(2), 210–215.

Myricks, N. (1983). The law and alternative lifestyles. In E. Macklin & R. Rubin (Eds.), *Contemporary families and alternative lifestyles* (pp. 343–361). Beverly Hills, CA: Sage.

Myricks, N., & Rubin, R. H. (1977). Sex laws and alternative lifestyles. *Family Coordinator, 26*(4), 357–360.

Nadler, J. H. (1976). *The psychological stress of the stepmother*. Unpublished doctoral dissertation, California School of Professional Psychology, Los Angeles.

Napier, A. Y. (1978). The rejection-intrusion pattern: A central family dynamic. *Journal of Marriage and Family Counseling, 4*, 5–12.

National Association of Social Workers. (1985, April.) *Presentation abstracts: Preventive/outreach and psychosocial issues*. Handout at the International Conference on Acquired Immune Deficiency Syndrome, Atlanta, GA.

Nelson, K. (1985). *On the frontier of adoption: A study of special-needs adoptive families.* New York: Child Welfare League of America.

Nelson, K. G., Key, D., Fletcher, J. K., Kirkpatrick, E., & Feinstein, R. (1982). The teen-tot clinic: An alternative to traditional care for infants of teenaged mothers. *Journal of Adolescent Health Care, 3*, 19–25.

Neugarten, B. L. (1973). The wariness of middle age. In B. L. Neugarten (Ed.), *Middle age and aging* (pp. 93–99). Chicago: University of Chicago Press.

New York Spaulding for Children. (1986). Survey shows 10% of group care population are adopted children. *Building Families, 2* (Spring–Summer).

Newcomb, M. D., & Bentler, P. M. (1980a). Assessment of personality and demographic aspects of cohabitation and marital success. *Journal of Personality Assessment, 44*(1), 11–24.

Newcomb, M. D., & Bentler, P. M. (1980b). Cohabitation before marriage: A comparison of married couples who did and did not cohabit. *Alternative Lifestyles, 3*(1), 65–85.

Newcomer, S., & Eldry, J. (1985). Parent-child communication and adolescent sexual behavior. *Family Planning Perspectives, 17*(4), 169–174.

Norton, A. J., & Glick, P. G. (1986). One-parent families: A social and economic profile. *Family Relations, 35*(1), 177–181.

Norvell, M., & Guy, R. F. (1977). A comparison of self-concept of adopted children. *Adolescence, 12*, 443–448.

Nungesser, L. (1980). Theoretical bases for research on social sex-roles by children of lesbian mothers. *Journal of Homosexuality, 5*, 177–187.

Nuta, V. R. (1986). Emotional aspects of child support enforcement. *Family Relations, 35*(1), 177–181.

Nye, I., & Berardo, F.M. (1973). *The family, its structure and interaction.* New York: Macmillan.

O'Connell, M., & Moore, M. (1980). The legitimacy status of first births in U.S. women age 15–24, 1939–1978. *Family Planning Perspectives, 12*, 16–25.

O'Leary, K. M., Shore, M. F., & Wieder, S. (1984). Contacting pregnant adolescents: Are we missing cues? *Social Casework, 65*, 297–306.

Ooms, T. (1981). *Teenage pregnancy in a family context: Implications for policy.* Philadelphia: Temple University Press.

Palmer, E. (1981). Comprehensive service for adolescent parents. *Child Welfare, 60*, 191–197.

Palmer, H. (1983). The alternative question. In R. Vogel & H. Palmer (Eds.), *Long-term care, perspectives from research and demonstration* (pp. 255–305). Washington, DC: Department of Health and Human Services.

Papanek, H. (1973). Men, women and work: Reflections on the two-person career. *American Journal of Sociology, 78*, 852–872.

Papanek, H. (1979). Family, status, production, The "work" and "non-work" of women. *Signs, 4*(4), 775–781.

Papernow, P. (1984). The stepfamily cycle: An experiential model of stepfamily development. *Family Relations, 33*, 355–363.

Parke, R., Power T. & Fisher, L. (1980). The adolescent father's impact on the mother and child. *Journal of Social Issues. 36*, 88–106.

Parkes, C. M. (1964). Effects of bereavement on physical and mental health, a study of the medical records of widows. *British Medical Journal, 2*, 274–279.

Parkes, C. M. (1972). *Bereavement: Studies of grief in adult life.* New York: International Universities Press.

Parkes, C. M. (1976). The broken heart. In E. S. Sneidman (Ed.), *Death: Current perspectives* (pp. 333–347). Palo Alto, CA: Mayfield.

Parkes, C.M., Benhamin, B., & Fitzgerald, R. G. (1969). Broken heart: A statistical study of increased mortality among widowers. *British Medical Journal, 1*, 740–743.

Pasley, K. (1985). Stepfathers. In S. H. Hanson & F. Bozett (Eds.), *Dimensions of fatherhood* (pp. 288–306). Beverly Hills, CA: Sage.

Pasley, K. (1986, April). *Summary of the findings from research on remarriage and stepparenting.* Paper presented at the annual meeting of the American Association of Orthopsychiatry, Chicago, IL.

Pasley, K. (1987). Family boundary ambiguity in remarriage: Perceptions of adult member. In K. Pasley & M. Ihinger-Tallman (Eds.), *Remarriage and stepparenting today: Research and theory.* New York: Guilford Press.

Pasley, K., & Ihinger-Tallman, M. (1982). Stress in second families. *Family Perspectives, 16*, 181–190.

Pasley, K., & Ihinger-Tallman, M. (1983). Remarried family life: Supports and constraints. In N. Stinnett, J. DeFrain, K. King, H. Lingren, G. Rowe, S. VanZandt, & R. Williams (Eds.), *Family strengths, Vol. 4: Positive support systems* (pp. 367–384). Lincoln, NE: University of Nebraska Press.

Pasley, K., & Ihinger-Tallman, M. (1985). Portraits of stepfamily life in popular literature: 1940–1980. *Family Relations, 34*, 527–534.

Pasley, K., & Ihinger-Tallman, M. (1987). The evolution of a field of investigation. In K. Pasley & M. Ihinger-Tallman (Eds.), *Remarriage and stepparenting today: Research and theory.* New York: Guilford Press.

Pasley, K., Ihinger-Tallman, M., & Coleman, C. (1984). Consensus styles among happy and unhappy remarried couples. *Family Relations, 33* 451–457.

Pearlin, L., & Schooler, C. (1982). The structure of coping. In H. McCubbin, A. Cauble, & J. Patterson (Eds.), *Family stress, coping, and social support* (pp. 109–135). Springfield, IL: Thomas.

Peplau, L.A., & Perlman, D. (Eds.) (1982). *Loneliness: A sourcebook of current theory, research and therapy.* New York: Wiley-Interscience.

Peterson, J., Moore, K., Furstenberg, F., & Morgan, P. (1985). *Starting early: The antecedents of early premarital intercourse.* Final Report to Office of Adolescent Pregnancy Programs, U.S. Department of Health and Human Services, Washington, D.C.

Peterson, J. A., & Briley, M. L. (1977). *Widows and widowhood.* New York: Associated Press.

Peterson, J. L., & Zill, N. (1986). Marital disruption, parent-child relations and behavior problems in children. *Journal of Marriage and the Family, 48*, 295–307.

Petty, J. A. (1975). *An investigation of factors which differentiate between types of cohabitation.* Master's thesis, Indiana University, Bloomington.

Polit, D. F. (1986). *Building self-sufficiency: A guide to vocational and employment services for teenage parents.* Jefferson City, MO: Humanalysis.

Polit, D. F., & Kahn, J. R. (1985). Project redirection: Evaluation of a comprehensive program for disadvantaged teenage mothers. *Family Planning Perspectives, 17*, 150–155.

Pollak, P. B. (1985). Family definition: A zoning barrier to housing choice. *Human Ecology Forum, 15*(2), 3–5.

Ponse, B. (1978). *Identities in the lesbian world.* Westport, CT: Greenwood Press.

Potter, S., & Darty, T. (1981). Social work and the invisible minority: An exploration of lesbianism. *Social Work, 26*(3), 192–197.

Presser, H. (1976, March). *Social factors affecting the timing of the first child*. Paper presented at the Conference on the First Child and Family Formation, Pacific Grove, CA.

Presser, H. (1977). Guessing and misinformation about pregnancy risks among urban mothers. *Family Planning Perspectives, 9*, 234–236.

Presser, H. (1978). Age at menarche, socio-sexual behavior and fertility. *Social Biology, 2*, 94–101.

Presser, H. (1980a). *Social and demographic consequences of teenage childbearing for urban women*. Final report to Center for Population Research, National Institutes of Health, Bethesda, MD.

Presser, H. (1980b). Sally's corner: Coping with unmarried motherhood. *Journal of Social Issues, 36*, 107–129.

Price-Bonham, S., & Balswick, J. O. (1980). The noninstitutions: Divorce, desertion and remarriage. *Journal of Marriage and the Family, 42*, 959–972.

Provence, S., & Naylor, A. (1983). *Working with disadvantaged parents and their children*. New Haven: Yale University Press.

Quint, J., & Riccio, J. (1985). *The challenge of serving pregnant and parenting teens*. (Available from Manpower Demonstration Research Corporation, New York, NY 10016.)

Raether, H. C. (1971). The place of the funeral: The role of the funeral director in contemporary society. In R. Fulton, E. Markusen, G. Owen, & J. L. Scheiber (Eds.), *Death and dying: Challenge and change* (pp. 289–300). San Francisco: Boyd Fraser.

Ramsey, S. H. (1986). Stepparent support of stepchildren: The changing legal context and the need for empirical policy research. *Family Relations, 35*(3), 363–369.

Rank, M. R. (1981). The transition to marriage: A comparison of cohabiting and dating relationships ending in marriage or divorce. *Alternative Lifestyles, 4*(4), 487–506.

Rawlings, E., & Carter, D. (1977). *Psychotherapy for women*. Springfield, IL: Thomas.

Reiss, I., & Miller, B. (1979). Heterosexual permissiveness: A theoretical analysis. In W. Burr, R. Hill, I. Nye, & I. Reiss (Eds.), *Contemporary theories about family*, vol. 1. New York: Free Press.

Rice, D. G., & Rice, J. K. (1986). Separation and divorce therapy. In N. Jacobson and A. Gurman (Eds.), *Clinical handbook of marital therapy*. New York: Guilford Press.

Rickels, K. (1985). *Final report: Study of unwanted pregnancy in adolescents*. Bethesda, MD: Center for Population Research, N.I.C.H.D.

Ridley, C. A., Peterman, D. J., & Avery, A. W. (1978). Cohabitation: Does it make for a better marriage? *Family Coordinator, 27*(2), 129–136.

Risman, B. J., Hill, C. T., Rubin, Z., & Peplau, L. A. (1981). Living together in college: Implications for courtship. *Journal of Marriage and the Family, 41*(1), 77–83.

Rivara, F. P., Sweeney, P. J., & Henderson, B. F. (1986). Black teenage fathers: What happens when the child is born? *Pediatrics, 78*, 151–158.

Rivera, R. (1982). Homosexuality and the law. In W. Paul, J. Weinrich, J. Gonsioreck, & M. Hotvedt, (Eds.), *Homosexuality: Social, psychological and biological issues*. Beverly Hills, CA: Sage.

Rivera-Casale, C., Klerman, L. V., & Manela, R. (1984). The relevance of child-support enforcement to school-age parents. *Child Welfare, 63*, 521–529.

Roberts, C. L. (1980, October). *Building developmental theory: A propositional inventory about stepfamily transitions.* Paper presented at the Theory Construction and Research Methodology Workshop at the annual meeting of the National Council on Family Relations, Portland, OR.

Rodgers, R. H. (1983, October). *Developing a propositional theory of the consequences of divorce/remarriage.* Paper presented at the Theory Construction and Research Methodology Workshop at the annual meeting of the National Council on Family Relations, Portland, OR.

Rodman, H., & Trost, H. (Eds.) (1986). *The adolescent dilemma.* New York: Praeger.

Rodman, H., Lewis, S., & Griffith, S. (1984). *The sexual rights of adolescents: Competence, vulnerability and parental control.* New York: Columbia University Press.

Roosa, M. & Vaughan, L. (1984). A comparison of teenage and older mothers with pre-school children. *Family Relations, 33*(2), 259–264.

Rosen, R. (1980). Adolescent pregnancy decision-making: Are parents important? *Adolescence, 15,* 44–54.

Rosen, R., Benson, T., & Stack, J. (1982). Help or hindrance: Parental impact on pregnant teenagers' resolution decision. *Family Relations, 31,* 271–280.

Rosen, R., Hudson, A., & Martindale, L. (1976). *Contraception, abortion and self-concept.* Paper presented at the American Sociological Association, Washington, DC.

Rosenthal, K. M., & Keshet, H. F. (1981). *Fathers without partners.* Otowa, NJ: Rowan & Littlefield.

Ross, H. L., & Sawhill, I. V. (1975). *Time of transition: The growth of families headed by women.* Washington, DC: Urban Institute.

Rubenstein, H., & Bloch. (1978). Helping clients who are poor: Worker and client perceptions of problems, activities, and outcomes. *Social Service Review,* 69–84.

Rubenstein, R. L. (1986). *Singular paths: Old men living alone.* New York: Columbia Studies of Social Gerontology.

Russ-Eft, D., Springer, M., & Beever, A. (1979). Antecedents of adolescent parenthood and consequences of age 30. *Family Coordinator, 28,* 173–178.

Russotto, J. (1980). Children of homosexual parents. In *The many dimensions of family practice: Proceedings of the North American Symposium on Family Practice* (pp. 112–120). New York: Family Service Association of America.

Sager, C. J. (1976). *Marriage contracts and couple therapy: Hidden forces in intimate relationships.* New York: Brunner/Mazel.

Sager, C. J. (1981). Couples therapy and marriage contracts. In A. Gurman & D. Kniskern (Eds.), *Handbook of family therapy.* New York: Brunner/Mazel.

Sager, C. J. (1986). Therapy with remarried couples. In J. Jacobson & A. Gurman (Eds.), *Clinical handbook of marital therapy.* New York: Guilford Press.

Sager, C. J., Brown, H. S., Crohn, H., Engel, T., Rodstein, E., & Walker, L. (1983). *Treating the remarried family.* New York: Brunner/Mazel.

Sager, C. T. (1976). *Marriage contracts and couple therapy.* New York: Brunner/Mazel.

Saghir, M., & Robins, E. (1973). *Male and female homosexuality.* Baltimore, MD: Williams & Wilkins.

Sandler, H. (1979). *Effects of adolescent pregnancy on mother-infant relations: A transactional model of reports to the Center for Population Research.* Bethesda, MD: National Institutes of Health.

Sandler J. (1986). *Working with teenage fathers: A handbook for program development.* New York: Bank Street College of Education.

Santrock, J. W. & Sitterle, K. (1987). Parent-child relationships in stepmother families. In K. Pasley & M. Ihinger-Tallman (Eds.), *Remarriage and stepparenting today: Research and theory.* New York: Guilford Press.

Sauber, M., & Corrigan, E. (1970). *The six year experience of unwed mothers as parents.* New York: Community Council of Greater New York.

Scales, P. (1983). Adolescent sexuality and education: Principles, approaches, and resources. In C. S. Chilman (Ed.), *Adolescent sexuality in a changing American society* (pp. 207–229). New York: Wiley.

Scarr, S., & Weinberg, R. (1986). The early childhood enterprise. *American Psychologist, 41*(10), 1140–1146.

Schaefer, E. S., & Finkelstein, N. W. (1975). *Child behavior toward parent: An inventory and factor analysis.* Paper presented at meetings of the American Psychological Association, Chicago.

Schafer, S. (1977). Sociosexual behavior in male and female homosexuals. *Archives of Sexual Behavior, 6*, 355–364.

Schaffer, J., & Lindstrom, C. (1984). *Denial of difference and insistence on difference in adoptive families.* Unpublished manuscript.

Schechter, M. (1960). Observations on adopted children. *Archives of General Psychiatry, 3*, 21–32.

Schiff, M., Duyme, M., Dummaret, A., & Tomkiewicz, S. (1982). How much could we boost scholastic achievement and IQ scores? A direct answer from a French adoption study. *Cognition, 12*, 165–196.

Schinke, S. P., & Gilchrist, L. (1984). The life skills approach. In S. P. Schinke & L. Gilchrist (Eds.), *Life skills counseling with adolescents.* Baltimore, MD: University Press.

Schofield, M. (1965). *Sociological aspects of homosexuality.* London: Longmans.

Schorr, A. (1986). *Common decency.* New Haven, CT: Yale University Press.

Schwartz, L. L. (1984). Adoption custody and family therapy. *American Journal of Family Therapy, 12*(4), 51–58.

Select Committee on Children, Youth and Families. (1986). *Teen pregnancy: What is being done?* Washington, DC: U.S. House of Representatives, U.S. Government Printing Office.

Seperberg, O., Jr. (1975). *The immortality factor.* New York: Bantam Books.

Shah, F., Zelnik M., & Kantner J. (1975). Unprotected intercourse among unwed teenagers. *Family Planning Perspectives, 7*, 39.

Shanas, E. (1979). The family as a social support system in old age. *The Gerontologist, 19*(2), 169–174.

Shanas, E. (1980). Older people and their families: The new pioneers. *Journal of Marriage and the Family, 42*, 9–15.

Shanas, E., & Sussman, M. (1977). *Family, bureaucracy and the elderly: An organizational/linkage perspective.* Englewood Cliffs, NJ: Prentice-Hall.

Shyne, A. W., & Schroeder, A. G. (1978). *A national study of social services to children and their families* (Publication No. OHDS 78-30150, pp. 109–123). Washington, DC: United States Children's Bureau.

Silverman, P. (1986). *Widow to widow.* New York: Springer.

Silverstein, C. (1977). *A family matter: A parents' guide to homosexuality.* New York: McGraw-Hill.

Silverstein, C. *Man to man: Gay couples in America*. New York: Morrow.

Simon, N., & Senturia, A. (1966). Adoption and psychiatric illness. *American Journal of Psychiatry, 122*, 858–867.

Simon, R. A., & Altstein, H. (1977). *Transracial adoption*. New York: Wiley.

Simon, W., Berger, A., & Gagnon, J. (1972). Beyond anxiety and fantasy: The coital experience of college youths. *Journal of Youth and Adolescence, 1*(3), 203–222.

Simos, B. (1987). Loss and bereavement. In A. Minahan et al. (Eds.), *Encyclopedia of Social Work*, Vol. 2 (pp. 72–81). Silver Spring, MD: National Association of Social Workers.

Slovenko, R. (1980). Homosexuality and the law: From condemnation to celebration. In J. Marmor (Ed.), *Homosexual behavior: A modern reappraisal*. New York: Basic Books.

Slovenko, R. (No date). Statement of position and purpose. Washington, DC: Dignity, Inc.

Smetana, J., & Adler, N. (1979). Decision-making regarding abortion. *Journal of Population, 2*, 338–357.

Smith, E. W. (1975). The role of the grandmother in adolescent pregnancy and parenting. *Journal of School Health, 45*, 278–283.

Smith, P. B., and Kimmel, K. (1970). Student-parent reactions to off-campus cohabitation. *Journal of College Student Personnel, 11*, 188–193.

Sorenson, R. (1973). *Adolescent sexuality in contemporary America*. New York: World.

Sorosky, A., Baron, A., & Pannor, R. (1975). Identity conflicts in adoptees. *American Journal of Orthopsychiatry, 45*, 18–27.

Spada, J. (1979). *The Spada report*. New York: Signet.

Spanier, G. B. (1983). Married and unmarried cohabitation in the United States, 1980. *Journal of Marriage and the Family, 45*, 277–288.

St. Pierre, T., & St. Pierre, R. (1980). Adolescent pregnancy: Guidelines for a comprehensive school-based program. *Health Education, 11*, 12–13.

Stanton, D. (1981). An integrated structural/strategic approach to family therapy. *Journal of Marital and Family Therapy, 7*, 427–439.

Staples, R. (1981). *The world of black singles*. Westport, CT: Greenwood.

Starr, P. (1986). Health care for the poor: The past twenty years. In S. Danziger & D. Weinberg (Eds.), *Fighting poverty* (pp. 106–132). Cambridge, MA: Harvard University Press.

Stein, L. M., & Hoopes, J. L. (1985). *Identity formation in the adopted adolescent*. New York: Child Welfare League of America.

Stein, P. J. (1978). The lifestyles and life changes of the never-married. *Marriage and Family Review, 1*(4), 1, 3–11.

Stein, T., Gambrill, E., & Wiltse, K. (1978). *Children in foster homes*. New York: Praeger.

Stein, T. J. (1987). Foster care for children. *Encyclopedia of social work*, 18th ed. (pp. 639–650). Silver Spring, MD: National Association of Social Workers.

Steiner, D. (1975). *Non-marital cohabitation and marriage: Questionnaire responses of college women and their mothers*. Master's thesis: North Dakota State University, Fargo.

Steinhart, F. (1977). Labor force participation as a resource for support systems. In H. Z. Lopata (Ed.), *Support systems involving widows in American urban areas*. Washington, DC: Social Security Administration, U.S. Department of Health and Human Services.

Stern, P. N. (1978). Stepfather families: Integration around child discipline. *Issues in Mental Health Nursing, 1*, 49–56.

Stokes, J., & Greenstone, J. (1981). Helping black grandparents and older parents cope with childrearing: A group method. *Child Welfare, 60*, 691–701.

Storm, V. (1973). *Contemporary cohabitation and the dating-marital continuum*. Master's thesis, University of Georgia, Athens.

Strothers, J., & Jacobs, E. (1984). Adolescent stress as it relates to stepfamily living: Implications for school counselors. *School Counselor, 32*, 97–103.

Sung, K. (1981). The role of day care for teenage mothers in a public school. *Child Care Quarterly, 10*, 113–123.

Talen, M., & Lehr, M. (1984). A structural and developmental analysis of symptomatic and adopted children and their families. *Journal of Marital and Family Therapy, 10*(4), 381–391.

Taylor, B., Berg, M., Kapp, L., & Edwards, L. E. (1983). School-based prenatal services: Can similar outcomes be attained in a nonschool setting? *Journal of School Health, 53*, 480–486.

Teen parents in Project Redirection have a better chance of avoiding pregnancy and finishing school. (1984). *Family Planning Perspectives, 16*, 38–40.

Terkelson, K. (1980). Toward a theory of the family life cycle. In E. Carter & M. McGoldrick (Eds.), *The family life cycle*. New York: Gardner Press.

Thompson, E. H., Jr., & Gongla, P. A. (1985). Single-parent families: In the mainstream of American society. In E. M. Macklin & R. H. Rubin (Eds.), *Contemporary families and alternative lifestyles: Handbook on research and theory*, 2nd ed. (pp. 97–124). Beverly Hills, LA: Sage.

Thornton, A. (1986). *Family and institutional factors in adolescent sexuality* (Final Report). Ann Arbor, MI: Institute of Social Research.

Tienari, P., Sorri, A., Lahti, I., Naarala, M., Wahlberg, K. E., Ronkko, T., Moring, J., & Pohjola, J. (1987). Family environment and the etiology of schizophrenia: Implications from the Finnish adoptive family study of schizophrenia. In H. Stirlin, F. B. Simon, & G. Schmidt (Eds.), *Familiar realities: The Heidelberg Conference*. New York: Brunner/Mazel.

Tizard, B., & Rees, J. (1977). A comparison on the effects of adoption, restoration to the natural mother and continued institutionalization on the cognitive development of 4 year old children. In A. M. Clarke & A. D. B. Clarke (Eds.), *Early experience: myth and evidence*. New York: Free Press.

Tousseing, P. (1962). Thoughts regarding the etiology of psychological difficulties in adopted children. *Child Welfare*, (February), 59–71.

Townsend, P. (1968). Isolation, desolation and loneliness. In E. Shanas et al. (Eds.), *Old people in three industrial societies* (pp. 258–287). New York: Atherton Press.

Tripp, C. (1975). *The homosexual matrix*. New York: Signet.

Troph, W. D. (1984). An exploratory examination of the effects of remarriage on child support and personal contact. *Journal of Divorce, 7*, 57–73.

U.S. Bureau of the Census. (1986). *Fertility of American women. June, 1985* (Current Population Reports Series P-20, No. 406). Washington, DC: U.S. Government Printing Office.

U.S. Bureau of the Census. (1986a). *Marital status and living arrangements: March 1985* (Current Population Reports, Series P-20, No. 410, November). Washington, DC: U.S. Government Printing Office.

U.S. Bureau of the Census. (1986b). *Households, families, marital status and living arrangements: March 1986 (Advance Report)*. (Current Population Reports, Series

P-20), No. 412, November). Washington, DC: U.S. Government Printing Office.

U.S. Bureau of the Census. (1981). *Marital status and living arrangements* (Current Population Reports, Series P-20, No. 365). Washington, DC: U.S. Government Printing Office.

U.S. Comptroller General. (1977). *The well-being of older people in Cleveland, Ohio.* Washington, DC: General Accounting Office.

U.S. Department of Commerce. Bureau of the Census. (1984). *Current population reports, consumer income* (Series P-60, No. 154). Washington, DC: U.S. Government Printing Office.

Udry, J., Bauman, K., & Morris, N. (1975). Changes in premarital coital experience of recent decades of birth cohorts of urban America. *Journal of Marriage and the Family, 37*(4), 783–787.

Unger, D. G., & Wandersman, L. P. (1985). Social support and adolescent mothers: Action research contributions to theory and applications. *Journal of Social Issues, 41*, 29–45.

Van Deusen, E. L. (1974). *Contract cohabitation: An alternative to marriage.* New York: Grove.

Verbrugge, L. (1979). Marital status and health. *Journal of Marriage and the Family, 41*(2), 267–285.

Visher, E., & Visher, J. S. (1978). Common problems of stepparents and their spouses. *American Journal of Orthopsychiatry, 48*, 252–262.

Visher, E., & Visher, J. S. (1979). *Stepfamilies: A guide to working with stepparents and stepchildren.* New York: Brunner/Mazel.

Visher, E., & Visher, J. S. (1985). Stepfamilies are different. *Journal of Family Therapy, 7*, 9–18.

Visher, E., & Visher, J. S. (1987). Treating families with problems associated with remarriage and steprelationships. In C. Chilman, E. Nunnally, & F. Cox (Eds.), *Families in trouble,* Vol. 5. Beverly Hills, CA: Sage.

Wagner, G., & Green, R. (1981). *Impotence: Physiological, psychological, surgical diagnosis and treatment.* New York: Plenum Press.

Wald, E. (1981). *The remarried family: Challenge and promise.* New York: Family Service Association of America.

Wald, E. Family: Stepfamilies. (1987). *Encyclopedia of social work,* 18th ed. (pp. 551–561). Silver Spring, MD: National Association of Social Workers.

Walker, E., & Emory E. (1985). Commentary: Interpretive bias and behavioral genetic research. *Child Development, 56*, 775–780.

Waller, W. (1951). *The family: A dynamic interpretation.* New York: Holt, Rinehart & Winston.

Warren, C. (1974). *Identity and community in the gay world.* New York: Wiley.

Washington Cofo Memo. (1986). December, VI, 4. *Newsletter of the Coalition of Family Organizations.* (Available from National Council on Family Relations, 1910 W. County Road B, St. Paul, MN 55113.)

Watson, R. E. L. (1983). Premarital cohabitation vs. traditional courtship: Their effects on subsequent marital adjustment. *Family Relations, 32*(1), 139–147.

Watzlawick, P., Weakland, J., & Fisch, R. (1974). *Change: Principles of problem formation and problem resolution.* New York: Norton.

Weatherley, R., Perlman, S., Levine, M., & Klerman, L. (1985). *Patchwork program: Comprehensive services for pregnant and parenting adolescents.* Seattle, WA: University of Washington Center for Social Welfare Research.

Weatherley, R., Perlman, S., Levine, M., & Klerman, L. (1986). Comprehensive programs for pregnant and teenagers and teenage parents: How successful have they been? *Family Planning Perspectives, 18*, 73–78.

Wein, K., & Lopez, D. (1985). *Overview of psychological issues concerning AIDS.* Paper presented at the NASW International Conference on Acquired Immune Deficiency Syndrome, Atlanta, GA.

Weinberg, M., & Williams C. *Male homosexuals.* New York: Oxford University Press.

Weingarten, H. R. (1980). Remarriage and well-being: National survey evidence of social and psychological effects. *Journal of Family Issues, 1*, 533–559.

Weingarten, H. R. (1985). Marital status and well-being: A national study comparing first-marrieds, currently divorced, and remarried adults. *Journal of Marriage and the Family, 47*, 653–662.

Weiss, R. S. (1973). *Loneliness: The experience of emotional and social isolation.* Cambridge, MA: The MIT Press.

Weitzman, L. (1981). *The marriage contract.* New York: Free Press.

Weitzman, L. (1985). *The divorce revolution. The unexpected social and economic consequences for women and children in America.* New York: Free Press.

Welter, B. (1966). The cult of true womanhood: 1820–1869. *American Quarterly, 18*, 151–160.

Whitam, F. (1980). The prehomosexual male child in three societies: The United States, Guatamala, Brazil. *Archives of Sexual Behavior, 9*, 87–99.

White, L. K., & Booth, A. (1985). The quality and stability of remarriages: The role of stepchildren. *American Sociological Review, 50*, 689–698.

Whittaker, J. K. (1987). Group care for children. *Encyclopedia of social work,* 18th ed. (pp. 551–561). Silver Spring, MD: National Association of Social Workers.

Wiegle, J. W. (1974, Sept./Oct.) Teaching child development to teenage mothers. *Children Today.*

Wilson, J., & Neckerman, K. (1986). Poverty and family structure. In S. Danziger & D. Weinberg (Eds.), *Fighting poverty: What works and what doesn't* (pp. 232–259). Cambridge, MA: Harvard University Press.

Wolf, D. (1979). *The lesbian community.* Berkeley, CA: University of California Press.

Woodman, N.J. (1982). Social work with lesbian couples. In A. Weick & Susan Vandiver (Eds.), *Women, power and change* (pp. 114–124). Washington, DC: NASW.

Yankelovich, D. (1981, April.) New rules in American life: Searching for self-fulfillment in a world turned upside down. *Psychology Today*, pp. 35–91.

Zelnik, M. (1980a.) *Determinants of fertility behavior among U.S. females aged 15–19, 1971 and 1976.* Final report to the Center for Population Research, NICHD-NIH, Bethesda, MD.

Zelnik, M., & Kantner, J. (1980b). Sexual activity, contraceptive use, and pregnancy among metropolitan area teenagers: 1971–1979. *Family Planning Perspectives, 12*, 230–237.

Zelnik, M., Kantner, J., & Ford, K. (1982). *Adolescent pathways to pregnancy.* Beverly Hills, CA: Sage.

Zill, N. (1985, May.) *Children in stepfamilies: Their behavior problems, school performance and use of mental health services.* Paper presented at the National Institute for Child Health and Human Development's Conference on The Impact of Divorce, Single-Parenting and Step-Parenting on Children, Bethesda, MD.

Zimmerman, S. (1982). Confusions and contradictions in family policy developments: Applications of a model. *Family Relations, 31*, July, 445–455.

Zitner, R., & Miller, S. (1980). *Our youngest parents*. New York: Child Welfare League of America.

Znaniecki, F. (1965). *Social relations and social roles*. San Francisco: Chandler.

Index

About The Editors and Authors

Jane K. Burgess, Professor of Sociology at the University of Wisconsin-Waukesha Campus, has her M.S. in sociology from the University of Wisconsin-Milwaukee and her Ph.D. in sociology from the University of Illinois, Champaign-Urbana. Her work experience includes teaching and research in the fields of family and social psychology. Her books include *The Widower, Straight Talk about Love and Sex for Teenagers,* and *The Single-Again Male* (now in press). She has also published chapters in many other scholarly books and journals and has served on many committees and councils involved with family-related issues.

Virginia G. Cartoof has an M.S.W. from Simmons College and a Ph.D. from the Heller School at Brandeis University. She operates her own consulting firm in Boston that specializes in social welfare research, program evaluation, and technical assistance to projects that serve pregnant and parenting adolescents. She is the author of several articles on pregnant teenagers' service needs and the impact of government policies on this population. Dr. Cartoof also teaches research at the Boston University School of Social Work.

Catherine S. Chilman, Professor Emeritus and part-time instructor at the School of Social Welfare, University of Wisconsin-Milwaukee, has her M.A. in social work from the University of Chicago and Ph.D. in psychology from Syracuse University. Her work experience includes direct service, administration, teaching, and research in the field of the family. Among other organizations, Dr. Chilman has served on the boards of National Council on Family Relations, the Council on Social Work Education, the International Conference of Social Work, and the Groves Conference on Marriage and the Family, of which she has been president. Her books include *Growing Up Poor, Your Child 6–12,* and *Adolescent Sexuality in a Changing American Society: Social and Psychological Perspectives for the Human Services Professions.*

Charles Lee Cole, Ph.D., is an Associate Professor of Family Environment at Iowa State University in Ames, Iowa, where he is a member of the clinical training faculty in the Marital and Family

Therapy Training Program. Dr. Cole is a clinical member of the American Association for Marriage and Family Therapy and maintains a private practice. He is the author of more than 30 journal articles and chapters in books and has conducted a number of research projects on marital quality, family wellness, and nonmarital cohabitation. His professional affiliations include the National Council on Family Relations, the Groves Conference on Marriage and the Family, and the editorial boards of six major journals in the field of marriage and family.

Fred M. Cox is Dean and Professor of Social Work at the University of Wisconsin-Milwaukee School of Social Welfare. He earned the M.S.W. degree from the University of California in 1954 and the D.S.W. from the University of California at Berkeley in 1968. From 1954 through 1957 he was employed as a social worker with the Family Service Bureau in Oakland, California. His specialties are social welfare policy and community organization practice. He is principal editor of two works, *Strategies of Community Organization,* now in its fourth edition, and *Tactics and Techniques of Community Practice,* now in its second edition. He served as secretary-treasurer of the National Association of Deans and Directors of Schools of Social Work between 1985 and 1987 and was recently re-elected to the Board of Directors of the Council on Social Work Education.

Joseph Harry, Professor of Sociology at Northern Illinois University, received his Ph.D. at the University of Oregon in 1968. His major publications include *The Social Organization of Gay Males* (with William DeVall), *Gay Children Grown Up,* and *Gay Couples.* His principal areas of interest include deviance, criminology, and sexual orientation.

Marilyn Ihinger-Tallman is Associate Professor of Sociology at Washington State University. She received her B.A. and M.A. degrees from the University of California, Riverside, and her Ph.D. from the University of Minnesota in 1977. With her colleague, Dr. Kay Pasley, she has written many scholarly articles and book chapters on the subject of remarriage, and she has recently published books on this topic, a textbook entitled *Remarriage* and the edited book *Remarriage and Stepparenting Today: Research and Theory.*

James J. Kelly is the Graduate Coordinator and Associate Director of the Social Work Department of California State University at Long Beach. He was chosen as 1987 Social Worker of the Year by the National Association of Social Workers in recognition of his work in graduate education, minority student recruitment, gerontology, and AIDS counseling. He has worked since 1985 with the AIDS Project in Los Angeles, leading a support group for parents and loved ones of AIDS patients. Dr. Kelly was also chosen in 1985 as the U.S. representative to a United Nations conference on aging held in the U.S.S.R.

Ron Kral is currently the Coordinator of the Adoptive Family Program at The Brief Family Therapy Center in Milwaukee, Wisconsin, where he does family therapy and researches effective therapeutic techniques with adoptive families. As a family therapist, adoptive parent, and practicing school psychologist, Mr. Kral has been involved in issues of parenting and adoption for over 10 years. His written work includes a monthly column in an adoptive parent group's newsletter and a manual for school personnel, *Strategies That Work: Techniques for Solution in the Schools*, and he has co-edited the book *Indirect Approaches in Therapy.*

Helena Lopata is Professor of Sociology and Director of the Center for the Comparative Study of Social Roles at Loyola University of Chicago. She obtained her Ph.D. from the University of Chicago in 1954, having come from Poland during World War II. She has published the following books: *Occupation: Housewife, Widowhood in an American City, Polish Americans: Status Competition in an Ethnic Community, Women as Widows: Support Systems, City Women: Work, Jobs, Occupations, Careers*, and *Widows and Dependent Wives: From Social Problem to Federal Policy* (with Henry Brehm). She is currently editing *Widows: The Middle East, Asia and the Pacific* and *Widows: North America.* She received a research grant from the International Exchange of Scholars to study the situation of widows in India during the winter of 1987–88.

Eleanor D. Macklin, Associate Professor and Director of the Marriage and Family Therapy Program at Syracuse University, has her M.A. and Ph.D. from Cornell University and has taught at Cornell and the University of Maryland. She is nationally known for her leadership in the study of nontraditional family forms and as one of the pioneers in the study of nonmarital cohabitation. Her professional affiliations include the editorial board of the *Journal of Marriage and the Family,* the National Council on Family Relations, the Groves Conference on Marriage and the Family, the American Association for Marriage and Family Therapy, and the American Association of Sex Educators, Counselors, and Therapists. Her publications include *Contemporary Families and Alternative Lifestyles: Handbook of Research and Theory.*

Elam W. Nunnally is a family life educator who is a co-designer of the (Minnesota) Couple Communication Program. He is also a marriage and family therapist who assisted in the development of solution-focused brief therapy at the Brief Family Therapy Center in Milwaukee, where he has his practice. He is Associate Professor in the School of Social Welfare, University of Wisconsin-Milwaukee, where he teaches marriage and family therapy, family development, and courses in parenting and parent education. During his summers he teaches Couple Communication and Brief Therapy in Scandinavia. He co-authored *Alive and Aware, Talking Together, Straight Talk,* and articles on communication and Brief Therapy. He holds a Master's degree in social work and a Ph.D. in sociology from the University of Minnesota.

Kay Pasley, Associate Professor of Human Development and Family Studies at Colorado State University, received both her M.S. and Ed.D. from Indiana University. Her primary research focus is remarriage and stepparenting, and in collaboration with Dr. Marilyn Ihinger-Tallman she has published numerous articles and two books on the topic. She is currently examining family functioning and financial management practices in remarriage and is also engaged in a follow-up study of 784 remarried individuals originally studied in 1980.

Susan Rice received her D.S.W. from the University of California at Los Angeles School of Social Welfare in 1982. She is currently an Assistant Professor at California State University at Long Beach in the Department of Social Work and has also been on the faculty of the School of Social Work at Michigan State University. Her work experience includes research, teaching, and practice in the field of gerontology. Her publications include articles in the *Journal of*

Gerontological Social Work and the *Journal of Teaching in Social Work* as well as chapters in social work textbooks, including *Helping the Sexually Oppressed*. Dr. Rice is also active in community peace organizations.

Roger H. Rubin is Associate Professor and Acting Chairperson of the Department of Family and Community Development at the University of Maryland, College Park. He received his Ph.D. in child development and family relationships from the College of Human Development at Pennsylvania State University. He has published in the areas of interpersonal lifestyles, human sexuality, and black family life. Dr. Rubin is co-editor of *Contemporary Families and Alternative Lifstyles: Handbook on Research and Theory,* and his professional affiliations include the National Council on Family Relations, American Association for Marriage and Family Therapy, and the Groves Conference on Marriage and the Family, of which he is currently president.

Judith Schaffer is Director of the Adoption Review Unit of New York City Special Services for Children. A co-founder and Director of Research at the Center for Adoptive Families, Inc., in New York City, she has her M.A. in psychology from the New School for Social Research. For the past 14 years Ms. Schaffer has been involved in the field of adoption and foster care as an administrator, researcher, educator, and advocate. Her current activities include training social services providers in brief solution-focused therapy techniques, training mental health providers in the special treatment needs of adoptive families, and preparation of a "Dr. Spock-like" book for adoptive parents.

Emily B. Visher, a clinical psychologist who received her Ph.D. from the University of California, Berkeley, in 1958, is in private practice in Palo Alto, California. Since 1976 she has specialized in working with stepfamilies and in 1979 founded the Stepfamily Association of America with her husband, Dr. John S. Visher. She has written numerous papers and book chapters on stepfamily issues and has co-authored with her husband *Stepfamilies: A Guide to Working with Stepparents and Stepchildren, Stepfamilies: Myths and Realities, How to Win as a Stepfamily,* and *Therapeutic Strategies with Stepfamilies* (in press).

John S. Visher, a psychiatrist and Lecturer in Psychiatry at Stanford University who specializes in working with stepfamilies, founded the Stepfamily Association of America with his wife, Dr. Emily B. Visher, in 1979. An M.D. from Indiana University School of Medicine, Dr. Visher was formerly Chief of Adult Outpatient Services at the North County Mental Health Center in Daly City, California. Dr. Visher's psychiatric papers include articles on a variety of topics including outpatient therapy, stepfamilies, community mental health, and administrative issues. He has also been a national officer in the American Psychiatric Association and other psychiatric organizations including the American College of Psychiatrists.

Carolyn Kott Washburne, who received her M.S.W. in community organization from the University of Pennsylvania School of Social Work, worked as a social worker for 15 years. She is now a freelance writer and editor and teaches English part time at the University of Wisconsin-Milwaukee.

Richard A. Weatherley has an M.A. in social work from the University of Chicago and a Ph.D. in political science from the Massachusetts Institute of Technology. He is an Associate Professor at the University of Washington School of Social Work, where he teaches courses in social policy and administration. He has conducted a number of studies of policy development and implementation, most recently concerning teenage pregnancy programs.